8 38-95

£7-99

The Lotus
and
the Lion

The Lotus
and
the Lion

Buddhism and the
British Empire

J. Jeffrey Franklin

CORNELL UNIVERSITY PRESS
ITHACA AND LONDON

First published 2008 by Cornell University Press
Printed in the United States of America

Library of Congress Cataloging-in-Publication Data

Franklin, J. Jeffrey.
    The lotus and the lion : Buddhism and the British Empire /
J. Jeffrey Franklin.
        p.   cm.
    Includes bibliographical references and index.
    ISBN 978–0–8014–4730–3 (cloth : alk. paper)
    1. Buddhism in literature. 2. English literature—19th century—
History and criticism. 3. Buddhism—Study and teaching—Great
Britain—History—19th century. 4. Great Britain—Religion—
19th century. I. Title.

    PR468.B83F73   2008
    820.9'382943—dc22

2008022869

Cloth printing   10 9 8 7 6 5 4 3 2 1

Contents

Preface

The idea for this book grew out of a simple observation in my reading of British literature from the second half of the nineteenth century. I kept encountering signs of Buddhism, signs that generations of critics seemed to have ignored or had read generically as signs of "the Orient" rather than specifically as evidence of the presence of Buddhism in Victorian culture. In the writings of mid century, Buddhism appeared only in passing reference. For instance, in Elizabeth Gaskell's 1851 novel *Cranford,* the ladies of the town mistake Peter Jenkyns, returning tanned and caftaned from India, for "the great Lama of Thibet" (111). How, I wondered, did Gaskell, whose life and writing revolved around provincial and industrial England, know there was such a person as the Dalai Lama of Tibet? As the century progressed, however, allusions to Buddhism became more visible and more significant in works of literature. Writers of romance novels, especially, began to employ the Hindu and Buddhist concepts of karma and reincarnation. H. Rider Haggard's best-selling romance-adventure *She* (1887) hinges on a particular understanding of reincarnation, and its sequel, *Ayesha: The Return of "She"* (1905), carries the action into the Himalayas and a Tibetan monastery there. What sources was Haggard drawing upon in his conception of reincarnation, or in his depictions of the ceremonies of a Tibetan monastery?

A series of other discoveries—some small, some revelatory—spurred my further interest. Having been guided to Victorian Buddhism first by works of literature, I then discovered what any professional religious studies scholar knows: that the discipline of comparative religion took shape in the nineteenth century; that it generated a substantial body of translations, analyses, and commentary, both scholarly and popular; and that its predominant object of study was Buddhism. Looking then at the periodical literature, I found hundreds of journal and newspaper articles published in the nineteenth century about Buddhism. Further, the number of articles increased significantly on a decade-by-decade basis between 1850 and 1900. A survey of them revealed a wide diversity of interests and concerns. Among them were reports of discovered manuscripts by East India Company officials, translations by newly created university chairs of Sanskrit, archeological surveys of ancient Buddhist holy sites in India, and travelogues of visits to Buddhist temples in Japan, Tibet, Siam (now Thailand), and China. There were articles on native religion by Methodist missionaries in Ceylon (now Sri Lanka), denouncements of Buddhist atheism by Catholic priests in Dublin, and anti-Catholic comparisons of Catholicism to Tibetan "Lamaism" by members of the Church of England. Many articles summarized the life of the Buddha, while others retold the folkloric Jataka tales about his past lives, birth, and childhood. Commentators summarized, with varying degrees of knowledge and sympathy, central doctrines like karma and reincarnation, and not a few addressed a topic of pointed concern: the perceived compatibility of the Dharma with Darwinian evolutionary theory. Later in the century, there were book reviews of recent scholarship on Buddhism, studies of medieval pilgrimage narratives of Chinese monks to India, and polemics by members of the Theosophical Society claiming Buddhism as their precedent. Even some defenses of Buddhism were penned by those who felt it had been unjustly attacked or who saw it as a viable alternative in an age of doubt. Nothing in a decade of doctoral studies, followed by research for my first book, had given me the slightest inkling that the intellectual and popular cultures of the time had been so steeped in Buddhism.

A similarly eye-opening experience for me came when, during a research trip to London, I visited the British Museum and the Victoria and Albert Museum, finding in each hundreds of Buddhist figurines, statues, paintings, scrolls, and manuscripts, the lion's share of which had arrived there in the nineteenth century. I felt as if I had walked into the "Wonder House" from Rudyard Kipling's novel *Kim* (1901), and in a sense I had. Rudyard Kipling, after all, had based it upon the Lahore Museum, of which his father had been the curator while in India, and some of its Greco-Buddhist statues of the Buddha, found at Gandhara, are in fact now held and displayed in those London museums.

Why then, I was compelled to ask, was there such a relative paucity of historical and literary research on Victorian Buddhism? With a few exceptions—most notably Christopher Clausen's essays in the 1970s, Philip C. Almond's landmark historical book, *The British Discovery of Buddhism* (1988), and Donald S. Lopez Jr.'s important work in the 1990s within the field of religious studies—little has been written. What Susan Thach Dean wrote in 1998 still is true: "In the many treatments of nineteenth-century religious controversies, relatively little attention has yet been paid to the development of knowledge about Buddhism in Britain and to the effect that this knowledge had on the Victorian's view of religion and of the world" (Dean 209). Even the most recent collections on Victorian literature and religion, such as those edited by Judith V. Nixon and by Carolyn W. Oulton, make no mention of Buddhism. The fact that Buddhist themes and allusions were pervasive in works of literature has received almost no serious attention in over a hundred years of criticism beyond that necessary to generate cursory endnote definitions. This situation seems somewhat akin to a critical work on John Milton's *Paradise Lost* devoid of informed cross-references to the Bible or serious investigation of the history of the Reformation and Restoration. Over the years it has become increasingly clear to me that this oversight is neither minor nor accidental. Rather, it represents a pervasive critical lacunae—at least within literary studies—that signifies a culture-specific blindness, a failure of critical self-reflection that demands the analysis given in this book.

On the topic of critical self-reflection, I feel required to acknowledge my own personal background, as it has a bearing on my motivations for writing this book. Like the majority of Victorians, I was raised as an Anglican (more precisely, an Episcopalian), but for over a decade I have been a practicing Buddhist. I cannot be fully aware of the extent to which this may or may not be apparent to my readers. In any case, the fact that I am Buddhist has deeply enriched my experience in researching and writing about Victorian Buddhism and has added personal to intellectual pleasure. Of course, the scholarship must stand on its own, regardless of my own beliefs as a Buddhist. Therefore I have worked to ensure that my arguments and interpretations are supported by textual and historical evidence.

While these scholarly responsibilities should go without saying, experience suggests that perhaps they should be said more often. One can read many a book of criticism in which the theoretical, ideological, or religious commitment of the scholar is all too apparent and yet is assumed to require no disclosure or reflection. In some cases one wishes for greater transparency and for argumentation not predetermined by the author's ideology or religion. It is dangerous to behave as if one is writing from a neutral position, especially with respect to such charged topics as race, class, ethnicity, gender, sexual orientation, and, certainly, religion. Among the most common examples of this in the history of Western letters is the tacit assumption by a critic that his or her immersion in Judeo-Christian culture in no way influences objective consideration of the religions of other cultures. Historically, this presumption has licensed those within a dominant religious group to pass judgment upon another religious group as if that judgment were merely stating a God-given fact, hence masking an exercise of power. One can observe this non-self-reflexive exercise of power by some popular, academic, and clerical critics of Buddhism in the nineteenth century, and I have used scholarship and argument to expose their lack of perspective.

Whether in Victorian England or twenty-first-century North America, what most non-Buddhist Westerners think they know about Buddhism consists largely of cultural stereotypes, many of which originated with the Victorians. Some stereotypes, such as the "martial arts Buddhism" popularized in films like *Crouching Tiger, Hidden Dragon* (2003) and *The Matrix* (1999), are as much or more a product of twentieth-century Western popular culture as of any Eastern culture and certainly do not represent the historical or doctrinal consensus of Buddhism. Western intellectual culture has developed its own stereotypes about Buddhism. For instance, as a North American Mahayana Zen Buddhist, I might have expected to find meditation as a central feature of Victorian Buddhism, but research suggests that there was little understanding of or interest in meditation within Victorian discourse about Buddhism. This may reflect the preference among Victorian scholars for the Theravada as opposed to the Mahayana canon, and surely it reflects their tendency to construct a textualized Buddhism at the neglect of Buddhist practice. But the expectancy of finding meditation as a central concern is itself a product of a specific culture and history, namely, the history of Buddhism in North America. The first Buddhist denomination to impact American culture in the early twentieth century was the Japanese Zen of such masters as D. T. Suzuki, and the two most influential styles of Buddhism in America today, Zen and Tibetan, both emphasize meditation. Thus a twenty-first-century American intellectual could be mistaken, for good reason, in expecting the Victorians to be concerned with meditation. Understanding, in their historical specificity, the assumptions about self and other that are embedded in such stereotypes is a primary concern of this book.

Unpacking Victorian conceptions and misconceptions about Buddhism, in addition to revealing a great deal about that culture and providing a more informed reading of that literature, has afforded me the indirect opportunity to cast light upon stereotypes that persist to the present day, stereotypes that I too may be reproducing. In this respect, I see myself as only one in a long line of Western writers on Buddhism that began in the nineteenth century with the likes of Hermann Oldenberg, Caroline Rhys Davids, Henry Steele Olcott, and Edwin Arnold. My reconstruction of the Victorian construction of Buddhism unavoidably reflects a certain early twenty-first-century, North American perspective, and, according to my own theoretical commitments, must say as much about my historical context as it does about nineteenth-century Britain, however objective and supportable I have worked to make the arguments of this book.

J. Jeffrey Franklin

Denver

Acknowledgments

My most general thanks go to the University of Colorado Denver—the College of Liberal Arts and Sciences and the Department of English—for the support and encouragement that made this project possible, and to Cornell University Press—the editors, outside readers, and staff who supported and worked hard to make this book a reality. I am grateful to two journals, *Victorian Literature and Culture,* which published a prior incarnation of chapter 3, and *ELH,* which published an earlier version of chapter 1. I also thank my colleagues and friends who belong to the Victorian Interdisciplinary Studies Association of the Western United States, who have listened to and commented upon pieces of this work at conferences over the course of seven years. Thanks are due to those scholars who read drafts of various chapters and provided valuable corrections and suggestions: Christopher Clausen, Pennsylvania State University, whose suggestion led to the title of this book; Gabriel Finkelstein, University of Colorado Denver; Peter Harvey, University of Sunderland (England); Bradford K. Mudge, University of Colorado Denver; Mark B. Tanzer, University of Colorado Denver, who monitored my treatment of philosophical texts; Steven J. Venturino, Loyola University Chicago; and Russell Webb and Sara Boin-Webb, former editors of *Buddhist Studies Review* (London). I am indebted especially to James Najarian of Boston College, who read the entire manuscript and whose knowledge and painstaking attention are evidenced throughout this book. Finally, my greatest debt of gratitude is owed to

Peter J. Potter, Editor-in-Chief at Cornell, who from the first envisioned what this book might be at its best and whose expertise and skillful means guided me through a process of revision without which this book would not have fulfilled its promise.

J.J.F.

The Lotus
and
the Lion

Introduction

> In the family temple [of the magistrate of Kolang, Tibet],
> in addition to the usual life-size images of Buddha and the Triad, there
> was a female divinity, carved at Jallandhur in India, copied from a statue
> representing Queen Victoria in her younger days—a very fitting
> possession for the highest government official in Lahul.
> —Isabella Bird Bishop, *Among the Tibetans* (1894)

> Should I be considered too bold if I were to go one step
> farther and suggest that there are really some points in the philosophy
> of the East, and especially of India, which are fated sooner or later
> to find their place in, and to exercise a not inconsiderable
> influence over, the thought of Western nations?
> —T. W. Rhys Davids, *The History and Literature of Buddhism* (1896)

The European "Discovery" of Buddhism

It would not be inaccurate to say that Buddhism did not exist in the West until near the beginning of the Victorian period (1837–1901), despite the fact that it had existed for over 2,400 years and was being practiced at that moment by millions of people throughout Southeast Asia, Tibet, China, and Japan. Prior to the early nineteenth century, few Europeans had heard of Buddhism at all, and the few who had heard of it pictured the Buddha as a minor Hindu deity or a celestial sun god in the pantheon of the "exotic Orient." Of course, Eastern thought long had trickled back toward the seats of Western empires along the same routes used for silk, tea, and opium, but serious engagement with that thought only began in the late eighteenth century with the first translations of the *Bhagavad-Gita* into French, German, and English.[1] Systematic study of Eastern sacred texts did not begin in Europe until around the 1820s, when collection and translation of ancient Buddhist manuscripts commenced. One of the earliest Western studies to focus exclusively on Buddhism was Edward Upham's *The History and Doctrine of Buddhism,* published in 1829. Only in subsequent decades did "the term 'Buddha' ('Buddoo', 'Bouddha', 'Boudhou', etc.)" begin to "gain currency" in common English usage (Almond 7). As late as the 1860s, but rapidly at that point, Buddhism "hit" Europe in general and England in particular, becoming a widespread topic both in the scholarly and popular literatures that peaked in London's "Buddhism-steeped Nineties" (Caracciolo 30).

Yet, despite this relatively recent dawning of awareness of Buddhism, by the end of the twentieth century there were an estimated 150,000 professed Buddhists in England practicing in 370 different groups representing lineages from Japan, Sri Lanka, Tibet, and Vietnam, among others (Coleman 19, 20). To understand why, according to the British census, Buddhism was second only to Christianity as the most widely observed religion in Devon and Cornwall in 2001, one might begin by asking about the events and discourses that moved John R. Ambereley to write during 1872 in London that "there is no religion the study of which is likely to be so useful to Europeans as Buddhism" (BBC; Ambereley 293). To understand why in the early twenty-first century many of the bestselling books from the religion sections of British and North American bookstores are about Buddhism, one should ask why in the latter decades of the nineteenth century three book-length poems recounting the life of the Buddha were published in London, of which Sir Edwin Arnold's *The Light of Asia* (1879) became an international bestseller. If one wishes to understand the chain of events by which the Fourteenth Dalai Lama of Tibet is now the patron and figurehead of the British Network of Buddhist Organizations, one well might follow those events back to Brian Houghton Hodgson, an employee of the British East India Company who, while on assignment in Nepal in the 1820s, collected ancient Buddhist manuscripts in Sanskrit, the delivery of which to the Royal Asiatic Society in London in 1835 and to the *Societe Asiatique* of Paris in 1837 launched the serious scholarly investigation of Buddhism in Europe. Within the Victorian period, if one wants to understand from which influences and sources Edwin Arnold created his character of Siddhartha Gautama, the Buddha, or how H. Rider Haggard derived his portrayal of a Tibetan Buddhist monastery in his novel *Ayesha: The Return of She* (1905), then one needs not merely some knowledge of the British Empire in India and Tibet but also some background on the Indian origins of Buddhism and on its history in Tibet, some insight into how Victorians responded to the figure of the Buddha and, quite differently, to Tibetan "Lamaism," and some knowledge of the broad range of sources available in England to Arnold and Haggard on Buddhism.[2]

In this book I tell the intriguing and multilayered story of the European encounter with Buddhism, which began in the first half of the nineteenth century and spread throughout British literature and culture in the second half of that century. I analyze the British constructions of Buddhism in popular novels, in particular Marie Corelli's *A Romance of Two Worlds* (1886) and *The Life Everlasting* (1911); H. Rider Haggard's *She* (1887) and *Ayesha: the Return of She* (1905); and Rudyard Kipling's *Kim* (1901). I both treat as objects of analysis and use as sources the primary works within the nineteenth century's new field of religious studies, comparative religion, two important examples of which are F. Max Müller's *Lectures on the Science of Religion; with a Paper on Buddhist Nihilism* (1872) and T. W. Rhys Davids's *Buddhism: Being a Sketch of the Life and Teachings of Gautama, the Buddha* (1877). I comparatively analyze two of the book-length poems that retold the life of Siddhartha Gautama, who lived in northeastern India from approximately 566 to 486 BCE: Richard Phillips's *The Story of Gautama Buddha and his Creed: An Epic* (1871) and Edwin Arnold's *The Light of Asia. Being The Life and Teaching of Gautama, Prince of India and Founder of Büddhism* (1879). A somewhat different object of analysis is *Isis Unveiled: A Master-Key to the Mysteries of Ancient and Modern Science and Theology* (1877) by Helena Petrovna Blavatsky. She was the co-founder of a new religion, Theosophy, that claimed its origins from "esoteric Buddhism" and was highly influential in both England and India. Finally, the last chapter traces the threads of the Victorian "nirvana debate" as they were woven into foundational texts of Western philosophical nihilism, in particular Friedrich Nietzsche's *The Will to Power* (1883–1888). Also discussed is a broad range of late-Victorian and Modernist literary texts, most notably Joseph Conrad's *Heart of Darkness* (1901), T. S. Eliot's "The Waste Land" (1922), and D. H. Lawrence's novels *Women in Love* (1920) and *Aaron's Rod* (1922), among others.

These texts, in their diversity, represent the range of Victorian responses to and constructions of Buddhism—with important implications for modernism and after. The analysis of them in subsequent chapters demonstrates that Buddhism pervaded, if diffusely, late-nineteenth-century British thought. If it existed largely at the margins and in the background, it even so was a critical component of central Victorian debates—those concerning the British Empire and its colonial obligations, those emanating from the confrontation between Christianity and Eastern religions at a time of religious upheaval in England, and those precipitated by the advent of Darwinian evolutionary theory. Indeed, the topic of Buddhism came to function as one nexus within

Victorian discourse, joining these issues. At a time when the Church of England was losing membership to Nonconformist Protestant denominations, and in the wake of the perceived assault on Christian faith by scientific naturalism, especially Darwinism, concerned Christians were primed to be wary of encroachment by a potentially competing Eastern religion. On the frontlines of empire, missionaries in Burma or Ceylon recognized Buddhism as the primary competition and understood explicitly that British occupation was wedded to Christianizing those populations.[3] The alignment between religion and empire meant that to question the superiority of the Christian faith was tantamount to questioning the God-given right of the British to govern Hindus, Muslims, and Buddhists.

On the home-front, Buddhism's compassionate founder and ethical system made it "the most appealing of non-Christian religions to the nineteenth-century mind" and, therefore, the most threatening alternative religion (Clausen, "Victorian" 13). The threat was intensified by the fact that many Victorians came to see Buddhism as compatible with evolutionary science, in sharp contrast to the dominant position across Christian denominations. This aligned it with the widely perceived nemeses of faith: materialism, science, and atheism. When Victorian Anglicans, Nonconformists, and, to a lesser extent, Catholics took a respite from inter-denominational contests and looked up from the immediate, shared threat of Darwinism, they recognized Buddhism as the next most dangerous enemy. Buddhism was the first non-Christian religion to be considered a threat to the West in its own home territory. Thus understanding the role of Buddhism in nineteenth-century Britain provides unique insights into the Victorians, their religious and social obsessions and fears, their aspirations and their prejudices, their self-understanding and their understanding of other cultures and religions.

I want to start the story of Victorian Buddhism with a relatively insignificant event, or rather with a chain of minor events that nevertheless are indicative of larger patterns. In 1797, Colonel Colin Mackenzie, an operative working under the auspices of the East India Company, visited the site of the ancient Buddhist Stupa at Amaravati, which had been in use from the third century BCE until perhaps as late as the fourteenth century, by which time Buddhism had died out in the country of its birth.[4] By the eighteenth century, nearly all signs that Buddhism ever had existed in India had been effaced; no living Indian knew the locations of most of the ancient Buddhist holy sites. Those sites would be recovered and preserved against loss through the efforts of European archaeologists in the nineteenth century. Though as part of colonial usurpation, and in the process of appropriating Buddhism as an artifact of Western knowledge, Europeans drove the effort to locate, unearth, collect, and archive the ancient record of Buddhism in India, which was on the verge of being lost to Buddhism and to world heritage. As part of this process, Colonel Mackenzie expropriated from the Stupa eleven stone bas-reliefs illustrating scenes from the time of the Buddha, and in 1821 he sent them to the Indian Museum in Calcutta. Nine of them were sent on to the East India Company collection in Leadenhall Street, London; to those were added 121 more, and in 1874 some of them were erected in the Sculpture Court at the Southern Entrance of the new India Museum in South Kensington. As a child, Rudyard Kipling, having been shipped by his parents from India back to England for education, spent many hours in that museum, as Kipling reports in his autobiography, *Something of Myself* (1937). In 1879–80, the collection was divided between the new Victoria and Albert Museum and the British Museum, where for sixty years they were on display in the main stairwell. I believe it is safe to speculate that every British author treated in this book, along with millions of other Britons, saw these and other Buddhist artifacts in one or both of these locations. I will use this small example as the ground for making several related points.

First, concerning the Western "discovery" of Buddhism, Philip C. Almond's *The British Discovery of Buddhism* argues in short that European scholars, predisposed by the ingrained Protestant belief that true religion is word and book-based, constructed through translation and analysis of the Buddhist canon an idealized textual Buddhism. He writes: "Originally existing 'out there' in the Oriental *present,* Buddhism came to be determined as an object the primary location of which was the West, through the progressive collection, translation, and publication of its textual *past*" (Almond 13). European scholars asserted the precedence of their textualized Buddhism over the indigenous practices of actual Buddhists in Asia. This represented a form of imperial appropriation of the religious other, a form of discursive violence that supplemented the physical violence of conquest and occupation. At its farthest remove from the violence that defines it, "discovery" must be understood as "construction": the process by which nineteenth-century British culture assimilated or failed to assimilate elements of Buddhism. And it is this very process that is the subject of this book.

This is a book about British culture and the British construction of Buddhism—not about indigenous Buddhist practices in Asia in the nineteenth century, nor about an ahistorical abstraction one might label "real" or "true" Buddhism, except to the extent that Victorians indeed did construct such an abstraction. My interest is in the fact that the young Rudyard Kipling's first exposure to Buddhism was in London, not India or Tibet or Japan; that he wrote the novel *Kim* for the most part from Rottingdean in Sussex; that most of the textual sources on which he drew were written and published in England, not Asia. My focus is upon the textualized Buddhism fashioned by Englishmen, which unavoidably said as much about nineteenth-century Britain as it did about Buddhism. Thus my objects of analysis are the very texts that Almond demonstrates appropriated Buddhism.

As a result, one risk that I confronted in the writing of this book was of perpetuating the assumptions and prejudices of my subjects—an unavoidable risk any historically based study must negotiate. One way that I have tried to ameliorate this risk is by treating works of comparative religion in a way similar to my treatment of literary works, not assuming that the former were objective or factual while the latter were strictly imaginative. Indeed, I have found imaginative misinterpretations of Buddhist doctrine in works of comparative religion, and I have found works of literature striving to be faithful to the historical record or the doctrinal consensus of Buddhism. All of these texts are cultural artifacts of that time and place, and I read them as such in relationship to one another. In all one can find signs—sometimes virulent, sometimes unintended—of the racism and cultural chauvinism that served the interests of the British Empire. After all, colonial invasion and occupation provided both the occasion and one motivation for the formation of the field of comparative religion: to gather knowledge in order to control. It was part of the textual appropriation of the Oriental other in order to form "the imperial archive"—what today we call "intelligence gathering" (Richards 1).

At the same time, however, in reading the works of comparative religion I developed considerable respect for its mission as expressed by its most even-handed proponents. That mission, in short, was to treat all religions as worthy of respect and to apply historical and textual analysis to each, even Christianity. As Max Müller wrote to his Christian readership in 1872, with a nice turn of reverse psychology: "Those who would use a comparative study of religions as a means for debasing Christianity by exalting the other religions of mankind, are to my mind as dangerous allies as those who think it necessary to debase all other religions in order to exalt Christianity" (Müller, *Lectures* 21–22). Scholars like Max Müller, and like T. W. and C. A. F. Rhys Davids, were able to build a body of translations and analysis that only could have come from the type of access colonial occupation afforded. They were able to bring together for comparative compositional analysis documents and artifacts that had been separated in time by hundreds of years; separated geographically between the northern Buddhism of Tibet or China and the southern Buddhism of Southeast Asia; separated doctrinally between the northern Mahayana and southern Theravada schools; and separated linguistically between the northern Sanskrit and the southern Pali. In this way, they distinguished what they judged to be the culture-specific elements of indigenous Buddhist practice from those elements that were duplicated across nations/cultures/languages and, therefore, that appeared to them most authentic. This was the basis for the idealized, textual Buddhism they "discovered." Yet, their work set the standard that still is relied upon by scholars of comparative religion today.

Therefore, while striving to remain critical, I compare Victorian literary representations of Buddhism to the best nineteenth-century scholarship. If one is to be able to assess various Victorian uses of key Buddhist concepts and doctrines, then one needs some standard definitions against which to compare them. It seemed reasonable to use definitions drawn from the best Victorian scholarship, not only because of the generally high quality of that work, but because one then is drawing upon a context-specific baseline. On the other hand, this may heighten the risk of uncritically re-inscribing Victorian prejudices.

Responding to this double-bind, I chose to supplement Victorian scholarship through comparison with twentieth and twenty-first-century sources, those written by renowned practitioners of Buddhism, both from Asia and from the West, and those by scholars of Buddhism working in Western universities. In this way, and borrowing a method from comparative religion itself, I triangulated sources in order to posit an abstraction that might be called "the historical and doctrinal consensus" of Buddhism. I deploy this abstraction throughout this book whenever I claim that a particular literary representation of karma or reincarnation, for instance, is or is not consistent with the predominant understanding of those concepts within Buddhism. I do this with full awareness that this abstraction reproduces the textualizing impulse of Victorian scholarship, ignoring denominational differences within Buddhism, and, though based on authoritative sources, unavoidably is in part my own construction. Without this or a similar assumption, however, it becomes impossible to comparatively analyze any context-specific use of Buddhist concepts—impossible to understand how the Victorian uses of "nirvana," for example, compare to a Buddhist norm.

Returning, then, to the question of how to understand the "discovery" of Buddhism, while concurring with Almond's conclusions, I want to complicate his thesis by making a point familiar from recent postcolonial theory: in constructing Buddhism in their own image, the Victorians were at the same time making their self-image subject to reconstruction by other races, cultures, and religions. The very nature of colonial contact opened Britain to what I have called a "counter-invasion" of the West by the East, and the resulting engagement with Oriental culture profoundly changed British culture. The counter-invasion had been building momentum for centuries as East-West trade and diplomacy gradually increased, but it culminated in the nineteenth century. This timing seems tied for obvious reasons to the fact that the British Empire had emerged in the first half of the century as the preeminent military and economic power in the world. As celebrations of the victories and duties of empire appeared with increasing frequency in journalism and literature, crescendoing around Queen Victoria's assumption of the title of Empress of India in 1876, an appropriately paradoxical counter-strain of fear also arose over the effects of Eastern ideas and products flowing back toward England.

Many Victorians recognized the counter-invasion as it was taking place. Ernest J. Eitel, writing in 1884 as the Boden Professor of Sanskrit at Oxford, warned: "The history of Eastern Asia is the history of Buddhism. But the conquests of Buddhism are not confined to Asia. The grand system of philosophic atheism, which discards from the universe the existence of a creating and overruling Deity and in its place deifies humanity, has, since the beginning of the present century, entered upon a course of conquest in the West, in Europe and America" (Eitel 3). The fear of counter-invasion was fanned by exaggerated comments such as the following, which originally appeared in the *Frankfurter Zeitung* on 25 April 1890: "It is known that the philosophy of Buddha has of late years won many adherents in Europe. What is less known is that the religion of Buddha is likewise beginning to spread in Europe.... Prominent persons call on me every day to tell me that they have been converted to Buddhism. I have been told that the number of Buddhists in Paris alone is 30,000" (*Literary Digest* 162). If, as some have argued, Romantic writers "embraced the Orient in a reconciling vision of wholeness," portraying it as a mysterious font of ancient wisdom, writers after the Opium War of 1839 and especially after the Indian Mutiny of 1857 were more likely to portray it as the seat of "corrupt and effete civilizations" whose decadent, nihilistic, or enervating ideas posed a threat to Western ideals (Batchelor 253; Lopez 2). As the novelist Wilkie Collins's evangelical old-maid Miss Clack puts it in *The Moonstone* (1868), with greater aptness than she understands, "How soon may our own evil passions prove to be Oriental noblemen who pounce on us unawares!" (Collins 198). Oriental nobleman—whether Brahmins, rajas, lamas, begums, yogis, or pashas—lurk at the margins of many Victorian texts, not to mention Indian jugglers, spies, assassins, and hookah-smoking caterpillars. These figures were signs of a process of cultural transformation underway in Britain as an unforeseen byproduct of the counter-invasion to which empire opened the doors.

The process I am describing is akin to the familiar postcolonial concept of "hybridity"—the relationship between colonizer and colonized within which the boundary of difference separating two nations, races, cultures, or religions becomes the connection of identity joining the two. As an antecedent to postcolonial theory, Mikhail Bakhtin theorized hybridity linguistically in terms of a "verbal-ideological decentering," which can "occur only when a national culture loses its sealed-off and self-sufficient character, when it becomes conscious of itself as only one among *other* cultures and languages" (Bakhtin, *Dialogic* 370). Homi Bhabha develops the concept as "a difference 'within'" identity, an " 'in-between' reality" separating and joining two cultures in a colonial relationship that generates a "*productive* ambivalence" between the self and "that 'otherness' which is at once an object of desire and derision, an articulation of difference contained within the fantasy of origin and identity" (Bhabha, *Location* 13, 67). The original nineteenth-century meaning of "hybrid" was as genetic cross-breeding, as in "Kipling's use of the term 'mule' to describe English-university-trained Indians," and with unavoidable reference to miscegenation

(Lahiri 99). Taking his cue from this point and building on the work of Bhabha, Robert C. J. Young focuses on racial hybridity in works such as *White Mythologies* and *Colonial Desire*. He demonstrates that the boundary between colonizer and colonized always is dangerously and excitingly permeable. The threat/promise of interpenetration, whether culturally or sexually, operates not only from the colonizer to the colonized but bi-directionally. This understanding of hybridity as a forced and unequal co-dependency between colonizer and colonized provides a model for explaining the impact not only of the self upon the other but of the other upon the self.

With this general definition in mind, I am most interested in pursuing the implications of the observation that "hybridity" "first entered social science via the anthropology of religion, through the theme of syncretism" and is "meaningless *without* the prior assumption of difference, purity, fixed boundaries," and "sacred origins" (Pieterse 223, 226). Different sacred origins come into conflict, and into the dialogue that invites hybridization, when two religions first come into contact. Contact leads to a "translation" between the two religions—how is Buddha like Jesus?, how is nirvana like heaven?, for instance—and this "desacralizes the transparent assumptions of cultural supremacy" (Bhabha, *Location* 228).

Consider the example of Victorian Anglicanism and Singhalese Theravada Buddhism. From early in the nineteenth century, news and commentary from British-occupied Ceylon blended political debate over colonial control with religious issues of Christian missionary access and indigenous Buddhist resistance. Buddhism thus became a topic about which some in Britain needed to be knowledgeable. Pioneers of Buddhist studies, such as Eugène Burnouf and George Turnour, had worked as members of the Ceylon Civil Service. Missionaries and tourists wrote letters, travelogues, reports, polemics, and, at least in the case of Samuel Landgon's *Punchi Nona* (1884), novels back from Ceylon. Founders of Theosophy H. P. Blavatsky and H. S. Olcott became among the first Westerners to publicly take layman's Buddhist vows while on a visit to Ceylon in 1880. They already had mixed elements of Buddhism into their new "hybrid religion," a subcategory of syncretism historically and culturally unique to late-Victorian Britain. Olcott went on to become a champion of the Singhalese Buddhist revival in opposition to pressure by Christian missionaries, mostly Anglicans and Methodists.[5] He wrote and distributed *A Buddhist Catechism* that still is used by Buddhists in Sri Lanka today, thereby creating a multi-hybrid of Buddhism mixed with his Protestant orientation and a Catholic genre. Thus my use in this book of the concept of hybridity is a specific application with special reference to religions.

My theory of cultural counter-invasion assumes the bi-directionality of hybridity and focuses on the impacts of colonization upon the colonizer. The British "discovery" of Buddhism was at the same time the beginning of the counter-invasion of Britain by Buddhism, or the discovery by Buddhism of

Britain, as evidenced by the number of Buddhists in Britain today. By the same token, it was the beginning of Britain's discovery of its own cultural identity through and as Buddhism.

Historical Background for the Counter-Invasion
of Britain by Buddhism

Though the counter-invasion of Britain by Buddhism did not fully commence until the nineteenth century, it must be understood within the context of the long history of Western contact with Buddhist cultures. That contact began certainly by the third century BCE, and may have begun as early as the sixth century BCE during the lifetime of Siddhartha Gautama, when Greek colonies first were established along the northwest border of current-day India.[6] But European contact with Buddhist cultures was not inaugurated until much later, around the mid thirteenth century, when Franciscan missionaries began opening pilgrimage routes into Mongolia, China, and Japan.[7]

The point that needs to be emphasized about the pre-nineteenth-century history of European interaction with Buddhism is that for at least six centuries, between the thirteenth and the early nineteenth centuries, there was no systematic study or synthesis of Buddhism in the West. While numerous individual contacts occurred—for the most part by missionaries and diplomatic envoys— "over the long scope of things, the information was never cumulative": "Time after time, it appears, writers either started from almost zero, without being aware of previous knowledge, or they worked without being able to articulate correctly the previous data with new knowledge" (Droit 15). Over centuries, disparate reports trickled back to Europe from Ceylon of "Godama," from China of "Fo," from Tibet of "Boud," from Japan of "Xaca" (Sakya), and from India of the ninth Hindu Avatar, an incarnation of Vishnu, named Buddha, all without being correlated. Roger-Pol Droit, among other historians of Buddhism, identifies fairly specifically the date by which a synthesized overview of Buddhism began to emerge.

> We must specify to what the very idea of a discovery of Buddhism refers. And this is fairly easy to circumscribe. There is a "discovery of Buddhism" from the moment that questions like the following are explicitly asked. Who is it that is referred to as the Buddha? What does his name mean? When did he live? What did he teach?...What are the main schools of Buddhism, and what are their main points of contention? And so forth....It is possible to date, with a certain amount of precision, the turning point at which the object "Buddhism" took form among the learned disciplines....; it was around 1820. (Droit 11–12).

Buddhism indeed did not exist in and for the West until near the beginning of the Victorian period.

Hinduism, however, became an object of systematic study at least fifty years prior to the Victorian period. What historian Raymond Schwab characterizes as "the Oriental Renaissance" began in Europe in the eighteenth century and, for political and colonial reasons, focused especially on India and thus Hinduism (Buddhism having ceased to be practiced in its country of origin by around the twelfth century). The watershed moment can reasonably be pinpointed as 1784, the year in which Sir William Jones convened the Royal Asiatick Society of Bengal and in which Sir Charles Wilkins published the *Bhagavad-Gita*, the first complete Sanskrit text translated into English. The impact of the *Bhagavad-Gita* on European intellectual discourse and, later, on the formation of American Transcendentalism, was critical: "No text could, by its profound metaphysics and by the prestige of its poetic casting, more irresistibly shake the hold of the tradition of a [presumed] superior race" (Schwab 161). In India and then Europe, an industry of Western Hindu studies burgeoned. Many commentaries, to the extent they mentioned Buddhism at all, conflated it with Hinduism. With no practicing Buddhists in India to consult, "no Sanskrit Buddhist texts [in English translation] to read, and in a climate of brahmanical anti-Buddhist prejudice, these pioneers of India studies gave little attention to the obscure figure they knew as Boudh" (Bachelor 233). William Jones, despite his considerable erudition, initiated what would become a popular myth linking the Teutonic god Wotan or Odin to Buddha, and his "On the Gods of Greece, Italy, and India" identifies the Hindu Rama as " 'the same person with Buddha' " (Jones, qtd. in Marshall 230).

When Wilkins's *Bhagavad-Gita* finally reached New England in 1843, Ralph Waldo Emerson referred to it as that " 'much renowned book of Buddhism' " (Emerson, qtd. in Field 60). Henry David Thoreau, who had studied the earliest French works of comparative religion, had a somewhat clearer understanding of the distinction between Hinduism and Buddhism. No less than Emerson, however, Thoreau hybridized concepts drawn loosely from a range of Eastern philosophies and religions—as well as from Protestantism, Romanticism, Deism, and American civil religion—in creating a uniquely nineteenth-century, New England Transcendentalism.[8] If Buddhism emerged as a distinct object from Hinduism in European scholarship in the 1820s, it did not do so in the United States until somewhat later. The eighteenth-century tradition of Orientalist studies both laid the foundations for the Buddhist studies that would commence in earnest in the 1830s *and* obfuscated any clear understanding of Buddhism until that time.

The first phase of scholarly Orientalism, then, can be dated roughly to the years between 1780 and 1820. If it was a phase of "philological and literary Romanticism" having very little to do with the history or doctrines of

Buddhism, the second phase, from approximately the 1830s to the 1850s, "was one of linguistic organization" (Schwab 121). The requisite first order of business was to locate and translate ancient manuscripts from the Sanskrit and, later, the Pali Buddhist canons. The pioneers of this phase of textual compilation and translation included, among others, Brian Houghton Hodgson, Alexander Csomo de Körös, Jean-Pierre Abel-Rémusat, Henry and James Princep, and Philippe Edouard Foucaux.

The moment identified by most historians of Buddhist studies as the culminating event was Eugène Burnouf's publication in 1844 of *Introduction à l'historie du Buddhisme indien.* Burnouf had drawn upon the Sanskrit manuscripts provided by Hodgson, the significance of which went largely unrecognized in London until Burnouf. Only after Burnouf did Buddhology emerge in Britain as the primary occupation of the newly forming field of comparative religion. Thus the third phase of Orientalism, the phase of "maturation," "became more pronounced around 1855" when Buddhist studies rose to the fore (Schwab 121). This phase was signaled by the immigration of F. Max Müller from Germany to England and his widely read studies on Buddhism published in the 1860s, and it was cemented especially by the work of T. W. Rhys Davids and C. A. F. Rhys Davids, who formed the Pali Text Society at Oxford in 1881.

Three characteristics of the third phase of Orientalism are critical. First, the object of study of Orientalist scholars increasingly became Buddhism rather than Hinduism, which is not to say that Hindu studies ceased. Second, the center of Buddhist studies shifted from Paris and the German universities to London (which, again, is not to say that they ceased on the Continent). Third, Buddhism rather dramatically entered not only scholarly discourse in Britain but also popular discourse. Works by F. Max Müller, Henry Alabaster, and the Reverend Samuel Beal, among others, were widely read and discussed. As a result, starting in the 1860s, Buddhist concepts began to appear with increasing frequency in poems, novels, and the popular periodical press.

That Buddhism entered the popular discourse in England in the second half of the nineteenth century explains the historical frame for this book. My analysis begins from the publications of comparative religion starting in the 1850s and1860s, incorporates the lively dialogue about Buddhism that occurred in the periodical literature soon thereafter, and then focuses on the works of fiction, poetry, religion, and philosophy that emerged especially in the 1870s to the 1890s. The primary works on which this book focuses are among those that engaged most fully with Buddhism, which is why I chose them. However, I hope that the current study demonstrates that they belonged to a body of scholarly, popular, and literary discourse of which they are representative.

The Religious Context for the Counter-Invasion

When Buddhism entered Victorian discourse at mid century, it became part of an environment of vital and divisive religious debates, not merely debates between the few dominant Christian institutions, but between a wide range of religious and spiritual positions. Some of those positions—such as the Spiritualism movement, Anglican Deism, and, later in the century, the Theosophical movement—are treated at length in this book. But even the dominant competing religious positions—Anglicanism and Nonconformity, "Church" and "Chapel"—were themselves very far from unified or stable. The dynamic complexity of the religious landscape of that century, which stands out in comparison with the preceding or succeeding century, meant that there could be no monolithic "Christian" response to Buddhism. Yet, there were consistent responses made in the name of Christianity as a whole by representatives of different denominations that spanned the many denominational differences. Some background is required in order to understand how the diversity of Christian positions and institutions alive in Victorian England not only conditioned a diversity of responses but generated certain shared responses to Buddhism.

In the first place, the Church of England was internally divided among three primary camps. The High Church or Anglo-Catholic position was championed by the Tractarian Movement of the 1830s–1840s and led by Oxford divines like Edward Pusey, John Keble, and John Henry Newman. It sought to reestablish the apostolic and therefore institutional authority of the Church in relationship to its Catholic origins. The Low Church movement began as part of the Evangelical Revival of the eighteenth century and was in the nineteenth century one attempt to compete with the growing popularity of Nonconformist evangelical and Biblical fundamentalist Christianity. Representative figures were the Seventh Earl of Shaftesbury, Bishop J. C. Ryle, and Bishop C. J. Ellicott. The Broad Church or Latitudinarian position was typified by A. P. Stanley, Benjamin Jowett, and John William Colenso, Bishop of Natal, and by the publication in 1860 of *Essays and Reviews*. The authors of those pieces strove for national unity among the diversity of Anglican positions, but instead they alienated evangelicals and Anglo-Catholics alike by advocating "for a thoroughly historical and critical approach to the Bible, for recognition of the moral and spiritual worth of religious traditions outside the Bible, and for acceptance of the findings of science concerning both the age of the earth and its geological history" (Parsons, "Reform" 41).

At the same time, the Church was under assault, both theologically and politically, from other denominations. By the 1830s there was intense pressure from Whig or Liberal parliamentarians in the direction of disestablishment of the Church's privileged status as the state-sanctioned institution it had been for most of three hundred years. The Test and Corporation Act of 1828 granted Nonconformists the right to hold public office, and Catholics were extended similar rights by the Roman Catholic Relief (or Catholic Emancipation) Act of 1829 (though with much less immediate impact, given that Catholics constituted only about 4 percent of the church-going population in England at mid century). These acts were precursors of religious legislation in subsequent decades that gradually reduced the legal exclusivity of the Church and extended greater political equality not only to Nonconformists, but to Catholics and Jews; indeed, the century charts the step-by-step, de facto disestablishment of Anglicanism.

A major turning point in this process came with the 1851 Census of Religious Worship.[9] It revealed two ground-shaking facts. First, in a nation that considered itself unequivocally and thoroughly Christian, the total percentage of the population that attended church of any kind was only around 60 percent. Second, of that number, the percentage who claimed to be Anglicans was only 51 percent, a number that would decline in the second half of the century to below 50 percent. The first of these facts became a clarion call to action for British Protestants regardless of denomination. The second finally toppled the long-standing claim that the Anglican establishment represented a substantial majority of Britons, which had been a primary rationale for its privileged status.

The 1851 census also revealed the extremely robust and diverse state of Nonconformity. It identified thirty different Nonconformist denominations or sub-denominations of adequate size in membership to merit separate counting.[10] The largest three were the Methodists, of which seven different subgroups were counted, the Congregationalists, and the Baptists, with six subgroups. It included the four most noted denominations of "Old Dissent"— Congregationalist, Baptist, Presbyterian, and Quaker—and the four largest denominations of "New Dissent" that had emerged from the Evangelical Revival: Methodist, Calvinist Methodist, Baptist (the minority of total Baptists), and Unitarian. One traditional distinction between old and new dissent concerns the difference between Calvinistic theology, according to which only the elect or predestined can be saved, and Arminian theology, according to which salvation is available to all through faith. But even in the eighteenth century only the minority of dissenters were true Calvinists, and the nineteenth century saw Calvinism become increasingly unpopular. What most distinguished new from old dissent was the heightened emphasis on evangelicalism, the spiritual and moral imperative to spread the word of God.

While evangelicals were motivated, as Elisabeth Jay notes, by "the heart's consciousness of sin and the need for Christ's redemptive power," the "insistence on the primacy of the individual's relationship with his Saviour, maintained through prayer and the search for guidance from Scripture, allowed considerable variation in the interpretation of these 'vital simplicities' " of evangelicalism (Jay 1). Indeed, the focus on individual responsibility for one's salvation and individual communion with Scripture and with God—unmediated by clergy, church, or state—was endemic to Protestantism from its beginning in the Reformation. It was part of the logical historical trajectory of Protestantism that each individual could in theory become his or her own minister and his or her own congregation. This explains why there were an estimated 63,000 non-denominationally-affiliated worshipers in "isolated Congregations" in England in 1851(groups like the Church of Christ or the Brethren, as vividly portrayed in Edmond Gosse's 1907 memoir *Father and Son* [Parsons, "Dissenters" 102]). Congregationalists and Baptists were so wary of hierarchical institutional control that they placed the first-order of authority over theology and practice with each congregation of individual worshipers.

For such reasons, Max Weber in *The Protestant Ethic and the Spirit of Capitalism* (1905) forwarded a theory of the parallel historical development of Protestant individualism and the self-satisfying individual of laissez-faire capitalism. That theory appears to be fully realized in the case of nineteenth-century Nonconformity. As Gerald Parsons writes in this regard: "Nonconformist theology, politics, social leadership, church organization and attitudes to social reform all reinforced one another. At the heart of this synthesis was a commitment to individualism....Thus, paradoxically, commitment to the moral priority of the individual conscience gave early and mid-Victorian Nonconformity a unity of purpose and an essential common identity and standpoint" (Parsons, "Dissent" 87). For very good reasons, then, the success of Nonconformity in the nineteenth century was founded upon "a network of Nonconformist banking, manufacturing and professional families committed to the ideals of mid-Victorian free trade and *laissez-fair* individualism" that later in the century was "peculiarly open to an alliance with Gladstonian Liberalism" (Parsons, "Dissent" 88). I will return to these features of Protestant individualism in analyzing Victorian constructions of Buddhism, but the point to be made now is that in theory there could have been as many "Christian" responses to Buddhism as there were individual Protestants, with Catholic responses added on top of these.

How then is it possible to address the Christian response to Buddhism in nineteenth-century Britain on any other than an atomized basis? Certainly there was a broad range of Christian responses to Buddhism, everything from categorical condemnation of it as the paganism of an inferior race to celebration of it as a moral system compatible with Christian ethics with a founder pleasingly similar to Jesus. One approach would be to look for clearly delineated patterns of response according to denomination, or even at the level of Anglicanism, Nonconformity, and Catholicism. However, I have not found that to be the case, at least not in any easily defined way. In the large body of periodical articles written in the nineteenth century comparing and contrasting Christianity and Buddhism, one finds articles by Methodists that treat the doctrines of karma and reincarnation as potentially valid, essays by Catholics that condemn Buddhist materialism, articles by lay Anglicans that praise the Buddhist ethical system, and pieces by university-based Anglicans who denounce Buddhism as atheistic nihilism. The difference is not primarily between denominations. Often one cannot tell the denomination of an author. If one published in *The Dublin Review,* the "leading Roman Catholic journal in Britain," or *Fraser's Magazine,* which was "Liberal Conservative with broad Church associations," or, even more clearly, in American journals like *The Methodist Review* or *Unitarian Review,* then one might have grounds for assuming the affiliation of the author (Fraser, *Gender* 215, 217). Even this assumption is risky. Authors generally do not announce their denominations. More significantly, they do not appear to respond to Buddhism primarily as Congregationalists or as Catholics or as Broach Church Anglicans or, for that matter, as humanist agnostics who still profess a Christian worldview and ethics. They nearly all write on behalf of Christianity as a whole, making general claims about the similarities and differences between Buddhism and "Christian belief," or about what "Christianity demands," or about "Christian tradition," or the "Christian world."

If there are patterns in the responses by Christians on behalf of Christianity to Buddhism, they probably had less to do with denomination than with position on the scale of latitudinarian to evangelical, pluralistic to fundamentalist, or, in twenty-first-century terms, liberal to conservative. Broad Church Anglicans may have had as much in common, theologically, with some Unitarians than with Low Church Anglicans. Evangelical Anglicans often found more in common with evangelical Nonconformists than with High Church Anglicans. What generalization can be made, then, about the difference between latitudinarian and evangelical responses to Buddhism? Perhaps obviously, the more religiously pluralistic the commentator, the more willing he or she might be to treat Buddhist history and doctrine either with an attitude of objectivity or with interest and sympathy. This description clearly identifies Broad Churchman, but it also includes a spectrum of liberal-intellectual Nonconformists and Catholics, as well as those who synthesized a pluralistic Christianity with elements drawn, for instance, from Spiritualism or from Buddhism directly.

That said, the more evangelical the writer, the more likely she or he might be to reject Buddhism outright or vehemently to defend Christianity while scathingly criticizing Buddhist tenets. The most fundamentalist of Victorian Christians—which, as in the case of Primitive Baptists, correlated with lower-class status—either would not have heard of Buddhism at all or, if they had, probably would have dismissed it out of hand as beneath consideration. They did not tend to publish essays in the *Westminster Review,* which is a reminder that educational level and class status—themselves correlated—also influenced

the nature of responses to Buddhism. They did not do so in any straightfor-
ward way, however, since some upper-class, university-based comparative religion scholars steered their treatment of Buddhism to reaffirm the preeminence
of Christianity, and some middle-class Nonconformists accommodated elements of Buddhism to their faith, even using Buddhist doctrine to critique the
failure of Christianity to remedy the excesses of the market and the inequalities
of society. Thus in discussing Victorian Christian responses to Buddhism, one
might be advised to distinguish at least between latitudinarian or pluralistic and
evangelical or fundamentalist positions.

Having emphasized the potential diversity of Christian positions on Victorian Buddhism, I want to note that there still existed a significant degree
of commonality, and certainly so among Protestants. On the Anglican side,
despite the apparent chasm separating Tractarians from evangelicals, there was
a solid foundation of agreement between them. Both "espoused the quest for
holiness of living...both agreed on the divine inspiration of scripture, both
agreed on the essentiality of the doctrines of divine judgment and eternal punishment, both held uncompromisingly supernatural view of Christianity, and
both firmly believed in miracles, revelation and the literal fulfillment of prophecy" (Parsons, "Reform" 34). Indeed, these features might apply to the large
majority of Victorian Christians of any type. A different, if not entirely different, consensus existed on the Nonconformist side. In 1846, the Evangelical
Alliance was formed in England, creating an elastic unity within diversity. Its
nine-point doctrinal statement included points familiar from the history of
Protestantism, such as the "utter Depravity of human nature in consequence
of the Fall," the "Justification of the sinner by Faith alone," and the "right
and duty of Private Judgement in the interpretation of the Holy Scriptures."
As Parsons argues, "it was precisely the cohesive and coherent *unity* of Nonconformity which explains its prominence and importance in Victorian public
life" (Parsons, "Dissent" 87). And, as I have suggested, that unity extended
beyond Nonconformity; the Evangelical Alliance included as signatories Low
Church Anglican congregations as well. Indeed, one of the overarching religious trends of the nineteenth century was toward increased evangelicalism,
not only across the spectrum of Nonconformists but among British Protestants in general, including Anglicans.

This trend toward evangelicalism was counterbalanced in certain respects by
another overarching trend: "By 1900 both Anglicanism and most of the major
Nonconformists denominations were doctrinally pluralist" (Parsons, "Dissent"
111).[11] Victorian Protestants, if more evangelical, became more tolerant of difference, at least among themselves. This may be one explanation for why they
became more willing to entertain Buddhist concepts toward the end of the
century. It would not be unsupportable to take the nine points of the Evangelical Alliance as representative of the major component of Victorian Protestant

Christianity by the end of the century, while still recognizing the importance of non-evangelical Protestantism and, in a separate but small category, Catholicism. It is this platform I cite when in the course of this book I refer to "Victorian evangelicalism" or "Victorian fundamentalist Christianity."

Here I make several final observations about Victorian Christians in general, including Anglicans, Nonconformists, and, to a limited extent, Catholics. First, as Hugh McLeod observes in opening his study, *Religion and Society in England, 1850–1914,* during this period "a relatively high degree of religious consensus existed, which had diminished by the early twentieth century, but had not yet broken down" (McLeod 1). This consensus, which was "accept[ed] by most of the population of Protestant Christianity," included "acceptance of the Bible as the highest religious authority, and of moral principles derived from Protestant Christianity, practice of the Christian rites of passage, and observance of Sunday" (McLeod 1). Second, Victorian Christians shared historically and culturally specific conditions, and this unity of experience generated a certain uniformity of response that spanned denominations. For example, British Christians in general experienced a shock from the 1851 census that church attendance, especially among the working classes, was lower than expected; this signaled a potential "decline of faith" and demanded some response in the form of "home missions." Of course, the more evangelical denominations and sub-denominations responded most vigorously. And all denominations experienced the threat that the authority of scientific materialism posed to the authority of the Bible. All experienced the advent of Darwinian evolutionary science as a crisis within the faith as a whole, while of course Biblical literalists were most reactive. In response to common crises, Christians of all denominations tended to speak in ways if not identical then at least using a shared vocabulary and to speak on behalf of Christianity as a whole. A lesser shared crisis was the counter-invasion of Britain by Buddhism. Spokespersons for Christianity from multiple denominations expressed concerns about Buddhism through a common repertoire of responses that focused on a discrete set of questions, assessments, and constructions. One goal of this book is to analyze the most prevalent of those responses and to identify the most commonly posed questions, assessments, and constructions.

Thus at times I make use of categories that threaten to lose significance through generality, namely, "Victorian Protestantism" and "Victorian Christianity." Where I reference the former of these, I am making a statement that I intend to encompass the most representative position shared by nineteenth-century British Protestants, Anglican and Nonconformist. Where I write of "Protestantism" without further qualification, I mean to generalize about the historical and doctrinal features that distinguish the collective of all denominations that trace their origins back to the Reformation, as for example the emphasis on individualism or on faith over works. Finally, where I refer to "Victorian Christianity," or to categories like "Christian sin and redemption," I mean the historical and doctrinal consensus of Christianity that distinguishes it from other world religions. The history and doctrines that virtually all denominations of Christianity share at however general a level, such as belief in the birth and crucifixion of Jesus of Nazareth, or belief in some version of sin, redemption, and heavenly reward. To put this in a more discrete and historically grounded way, in certain moments in the analysis I take as my exemplars those Victorians who, regardless of denomination, felt it appropriate to refer to Christianity as a whole in comparing it with Buddhism.

Forms of the Counter-Invasion

The counter-invasion of Britain by Buddhism took place via a diversity of vehicles and media. The earliest of these was through human contact itself: the hundreds and then thousands of Britons who traveled to the Orient and returned; the much smaller number of people from Eastern countries who visited or immigrated to England; and, as Robert Young and others argue, the real and imagined contact between bodies, the most threatening being sexual contact across racial boundaries. Other primary vehicles of the counter-invasion were the artifacts brought back to England: the thousands of scrolls, robes, prayer wheels, figurines, singing bowls, tapestries, statues and other items, including the Amaravati bas-reliefs, accumulated in London museums, as well as the thousands of pages of ancient and contemporary religious manuscripts in many different languages, including those in Sanskrit that Brian Hodgson had delivered to London.

But the primary vehicles for the counter-invasion were texts produced primarily in Europe, though also in Anglo-India and other imperial enclaves, in response to the foreign human contacts, artifacts, and manuscripts already mentioned. The end of the eighteenth century saw accelerated publication of translations, government reports, travelogues, and missionary narratives, among other types of texts, issued from or pertaining to countries with ties to Buddhism. Many examples of each of these genres exist, but then genre boundaries often were far from distinct. Some early works mixed bits of translation and travelogue with missionary report, study of a foreign religion, or polemic against that religion. This was true in part of two of the most widely read works on Buddhism at mid-century, the Reverend R. Spence Hardy's *A Manual of Buddhism, in its Modern Development; Translated from Singhalese Mss.* (1853) and The Right Reverend P. Bigandet's *The Life or Legend of Gaudama, The Buddha of the Burmese* (1858).

But perhaps the single most influential source of texts was comparative religion: scholarship was a primary vehicle for Buddhism into Western culture. Burnouf's groundbreaking work was followed by an outpouring of scholarly production, of which these, along with those already cited, are representative: Jules Barthélemy Saint-Hilaire's *Le Bouddha et Sa religion* (1860); Hermann Oldenberg's *Buddha: Sein Leben, seine Lehre, seine Gemeinde* (1881); T. W. Rhys Davids's *Lectures on the Origin and Growth of Buddhism* (1884); Ernest J. Eitel's *Buddhism: Its Historical, Theoretical and Popular Aspects* (1884); and Monier Monier-Williams's *Buddhism, in its Connexion with Brāhmanism and Hindūism, and in its Contrast with Christianity* (1889). Every author treated in this book was exposed to works of comparative religion and to the popular commentary upon them in the periodical literature. All of them directly referenced or alluded to those works in their writings.

However, the British reading public at large, including some indeterminate percentage of those outside university-educated circles, would have been exposed to Buddhism primarily through the periodical press. The numbers of newspaper and journal articles with "Buddha" or "Buddhism" in their title increased significantly on a decade-to-decade basis between 1850 and 1900.[12] The counter-invasion arrived in no small part on the flood of periodical literature about Buddhism that occurred after mid century. In order to illustrate this point, I will focus on one debate that persisted over the course of several decades, the Christianity-versus-Buddhism debate. Perhaps the largest percentage of the newspaper and journal articles on Buddhism addressed similarities and differences between it and Christianity, not infrequently denouncing Buddhism while defending Christianity against encroachment. More than a few articles were titled simply "Christianity and Buddhism," and these ranged from thoughtful comparisons to polemics against Buddhism to, in a few cases, advocacies for Buddhism.[13] Other articles clearly announced their mission in their titles, for instance, C. de Harlez's "Buddhist Propaganda in Christian Countries" from the *Dublin Review* in 1890, or F. F. Ellinwood's "Buddhism and Christianity—a crusade which must be met," published in *The Missionary Review of the World* in 1891.

But it was the apparent similarities between Buddhism and Christianity that afforded the best opportunities for Europeans to begin to approach it. Three such features of Buddhism were potentially attractive: (1) its presumed historical similarities to Protestantism; (2) the life and personality of its founder; and, (3) its ethical system. One common conception of Buddhism was as the "Protestantism of Asia" (Clausen, "Victorian" 7). Some argued that Siddhartha Gautama had broken from the Brahmanical hierarchy in a way similar to Jesus's break from the Hebraic elders, Martin Luther's launching of Protestantism, and the emergence of the Church of England from Catholicism. One author in the *Journal of Sacred Literature and Biblical Record* in 1865 commented,

"Caste or Brahmanism, which is the same thing, is the system, Buddhism is the protest against the system" (J. M. M. 282).[14] According to the story of his life popularized in poems and essays, Gautama had forfeited wealth and royal blood, opposed the "priest-ridden" hierarchy to found a religion of individual practice, and transcended the inequalities of the caste system to offer a path that all could walk in equality (Max Müller, *Chips* 241). Thus a qualified pro-Buddhism strain, even in the mouths of some Anglican clergymen, became a part of Victorian anti-Catholic discourse. This Protestant construction was supported by a general acceptance of the Buddha's saintliness. Even detractors of Buddhism drew comparisons between Buddha and Jesus; the "founder's personality" became a major draw, as Richard A. Armstrong observed in an 1870 piece in *The Theological Review* (Armstrong 198). Many Victorians were fascinated by the life story of the Buddha, and, following half-a-dozen book-length accounts by prominent scholars, numerous journal articles summarized his biography with varying degrees of sympathy and accuracy to the available historical sources.[15]

Perhaps the single most attractive feature of Buddhism was its ethical system as outlined in the Five Precepts and the Noble Eightfold Path, partial corollary to the Ten Commandments, though the differences between the two sets of tenets are much more profound than the similarities. Buddhism arrived in England at the time when mid-Victorian liberal intellectuals like John Stuart Mill, George Eliot, and Matthew Arnold were striving to generate non-theological ethical systems to provide a basis for moral order in society.[16] It arrived in this context as a fully articulated, rigorous, and historically tested ethics that did not depend on a supernatural source but still was part of a religion, as opposed to a strictly humanistic philosophy. Thus John R. Ambereley, writing in *The Theological Review* in 1872, proclaimed that Buddhism "has the credit of placing morality far above everything else as a means of obtaining the blessings promised to believers," and Helen Graham McKerlie, in the *Asiatic Quarterly Review* in 1890, concluded that "we owe much of the morality and civilization of the world to the life of renunciation and self-sacrifice of Gautama Buddha" (Ambereley 316; McKerlie 225).[17] Monier Monier-Williams, an outspoken critic of Buddhism, admitted a laudable similarity to Christian morality of the Buddhist ethical system, which he called "one of the most perfect which the world has ever known," though he goes on to argue, as many Victorians did, that Buddhism is "no religion at all, but a mere system of morality and philosophy founded on a pessimistic theory of life" (Monier-Williams, *Buddhism* 217, 537).

While the perceived similarities of Buddhism to Christianity and the strengths of its ethical system made it appealing to some, those qualities also heightened the potential threat of Buddhism as a rival. A number of its features must have been especially threatening, since they received repeated commentary in the periodical literature. In the first place, the realization, which emerged as data on the ancient history of India amassed, that Buddhism had preceded Christianity by over five hundred years brought with it the implication that Jesus of Nazareth may well have studied at the feet of "wise men from the East." By the 1890s, the thought that "Buddhists had been in the Holy Land during Christ's life-time was an idea very much in vogue" (Whitlark, "'Nirvana Talk'" 27). It was only a step from there to speculating about the influence of Buddhist parables on the Bible, for which there was some historical support.[18] Ernest J. Eitel was not alone in 1884 in asking, incredulously, "Are we to conclude then, that Christ—as a certain sceptic would make us believe—went to India, during the eighteen years which intervened between his youth and manhood, and returned, thirty years old, to ape and reproduce the life and doings of Shâkyamuni Buddha?" (Eitel 15). Consider, for example, the title of J. G. R. Forlong's article "Buddhism, Through what Historical Channels did it influence Early Christianity?," which appeared in *Open Court* in 1887, or Feliz L. Oswald's "Was Christ a Buddhist?" from *The Arena* in 1890, which was reprinted in the London *Review of Reviews* in February of 1891.

A lesser but persistent concern among commentators was whether the world population of Buddhists outnumbered the Christians. As Richard Armstrong put it in 1870, "The God of Sinai and the gods of Olympus are not representative of the general faith of humanity," yet "we have run to our next-door neighbours for a declaration of their views, and given out these as the opinions of all mankind" (Armstrong 178). A scare arose when early estimators designated, inaccurately, the populations of China and the entirety of Southeast Asia as Buddhist, sparking a mixture of a Malthusian fear of being out-peopled with a Darwinian anxiety over the statistics of competition and survival.

To make matters worse, John Stuart Mill, in "The Utility of Religions," used the large number of Buddhists to argue, as one contemporary critic summarized his point, "that mankind can perfectly well do without belief in a heaven or a future life" (Gordon 527). Other critics tried to discount the apparent population advantage by turning into an indictment what some other Victorians saw as an admirable feature of the history of Buddhism: its tolerance of other religions and general refusal to use violence as part of its evangelism. John Ambereley, in his 1872 article, wrote that "Buddhism does not teach the necessary damnation of those who do not believe in Buddha, and in this respect I think it is more excellent than the other religions which teach that all but their own followers will surely go to hell" (Ambereley 317). But Reginald Copleston, Bishop of Colombo, in a well-argued 1888 polemic against Buddhism, answered the threat of being outnumbered with the argument that Buddhism "is a parasitic religion, ready to thrive where it can, without displacing or excluding others" and so never could mount a unified assault on Christianity, being too impurely mixed with each country's indigenous practices

(Colombo 121). It seemed undeniable, however, that adaptability had proved to be a historical advantage for the spread of Buddhism. In relation to a nation like England that, while intolerant not only of non-Christian religion but of non-Anglican Christianity, was perhaps exceptionally tolerant of the free exchange of ideas, Buddhism's tolerance and adaptability suited ideally the purposes of cultural counter-invasion.

The Christianity-versus-Buddhism debate was a primary response to and expression of the nineteenth-century counter-invasion of Britain by Buddhism. As such, it usefully demarcates the boundary between what Victorians could accept and what they could not accept about Buddhism. It therefore points to a related question that underlies this book's analysis. Which aspects of Buddhism were assimilable by Victorian culture, and which were not? Also, what can we learn about that culture from those differences? Victorians recognized certain elements of Buddhism, by which I mean they could perceive the meaning of those elements as expressed in their sources and could respond through agreement, qualification, or counter-argument. Those elements were assimilable in varying degrees. Assimilability implies some degree of compatibility, "assimilating Buddhism in so far as it correlate[d] with normative Victorian ideas and values" (Almond 132). In these cases, we can observe the re-presentation of those elements within Victorian discourse in ways that mixed efforts at even-handed treatment with appropriation of Buddhism for purposes that served those normative ideas and values. Thus even the elements of the Buddhist ethical system with which Victorians took exception were recognizable and, to some extent, assimilable.

But certain other elements of Buddhism could not be recognized. These were the aspects most antithetical to Victorian ideology and to Western metaphysics generally, so far outside of the Victorian worldview as to be incommensurable and, therefore, incomprehensible, beyond meaning. While some assimilable elements of Buddhism also were threatening and therefore required reinterpretation, the unassimilable elements were utterly heretical, blasphemous, horrifying, and so could not be expressed within Victorian discourse except as denial or trauma. To summarize only briefly here, those included the absence of a creating deity, the replacement of the system of personal sin/redemption by the impersonal system of karma, the abandonment of individual heavenly reward for continuous reincarnation without continuous identity, the perceived annihilation of nirvana, and the Buddhist "no-self" doctrine, which was directly antithetical to the foundational principles of Protestant and capitalist individualism. Thus unassimiliability signals much more than foreignness; it identifies those elements of the other that perfectly correspond to blind spots within the self, the most potentially disruptive and revealing sites. Assimilability is an extremely useful index of the boundaries, adaptability, and absolute limits of Victorian culture.

Thus while the Christianity-versus-Buddhism debate was a significant expression of and response to the counter-invasion, it serves largely as historical background for the purposes of this study. The real frontier of the counter-invasion, the more difficult interface to locate and analyze, was the boundary between assimilability and inassimilability. Locating and analyzing that boundary must be the ultimate object, as crucial as it is illusive, of this book.

Chapter 1

The Life of the Buddha in Victorian Britain

Competing Victorian Buddhas

Thousands of late-Victorian Britons went about with images of the Buddha floating in their heads. While this may sound like a statement out of Lewis Carroll—who indeed did allude to Buddhism in the Alice books—it is nonetheless a fact, if for no other reason than that three book-length poems recounting the life of the Buddha were published in London in the 1870s and 1880s: Richard Phillips's *The Story of Gautama Buddha and his Creed: An Epic* (1871), Sir Edwin Arnold's *The Light of Asia. Being The Life and Teaching of Gautama, Prince of India and Founder of Büddhism* (1879), and Sidney Arthur Alexander's much briefer verse narrative, *Sakya-Muni: The Story of Buddha* (1887), which won the Newdigate Prize that year at Oxford. Arnold's *The Light of Asia,* beyond being a bestseller, was a cultural phenomenon in England, as well as in America and India. Though it has received scant critical attention since the nineteenth century, "Immediately after its first publication in 1879 it became one of the most popular long Victorian poems; its author...achieved overnight fame throughout the English-speaking world, and for two or three decades the poem exercised an intellectual and religious influence out of proportion even to the hundreds of thousands of copies which it sold" (Clausen, *Light* 1). Arnold's work marked and to a limited extent caused a cultural attitude shift in the West concerning perceptions of the Buddha and receptivity to Buddhism. Reading it moved Charles Bennett in 1901 to become Ananda Metteyya, the first British Buddhist monk. "Like many before him and untold thousands since, [he] found that a new world of spiritual adventure was opened before his eyes," as illumined by *The Light of Asia* (Humphreys 13). Arnold's work inspired Rudyard Kipling's creation of the Teshoo Lama in *Kim* (1901) and influenced, however diffusely, a generation or more of British writers, including W. B. Yeats and T. S. Eliot.[1] In one of the many favorable contemporary reviews, Oliver Wendell Holmes wrote from America that "its tone is so lofty that there is nothing with which to compare it but the New Testament" (Holmes 347). For this very reason, however, the poem motivated no less than four book-length rebuttals, all written by clergymen who were alarmed that it "had enormously increased an already existing interest in Buddhism which threatened the predominance of Christianity" (Clausen, "Sir" 185).[2] What conditions laid the groundwork for the tremendous response—both positive and negative—elicited by *The Light of Asia?* Why were late Victorians so primed to be fascinated with the life story of a religious figure who lived in India over 500 years before Christ, and what does the fact that they were fascinated tell us about them?

Three preliminary answers to the first of these questions come to mind, which though obvious and sweeping are nonetheless pertinent, namely, the much-analyzed Victorian "crisis of faith," the advent of Darwinian evolutionary theory, and the culmination of the British Empire in the second half of the nineteenth century. It is not insignificant for Arnold's writing of *The Light of Asia* or for the popularity of the poem that it was published eight years after Charles Darwin's *The Descent of Man* (1871) and only three years after Queen Victoria was named Empress of India. The British occupation of India and colonial presence throughout Southeast Asia had laid the groundwork for Arnold's poem decades earlier by opening the channels through which the sacred texts of Eastern religions would filter back to Europe.[3] The years between 1860 and 1890 saw an outpouring of scholarly translations from Sanskrit and especially from Pali, as well as a rush of scholarship that focused more on Buddhism than on Hinduism or Islam. During the same decades in which Darwin published his paradigm-shifting works, the formation of the new discipline of comparative religion shifted the paradigm of religious studies. One of its founders, Friedrich Max Müller, helped define it with such works as *Lectures on the Science of Religion; with a Paper on Buddhist Nihilism* (1872). In 1881, T. W. Rhys Davids and his wife, C. A. F. Rhys Davids, formed the Pali Text Society, which continues to be active at Oxford and that in the nineteenth century produced thousands of pages of translations that still are considered authoritative today.

The general point here is that Darwinian evolutionary theory, comparative religion, and the first major object of its study, Buddhism, entered British public consciousness at roughly the same time, contributing separately and conjointly to the ongoing crisis of faith within the Church of England, especially. In part as a result of this confluence, comparative religion and the understanding of Buddhism in Britain intermeshed with the discourses surrounding the evolutionary theory debate. Thus comparative religion drew on the historicizing trend that also characterized recent "Higher Criticism" of the Bible and took as its purpose the "scientific" comparative analysis of the origins and evolution of religions. Every aspect of this approach was threatening to divine mystery and to any claim for the one true religion. Similarly, the British construction of Buddhism emphasized the parallels between scientific law, especially as described by evolutionary theory, and the Dharma, often translated as "Law," or between natural causality and the causal necessity of karma, or between the evolution of species and the progressive evolution that many Westerners assumed occurred between lives in the cycle of reincarnation.[4] These parallels lent credibility to Buddhism in the eyes of those who subscribed to some form of evolutionary theory and made Buddhism all the more persuasive as a potential spiritual or ethical alternative to those who had lost (or never held) their faith in Christianity. By the same token, these associations with Darwinism made Buddhism all the more damnable for some concerned Christians, particularly fundamentalist and evangelical Protestants, Anglican as well as Nonconformist. Any analysis of Victorian portrayals of the life of Buddha must consider how they incorporate and respond to evolutionary theory.

The more specific point to be made is that Edwin Arnold's *The Light of Asia,* rather than springing without precedent from an individual man's Oriental infatuation, was the culmination and expression of an historically specific wave of interest in the Buddha in the West. A large amount of scholarship provided the foundation for the success of Arnold's poem, and a heated public dialogue followed on the heels of the scholarship. As comparative religion focused on Buddhism, so the debate that soon swelled the intellectual, popular, and religious presses focused on the figure of the Buddha. Multiple articles published in France, Germany, England, and America offered accounts of the life of Buddha to a newly fascinated readership. Many of those contributed to what might be called the Victorian Jesus-versus-Buddha debate.[5] Even some critics of Buddhism acknowledged the saintliness, wisdom, and compassion of its founder. Some who were attracted to Buddhist thought became interested in pursuing the implication, made with increasing frequency, that early Christianity had borrowed from Buddhism.[6] In addition, the picture of Siddhartha Gautama emerged as one who had broken from the "Brahmanical hierarchy" much as Jesus later broke from Judaism and as the Church of England broke from "priest-ridden" Catholicism (Almond 72). As James Freeman Clarke, a Unitarian minister, wrote in 1869, "Buddhism in Asia, like Protestantism in Europe, is a revolt of nature against spirit, of humanity against caste, of individual freedom against the despotism of an order, of salvation by faith against salvation by sacraments" (Clarke 713). Max Müller summarized the resulting dilemma: "In no religion are we so constantly reminded of our own as in Buddhism, and yet in no religion has man been drawn away so far from the truth as in the religion of Buddhism. Buddhism and Christianity are indeed the two opposite poles with regard to the most essential points of religion"; yet, Jesus and Buddha remain strikingly similar (Max Müller, *Lectures* 113). Thus any study of Victorian portraits of the Buddha must take into account parallels and divergences from traditional conceptions of Jesus.

This chapter pursues these questions and issues through a comparative analysis of Edwin Arnold's *The Light of Asia* and Richard Phillips's *The Story of Gautama Buddha*. The analysis is motivated and organized by one additional question: why was Arnold's poem such a tremendous success with such far-reaching influence when Phillips's poem received so little notice, indeed, no notice of any kind in print that I have been able to find? Arnold was knighted and nearly made the Poet Laureate; Phillips appears to have dropped forever from public sight after the publication of his poem. Yet, both poems focus on the same subject, only eight years separate their publication dates, and each was published by a nationally known house. What, then, accounts for such a wide disparity in reception and impact, and what do the answers to this question tell us about the Victorian engagement with the life of the Buddha?

Sources for the Victorian Buddha

Either factors external to *The Story of Gautama Buddha* and *The Light of Asia* or factors internal to them, their portrayals of the character of Buddha—or both—must account for the difference in reception and impact. The short period of time that separates the publication of the two poems argues against the possibility of a significant change in receptivity. However, evidence suggests that such a change did indeed take place in those eight years. In his preface, Phillips himself claims that "Gautama Buddha is at present hardly known to any but oriental scholars and literary men" (Phillips v). Yet, only eight years later, T. W. Rhys Davids, in favorably reviewing Arnold's work, worried that the story was "too familiar to the reading public for the poem to become popular" (Clausen, "Sir" 184). That a contextual change did occur during these years is supported by comparing the articles on Buddhism in successive editions of the *Encyclopaedia Britannica*. The 1810, 1842, and 1854 editions, for instance, use their definitions of "Hinduism," "Buddhism," and "Islam" as opportunities to assert the superiority of Christianity. In the 1842 article on Buddhism, as Sheila McDonough argues, "little is said save that Buddha was an incarnation of Vishnu, and that the sceptical doctrines which he disseminated in the course of that delusive manifestation became afterwards blended with a variety of other ideas and practices" (McDonough 779). However, "by 1880 the tone of the Britannica articles has again changed," thanks to the work of scholars of comparative religion: "The work of these men in translating the source material for the major world religions, in attempting to enter imaginatively into the inner meaning of the religious experience of persons in other traditions, and in conveying their knowledge in a dramatic and effective manner to western readers, seems finally to have broken through the wall of prejudice in the West, and to have made it possible for the authentic voice of the eastern traditions to begin to be heard in the pages of the Encyclopaedia" (McDonough 783). McDonough goes on to note that "by far the most striking instance of the changed attitude in this edition is the presentation of the life and teaching of Buddha," a change undoubtedly influenced by *The Light of Asia*.

Another factor to consider is which primary sources were available in translation to Phillips and Arnold. If one considers only those books available in English prior to 1870, then the primary sources for Phillips would have been The Right Rev. P. Bigandet's *The Life or Legend of Gaudama* (1858), derived from Burmese sources, and R. Spence Hardy's *A Manual of Buddhism* (1860), which relies on ancient Ceylonese texts. Though each of these authors worked toward accuracy and evenhandedness, neither was sympathetic to Buddhism; both were missionaries, and they wrote in large part to give those who followed the information necessary to know what they were up against and, therefore, the best strategies for converting Buddhists to Christianity. This lack of sympathy is evident in Phillips's poem, but not in Arnold's. Though Arnold in fact includes more Biblical allusions than does Phillips, Phillips's purpose was to show that Buddha suffers by comparison with Jesus, while Arnold's purpose was to draw upon the parallels in fashioning a sympathetic Buddha. Arnold had read Bigandet and Hardy, but by the time of his writing a much different body of source materials was available. In 1871, Henry Alabaster published his still influential work, *The Wheel of the Law: Buddhism Illustrated from Siamese Sources;* it includes a sympathetic retelling of the life of the Buddha and an articulate defense of Buddhism addressed specifically to Western readers by the Singhalese intellectual Chao Phya Thipakon. Two of the most important other sources for Arnold were Samuel Beal's *The Romantic Legend of Śākya Buddha* (1875) and T. W. Rhys Davids's widely read *Buddhism: Being a Sketch of the Life and Teachings of Gautama, the Buddha* (1877).[7] The first of these, a translation of the Chinese version of the Sanskrit *Abhinishkramana Sutra,* is indeed romantic, colorful, and full of miracles. By contrast, Rhys Davids's book, based on the Pali canon, strives to be historically factual and to demythologize Buddhism; it is considered one of the most thorough and balanced sources in English prior to the twentieth century. Thus Arnold had a larger, more sympathetic, and perhaps more objective body of sources from which to draw, and he actively incorporated what he learned from them.

Arnold was more informed and influenced by comparative religion. Victorian Buddhologists such as Max Müller and the Rhys Davidses spent their professional lives translating and comparatively analyzing ancient texts from disparate locations—Tibet, China, Ceylon, and Burma. Driven by a Protestant belief in the truth-telling authority of the most ancient textual sources, they unavoidably participated in the appropriation of Buddhism from its indigenous contexts by attempting to strip it of local mythologies so that it could be turned into a "purified" textual object of Western knowledge, a project that was inseparable from the British national project of imperialism.[8] Their analysis of the writings enabled them to triangulate between accounts of the life of Buddha that had been separated by centuries, separated by geography (between the northern Buddhism of Tibet and China and the southern Buddhism of Ceylon and Southeast Asia), separated by doctrine (between northern Mahayana Buddhism and southern Theravada Buddhism), and separated by language (between the northern Sanskrit and the southern Pali). In this way, they were able to identify the culture-specific elements of Buddhist practice and doctrine from elements that were duplicated across nations, cultures, and languages and that therefore appeared to be authenticated. Rhys Davids applied this method in relation to the story of the life of the Buddha, concluding: "I would maintain, therefore, that some parts of the story—few indeed, but very important, and sufficient to throw great light on the origin of Buddhism—may already be regarded as historical; other parts may be as certainly rejected; and many episodes remain, which may be altogether or partly fictitious" (Rhys Davids, *Buddhism* 17). It is clear from the array of sources Arnold draws upon that he adopted a not dissimilar strategy of triangulation and synthesis. If he was more confident than Phillips in what he thought were the facts of the story and more possessed of the sensibility of retelling verifiable history, this may be one factor in explaining why his poem was more pleasing and convincing to Victorian readers.

This is not to claim that Arnold's poem is more "accurate" than Phillips's, though it is much more sympathetic to Buddhism, and though it is true that Phillips takes greater license in boldly rewriting part of the traditional story for polemical purposes.[9] Both Arnold and Phillips touch with varying degrees of poetic license and fealty to primary sources on the most frequently recounted historical events in the life of the Buddha. Those events are as follows. In the year 563 BCE, a child named Siddhartha was born near Kapilavastu into the royal family of King Suddhodana and Queen Mayadevi of the Gautama family in the Sakya tribe ("Sakyamuni" means "sage of the Sakya tribe").[10] He grew toward manhood as a prince sheltered from witnessing the suffering of life by his station and by his father, who was determined that he should become a great ruler instead of a great Buddha, as had been prophesized. His father therefore arranged a marriage between the sixteen-year-old Siddhartha and the beautiful Yashodhara, with whom he had a son, Rahula. He continued to live a sheltered life, but on four excursions out of the palace compound he witnessed four events that served as life-changing signs—an old man, a sick man, a dead man, and, finally, a peaceful monk. He experienced the "Renunciation," his decision to leave his life of luxury, privilege, and family in order to become a monk and seek the truth about human suffering and made his "Great Departure." After finding that the most renowned spiritual teachers could not show him the truth, he committed himself to extreme asceticism. After six years of this, he realized that such mortification does not lead to enlightenment and so discovered the "Middle Way" between the extremes of self-indulgence and self-denial. He determined to sit under the Bodhi tree until he found the truth, and after intense struggle (with Mara, the god/devil of death and desire) he attained enlightenment on the day of his thirty-fifth birthday. He traveled to the Deer Park at Sarnath, near Benares, and delivered his first sermon, the "Setting into Motion of the Wheel of the Dharma," in which he preached the Middle Way, the Four Noble Truths, and the Noble Eightfold Path, the cornerstones of Buddhism; later, and for forty-five years, he built up the community of monks, or Sangha, and traveled India teaching the Dharma (truth, law, reality—no cognate exists in English); on his eightieth birthday in the year 483 near the town of Kushinagara, he died, or entered Paranirvana, the state into which one passes who already has attained nirvana.[11] If accuracy means in some way representing these events, on which nearly all primary sources, whether Theravada or Mahayana, agree, then both poems are "accurate."

But historical accuracy or faithfulness to primary sources is not really the issue, nor is it a principle explanation for the differing receptions that the two poems received. Both poems are rife with imaginative projections and divergences from anything in any primary source available to the Victorians. For that matter, there is no single, authoritative source for the life of the Buddha, and different sources vary significantly, especially when it comes to the inclusion or not of miraculous phenomena, though they agree on key historical places and events. The important point is that *The Light of Asia* and *The Story of Gautama Buddha* are themselves cultural artifacts.

I draw three conclusions from this. First, each poem presents specific interpretations of the figure of the Buddha that say more about England in the 1870s–1880s than about India, whether in 500 BCE or in the late nineteenth century. Second, both poems therefore construct images of the Buddha that unavoidably participate in the discourses of cultural superiority/inferiority, West/East, and colonizer/colonized that were part of the fabric of British Orientalism. Third, just as the ancient texts of Buddhism deserve to be read nonreductively, so these two poems need to be read to reveal the full complexity of the constructions that they place upon the figure of the Buddha, which are far from simple, one-sided, or monological. Both poems simultaneously duplicate dominant ideologies of late-Victorian society *and* throw them into crisis, whether by introducing "other 'denied' knowledges [that] enter upon the dominant discourse and estrange the basis of its authority," or by constructing a hybridized figure of the Buddha, or by injecting extreme ambivalence between "us" and "them," British and Indian, Christian and Buddhist (Bhabha 114).

A Secular, Exotic, Protestant Buddha

The Light of Asia and *The Story of Gautama Buddha* share a number of meaningful similarities, the identification of which also will assist in bringing the more significant differences into relief. The first issue to address is literary merit. Suffice it to say that Phillips's 220 pages of heroic octaves are within the same range of accomplishment as Arnold's 231 pages of blank verse. Each author handles the challenges of prosody and of narrative with admirable facility; each poem can be criticized for metrical predictability and narrative awkwardness, though I am not concerned here with evaluation. Literary quality is not a deciding factor.

Both poems largely strip the Buddha story of supernatural phenomena, hence reflecting the influence of comparative religion that embodied the empirical and historicizing tendencies of its age. British scholars came to favor the scriptural accounts in the *Tripitaka* (the "Three Baskets" of canonical scripture) over the popular *Jataka,* a folkloric collection recounting miraculous events surrounding the birth and previous lives of the Buddha. They similarly favored the older Theravadan, Pali canon over the Mahayanan, Sanskrit canon, because they thought the former more "original" or "pure" and the later too heavily colored with demons and miracles.[12] Following this line, Max Müller concluded: "In these three recitation-portions [of the *Vinaya Pitaka,* one third of the *Tripitaka*] then, we have 'in a nutshell' the authentic kernel of Buddhism. The rest of the 'sacred books' and Commentaries are the expansion of its teaching: the Jataka Life, the Lalita Vistara, and the 'Light of Asia' are the fanciful development, in successive degrees, of his biography" (Müller, "Buddhism" 334). It is true, as Müller suggests, that Arnold's poem surrounds the birth of Siddhartha with a selection of the traditional miraculous signs and incorporates several of the *Jataka* talcs. Phillips's poem more strenuously excludes the supernatural, and perhaps this is a small part of the reason that Victorian readers found it less entertaining than Arnold's poem. But Arnold, too, "by excising many miracles and reducing the dependence of the narrative on those that remained,...made the story more coherent and increased its appeal for post-Darwinian readers" (Clausen, "Sir" 177). The fact is that both Phillips and Arnold entirely excluded from their accounts the "Eight Great Events," the primary miracles that are most frequently attributed to the Buddha within certain traditions, choosing instead to focus largely on the "historical Buddha."[13]

As might be expected, both poems appeal to the "exotic Orient" through figures that were long familiar to Westerners by the nineteenth century. The settings, the foreign cultural references, and the use of vocabulary from ancient languages provide an exotic mise-en-scene. Here is one sample of Arnold's cataloguing of exotic elements:

> Its beams were carved with stories of old time—
> Rādhā and Krishna and the sylvan girls—
> Sitā and Hanumān and Draupadi;
> And on the middle porch God Ganesha,
> With disc and hook—to bring wisdom and wealth—
> Propitious sate, wreathing his sidelong trunk.
> By winding ways of garden and of court
> The inner gate was reached, of marble wrought,
> White, with pink veins; the lintel lazuli,
> The threshold alabaster, and the doors
> Sandal-wood, cut in pictured paneling;
> Whereby to lofty halls and shadowy bowers
> Passed the delighted foot, on stately stairs,
> Through latticed galleries, 'neath painted roofs
> And clustering columns, where cool fountains—fringed
> with lotus and nelumbo—danced; and fish
> Gleamed through their crystal, scarlet, gold, and blue.

(Arnold 2:46–47)

This passage continues with a listing of animals—gazelles, peacocks, parrots, snakes, musk-deer, monkeys, and so on—that could have come from, or rather will reappear in, Kipling's *Jungle Book*. In smaller doses, Phillips too dwells on "The luscious fruits that Eastern lands produce" (Phillips 1.23). Predictably, both poems also invoke the figure of the harem and draw on the character-ization of the Oriental other in terms of female seductiveness and receptivity. While both exploit these stereotypes of patriarchal, imperialist wish fulfillment, neither gives them a central focus.[14] Arnold, unlike Phillips, and "unlike any of his predecessors," "was mainly interested in a system of ideas which India had to offer, and everything in the poem is subordinated to a sympathetic (if not always accurate) presentation of the Buddha and his religion" (Clausen, "*Light*" 5). At the same time, however, Arnold enlists the "exotic Orient" more than does Phillips to sell those ideas—and his books—to a Victorian readership, which may be one part of the explanation for the greater appeal of his poem.

The final similarity is that both poems adopt the commonly held but par-tially mistaken perception that Buddha was a reformer who "did for India what

Luther and the Reformers did for Christendom" (J. M. M. 287). It is true that Siddhartha violated the caste system when he abandoned his status, cut his hair, and donned his robes and begging bowl. It is true, as T. W. Rhys Davids observed, that "all of his first disciples were layman [rather than Brahmins], and two of the very first were women," and, as another nineteenth-century commentator wrote, that "Buddha made provision for the diffusion of his doctrines among all classes of the community" (Rhys Davids, *Buddhism* 54; Neale, "Buddha" 445). Buddhism was much more egalitarian than contemporary Brahmanism, but it was not initially socially revolutionary, and its break from tradition was less dramatic than Victorians liked to think. The desire to conceive of Buddhism as a confirmation of Protestantism was so pervasive that Max Müller felt it necessary to rebuke "romantic" conceptions of the Buddha as a "daring reformer" (Max Müller, "Buddhism" 318). *The Light of Asia* was one of Max Müller's targets. The poem indeed portrays the Buddha as ready to question and break from Brahmanic—read "popish"—authority, and it turns his compassion for all sentient beings into something that often resembles nineteenth-century middle-class ideology, as in these lines: " 'Pity and need / Make all flesh kin. There is no caste in blood" (Arnold 6:143). Phillip's *The Story of Gautama Buddha* also contributed to this conception, for example, in these lines in which Buddha casts the Brahmins out of the temple, so to speak: " 'How should they / Who profit most by error lead the way / To reformation, when the same must cost / The giving up of what they value most? / Their hearts are narrow. I must look elsewhere / For that salvation wherein all may share' " (Phillips 6.102). Thus both poems underwrote and helped create a popular understanding of Buddhism as the original protesting reformation. This certainly did contribute to its appeal among the large majority of British Christians who were Protestants, though not enough, apparently, to make Phillips's poem as successful as Arnold's.

Darwinism and Buddhism

It is the differences between the two poems that are most significant in explaining the gap between the receptions that they received. One critical difference is the way that each incorporates and responds to the evolutionary theory debates. Both poems expand upon one stereotypical Victorian image, articulated by Tennyson in *In Memoriam* prior to *Origin of Species*, of nature "red in tooth and claw." Here Arnold improvises upon a common story of the youthful Siddhartha witnessing a worm cut in half by a plow:

> ...then marked he, too,
> How lizard fed on ant, and snake on him,

> And kite on both; and how the fish-hawk robbed
> The fish-tiger of that which it had seized;
> The shrike chasing the bulbul, which did hunt
> The jewelled butterflies; till everywhere
> Each slew a slayer and in turn was slain,
> Life living upon death. So the fair show
> Veiled one vast, savage, grim conspiracy
> Of mutual murder, from worm to man.
>
> .   .   .   .
>
> The rage to live which makes all living strife—
> The Prince Siddhãrtha sighed.

(Arnold 1:25–26)

Siddhartha then meditates upon "this deep disease of life, / What its far source and whence its remedy" (Arnold 1:26). In a similar vein, Phillips writes: "To him the endless war of Nature seemed / Not otherwise than evil, for he dreamed / Of rest and peace and brotherhood" (Phillips 7.112). But here Phillips and Arnold part ways.

Arnold's poem develops three other perspectives on evolutionary theory, the first two of which are potentially contradictory. The poem in places adopts a naively progressive understanding of evolution, an understanding that also was adopted by one strain of Social Darwinism in order to justify "survival of the fittest" as the "natural" condition of the marketplace, a worldview that was on the way to becoming the dominant model for the "natural order" of society.[15] Thus he writes that "Life runs its rounds of living; climbing up / From mote, and gnat, and worm, reptile, and fish, / Bird and shagged beast, man, demon, Deva, God," according to the "fixed decree at silent work which wills / Evolve the dark to light, the dead to life, / To fullness void, to form the yet unformed, / Good unto better, better unto best" (Arnold 4:97, 6:164). This collapses Buddhist concepts of karma and reincarnation into Darwinism, misinterpreting both. In addition, "This notion of progressive evolution bears little relation to anything in Buddhism or in Arnold's sources" (Clausen, "*Light*" 221). Nevertheless, it is consoling, optimistic, especially in a society that conceives of nature as threatening extinction to those who fail to adapt and that therefore chooses to relieve its anxiety by positing infinite progress as the means of escape from the grasp of this avaricious nature.

Arnold's poem develops a second perspective on natural violence that is antithetical to the progressive model, or perhaps simply the other side of the same coin. It suggests that the Buddha did, and humankind should, cultivate compassion and insight in order to control the desire that produces striving, violence, and suffering. This desire is described in the first and second of the Noble Truths, *Dukkha* and *Samudaya,* which state, very roughly, that to live unavoidably involves suffering and that the origin of suffering is *trishna* (literally "thirst"), the desire for everything that one does not and can never possess, namely, unassailable comfort, security, identity, and fulfillment (see appendix 2). Thus Arnold has the Buddha say, "So flameth *Trishnā,* lust and thirst of things / Eager ye cleave to shadows, dote on dreams; / A false Self in the midst ye plant..." (Arnold 8:220). This also is what Thomas Henry Huxley meant by "fountain of desire" in *Evolution and Ethics* (1893): "IF the cosmos 'is just and of our pleasant vices makes instruments to scourge us,' it would seem that the only way to escape from our heritage of evil is to destroy that fountain of desire whence our vices flow; to refuse any longer to be the instruments of the evolutionary process" (Huxley 122). Huxley's purpose was to challenge Social Darwinist assumptions and to argue for controlling those natural desires—celebrated by captains of industry and masters of empire—in order to create a more civilized, equitable, and ethical society. Arnold was a precursor of Huxley, or, more accurately, comparative religion was the precursor, since Huxley draws on the scholarship of T. W. Rhys Davids, identifies the origins of evolutionary theory in "the early philosophies of Hindostan," and writes that "it is a remarkable indication of the subtlety of Indian speculation that Gautama should have seen deeper than the greatest of modern idealists" (Huxley 111, 124). *The Light of Asia* also finds in Buddhism the call to see natural competition and violence not as inescapable but precisely as that which must be understood and controlled in order to escape the cycle of violence that generates suffering in life. As Arnold's young Siddhartha cries, "There must be refuge!" (Arnold 4:97).

Phillips's poem does not share either of these two perspectives on natural violence and evolutionary progress. His argument expresses greater unresolved ambiguity. It surfaces near the end of canto 7, which summarizes Gautama's six years of extreme asceticism, concluding that those years were "not wholly barren of all good," "For he, beholding the continual strife / Of all that therein drew the breath of life—/...felt compassion steal / Into his heart" (Phillips 7.112). The narrator then shifts rather oddly to interrogation of a generic modern Buddhist monk about his efforts to spare the lives even of insects, addressing him in present tense as "Priest of the yellow robe and shaven crown" (8.113). After the monk explains the precept against taking any life, the narrator then turns directly to the reader, or the addressee of the poem, with this admonition: "Be not too lavish of thy scorn on these / Deluded heathen and their practices; / Nor slow to read herein the evidence—/...Of Buddha's doctrine, which somewhat at least / Has changed the hard heart of the cruel East" (7.114). Here, then, is a conflict that is reproduced throughout the poem: the Buddha's compassion is good, but it is deluded. The narrative compounds this contradiction, first claiming that "No great voice bids you

let all creatures live," then staging a debate between an Eastern voice (the generic monk?), which says, " 'But let all breathing things live on in peace,' "
and a Western "you" to whom "the voice" (God?) cries: " 'Freely take and
eat / Whate'er ye lust for; all things are your meat: / All things are yours, do
with them as ye will.' / And yet amid your feasting, thinking still / Of blood-
less Eden, sigh ye for the same, / Nor be of those who glory in their shame"
(7.115). Whose side is the narrator on? There seems to be a genuinely conflicted dialogical exchange here about the merits of resisting the "natural order"
of violence, domination, and, yes, imperial conquest.

The Story of Gautama Buddha conducts this conflicted dialogue throughout
in relation to the topic of empire, with unavoidable reference to British colonial
occupation of India, for which the text both apologizes to the East and defends
the West.[16] From its opening page, the poem reflects an uneasy consciousness
about the violent relationship of West to East, which it expresses through the
logic of paradox by inverting that relationship and making the Orient into the
imperial invader: "I sing not of great heroes who have warr'd, / And reapt
the harvest of the bitter sword: / And yet I mean to tell a wondrous tale / Of
Asian conquest,..." of Asia (Phillips, "Intro." 1). From this opening on, one
subtext of the poem is the difficulty of justifying British imperial violence. The
dilemma that the poem is ambitious or honest enough to set for itself is how
to defend a theory that justifies aggressive conquest relative to a creed that prescribes non-violence and compassion within a religion that is singular among
world religions in not having a history characterized primarily by violence.[17] It
is as if the poem conceives of the Orient and, in this case, the Buddha as the
competition that the British must overcome in conquering the Orient in order
to save it from itself. This is of course similar to how some British missionaries
and colonial governors viewed the indigenous religions and peoples of Asia.

"Militaristic Social Darwinism" was a primary theory used to justify conquest, and, as Patrick Brantlinger has detailed, Victorian debates about Darwinian theory and about empire unavoidably intertwined, as they do in Phillips's
poem (Crook 271). Thus the debate in canto 7 is part of a subtext that questions and, with difficulty, justifies imperial violence as an expression of "natural
law." This debate shows itself, again ambivalently, in the treatment in canto 11
of the third-century Buddhist emperor of northern India, Asoka, who disseminated Buddhism from the Mediterranean through Southeast Asia, "But not
with arguments of sword and flame / Did this man spread his creed—would
that the same / Were true of nations of the prouder West!" (Phillips 11.176).
The debate fully surfaces in the final canto, which struggles to praise Buddha while condemning his teachings: "We will not hate him, but shall we be
blamed / If we admire and love the man who shamed, / By love and gentle-
ness in word and deed, / The hard disciples of a nobler creed?" (13.210). The
monological imperial "we" finally emerges, asserting that it is one thing for

Buddha to "rule the multitudes that dote and dream; / But we are children of the North" (13.215). There is a hint here of concern about the possible counter-invasion of the West by the East, of Christianity by the much older and perhaps more populous Buddhism. But, no: "Our sires of old were worshipers of Thor / And all the hearty Norse gods: they made war / Against the West and conquered.... / ...We have still / The olden vigour and the ancient will"; thus, "we have not ceast / To hold the empire of the slothful East" (13.216). Phillips succeeds at last in justifying the "natural" violence of imperialism, but only through the strained methods of essentializing both East and West and trotting out old stereotypes of the indolent Orient. What is more interesting is the discomfort that the poem generates in arriving at this necessary conclusion, which renders it less than fully convincing. One might think that Victorians would rally to a poem that justified their society's Christian and imperial supremacy, but they did not. Perhaps what they read, accurately, was the moral ambiguity, the "process of *ambivalence,* central to the stereotype" (Bhabha 66). Perhaps they recognized the patriotism required to cover the shame of aggression, the disturbing oscillation between condemnation of Buddhist doctrine and praise of the Buddha's compassion, the dialogical struggle between the voice of the colonizer and the voice of the colonized, which the poem to its credit includes.

Arnold's *Light of Asia*—less gloomy and less self-justifying—provides a third response to evolutionary theory and natural violence not included in Phillips's poem. Phillips subscribes to a dog-eat-dog natural order as the inescapable condition to which humans, and nations, must adapt or die. Far from celebrating this "natural law," he convinces himself to grasp that nettle only because he cannot convince himself that any other alternative has as much scientific or practical force. Arnold, in contrast, forwards the alternative that Buddhism offers: the law of the Dharma. He first portrays the Dharma as a sort of universal natural force, which he refers to as "a Power" and "the great Law," overseeing all living things and connecting them to "The ordered music of the marching orbs" (Arnold 8:212). This is a combination of Romantic organicism with Victorian progressivism, but it also is not entirely divorced from Buddhist metaphysics, which does posit an interconnectedness not only between all living beings but between each one of them and all of the actions that he/she/it ever has committed.[18] This is Karma. Arnold puts these words into the mouth of the Buddha, who speaks for most of book 8 in rhyming quatrains:

> It seeth everywhere and marketh all:
> Do right—it recompenseth! do one wrong—
> The equal retribution must be made,
> Though DHARMA tarry long.

It knows not wrath nor pardon; utter-true
It measures mete, its faultless balance weighs;
Times are as nought, tomorrow it will judge,
Or after many days.

By this the slayers' knife did stab himself;
The unjust judge hath lost his own defender;
The false tongue dooms its lie; the creeping thief
And spoiler rob, to render.

Such is the Law which moves to righteousness,
Which none at last can turn aside or stay:
The heart of it is Love, the end of it
Is Peace and Consummation sweet. Obey!

(8.211, 214)

If not entirely Buddhist, here is a Buddhism-inspired alternative that not a few late Victorians understood as having as much basis in natural law as the law of the survival of the fittest. One 1890 study titled "Buddhism, Positivism, and Modern Philosophy" compared Buddhism to the Law of Conservation of Energy and argued that "Gautama Buddha's doctrine... is the only doctrine as yet known that includes all the elementary processes of this world, both physical and mental; it is the highest generalisation yet proclaimed by man" (Salzer 8). Ernest J. Eitel, a noted scholar and fierce critic of Buddhism, wrote indignantly in 1884 that a "Buddhist may adopt all the results of modern science, he may become a follower of Newton, a disciple of Darwin, and yet remain a Buddhist" (Eitel 63). For this very reason, however, Victorians ranging from liberal intellectual humanists to Broad-Church Anglicans to devout Spiritualists or Theosophists approved of the assumed scientific nature of Buddhism, however accurately or inaccurately understood. A more accurate Buddhist conception than Arnold's would remove his implication of a benevolent inclination on the part of the universe, but it would adhere to an inexorable natural order to the universe, one that is impersonal but just.

In the face of an understanding of nature as not only potentially hostile but indifferent to the survival of the human race and a natural law regulated only by the chances of "random selection," *The Light of Asia* offered a positive alternative: a universe governed neither by God nor by chaos or randomness, but rather governed by an orderly and just natural law.[19] While Phillips's poem projects the Victorian crisis of faith, the Darwinian debates, and reservations about imperial violence back onto the story of the Buddha, Arnold's poem palliates these very anxieties by having the Buddha offer a comforting alternative, partly Buddhist and partly Victorian. Surely this is one reason Victorian readers preferred Arnold's poem.

The Nirvana of the British Empire

The Story of Gautama Buddha and *The Light of Asia* differ significantly in their representations of Buddhist doctrine and philosophy. Indeed, Phillips's poem contains very little indication of what the primary doctrines of Buddhism are, despite the phrase "and his Creed" in its title. Phillips's canto 12 is dedicated to a baffling summary of a Buddhist cosmology (his source for which I do not know), which is at best peripheral to the primary teachings of the Buddha and says nothing of the central tenets of the Four Noble Truths, the Middle Way, and the Noble Eightfold Path. *The Light of Asia,* in contrast, does summarize those tenets and the moral precepts of Buddhism generally and spends much more time on the ideas behind Buddhism than does *The Story of Gautama Buddha.* Demonstrating that would require a thorough analysis of Arnold's book 8 and a more detailed consideration of Buddhist philosophy than is appropriate to my purposes here. Suffice it to say that *The Light of Asia,* unlike *The Story of Gautama Buddha,* provided an extremely rudimentary but "substantially accurate" primer on the basic teachings of the Buddha, which could account for some of its appeal to interested Victorian readers (Clausen, *"Light"* 273).

The more significant difference between the two poems is that Arnold's poem diffuses or reverses several of the most commonly held Victorian stereotypes about Buddhism, which Phillips's poem tends either to reinforce or to redirect to yet harsher criticism. Three of those prejudices can be summarized as follows: (1) Buddhists, like all Orientals, are weak-willed and passive when they should be active; (2) as a result, they are fatalistic, subjecting humankind to predetermination and thereby denying the power and responsibility of the human will; and, (3) worst of all, they are pessimistic and nihilistic and deny the value, not to mention the joy, of life, as evidenced by their inexplicable longing for the annihilation of nirvana.[20]

In challenging the first of these stereotypes, Phillips and Arnold present a Buddha who is far from passive, even if the motives of the two poets could not be farther apart. Both show young Siddhartha winning the hand of Yashodhara through the demonstration of his masculinity at riding and archery, for instance; both show him asserting his will in defying his father's wishes and choosing to cast himself out of the relative Garden of Eden of the palace in order to seek the truth. But there the similarity ends. From that early stage of the story onward, Phillips's Buddha becomes more virile and self-determined, if also haunted by what the poem portrays as a morbid fixation on existential questions—an extremely odd portrayal to anyone familiar with Buddhist literature. His Buddha emerges as possessed of great intellectual as well as physical daring, standing up to and out-thinking the most renowned Brahmins.[21] The poem then casts the Buddha's six years of asceticism as a very Victorian but extremely non-Buddhist struggle over the unresponsiveness of God. He fails to find God because he does not know the correct name by which to call Him, as the narrator concludes: "Yet God is good, tho' Baal hear us not, / And Belus disregard, and tho' our lot / Be nothing bettered by our cries to Zeus / Tho' prayer to Jupiter prove of no use; / Tho' Brahm still slumber in a slothful rest" (Phillips 7.109). The Buddha, whom according to all ancient scriptures chose not to address such unanswerable metaphysical questions as whether or not God exists because they merely distract from genuine practice, then, according to Phillips, becomes an atheist. But, at least he is not a passive atheist.

Here, if not before, is the point at which Phillips's story departs entirely from any source and differs most dramatically from Arnold's account. Canto 8 elaborates a theory about the Buddha's enlightenment that is entirely Phillips's invention. He represents the Buddha as one who believes that he has confirmed the non-existence of God, reasons that he had best not reveal his knowledge to humankind, since that might result in moral anarchy (precisely what liberal intellectuals like Matthew Arnold feared), and concludes that the most compassionate course, under these circumstances, would be to design a new humanist religion. He muses to himself, " 'Thou shalt incur no guilt, / Tho' teaching error and concealing truth; / Because thou doest it from love and ruth, / And these flow not from a polluted fount. / There is no God to call thee to account' " (Phillips 8.128). Through a sort of reverse engineering, Phillips builds a portrait of the Buddha systematically constructing the components of what will become Buddhism, as in this representative stanza:

> Concerning death I will invent a most
> Refined and subtle doctrine that may boast
> Of being better far than truth; for all
> The elements of man at death shall fall
> Apart for ever; yet what he has done
> As a creative power shall still live on,
> and build another life which shall inherit
> Its predecessor's merit or demerit.

(Phillips 8.131)

This Buddha is at once a representative Victorian liberal intellectual humanist—a John Stuart Mill or an Auguste Comte—and an updated version of Milton's Satan. His heart is to some extent in the right place, but he is, as Phillips first calls him in his "Preface," "a willful deceiver, beguiling men to virtue" (Phillips vi). If Phillips's poem debunks the stereotype of the impassive Oriental, it is only because he needs an ambitious Buddha in order to justify a uniquely Victorian theory about the origins of Buddhism.

Arnold's purpose is utterly different, and his diffusion of the active/passive dualism more subtle. No doubt Tennyson's "Ulysses" spoke more directly to many Victorians than did Arnold's response to that poem's last line with these lines: "To seek not, strive not, wrong not; bearing meek / All ills which flow from foregone wrongfulness" (Arnold 6:166–67). At the same time, however, Arnold also portrays an active Buddha, one who seeks the truth about human suffering and who practices active compassion, not passive withdrawal from the world. Starting on his search, Arnold's Buddha says, "Since there is hope for man only in man, / And none hath sought for this as I will seek, / Who cast away my world to save my world" (4:108). He later rebukes the extreme asceticism and apathy of fellow monks: " 'Twere all as good to ease one beast of grief / As sit and watch the sorrows of the world / In yonder caverns with the priests who pray' " (5:124). And here he celebrates the human freedom to exercise will and thereby change one's future: "If ye lay bound upon the wheel of change, / And no way were of breaking from the chain, / the Heart of boundless Being is a curse, / The Soul of Things fell Pain. // Ye are not bound! the Soul of Things is sweet, / The Heart of Being is celestial rest; / Stronger than woe is will: that which was Good / Doth pass to Better—Best" (8:210).

In thus providing a counter-image to the stereotype that Buddhists lack active will, Arnold also addresses the second stereotype of Buddhist fatalism. His Buddha presents karma not as inescapable fate but as the conditions that one has made for oneself and from within which one can choose to advance by intentions and actions in each present moment (a model not dissimilar to George Eliot's "web" of "sympathy" in *Middlemarch*).[22] He shows "how man hath no fate except past deeds, / No Hell but what he makes" (7:183). Arnold understood Buddhist morality as placing greater responsibility on the individual for his/her past actions and more, not less, emphasis on the exercise of will and choice in every moment of life. As Helen McKerlie wrote in 1890, "The hardness of attainment and apparent impossibility of Buddhist holiness lies in this doctrine of free will and responsibility of action," and Reginald Copleston, Bishop of Colombo and no friend of Buddhism, lamented the Buddhist evasion of God's redemption in placing so much moral responsibility on individual " 'Effort,' 'exertion,' 'self-training,'...Gautama's key to morals" (McKerlie 129). Thus Arnold, whether unintentionally or shrewdly, appeals in his portrait to the Victorian discourses of "improvement" and "self-help."[23] As one is responsible for one's own actions and the resulting suffering—"Ye suffer from yourselves. None else compels"—so one has the freedom to exercise discipline and self-control in order to overcome suffering, enjoy life more, and advance toward enlightenment: "Within yourselves deliverance must be sought" (8:210, 208). At the same time, Arnold also calls upon those elements of Victorian middle-class ideology that privileged one's work and worthiness over one's bloodline and status, as in this passage: "Each hath such lordship as the loftiest ones; / ...Act maketh joy and woe // ...Who toiled a slave may come anew a Prince / For gentle worthiness and merit won; / Who ruled a King may wander earth in rags / For things done and undone" (8:209). In these ways Arnold's poem not only worked to undermined key prejudices but to replaced them with appealing aspects of Buddhism presented in recognizable terms.

One of the strongest prejudices against Buddhism that hardly could be rebutted, since it is all but undeniable, is that Buddhism is atheistic.[24] Arnold, unlike Phillips, therefore chose largely to avoid confronting it directly. In one of the few places where it does arise, Arnold's Buddha, on the brink of his renunciation, criticizes "Brahm," not "God": "How can it be that Brahm / Would make a world and keep it miserable, / Since, if all-powerful, he leaves it so, / He is not good, and if not powerful, / He is not God?" (Arnold 3:80). Many Victorians had this very thought. For the most part, *The Light of Asia* strives to ameliorate this concern in less direct ways. As already shown, it mildly anthropomorphizes the Dharma, making it if not God then at least benevolent and progressive in tendency. Arnold also enlists the commonly acknowledged parallels between Jesus and Buddha, characterizing the Buddha and his mission in the Christ-like terms of saving suffering humanity, thereby figuratively preserving one part of the Christian deity.[25] Moreover, the poem never directly denies or defends the absence of a monotheistic deity from Buddhism but rather redirects attention that might go to this issue to descriptions of the doctrines within Buddhism that effectively take the place of God (from a Western perspective). The descriptions of doctrines such as karma and reincarnation then enlist terms from familiar Victorian discourses—self-help, for example—to make those doctrines seem a reasonable and not unpalatable alternative to the moral economy of sin/redemption or hell/heaven. Without doing excessive violence to Buddhist concepts, though obviously appropriating them, Arnold skillfully translates them for Victorian culture and subtly maneuvers through the minefield called "the death of God."

These same strategies also serve Arnold's presentation of the most troubling of Buddhist concepts for Victorians: nirvana. Since there is "no way to isolate a simple, primordial meaning of nirvana in the Buddhist usage," and since different schools of Buddhism themselves disagree over whether the Buddha offered a definitive statement about nirvana, it is understandable that the Victorians failed to arrive at a consensus definition (Welbon 299).[26] Attempts to do so generated tremendous debate among scholars of Buddhism and, following the publication of *The Light of Asia,* "the nature of nirvana was a relatively common topic of conversations among people more interested than knowledgeable" (Whitlark, "Nineteenth" 17). Three understandings of the nature of nirvana dominated nineteenth-century Western debates: (1) that nirvana is annihilation, the utter cessation of being, sans afterlife, sans any continuing soul (especially since in Buddhism there is no soul, in the Western sense, to continue); (2) that nirvana is the merging of individual consciousness into the godhead or the universe, Brahm or the Oversoul; and, (3) that nirvana is an enlightened state that one can attain while still living on the earth, a transcendence of all attachment and aversion. The first two of these were by far the most common, the former being adopted by the first generation of Buddhologists and by those throughout the century least sympathetic to Buddhism, and the second being adopted by those who were sympathetic to Buddhism, if generally not very knowledgeable, and who therefore wanted to believe that nirvana approximates the Christian heaven.[27] Phillips's *The Story of Gautama Buddha* falls into the first camp; his Buddha says, " 'Cessation of existence I will call / Nirvána and my rest" (Phillips 8.132). Arnold's poem partially adheres to the second position, and its challenge to the general opinion of nirvana as annihilation helped many of its first readers to be open to a concept that otherwise would seem to them to be inconceivably nihilistic. Here, for example, Arnold's Buddha says, "Seeking nothing, he gains all; / Foregoing self, the Universe grows 'I': / If any teach NIRVANA is to cease, / Say unto such they lie. // If any teach NIRVANA is to live, / Say unto such they err; not knowing this, / Nor what light shines beyond their broken lamps, / Nor lifeless, timeless, bliss" (Arnold 8:226). As these lines illustrate, Arnold also was either canny enough or knowledgeable enough—or perhaps purposefully vague enough—to avoid simple definitions. The statements that his Buddha makes skirt the abyss of annihilation while painting nirvana less as a facsimile of heaven than as the cessation of earthly suffering, as in these stanzas:

> He [who has ceased to cling to
>   life]—dying—leaveth as the sum of him
> A life-count closed, whose ills are dead and quit,
> Whose good is quick and mighty, far and near,
> So that fruits follow it.
>
> No need hath such to live as ye name life;
> That which began in him when he began
> Is finished: he hath wrought the purpose through
> Of what did make him Man.
>
> Never shall yearnings torture him, nor sins
> Stain him, nor ache of earthly joys and woes
> Invade his safe eternal peace; not deaths
> And lives recur. He goes

Unto NIRVĀNA. He is one with Life,
Yet live not. He is blest, ceasing to be.
OM, MANI PADME, OM! the Dewdrop slips
Into the shining sea!"

(Arnold 8:216)

It is indicative of Arnold's success in ameliorating Victorian trepidations about
nirvana that "the Dewdrop slips / Into the shining sea!" was the poem's most
quoted phrase (Clausen, "*Light*" 271). The use here and elsewhere of familiar
Christian markers, such as "sin" (which does not exist in the Christian sense
in Buddhism), is less an attempt to make Buddhism into Christianity, I would
argue, than an attempt to express Buddhist concepts in terms recognizable to
a Victorian audience. For similar reasons, Arnold avoids dwelling directly on
the most incendiary topics while at the same time intimating them in non-
threatening terms. In "Foregoing self, the Universe grows 'I'," for example, he
alludes to the concept of *anatman* ("no self") but without rubbing his readers'
noses in a central Buddhist idea that is antithetical to Western metaphysics and
directly threatening to foundational beliefs of both Protestantism and capitalism, such as the body/soul dichotomy and the self-originating individual.[28]
Thus, in the face of arguments by early scholars and divines that Buddhism was
"a system of cold Atheism and barren Nihilism," Arnold was able to provide a
much warmer and less barren counter-image (Eitel 97). However accurate or
inaccurate, his image was more influential than that of most of his critics, both
because of the circulation of *The Light of Asia* and because it simply was more
pleasing for late-Victorians to contemplate.

The Role of Woman

The final, significant difference between Phillips's *The Story of Gautama
Buddha* and Arnold's *The Light of Asia* is the representation of women. The
difference is dramatic in the first place because Phillips's poem portrays no
significant female characters. Siddhartha's mother, Mayadevi, gives birth and
dies; Yashodhara appears briefly as the sexually attractive wife; the only comment about women made by Siddhartha is a slight to one of the other suitors
trying his manhood for Yashodhara's hand: "Go home, thou girl, and help
the women spin" (Phillips I.37). Arnold's poem, by contrast, gives meaningful roles to three female characters: Yashodhara, Kisagotami, and Sujata.
Arnold spends much more time on Siddhartha's married life with Yashodhara than do any of his sources. His Siddhartha not only expresses love for
Yashodhara but consults her in the early stages of his spiritual struggles. Seeing
him distracted, she asks, "'Hath not my Lord comfort in me?'" He responds,

"'Ah Sweet!...such comfort that my soul / Aches, thinking it must end, for it will end /...And all my heart is fixed to think how Love / Might save its sweetness from the slayer, Time" (Arnold 3:64–65). The entirety of book 4 concentrates on Siddhartha's decision to renounce family and caste, but the real focus is on the painful separation from Yashodhara, often from her perspective. She wakes him, saying "'Awake, my Lord! / Give me the comfort of thy speech!'" and reports three dreams of premonition that she has had. He comforts her, asking her in future to remember that "Always I loved and always love thee well, / And what I sought for all sought most for thee" (4:89, 93). More significantly, he then explains to her at length the reasons for his pending renunciation, whereas in none of Arnold's sources does Siddhartha "conduct philosophical discussions with his wife" (Clausen, "*Light*" 232). In parting, "thrice he made to go, but thrice came back" to Yashodhara's side, a scene that appears in no primary source. Nearly all of this is sheer romantic invention, but it served a very important function in relation to Arnold's initial readership. It provides an image of married love that spoke to Victorian readers, recognizes Yashodhara's partnership with Siddhartha, and acknowledges the validity of a woman's painful emotional experience in finding herself married to a Buddha.

Kisagotami and Sujata are relatively minor characters in ancient accounts to whom Arnold gives his own interpretation and significance. Kisagotami was a woman who came to the Buddha in grief over the death of her child.[29] The parable recounts how he told her that she would find relief from black mustard seed (suggestive of the subsequent Christian parable), but only if "Thou take it not from any hand or house / Where father, mother, child, or slave hath died" (5:126). After many unsuccessful tries, she finds through the Buddha's compassionate teaching that "The grief which all hearts share grows less for one" (5:128). Clausen's comment on Arnold's rendition is telling: "A more crucial difference is that in Arnold the sorrow of Kisagôtami and of those whose relatives have died is one of the motivations for Siddârtha's quest, while in the source it is simply a proof that 'among all living things there is no permanence'" (Clausen, "*Light*" 246). In Arnold's telling, Kisagotami functions not only as the vehicle for a very touching story about the sorrow of mothers but also as a spiritual guide to Siddhartha.

And this is very much how the poem presents the story of Sujata. In Arnold's telling, Sujata's story is preceded by the Buddha witnessing on the road "a band of tinseled girls, the nautch-dancers" who sing, "*The string o'erstretched breaks, and music flies; / The string o'erslack is dumb, and music dies; / Tune us the sitar neither low nor high*" (6:143, 144). Weakened from years of extreme asceticism, he comments to himself "'I strain too much this string of life'," and thus is guided by a group of women toward realization of the Middle Way, the balance between utter denial of desire and compulsive gratification of desire (4:144).

Near death, he sits beneath a tree to meditate and is encountered by Sujata, the daughter of a local landowner, a recent mother herself, who offers him a bowl of ceremonially purified milk. This, according to Arnold, is a major turning point, more so than in any primary source.[30] Sujata shows the Buddha The Way in the act of giving him the sustenance essential to pursue it. Moreover, the Buddha then asks Sujata for guidance: "Yet doest thou truly find it sweet enough / Only to live? Can life and love suffice?" (6:149). What follows is a multi-page soliloquy by Sujata about the joys and trials of her life, one full of family and love and faith in the goodness of life, which ends, " 'What good I see humbly I seek to do, / And live obedient to the law, in trust / That what will come, and must come, shall come well' " (6:151–52). Gautama responds: " 'Thou teachest them who teach, / Wiser than wisdom in thy simple lore. / . . . In this is seen why there is hope for man / And where we hold the wheel of life at will" (6:152). Sujata's character replicates certain elements of Victorian patriarchal ideology as the poem transposes the image of the domestic, middle-class "good wife" onto ancient India. However, it also gives Sujata her own story and, perhaps, her own voice, though this might be debated. Most importantly for the question of reception, it was these very elements of ideology and this image of domestic sympathy that "hailed" Victorian readers and contributed to the success of Arnold's poem.

The inclusion of women in *The Light of Asia* served several important purposes for Arnold and for his Victorian readers. It was instrumental in providing a humanized and life-affirming image of the Buddha. It suggested, regardless of fealty to primary sources, that it was this life-affirming impulse, rather than fatalism or nihilism, that prompted the Buddha to sit beneath the Bodhi tree and attain enlightenment, which he commits himself to do following his encounter with Sujata. It made female characters integral to the Buddha story and attributed to them the extremely important role of serving not only as comforters and providers but as spiritual guides. Finally, it thereby affirmed certain middle-class values concerning love, domesticity, and mutuality between women and men (which of course is not the same thing as equality). Certainly these features would have contributed to the greater appeal for Victorian readers of *The Light of Asia* as opposed to *The Story of Gautama Buddha*.

How Victorians Preferred Their Buddha

The success of *The Light of Asia* compared to *The Story of Gautama Buddha* indicates a preference on the part of a large number of late-Victorian readers for a life of the Buddha that presents itself as objectively historical, as opposed to one that presents itself obviously as a critical reinterpretation, even when (or perhaps particularly because) that reinterpretation serves certain dominant Christian, capitalist, and imperialist ideologies. These Victorian readers preferred the "historical Buddha" over the supernatural Buddha, though a few devas, demons, and miracles are good to spice up the story. They preferred a Buddha who could be thought of as the original protestant reformer, a precursor and justification for the majority of their own Protestantism. They preferred a sympathetic portrayal of the Buddha over a critical characterization of him as a brilliant and compassionate but misguided and unprincipled schemer. They preferred a Buddha whose similarities to Jesus recommended rather than condemned him. They preferred an accessible summary of the primary doctrines of Buddhism over a reduction of them that precluded further assessment by the reader. They sought an intellectual understanding of spiritual matters, and, as subjects of the history of Protestantism, they felt capable as individuals of assessing spiritual claims for themselves. It would appear that many preferred to hold open for consideration an alternative religious or moral system rather than condemn it peremptorily on the grounds that it was non-British and non-Christian, at least in the case of Buddhism. They were interested in considering spiritual options, not least because the Christian worldview increasingly was being called into question. They preferred a story of the life of the Buddha that included significant female characters and the domestic experiences they typically associated with women, as opposed to one that excluded women and did not represent romantic, matrimonial, or familial concerns. They preferred to see the Buddha both as titillatingly exotic and, more importantly, as familiar, as a human being who not only practiced great compassion but who also seems to have endorsed certain cherished, middle-class ideals, such as moral earnestness, self control, responsibility for one's actions, reward according to merit, improvement through the exercise of will and choice, and discipline in achieving spiritual growth.

Victorian readers, it would seem, also preferred *not* to be confronted baldly either with the most perturbing and threatening aspects of Buddhism or with the most painful dilemmas facing their own society. Arnold therefore handles with great discretion the atheistic nature of Buddhism, the potential nihilism of nirvana, and the Buddhist conception of self as ever-changing, non-unified, and non-continuous after death. Phillips's poem instead takes "the death of God" head on, and, though the purpose is to refute it, the effect is to stir up a painful consciousness of an ongoing crisis within Christianity, in particular Broad-Church Anglicanism. It is doubtful that the poem offered balm to any other than those whose faith already had placed them beyond the need for it. Similarly, Phillips's poem thematizes Victorian anxieties over evolutionary science and British imperial violence by enacting them in the life and time of the Buddha; it brought into glaring focus some of the most troubling issues for late Victorians. Arnold, to the contrary, soothed or sublimated those anxieties while at the same time using them subtly to invite receptivity to Buddhism. Arnold's genius was not in his prosody or his story-telling ability but rather in his ability to read the concerns of late-Victorian society and to respond to them by "skillful means," to use a Buddhist phrase. Thus he redirected potentially inflammatory anxieties about God, natural violence, and empire in the process of translating Buddhism into terms that both subtly addressed those anxieties and constructed a Buddha that middle-class Victorians might embrace.

This is not to claim that *The Light of Asia* was less of a vehicle for Victorian ideologies than *The Story of Gautama Buddha,* nor to say that Arnold's poem provides a platform for the voice of the colonized other while Phillips's poem only silences it with the monological voice of God/Queen/Empire. Each of these poems is more complex than that. If Phillips's poem finally reasserts the supremacy of that monological voice, it also interjects an extreme ambivalence throughout that undermines that authoritative voice and permits a Buddhist voice to emerge, however faintly, from the background. Arnold's poem intends to destabilize certain prejudices and to offer a genuine alternative, but at the same time it unavoidably reproduces elements of dominant ideology, for example, in Christianizing Buddhism and in marshalling the middle-class discourses of domesticity, progressivism, and self-help. In one sense, Phillips was more direct and transparent and Arnold more subtle and manipulative, which only made Arnold's poem more palatable and convincing. Thus, for instance, while Phillips directly expresses shame for the violence of British imperial aggression, Arnold represses that issue, covering it with a positive image of the Buddha that both refutes and partakes of Orientalist assumptions. Perhaps the fact that Arnold gave Victorians a Buddha they might embrace only evidences a greater complicity than Phillips in the cooption and conquest of the Oriental other.

I take the view that Arnold's Buddha, and Phillips's Buddha to a lesser extent, is a genuinely hybrid figure and cuts both ways: toward imperial appropriation *and* toward self-effacing acknowledgment of the other. Certainly many concerned Victorian Christians recognized this latter point in viewing *The Light of Asia* as heretical, as blasphemous in the sense described here by Homi Bhabha: "Blasphemy is not merely a misrepresentation of the sacred by the secular; it is a moment when the subject-matter of the content of a cultural tradition is being overwhelmed, or alienated, in the act of translation" (Bhabha 225). In the act of translating Buddhism into a form recognizable within Victorian culture, Arnold also translated his culture away from its own tradition, drawing it blasphemously toward Buddhism. To the extent that his Buddha is "a narcissistic image of the Other," it at the same time "effects a comparable antithetical alienation of European selfhood" (Young, *White* 156). The Victorian Buddha was an identification by Westerners with an Eastern way of knowing, and "what is most graphically enacted in the moment of colonial identification is the splitting of the subject in its historical place of utterance" (Bhabha 46). Victorian identity was split by *The Light of Asia,* and many Victorian readers found that experience exciting, instructive, and enjoyable.

Chapter 2

Buddhism and the Emergence of Late-Victorian Hybrid Religions

The last quarter of the nineteenth century witnessed the generation of new, alternative or syncretic religions in Europe at a rate perhaps unprecedented in modern Western history. Examples include The Church of Christ, Scientist; the Hermetic Order of the Golden Dawn; the Theosophical Society; and Anthroposophy. Some scholars would challenge this broadened use of the term "religion"; I would open the definition even further by including a number of humanist institutions that likewise emerged during that period as surrogates for Christian institutions.[1] For example, the Positivist Political and Social Union, inspired by the writings of Auguste Comte (1798–1857), was founded in London in 1867 and became so ceremonial that Thomas Henry Huxley quipped that "Positivism was Catholicism minus Christianity" (W. Smith 92). In a statement that now appears at least cultural-centric and at worst racist, one commentator in 1889 observed that "for some reason that is not very immediately apparent, the Anglo-Saxon is the only one among modern races that has been fertile in the invention of new religions" (Legge 10). Though most religions claim to have been revealed by a deity, all religions are in fact syncretic, having been formalized through context-specific social processes within history, and all societies invent religions, at the least by reshaping the beliefs and rituals handed down to them to serve new social conditions and cultural urgencies.[2] Given that, the Victorians nevertheless appear to have been extraordinarily active in the invention of new religions. Why? Explanations must come from consideration of the convergence of events and discourses that occurred in nineteenth-century England as in no other time and place. The reason that will be of particular interest here is the European encounter in the first half of the century with Buddhism. Buddhism—the Western construction of it—was a necessary though not in itself sufficient source for the formation of a number of late-Victorian hybrid religions. Indeed, this was one of the most immediate as well as most far-reaching impacts of the encounter with Buddhism upon Western culture. The ways in which new hybrid religions sampled from and modified elements of Buddhism is a study in cultural assimilation and, more telling, failed assimilation.

After attempting to summarize the range of discourses and events that contributed to the late-Victorian flurry of religion production, and after theorizing a working definition of "hybrid religion," this chapter focuses on a case study of a representative example: Theosophy.[3] I analyze the specific ways in which the founders of Theosophy borrowed elements from Buddhism and combined them with elements drawn from other theologies, mythologies, and contemporary ideologies for the purpose of synthesizing a new hybrid religion.

Background: Spiritualism versus Materialism

One of the most pervasive and persistent tensions within the history of European culture is the conflict between materialism and spiritualism, most broadly conceived. One manifestation of this conflict finally erupted in the nineteenth century in full-scale public combat between evolutionary scientists and Church of England apologists following Darwin's publication of *The Origin of Species* (1859). The stage long had been set, not only by immediately preceding scientists like Charles Lyell and Jean-Baptiste de Lamarck, nor alone by the culmination in the preceding century of Enlightenment skepticism, but as far back as the materialist philosophy of the pre-Socratics.[4] Prior to the connotation of "materialism" as a desire for material possessions, "materialist" meant "one who denies spiritual substances," according to Samuel Johnson's 1755 *Dictionary* (Johnson, np). Throughout the first half of the nineteenth century, commentators increasingly associated materialism in this sense with scientific naturalism, the ideology of science's truth-telling authority, as well as with atheism. Many Victorians saw materialism as the historical nemesis not only of Christian belief but of spirituality at the most fundamental level of belief in the human soul. Indeed, "materialism was widely perceived as the arch-villain of the [Victorian] age" (Oppenheim 61).

The Victorian "crisis of faith" was to no small degree the product of the erosion of the credibility of key Christian truth-claims as a result of the widely perceived failure of the Church of England to mount a convincing rejoinder to the challenges of materialism and, in particular, scientific naturalism. Anglicanism, among all denominations, was compromised by the fact that from early in its history it had accommodated the Natural Theology of Deism. Natural Theology, defined as early as Aquinas (1224–74), subscribed to "a body of truths about God and his relationship to the world discoverable by the use of unaided human reason" (Byrne 1). Deists questioned not the existence of God but rather the necessity of demonstrating the existence of God through revelation, miracle, or the supernatural as opposed to the immanence of God in the natural order of the universe. Enlightenment Deism thus was one source for the organic naturalism of Romanticism and the Over-Soul of Transcendentalism, and it became an integral component of late-Victorian hybrid religions. Deism drew upon a number of key distinctions, including these: (1) revealed or supernatural religion versus Deism's claimed natural religion; (2) historical religion, founded upon revelation at a specific historical time and place to a specific people, versus universal religion, the essential religiousness common to humanity and thus to all religions; (3) religion founded on God's judgment and the fallenness of humankind versus religion founded on a model of the universe as naturally just and of humans as innately religious; and 4) religion wedded to the social and political agendas of human institutions versus religion that claims, like Deism, to be original and therefore pure.[5]

Thus Deism represented a compromise between the traditional foundation of Christianity in revealed theology and the rationalism and humanism of the Enlightenment. From the seventeenth century, "natural religion was used to uphold the centrality of a reasonable religion embodied in the faith and liturgy of the Church of England" (Turner, *Contesting* 47). The signature expression of Deism was the well-known "argument from design," which was given clearest articulation in *Natural Theology* (1802) by William Paley, an Anglican clergyman and naturalist. The large majority of eminent scientists in eighteenth and nineteenth-century England were in fact good Anglicans; the history of British science overlaps significantly with the history of the Church. That is, until Darwin, when "the house of science so carefully constructed by the primarily Anglican founders of the British Association [of Science] collapsed as did the tradition of British natural theology that had flourished for two centuries" (Turner, *Contesting* 57). The *Descent of Man* (1871) undercut the consoling belief in a benevolent natural universe centered by its creator on the privileged species, humankind. The failure at mid-century of natural theology to stand up to scientific naturalism created a crisis within the Anglican establishment and only confirmed the suspicions of those who from early in the century had argued not only that the Anglicans were complicit with materialism but that Christianity in general, however purified by the Protestant Reformation, had lost touch with genuine spirituality.

The most direct rejoinder to materialism in the nineteenth century came in the form of the Spiritualism movement. Spiritualism, which now may seem easy to dismiss as little more than superstition and fraud, was a widespread and immensely important cultural movement that expressed some of the most deeply held doubts, fears, and hopes of the Victorians. As Hudson Tuttle, a proponent, argued in *Arcana of Spiritualism: A Manual of Spiritual Science and Philosophy* (1867), if a few people are seeing ghosts, then we call them insane, but if "it is not a single case of insanity, but of millions, all infatuated alike," then we must take such phenomena seriously (Tuttle 48). The movement was sparked in New England in the late 1840s, and in certain ways it was a unique product of North American Puritanism. However, it spread "like a contagious infection" to the Continent and to England, where thousands of séances, both private and public, were held over the course of decades (Brandon 43). By the time the movement had begun to wane in the 1880s—or, rather, by the time it was replaced by the "new occultism" of hybrid religions—it had graced the lips of nearly every British citizen and had drawn royalty, eminent scientists, literary luminaries, and even clergymen into the darkened room of the séance chamber.[6] It spurred the founding of a plethora of spiritualist societies, for example, Birmingham's Midland Spiritual Institute, Nottingham's Association of Spiritualists, or the Union of London Spiritualists; caused the founding in 1882 of an influential scientific society, the Society for Psychical Research; and launched a dozen spiritualist newspapers, including the *British Spiritual Telegraph, Spiritual Magazine, Spiritualist, Medium and Daybreak,* which ran from 1870 to 1895, and *Light,* which began publication in 1881 and continues today.[7]

Though Spiritualism became institutionalized in various ways, and though proponents claimed it as a religion, it was far from uniformly practiced or organized.[8] Its true center, from beginning to end, was really a discursive network linking thousands of parlors and kitchen tables (not unlike the internet today). The tenets shared by Spiritualists of all persuasions were few and basic, as summarized here by an advocate in 1875: "It is simply a belief, first, that man has a Spirit; second, that this Spirit lives after death; third, that it can hold intercourse with human beings on earth" (M. Davis 5). In addition, the Spiritualism movement exhibited five characteristics that I would note because each of them directly influenced the subsequent formation of hybrid religions: (1) a mission to defeat materialism; (2) a claim to an empirical basis; (3) a commitment to radical individualism, coupled with a progressive model of individual spiritual evolution; (4) a debt to the history of European and Judeo-Christian occultisms; and, (5) a recentering of spiritual authority to empower women.

Spiritualism arose in part out of an historically specific cultural imperative to disprove materialism. The Victorian séance was the acting out of that culture's own worst fears. Those fears were not of seeing ghosts; on the contrary, many Victorians desperately wanted to see ghosts. The fear was of *not* seeing ghosts. Not to see ghosts meant for the many followers of Spiritualism the extinction of the human soul. The situation as spiritualists saw it was this: "There is no alternative, material science is fast driving Christianity to the wall. It has taken all the thinkers of the world. The church holds only those who do not think. Spiritualism is the last stronghold against the tide of materialism, and if it fail to establish its claims, the former will be supremely triumphant" (Tuttle 56). However, Spiritualism drew substantial credibility from its claim to be founded on the materialist grounds of empirical proof. The movement had been preceded by the "Mesmerism Mania" that swept through Europe in the first half of the century (Winter 284). Mesmerism was founded on a purportedly scientific theory "derived from the concept of an imponderable fluid permeating the universe," which was theorized variously as gaseous, magnetic/electrical, or atomic (Tatar 4).[9] Those who could master this "animal magnetism" could impose their wills on receptive others through what would come to be called hypnotism (which therefore represents a clear link between Mesmerism early in the century and the "science" of psychoanalysis late in the century). Spiritualism sampled directly from Mesmerism: the mesmeric trance translated into the medium's trance; mesmeric "table turning" morphed into table rapping; and the "imponderable fluid" became the medium through which spirits communicated with the living.[10] Spiritualism also retained Mesmerism's claim to a scientific basis.[11] As Christians of various denominations struggled to defend the unverifiable truths of faith in the face of scientific naturalism's apparently verifiable truths, "many thousands of women and men became spiritualist believers precisely because spiritualism did not demand faith, but instead offered actual demonstration and thus objective 'proof' of its claims" (Owen, *Place* 245). Spiritualism was directly experiential; sensory contact with departed souls was personal proof of the existence of one's own soul, of the existence of a Spirit World, and thus of life after death. As James Robertson put it in 1893, "one single echo, a tiny rap from the [deceased] loved ones, was more value than book revelations, more comforting than what without evidence were simply speculations" (Robertson 66). There was no intended irony in the common argument forwarded on behalf of Spiritualism that it was anti-supernatural. Spiritualists "believed that the erratic phenomena of the séance could be reduced to natural laws and that their enterprises could thereby gain scientific credibility" (Noakes 24). The central contradiction of the Spiritualism movement—one subsequently inherited by hybrid religions—was that while vehemently decrying the march of materialism, it founded itself on terms borrowed if not from that very same materialism then from its assumed ally, scientific naturalism.

Also contradictory within Spiritualism was the fact that, on the one hand, it was a product of the history of Protestant Christianity in Europe and, on the other hand, a trenchant critique of that tradition. Many spiritualists continued to practice as Christians of one denomination or another.[12] They argued that it only revitalized Christianity, furthered a shared anti-materialist agenda, and provided modern proof of the miracles performed by Jesus, whom they

claimed was but the most exemplary, early practitioner of Spiritualism. However, anti-Christian sentiment, with opposition in particular to Calvinist sever-
ity and the doctrines of original sin and eternal damnation, was widespread
among spiritualists. Anti-Christian spiritualists even so shared with Christian
spiritualists a thoroughly Protestant distrust of the "exoteric" trappings of institutionalized religion. Louisa Lowe, addressing a convention of spiritualists in
1877, exhorted her colleagues to " 'overthrow all external authority in matters
of thought; to free mankind from religious dogma and the trammels of priest
craft—in a word, to teach the individual to make his own reason an ultimate
court of appeal in all matters of personal concernment' " (Lowe, qtd. in Oppenheim 99). And this is what Spiritualism asserted: the right of the individual
entirely to control his or her own spiritual practice. In striving for unmediated
personal contact with the Spirit World, spiritualists one-upped Protestantism.
Protestantism had claimed to remove the impediment of church-and-clergy
from between self and God; Spiritualism removed the further layer separating
humankind from Spirit, namely God Himself. Every spiritualist became his or
her own clergy, his or her own congregation, and, ultimately, his or her own
divine Spirit. The individual was freed from the strictures of divine judgment
to pursue what Arthur Conan Doyle, one of the last great public advocates for
Spiritualism, in his 1926 *History of Spiritualism* called the "Eternal progress
open to every soul" (Doyle, *History* 260). Frederic Myers, a champion of psychical research whose lifework was to close the gap between post-Darwinian
science and Spiritualism, likewise championed the "progressive moral evolution" of the soul (Myers 37, qtd. in Oppenheim 269).[13] Spiritualism was in one
sense the logical culmination of Protestant individualism, but to such an extent
that it appeared as the end-point of that historical trajectory and, therefore,
appeared from a Protestant perspective to spell the demise of Christianity.

The opposition between Spiritualism and Christian institutions was endemic to their shared history. The Spiritualism movement was the most recent
manifestation of a long history of occultisms in Europe, the most virulent persecutor of which had been the Catholic Church. The ashes of burned witches
smoldered nearly to the end of the eighteenth century; the Spanish Inquisition
officially ended as recently as 1834 when the Tribunal of the Faith was abol-
ished.[14] A century earlier than this date, séance mediums would have been at
bodily risk; yet, some mid-Victorian mediums became highly-paid celebrities
courted by eminent men and women and invited by royalty. Frank Podmore's
1902 history of Spiritualism starts from the position that it must be analyzed
as "an organic outgrowth from previous forms of mysticism" (Podmore xii).
His two-volume study traces the histories of witchcraft, alchemy, magicianship,
Rosicrucianism, and Mesmerism as the antecedents of modern Spiritualism.
The "recognition of the trance phenomena, as testifying to the existence of a
spiritual world" long preceded Victorian Spiritualism, and, therefore, "the raps

and movement of tables did not, in the ultimate analysis, originate anything; they served merely to confirm a pre-existing belief" (Podmore xiv–xv). In centuries prior to the nineteenth century, entranced or ranting people were thought to be possessed by angels or devils and to demonstrate this by speaking in foreign or unknown languages. Victorian Spiritualism replaced the witch with the medium, replaced "possession" with "channeling," and replaced "speaking in tongues" with common English—sometimes delivered with a regional accent and bad breath, as some séance sitters observed. Possession by devils and angels gave way to visitations from the souls of dead family members (as well as by the souls of famous people like Shakespeare and Napoleon), and indeed the séance was, among other things, a dramatic new form of public mourning. Bolstered by a reinforced ideology of individualism and armed with the modern discourse of science (as opposed to the old science of alchemy), Spiritualism nevertheless belonged to an identifiable lineage of European occultisms.

Representative of that lineage, the Spiritualism movement also was woman-centered. The movement had been launched by the special receptivity of teenage girls and young women; the majority of professional mediums were women; the setting for most séances was the home, that bastion of a "woman's sphere." The domestic séance brought the public, masculine domain of religion back into the private, feminine domain of the dining table or the parlor. Recent scholarship thus has focused on the central role of woman in Spiritualism and the role that Spiritualism played in empowering women in the nineteenth century. Alex Owen opens her study of the gendering of Spiritualism by noting that the movement "emerged contemporaneously with the consideration of women's proper role and sphere which became known as 'the woman question'" (Owen, *Darkened* 1).[15] Janet Oppenheim broaches the issue of Spiritualism and female sexuality with this point: "Without exaggerating the extent of sexual repression in Victorian society, one can surmise that the holding of hands and caressing of spirit forms might have been stimulating not only to the sitters, but also to the young women whose emerging sexuality was denied natural means of expression" (Oppenheim 21). This observation, coupled with Owen's that the "years which witnessed the expansion of women's horizons and the forging of new forms of feminist political consciousness were paralleled by the rapid decline of [full-body] materialized 'forms,'" cleared the way for Marleen Tromp's more recent argument that "full-form materialization mediumship may have made itself obsolete by participating in a shift of codes that made increased sexual freedom less a subject of spectacle and more a part of the norm" (Owen, *Darkened* 234; Tromp 78). Tromp concludes that "Victorian mediums were doing more than locating and carrying on conversations with the angel in the house; they were channeling her to reshape their lives" (Tromp 78). All that I would add to these studies is the broader observation that the Spiritualism movement enacted the cultural assimilation, rebuttal, and triumph over a long history of persecution of women's heretical spirituality. The witches—Wiccans—had come home at last, reclaiming a feminine strong-hold for spiritual practice.

During the same decades in which the Spiritualism movement was striving to staunch the spread of materialism, a new paradigm for religious scholarship emerged that, while arising out of the long European tradition of theological and exegetical studies, diverged from that tradition in critical ways that appeared to align it with materialism. Comparative religion rose to prominence in England in the 1860s, little more than a decade after the advent of Spiritualism, and, along with Spiritualism, proved to be a critically important source for the formation in the following decades of new hybrid religions. By making widely available for the first time the histories and doctrines of a range of Eastern religions, the discipline infused radically new concepts into European discourse. Its rapidly expanding textual base of translations and analyses provided much of the raw material from which the founders of hybrid religions acquired the knowledge of other traditions upon which they drew in synthesizing new ones. It also demonstrated a method for comparing and contrasting diverse traditions that some founders of hybrid religions would apply in sampling components from across those traditions.

Comparative religion, in conjunction with the most dramatic event contemporary to it, the Darwinian revolution, was an essential catalyst for the formation of late-Victorian hybrid religions. Its practitioners in fact adopted the general template of Darwinian science in shaping their research project to find the origins of religions and trace their evolution. The very nature of this project was threatening to some Christian observers and was to spiritualists but further proof of the materialism of the age. To probe the origins of a religion is to dwell upon its historicity, which cannot but cast doubt upon its status as divine revelation. This of course also was what had made the Higher Criticism of the Bible controversial, and, in adapting that same approach to other religions, comparative religious scholars poured additional salt on the painful "European awareness of the fragile historicity of their own God" (Silk 182). F. Max Müller, the most outspoken advocate for the discipline, argued strenuously that all religions were equally worthy of historical and comparative analysis. His intention was not to diminish Christianity, but, any such "discussion of another religion in open-minded and favourable terms naturally weakened the exclusive hold of Christianity, the assumption that the world was divided between one true faith and many pagan cults" (Clausen, "Victorian" 13). Comparative study of religions provided a basis for a pros-and-cons discussion that was threatening by way of its potential evenhandedness. It might provide a basis for the perceived shortcomings of Hinduism, Islam, or Buddhism relative to Christian doctrines and institutions—as indeed many public commentators used it to do—but by the same token it might open Christianity to similar critical scrutiny, within which there was no guarantee that some aspects of other religions might not appear more convincing or attractive. Whether in subject matter or theory and method the "science" of comparative religion, as Müller labeled it, seemed an instrument of materialism that was wielded against spirituality.

This judgment was bolstered by the fact that the predominant object of study of comparative religion in the nineteenth century was Buddhism, which most Victorians understood as a materialist-humanist-atheistic religion, or as no religion at all, merely a philosophy. As T. W. Rhys Davids, perhaps the most prominent Buddhologist of the last quarter of the century, wrote in 1881, Buddhism "proclaimed a salvation which each man could gain for himself, and by himself, in this world, during this life, without any the least reference to God, or to gods, either great or small" (Rhys Davids, *Lectures* 28). This is one reason why the scholar Monier Monier-Williams coupled in the introduction to his *Buddhism, in its Connexion with Brāhmanism and Hindūism, and in its Contrast with Christianity* (1889) a claim to scientific disinterestedness with this condemnation: "I hold that Buddhism...contained within itself, from the earliest times, the germs of disease, decay, and death...and that its present condition is one of rapidly increasing disintegration and decline" (Monier-Williams xv). His summary of definitions of Buddhism is representative of the range of commonly held views at that time: "It is under one aspect mere pessimism; under another pure philanthropy; under another monastic communism; under another high morality; under another a variety of materialistic philosophy; under another simple demonology; under another a mere farrago of superstitions, including necromancy, witchcraft, idolatry, and fetishism" (Monier-Williams 13).

Monier-Williams defeated Müller in the highly politicized 1860–61 contest for the Boden Professorship of Sanskrit at Oxford. Müller represented the "new continental tradition of comparative philology," as opposed to Monier-Williams's more clearly British and Anglican allegiances, and did not appear sufficiently committed to the Boden mandate of "'enabling Englishmen to proceed in the conversion of the natives of India to the Christian religion'" (Beckerlegge 188, 198). Another well-known scholar, Ernest J. Eitel, in his book *Buddhism: Its Historical, Theoretical, and Popular Aspects* (1884), pointed to the feature of Buddhism, after its atheism, that most aligned it with materialism: its perceived compatibility with evolutionary science. Eitel wrote that "Buddhist scriptures have not observed the wise reticence with regard to natural science by which our Christian bible is marked," since Buddhism attained "even so long as two thousand years ago, to that remarkable Darwinian idea of a pre-existing spontaneous tendency to variation as the real cause of the origin of species, but—like Darwin and his School—it stopped short of pointing out Him, who originated the first commencement of the so-called spontaneous tendency" (62, 66). Eitel alludes here to the central Buddhist doctrine of the Dharma, which scholars often translated as "Law."[16] Many commentators writing in the periodical literature assumed a parallel between scientific law and the Dharma, its law of karmic causality, or between the evolution of species and the evolution that many Westerners presumed occurred between lives in the cycle of reincarnation. Buddhism and the first major vehicle for it into the West, comparative religion, hit England arm-in-arm at the historical moment when Christianity, or the main Protestant denominations, were declaring war on evolutionary science. Buddhism entered the fray both damned by its perceived compatibility with that science and, from the point of view of some looking for an alternative religion, advantaged over Christianity for the very same reason.

The Spiritualism movement, the Darwinian revolution, the rise of comparative religion, and the encounter with Buddhism—these were primary sources for the formation of late-Victorian hybrid religions. Each of these broad cultural and intellectual trends was part of the even broader dialectic between spiritualism and materialism. The "spiritual science" of Spiritualism, the "science of religion" of comparative religion, the "scientific religion" of Buddhism, and, as will be shown, the "esoteric science" of Theosophy, participated in the same cultural imperative: to resolve the long-standing and deeply embedded conflict between materialism and spiritualism, science and religion. Figuratively speaking, each functioned as a circuit, or a deconstructing third term, both joining and separating the soul and the body of the Victorian era. The encounter with Buddhism was especially catalytic. Victorians constructed Buddhism as exemplary of the possibility of bridging the gap between materialism and spiritualism, as both apparently scientific and deeply ethical. Victorian Buddhism was both a model of a just universe and a model of a universe without the need for God.

Defining Late-Victorian Hybrid Religions

The traditional term for hybrid religions is "syncretism." Among the oldest uses of the term was that used by Plutarch to refer to the Cretans; his pejorative connotation has dominated its use.[17] It continues today as "a contentious term, often taken to imply 'inauthenticity' or 'contamination,' the infiltration of a supposedly 'pure' tradition by symbols and meanings seen as belonging to other, incompatible traditions" (Shaw and Stewart 1).[18] It rings with a tone not far removed from that of "cult" or "sect." These connotations were cemented by nineteenth-century British discourse in which it came to be used by clergymen and scholars to distinguish the "pure" religion of Christianity from those—including Buddhism—whose "sacred origins" could be questioned (Eliade 218; Pieterse 226).

As this distinction suggests, syncretism as a concept had been implicit in Natural Theology, according to which the same religious impulse is naturally shared by all religions while the institutions and practices of each are context-specific and thus limited.[19] Missionary engagement with other cultures/religions, which for Britain increased dramatically in the nineteenth century, "almost inevitably lead[s] to syncretism" (Droogers 9). Empire is the historical vehicle of syncretism. Understandably, then, it was from the beginning the ultimate subject of comparative religion. Once one begins looking at the origins of religions and the processes by which they distinguished themselves from pre-existing religions, one must recognize that all religions are syncretic. To say that a certain religion is syncretic therefore "tells us very little and gets us practically nowhere, since all religions have composite origins and are continually reconstructed through ongoing processes of synthesis and erasure" (Shaw and Stewart 7). The emergence of Christianity from Judaism and its formalization through a series of councils in the third and fourth centuries was a long and highly political historical process of religion building. However, all religions that claim an origin in divine revelation disclaim their syncretic roots, focus attention on their sacred origin, and strive to place it either outside of history or as the beginning of historical time.

Thus it is that syncretism almost always refers to the religious other. A recent trend in the postcolonial study of religion has been to reopen the topic of syncretism for debate and to attempt to salvage the utility of the concept. The outcome has been the useful recognition that it is best to use "syncretic" not to designate a specific religion or type of religion but rather to describe a process to be studied longitudinally as "a *field of investigation*" (Kraft 148). Syncretism is a process, one shared by all religions but historically unique in each case, through which different traditions and practices come into contact with one another, interact (peacefully or violently), maintain certain boundaries, and interpenetrate one another through influence, assimilation, domination, blending, creolization, etc. It concerns the identity boundaries of a religion and how they change over time as a result of contact with foreign or alien peoples.

I propose not to jettison or replace the concept of syncretism but rather to forward "hybrid religion" as a historically specific case, an event or trend that occurred in the West in the latter decades of the nineteenth century. I choose "hybrid" in part because it avoids the still pejorative flavor of "syncretic," a term that has been used to denigrate the religions about which I am writing, but, more importantly, because it seems especially appropriate to the conditions and phenomena under consideration. It is appropriate to the climatic convergence of multiple, competing discourses of spirituality and of science that occurred in the Victorian era. As the following analysis of Theosophy will demonstrate, the hybridity of late-Victorian hybrid religions often was manifold, mixing and matching elements drawn not just from two but from half-a-dozen religious traditions, and not solely from religions but also from secular discourses, such as scientific naturalism. Here I draw upon an observation by André Droogers that syncretism is not limited to a relationship between two religions but "may occur between currents of one religion, between a religion and an ideology, between religion and science, and between religion and culture" (Droogers 13). All of these combinations are evident in late-Victorian hybrid religions, which, in addition, did not limit the number of any of these variables.

The concept of the hybrid also seems especially fitting for the pressurized amalgamating of cultures precipitated by the British Empire. It is apt for describing the uneasy splicing of alien voices within late-Victorian hybrid religions, a process that resonates with Mikhail Bakhtin's description of "two languages, two belief systems that intersect in a hybrid construction" (Bakhtin 305). The term also draws upon its more recent connotations in the postcolonial theory of Homi Bhabha, Robert Young, and others. Describing Indian responses to Christian missionaries, for example, Bhabha writes, "When the natives demand an Indianized Gospel, they are using the powers of hybridity to resist baptism and to put the project of conversion in an impossible position" (Bhabha 118). As Bhabha would be aware, according to the same logic when a native of whichever hemisphere demands an Eastern-Western, mystical-scientific religion, she too is using the powers of hybridity, and doubly so, both to co-opt— as well as honor—another religion and to renew—and thus subvert—her own religious tradition. Late-Victorian hybrid religions enacted this splitting/ splicing of both self and other simultaneously. Thus a final characteristic that distinguishes late-Victorian hybrid religions is the unusual extent to which their founders consciously set about designing and manufacturing them from an array of components (which is not to deny the unavoidable effect of unconscious cultural assimilation). The founders especially of Theosophy and Anthroposophy adopted an "*intentional programme for syncretism*" (Kraft 156). Since syncretism most typically describes an unintentional historical process that unfolds as the result of two religions coming into contact and, as it were, naturally interbreeding, it is reasonable to distinguish these late-Victorian religions as a special case of arranged, hot-house breeding—hybridization.

What follows is a working definition of late-Victorian hybrid religions. It is a theoretical model and therefore offers many opportunities for future correction and revision. Some of the listed features may apply more to one of the hybrid religions than another. Given the fact that the primary example in the current analysis is Theosophy, some of these features may most accurately describe that hybrid religion, which is to acknowledge that a more detailed treatment of each of the religions that I have grouped together because of their historical proximity is warranted. Given these caveats, I propose that late-Victorian hybrid religions exhibited these features:

1. They were a product of the nineteenth-century "crisis of faith" and the perceived failure of Christian institutions to defeat materialism; thus they all shared a mission to save spirituality from materialism. They strove *either* to renew or reinvent Christianity, as in the case of Christian Science (and the fictional hybrid religion in Marie Corelli's novels), *or* to prove that Christianity was defunct and therefore needed a replacement, as in the case of Theosophy. In both cases, they took part in a flight away from the strictures of fundamentalist, Calvinist, or Puritanical doctrines.

2. They nevertheless were unavoidably a product of the history of Protestantism. They carried Protestant individualism to its logical extreme, centering heavily on individual vocation and will, and they distrusted the imposition of institutional structure on spiritual practice. They also were inherently if not explicitly anti-Catholic.

3. They were a product of the history of Natural Theology or Deism. They shared with the Spiritualism movement and American Transcendentalism a belief in Spirit as a natural universal order or law that stands above and effectively obviates the traditional anthropomorphic God. They claimed that they were an expression of the original and innate religious impetus of humankind that underlies all religions.

4. They were a product of the history of European and Judeo-Christian occultisms and mysticisms. Some cited roots in ancient Hebraic Kabbalahism, early Christian Gnosticism, the Knights Templar, or Rosicrucianism. All shared a debt to the immediately preceding occultisms of the Mesmerism and Spiritualism movements. At the same time, they strove to distinguish themselves from modern movements by claiming privileged access to a more original source (as in Deism) or an ancient wisdom tradition.

5. They combined elements not only from diverse religious discourses but also from humanist and social discourses. They all unavoidably reproduced elements of Victorian ideology, such as "self-help" and progressivism. Most significantly, all were a product of scientific naturalism, enlisting its authority by claiming a scientific basis. They enlisted the language of materialism to disprove materialism. More specifically, all of them incorporated the language of evolutionary science by formulating versions of spiritual progress.

6. They asserted the equality—if not the primacy—of women relative to men in the realm of spiritual and religious practice. Some of them did this as a matter of course at an operational level by the predominance of women in the leadership and membership; some of them stated this explicitly at the level of doctrine. The (re)emergence of woman-centered religion in the late nineteenth century can be viewed as a correction to the history of Catholicism and then Protestantism. It can be viewed both as a component of the emerging women's rights movement and as a manifestation of the positioning within Victorian literary and cultural discourse of woman as the "angel in the house."

7. As the preceding features suggest, they tended to disclaim the very religious and secular discourses to which they were most indebted. For example, they strove to distance themselves from Spiritualism as too undisciplined and popularized while drawing upon its formulation of Spirit.[20] They lambasted scientific materialism while claiming a scientific and entirely natural basis. In this (and like Deism), they claimed to be anti-supernatural, yet some of them cited miraculous phenomena or ancient, revealed origins.

8. Finally, they were the product of empire (which may be true for nearly all occurrences of syncretism). The lynchpin event for the formation of late-Victorian hybrid religions was the influx to European cultures of Eastern religions. Buddhism, as both the privileged subject of comparative religion and the non-Christian religion of greatest interest to Victorians, was among the most important non-European sources for hybrid religions.[21]

To amplify this last point, late-Victorian hybrid religions like the Order of the Golden Dawn or the Anthroposophical Society could not and would not have arisen as they did had the European imperial powers not invaded and colonized Northern Africa, the Middle East, the Indian subcontinent, and Asia. The point is familiar enough: empire provided the means and the motivation for collecting and translating the artifacts and scriptures of ancient Egyptian polytheism, Zoroastrianism, Hinduism, Buddhism, and Islam, among others, and filtering them back into Western cultures. A counter-invasion occurred as these artifacts and translations streamed back toward the seats of empire and began to infiltrate Western discourse. This process was well underway by the time of Charles Wilkins's landmark translation in 1785 of the *Bhagavad Gītā*. That event alone profoundly influenced Western thought, injecting concepts such as karma and reincarnation—as well as vivid images of the "exotic Orient"—into the philosophy of Arthur Schopenhauer, the literature of the Romantics, and the Transcendentalism of Ralph Waldo Emerson. The signs of this counter-invasion can be read throughout the literature of the nineteenth century in all of the Egyptian, Hindu, Islamic, or Buddhist figures that appear in works by Samuel Taylor Coleridge, Edward Bulwer-Lytton, Wilkie Collins, Edward FitzGerald, D. G. Rossetti, H. Rider Haggard, Marie Corelli, George MacDonald, Rudyard Kipling, Arthur Conan Doyle, Joseph Conrad, W. B. Yeats, and T. S. Eliot, among many others.

The Case of One Late-Victorian Hybrid Religion: Theosophy

The Theosophical Society was launched on 7 September, 1875 in New York City by a small group of ardent spiritualists, the most noted members of which

were Madame Helena Petrovna Blavatsky, Henry Steele Olcott, and William
Quan Judge.[22] Blavatsky, the daughter of a Russian colonel and a noble-born
writer, had experienced paranormal phenomena and read Hermetic, alchemical,
Kabbalah, Rosicrucian, and other occult texts since girlhood. A well-traveled
citizen of the world who reportedly had studied mysticism in Egypt and rid-
den with a caravan of Buddhist pilgrims to Tibet, she followed the Spiritualism
movement to its epicenter in New England. Her apartment in New York became an occultist gathering place known famously as "the Lamasery." She and
Olcott met because he had been reporting in the press on the séances that were
occurring in 1875 at the William Eddy farmhouse in Chittenden, Vermont.
The founding principles of the Society, recorded in 1882 and restated here by
Olcott in 1889, were as follows: (1) "To form the nucleus of a Universal Brotherhood of Humanity, without distinction of race, creed, sex, cast or colour";
(2) "To promote the study of Aryan [which then primarily meant originating
in northern India] and other Eastern literatures, religions, philosophies, and
sciences"; and, (3) "To investigate unexplained laws of nature and the psychic
powers of man" (Olcott, "Genesis" 210).[23] Blavatsky recognized that the Spiritualism movement had peaked and was waning and that the Theosophical Society could be the vehicle for her ambition, which was to found a new religion
as an alternative to Christianity. She and Olcott decided to leave New York in
1878 and spread their new religion first to London and then on to India in
1879, where in 1882 they built the current headquarters of the Theosophical
Society International in Adyar (now Chennai). Judge, who became the president of the American branch, broke with Blavatsky and the International in
1895. That branch subsequently moved its headquarters to California, where
today it operates as The Theosophical Society Pasadena (not to be confused
with the American branch of the International in Wheaton, Illinois). But it was
Blavatsky who became the most famous—and infamous—spokesperson for
Theosophy, and I therefore focus on her, Olcott, and A. P. Sinnett, another
primary British spokesperson for Theosophy.

Blavatsky furnished the Society with its spiritual doctrine, its historical underpinning, and its textual foundation. Her major works, *Isis Unveiled* (1877),
The Secret Doctrine (1888), and *The Key to Theosophy* (1889), were best-sellers
representing over three thousand pages and became, in effect, the bibles of
Theosophy. She founded theosophical journals in Bombay, London, Paris, and
New York, and published, over the course of her career, an estimated one
thousand articles in English, French, and her native Russian in these as well as
in other, national newspapers and magazines (Zirkoff ix). At the time of the
Society's Jubilee in 1925, over fifteen thousand theosophical "lodges" were
reported across 41 nations.[24] Few other Victorians—or people of any period,
for that matter—can be said to have founded a religion that continues to be
actively practiced by thousands over a century later.

But Blavatsky's accomplishments were overshadowed in the popular imagination by the scandals in which she was involved. Her detractors charged her with plagiarism in her writings and with fabricating the "Mahatma letters," letters purportedly penned by spiritual guides, whom she and many followers called "The Masters" or "The Mahatmas," and delivered to her from Tibet via psychic airmail.[25] The largest scandal came to a head in 1884 when the Society for Psychical Research, which had been formed in London in 1882, sent Richard Hodgson to Adyar to investigate the authenticity of the Mahatma letters. In his report, published in *The Proceedings of the Society for Psychical Research* in 1885, Hodgson denounced Blavatsky as "one of the most accomplished, ingenious and interesting impostors in history" (Hodgson, qtd. in Sinnett, *Early Days* 66). It is this image of Madame Blavatsky that dominates popular and perhaps academic conceptions of her to this day. The concern here is not with these scandals nor with the question of the authenticity of the paranormal phenomena that Blavatsky marshaled, quite successfully, to popularize Theosophy. Aside from the sensational publicity it generated, the whole furor over the Mahatma letters is irrelevant to my purposes. "Surely," as one skeptical historian of religion put it, "the physical and mental effort expended in incessant letter writing in various hands, the production of multi-volume works of incomprehensible philosophy and pseudo-anthropology, the continuous behind-the-scenes arrangement of marvels—and, interspersed, the seemingly placid at-homes, charged with quiet electricity, delighting the most unsusceptible of guests—surely all this was more than a great hoax or a great joke" (W. Smith 154).

Indeed, anyone who reads Blavatsky's work knows that she was in deadly earnest, even if part of what she was doing elsewhere was smoke and mirrors. *Isis Unveiled* and *The Secret Doctrine* are mammoth accomplishments, vertiginous compendiums of arcane ancient and medieval philosophy and theology of every variety, all packed together with the density of stream-of-consciousness dictation, but all the while maintaining the appearance, if not the actuality, of scholarly rigor. Blavatsky blazed the trail that would be followed by Sir James Frazer, Jessie Weston, and Joseph Campbell, though they might not choose to acknowledge her. I suspect that Blavatsky, though not always the wisest publicist, understood both the coincidence and the difference between the public spectacle she conjured out of thin air and her real work. Her real work was to synthesize a new, hybrid religion, one that could stand up to what she viewed as the hegemonic patriarchal institutions of Christianity, on the one hand, and scientific materialism on the other. My concern is with the processes and sources from which that hybrid religion was constructed and, in particular, the nature of its debt to Buddhism.

Theosophy exhibited all of the features listed in the previous section as part of the working definition of "late-Victorian hybrid religion," and then some.[26]

Like the Spiritualism movement before it, Theosophy joined the Manichean battle against materialism, as Blavatsky writes here in the first volume of *Isis Unveiled*: "Deeply sensible of the Titanic struggle that is now in progress between materialism and the spiritual aspirations of mankind, our constant endeavor has been to gather into our several chapters, like weapons into armories, every fact and argument that can be sued to aid the latter in defeating the former.... Our voice is raised for spiritual freedom, and our plea made for enfranchisement from all tyranny, whether of SCIENCE or THEOLOGY" (Blavatsky, *Isis 1*:xlv). A. P. Sinnett, in *Esoteric Buddhism* (1883), argued that the "esoteric doctrine" of Theosophy was "really the missing link between materialism and spiritualism," because it was a "spiritual science" (Sinnett, *Esoteric* 66). In referring to the "tyranny of theology" Blavatsky meant what she perceived as the repressiveness of "exoteric," institutional Christianity, Christianity that had lost touch with its spiritual origins and become about form and ceremony, politics and power, instead of about "esoteric" spirituality. While Theosophy was like other hybrid religions in responding to the apparent failure of Christianity to defeat materialism, Blavatsky's brand of Theosophy was the only one (of which I am aware) to posit Christianity itself as the major culprit for the ascendancy of materialism. The "Preface to Part II" of *Isis Unveiled* launches itself in this way: "An Analysis of religious beliefs in general, this volume is in particular directed against theological Christianity, the chief opponent of free thought. It contains not one word against the pure teachings of Jesus" (Blavatsky, *Isis 2*:iii, iv). *Isis Unveiled* is in one sense a history of Catholicism in particular from the perspectives of all those whom, according to Blavatsky, it had silenced or persecuted. It may be one of the most sustained critiques of a religion's historical record ever written. By contrast, Christian Science, Anthroposophy, and even Christian Socialism, for example, tried to revitalize Christianity itself in order to breed a more vigorous hybrid for battle against materialism and skepticism.

Blavatsky positioned Catholicism as the primary straw figure to be knocked down, in part for strategic reasons, using it as a foil against which to define her alternative religion; in part because she honestly viewed the Catholic church as the most repressive institution in history; and in part for what must have been personal reasons, given the virulence of her attack on it. Though Theosophy reflected the influence of the history of Protestantism in its emphasis on individualized spiritual practice and its anti-Catholic stance, Blavatsky at the same time disdained as undisguised narcissism the anthropomorphic Personal God or "P.G.," as she called it, that had come to be claimed especially by evangelical Protestants (Godwin 328). She likewise assessed the God of the Talmud and the Old Testament as a small-minded, repressive patriarch who should not be mistaken for the higher-order Divine Spirit that embraces the universe and all of the life that It had created. This is not to say that *Isis Unveiled* casually dismisses Christian belief. On the contrary, Blavatsky in fact wrote "toward the Western and particularly Christian world" in order to offer it a spiritual practice that she argues is more truly Christ-like than the institutional Catholicism that had capitalized on the teachings of Jesus not long after the crucifixion and, in the course of two centuries, consolidated its power in true Roman fashion (Neufeldt 235). Thus *Isis Unveiled* claims to uphold the teachings of Jesus, while simultaneously mounting a series of assaults on the institutions founded in his name, the goal apparently being to convince a Christian readership that Christianity is not the religion they might imagine. The teachings of Jesus about the Holy Spirit, for instance, are the true, founding, esoteric roots of Christianity and, as such, are linked to the "'Secret doctrines' of the ancient universal religion," which Blavatsky posits as the shared foundation for all religions and the source of Theosophy (Blavatsky, *Isis 1*:xi). But, according to Blavatsky's telling, the esoteric aspects were suppressed from the beginning, then officially written out of existence, for instance, at the Council of Nicaea (CE 325), and then violently persecuted as heresy in the Inquisition. As a result, "the true Christ-like principles have been exemplified, and true Christianity practiced since the days of the apostles, exclusively among Buddhists and 'heathen,'" and "the Christian virtues inculcated by Jesus in the sermon on the mount are nowhere exemplified in the Christian world" (Blavatsky, *Isis 2*:81). The best thing that a true Christian could do, according to Blavatsky, would be to adopt "Christism," the worship of Jesus, "in place of Christianity, with its *Bible,* its vicarious atonement" (through the crucifixion, as opposed to direct karmic atonement), and its "personal devil," Satan, that "patron genius of theological Christianity" (Blavatsky, *Isis 2:* 472, 478, 506).

Theosophy was like other hybrid religions in reflecting a debt to Natural Theology. Deism is evident in the conception, familiar from the Spirit World of Spiritualism, of Spirit as the universal, divine source and essence of all being, a concept not unrelated to that of "Providence," which is both more general and less gendered than the masculine "God." Natural Theology also was one source for the theory, central to Theosophy, of the ancient wisdom religion, which is recognizable as a variant of what Peter Byrne in *Natural Religion and the Nature of Religion* characterizes as innate "human religiousness," with "some of the meaning of 'original religion'" (Byrne 10). Blavatsky writes: "What we desire to prove is, that underlying every ancient popular religion was the same ancient wisdom-doctrine, one and identical, professed and practiced by the initiates of every country, who alone were aware of its existence and importance" (Blavatsky, *Isis 2*:99). She summarizes the fundamental beliefs of this ancient wisdom religion as follows: (1) "The unity of God"—though she will define "God" not as the Judeo-Christian deity but rather as "the one infinite and unknown Essence," which predates and supersedes the anthropomorphic deity; (2) "the immortality of the spirit"—where "spirit" is the highest element in a trinity with the "body" and the "astral body" (a partial corollary to the traditional soul), both of which are perishable while Spirit is immortal and unchanging; and, (3) "belief in salvation only through our works, merit and demerit"—which flies in the face of most Christian models of sin and redemption and alludes to the Hindu and/or Buddhist concepts of karma and reincarnation (Blavatsky, *Isis* 2:116, 264). Blavatsky very cannily enlisted a long-standing and widely disseminated popular belief, derived from Deism, in something similar to an ancient wisdom religion. By founding Theosophy upon that belief, she was able to position it as having historical precedence over Judaism and Christianity and as being truer to the original, pure religion (purer than Puritanism, as it were), which Judaism and Christianity had suppressed and forgotten.

She also thereby set the agenda for one of the organizing objectives of *Isis Unveiled:* to trace the history of the Secret Doctrine from around a thousand years before the Common Era up to the nineteenth century as it had been practiced and handed down by the "adepts" of each generation in an historical chain linking ancient Egyptian Isis worship to pre-Hindu Vedanta to Platonic idealism to Hebraic Kabbalah to Jewish and Christian Gnosticism, and so on. By characterizing the vehicle for the ancient wisdom religion as "esoteric knowledge," knowledge known only to initiated adepts and kept secret from the majority of the population, Blavatsky established a number of critical safeguards for Theosophy. She explained why the ancient wisdom was not common knowledge. She placed verification or falsification of that knowledge beyond access by her critics. At the same time, however, she enlisted as examples of former adepts a number of landmark figures—Gautama Buddha, Pythagoras, Plato, and Jesus of Nazareth, for example—whom she argued had been among the most important adepts of the ancient wisdom religion and from whom she therefore could garner immense credibility for Theosophy.

Isis Unveiled recounts the story of how the ancient esoteric knowledge was shared and preserved among various ancient and then medieval visionaries and sects. It does this through a strategy of pseudo-historicism that even so is anchored here and there in recognizable facts and figures drawn from the historical record. The book's argument about cross-pollination between various mythologies and esoteric doctrines across the ancient world is tied to a theory of historical population migrations. The flavor of this approach is indicated when Blavatsky writes, for example, "History tells us of the stream of immigration across the Indus, and later of its overflowing the Occident; and of the populations of Hindu origin passing from Asia Minor to colonize Greece" (Blavatsky, *Isis* 2:428).

The result is a sweeping historical saga, but a saga grounded in periodic reference to events if not fully verifiable then entertained at least by some trained historians, for example: the cross-fertilization in the sixth century BCE between philosophers in what is now northern India and Pythagoras in Greece, which later influenced the idealism of Plato (c. 427–c. 348 BCE);[27] the cultural transference from West to East effected by the march of Alexander the Great (356–323 BCE) into northern India; the subsequent transference from East to West effected by missionaries sent out by the northern Indian, Buddhist emperor Asoka (c. 299–c. 237 BCE), specifically the likely contact between Buddhist thought and the neo-Platonists, the Essenes, and the Gnostics;[28] and, the influence of the Essenes and the Gnostics on the Nazarenes, as in Jesus of Nazareth, suggesting the possibility of a partially Eastern source for the asceticism and the doctrine of compassion for which he became known.[29] Thus for a large number of Victorian readers, as for many Theosophists today, *Isis Unveiled* succeeded in giving a believable impression of historicity, regardless of whatever the actual historical basis may be.

The next step in Blavatsky's genealogy of Theosophy was to trace the esoteric knowledge from the ancient world to the subsequent European occultisms, for example the Hermetic tradition, medieval alchemy, the Knights Templar, and Rosicrucianism. Like other late-Victorian hybrid religions, Theosophy unavoidably owed a debt to the history of European, Judeo-Christian (or anti-Christian) occultism, especially the most recent manifestations, Mesmerism and Spiritualism. Though Blavatsky had practiced as a spiritualist, and though in a limited sense "theosophy originated in spiritualism," once she recognized that Spiritualism was in effect too populist and therefore would not accommodate the doctrinal authority, textual basis, and institutional structure necessary for her purposes, she worked to distance herself and Theosophy from Spiritualism (Prothero "From," 198). Some spiritualists returned the favor by denouncing Theosophy as an appropriation of their ideas. She resented the fact that "Theosophy seemed wedded in the public mind to Spiritualistic phenomena instead of to the high ideals of true wisdom and brotherhood on which the Society was based" (W. Smith 146). An early agenda of the first volume of *Isis Unveiled* is to distinguish the basis of her new religion from the "strange creed" and "fanaticism" of the table rappers and séance mediums (Blavatsky, *Isis* 1:x). She replaces the apparitions of Spiritualism with a concept of Spirit that is above parlor tricks; she replaces the petty (but, she held, authentic) magic of spirit materializations, which might be exposed by scientific investigation, with the "law" of ancient "esoteric science"; and she replaces "mediumship" with the much more exclusive concept of "adeptship." Near the end of the second volume of *Isis Unveiled,* she finally provides a "Summary of the points of the Wisdom-religion" in ten points, the sixth of which is: "Mediumship is the opposite of adeptship; the medium is the passive instrument of foreign influences, the adept actively controls himself and all inferior potencies" (Blavatsky, *Isis* 2:588). Blavatsky's writings theorize an historical and philosophical basis for a spiritualism (in the most generic sense) for the elite "educated intellectual," leaving the Spiritualism movement for "the masses," as one commentator observed in 1891 (Pember 50).

Yet, "Theosophy could not have made a serious bid for attention among Londoners—or elsewhere—if a revival of Spiritualism had not preceded it" (W. Smith 142). Blavatsky understood that Theosophy required not only an historical pedigree but a supernatural endorsement, one more authoritative than the phenomena of Spiritualism. The Masters or Mahatmas and their miraculously materializing letters served that purpose. They provided the proof of the authority invested especially in Blavatsky as a spiritual leader and of the legitimacy of Theosophy as a path. As Blavatsky shrewdly argued, all of the major religions, especially Catholicism, her chosen nemesis, rely for proof of divine sanction on ancient "miracles," which, if taken as true, must demonstrate the efficacy of supernatural phenomena; therefore, the miraculous Mahatma letters only similarly demonstrate the authenticity of Theosophy, as well as suggesting that the miraculous now had gone out of Christianity by comparison. Playing both ends against the middle, Theosophy remained necessarily wedded to the supernaturalism inherited from Spiritualism while it just as necessarily claimed to rest, in addition, on something more solid and demonstrable.

That solid and demonstrable something was the discourse of scientific naturalism, another source to which all late-Victorian hybrid religions were indebted. *Isis Unveiled* opens by invoking the authority of science, if not exactly the science of the Royal Institute: "The work now submitted to public judgment is the fruit of somewhat intimate acquaintance with Eastern adepts and study of their science" (Blavatsky, *Isis* 1:v). Those adepts had showed her, she reports, "that by combining science with religion, the existence of God and immortality of man's spirit may be demonstrated like a problem of Euclid" (Blavatsky, *Isis* 1:vi). Physics had failed to account for paranormal phenomena not because they are inexplicable but because modern science, blinded by centuries of religious dogma, had failed to retain or reach the level of understanding that had been attained by ancient science. Blavatsky concludes the preface, "*We wish to show how inevitable were their* [modern scientists'] *innumerable failures, and how they must continue until these pretended authorities of the West go to the Brahmans and Lamaists of the far Orient, and respectfully ask them to impart the alphabet of true science*" (Blavatsky, *Isis* 1:xlv). The first volume then sets about showing how esoteric knowledge had been codified in an "alphabet of true science" that was shared by adepts all across the ancient world. Not only had these scholar-priests gained insights that anticipated discoveries of modern science, they had discovered "laws of nature" that still eluded modern scientists. "Law" becomes a critical term in establishing credibility for Theosophy, as for some other hybrid religions. The first point in Blavatsky's "Summary of the points of the Wisdom-religion" is this: "There is no miracle. Everything that happens is the result of law—eternal, immutable, ever active"

(Blavatsky, *Isis* 2:587). Here Blavatsky intends "law" simultaneously in two specific, related ways: as the Buddhist Dharma or the "law of karma and reincarnation," and as "natural law," in particular the law of evolution or the "law of survival of the fittest."[30]

Theosophy was built upon an evolutionary model of spiritual development. Sinnett carried this idea to its extreme in *Esoteric Buddhism,* writing, for example: "But through successive incarnations in forms whose physical improvement, under the Darwinian law of evolution, is constantly fitting them to be its [the soul's] habitations at each return to objective life, it gradually gathers that enormous range of experience which is summed up in its higher development" (Sinnett, *Esoteric* 14).[31] Taking one additional step, Blavatsky and, following her, Sinnett merged evolutionary spiritualism with Victorian progressivism. "Progress" was for Blavatsky "simply another term for evolution"; her concern was with "the laws governing spiritual progress" (Neufeldt 248; Sinnett, *Early Days* 31). Theosophy, and popular conception beyond the Theosophical Society, was attracted to the idea of a personality or consciousness that continues after death and progresses from incarnation to incarnation, learning from past moral errors and carrying that knowledge with it in order to make spiritual progress in the next lifetime. However, this was not Darwinism; it was Lamarckian evolutionary theory seasoned with Social Darwinism.[32] Nevertheless, Blavatsky had enlisted if not Darwin then a popular conception of science at its most powerful. Works by Darwin and Huxley are among the most frequently cited sources in *Isis Unveiled,* and Alfred Russel Wallace, the co-discoverer of evolutionary theory with Darwin as well as a famous spiritualist, returned the favor by writing to Blavatsky, " 'I am amazed at the vast amount of erudition displayed in [your volumes] and the great interest of the topics on which they treat' " (Wallace 559, qtd. in Gomes, *Dawning* 143). Blavatsky thus garnered for her hybrid religion a credibility with her contemporaries that was borrowed from the very modern science she otherwise denigrated as materialism. In effect, she immunized Theosophy from the threat of materialism by inoculating spirituality with the most virulent strain of science: evolutionary theory.

The resulting amalgam of evolutionary theory with loosely compatible elements drawn from Eastern philosophy as well as from Victorian ideology is characteristic of late-Victorian hybrid religions. New religions ranging from Christian Science to Anthroposophy faced the challenge of merging an appeal to a source of truth "higher" than science with an appeal to the authority of science itself. In the nineteenth century, revelation needed to be bolstered by scientific rationality or, as Marie Corelli wrote in the prologue to her novel *A Romance of Two Worlds,* "men and women of to-day must have proofs" (Corelli, *Romance* 2).

Another defining feature that Theosophy shared with other late-Victorian hybrid religions was that if it was not explicitly woman-centered, it raised women to equality with men in spiritual matters. This was but one of many outcomes of the pervasive Victorian spiritualization of the feminine and "feminization of religion," which simultaneously idealized and constrained women but also was an important historical event with real benefits for the women's movement (Dixon 7). Ann Braud, writing particularly about Spiritualism and Christian Science, notes that "instead of viewing the qualities that inclined women toward piety as disqualifications for public roles," these religions "made the delicate constitution and nervous excitability commonly attributed to femininity a qualification for religious leadership" (Braud 57). Many hybrid religions were founded or led by women, for example Mary Baker Eddy for Christian Science; Katherine Tingley, who succeeded W. Q. Judge in the Theosophical Society Point Loma (later in Pasadena); and of course Blavatsky and her successor, Annie Besant. The example of these women in roles of leadership alone "suggested (a) that women could take full control of their lives, (b) that such self-controlled female lives could be eminently productive and useful to the world, and (c) that women in such cases could have direct, unmediated access to spiritual truth and power, outside the male-written scriptures or man-powered churches" (Ellwood and Wessinger 76). Not a few women in the last quarter of the century in England mixed a progressive spiritual agenda with a progressive social agenda in order to see the two as directly related. Anna Kingsford, for example, one of the first women in England to be certified as a physician, was both an active feminist and an active Theosophist, and Annie Besant was outspoken on women's suffrage as a leading member of the Fabian Society before converting to Theosophy and becoming first a disciple of Blavatsky and then the president of the Society. As Diana Burfield notes, "The renascence of the feminine principle (Isis, Sophia, the Great Mother) with its mission of renewal was a dominant theme in the esoteric teaching of the time, and one that recommended itself to mystical feminists" (Burfield 41). Theosophy, in particular, was appealing to women seeking a spiritual alternative, because, in the first place, its founding tenets explicitly decreed against discrimination on the basis of gender, as well as race or creed, and, in the second place, it recognized the female principle as co-equal to the male principle in the Godhead and, therefore, in the order of the universe. Theosophy thus provided "a theoretical legitimation at the highest cosmological level for mundane notions of equality between the sexes" (Burfield 36). While not programmatically feminist, Theosophy's "links to the English feminist movement were particularly marked," and "the Theosophical worldview and institutional expressions have been very supportive of the equal leadership of women" (Dixon 5; Ellwood and Wessinger 83). Blavatsky cleared the way for a range of twentieth and twenty-first-century woman-based spiritual practices, such as the Wicca movement. Though she generally is not included in the list of prominent Victorian feminists such as Barbara Bodichon, Josephine Butler, or Frances Power Cobbe, she did work consciously for the equality of women, if on what she would have considered a higher plane, and Anne Besant later became a prominent spokesperson for a mixed colonialism-feminism in Indian politics.[33]

Isis Unveiled works for the spiritual equality of women in two pronounced ways: it defends occult and woman-based spirituality against its historical persecutor in Europe, the Catholic Church (thereby also participating in the anti-Catholic discourse that was rampant in mid-Victorian England), and it centers Theosophy on the figure of the Goddess. The true, historical enemy of esoteric spirituality was Catholicism, which for Blavatsky meant the Church of inquisitions and crusades, exorcisms and witch burnings. At its earliest stages, she argues, the Church undertook purgings of "heretics" in order to conceal its own debt to pre-existing esoteric doctrine and to maintain its monopoly over the miraculous: "In their insatiable desire to extend the dominion of blind faith, the early architects of Christian theology had been forced to conceal, as much as it was possible, the true sources of the same. To this end they are said to have burned or otherwise destroyed all the original manuscripts of the Kabbalah, magic, and occult sciences upon which they could lay their hands" (*Isis* 2:26). This led before long to the burning of people, as the Inquisitors "persecuted the Gnostics, murdered the philosophers, and burned the kabalists and the masons" (*Isis* 2:37). Volume 2 of *Isis Unveiled* puts the Inquisition on trial. The second chapter in particular moves from a list of the Church's atrocities to the Church's own list of some of the estimated 600 burned at the stake in Germany alone in the decade of the 1620s. The list includes both men and woman, and many are listed anonymously, for instance, simply as "a stranger." However, many are children and women, as in "The wife of...," "A strange woman," and "The little daughter of...," generally giving names only for the men to whom the women belonged (Blavatsky, *Isis* 2:62). Though Blavatsky is protesting on behalf of all occultisms and all victims of the Inquisition, she clearly views the Church as a masculine institution and its victims as the most vulnerable and innocent. *Isis Unveiled* speaks at times from a place of deep and bitter trauma—a personal dislocation of a perceived historical trauma—in response to the long history of persecution by masculine religious institutions of women and children.

This reading is supported by the way that Blavatsky tells her version of the plight of the female deity at the hands of patriarchal world religions. A primary mission of the second volume of *Isis Unveiled* is to reintroduce the female component of the divine back into Western religious discourse. The first move in the argument toward that end is to show how the Virgin Mary can be "unveiled" as a figure derived mythologically from Nari, the Universal Mother in Brahmanism, and from Isis, whom ancient inscriptions describe with the phrase, " 'Immaculate is Our Lady Isis' " (Blavatsky, *Isis* 2:41). The second move is to show how in a range of ancient religions the Creator of the universe was ungendered, but "whenever the Eternal awakes from its slumber and desires to manifest itself, it divides itself into male and female" (*Isis* 2:170). Thus pre-Hindu Brahmanism, the doctrine of the ancient Chaldeans, and that of the Gnostics all recognized a "Double-Sexed Deity." However, "as neither the male nor female principle, blended into the idea of a double-sexed Deity in ancient conceptions, could be comprehended... the theology of every people had to create for its religion a Logos, or manifested word, in some shape or other" (*Isis* 2:171). The third move is to show, in short, how Judaism and then Catholic Christianity had denied the ungendered, originating Spirit; collapsed the double-sexed deity spawned from that Spirit into one gender by promoting the masculine component to the Logos and demoting the female component to human status; demonized the female component (Sophia, as in Theo-Sophy) in the form of Eve while domesticating and unsexing her counterpart, the Virgin Mary; and thereby rendered the deity as an entirely masculine authority, "a spouseless Father with one Son, who is identical with Himself" (*Isis* 2:2).

All the while Blavatsky forwards a parallel argument aimed at reestablishing the historical-mythical foundation for the Goddess. That argument culminates in passages such as this: "Sophia-Achamoth, the half-spiritual, half-material LIFE, which vivifies the inert matter in the depths of chaos, is the Holy Ghost of the Gnostics, the *Spiritus* (female) of the Nazarenes. She is—be it remembered—the *sister* of *Christos,* the perfect emanation, and both are children or emanations of Sophia, the purely spiritual and intellectual daughter of Bythos, the Depth" (*Isis* 2:226–27). Thus the overall argument's fourth move, and its ultimate purpose, is to reinstate the female divinity by showing, through a sort of archaeology, how the Goddess functioned in ancient religions prior to repression by Judaism and Christianity, linking Her to the complex of suppressed esoteric doctrines that Blavatsky is set upon resurrecting, thereby building Her into the very foundation of Theosophy. Theosophy is unique among late-Victorian hybrid religions and, for that matter, among world religions in being founded on a cosmology and a deity that is as much if not more woman-centered as man-centered.

Buddhism and Theosophy

Buddhism was not the primary ingredient of Theosophy, but it completed the recipe, so to speak. Selected and reinterpreted elements drawn from Buddhism, as well as Hinduism, came to provide the ethical system, part of the cosmology, and a central rhetorical justification for Theosophy. This was not necessarily the case from the start. At its inception, the Theosophical Society committed itself to study "Eastern literatures, religions, philosophies, and sciences," but at some point after that Blavatsky, followed by Olcott (but not by Judge), chose to move from studying it to using it as a primary source of concepts and terms from which to build the new religion (Olcott, "Genesis" 210). In 1877, the *New York World* published an interview with Blavatsky in which she "proclaimed herself a Buddhist" (Gomes, *Dawning* 137). This became technically true in 1880 when Blavatsky and Olcott became two of the earliest Westerners to take Buddhist layman's vows during a stay in Ceylon (now Sri Lanka). Olcott would later become an outspoken champion of the Ceylonese Buddhist revival and a public critic of the Christian missionary organizations there.[34] By Blavatsky's account, her engagement with Buddhism began much earlier, perhaps as early as the mid 1850s when she purportedly was trekking in the north of the Indian subcontinent in or near Tibet.[35] Whether intentionally or through replication of what was becoming a cultural stereotype, Blavatsky appealed to a popular conception of Tibet as the ancient seat of esoteric spiritual knowledge. Peter Bishop observes: "Blavatsky's all-wise, eternal mahatmas were an obvious manifestation of this archetypal quality, but the fantasies of theosophy reached a far wider audience than its followers. Time and again travelers *looked* for the mahatmas—or commented upon their absence. Blavatsky's fantasies struck a chord in the Western psyche that continues to echo to this day" (Bishop 181). By choosing to seat the Mahatmas in Tibet, Blavatsky had chosen to wed Theosophy to Buddhism, as well as placing them conveniently beyond the reach of almost all Westerners.

Thus *Isis Unveiled* places at the center of the ancient wisdom religion, as the ur-religion from which all others had issued, something called "prehistoric Buddhism." Statements such as this appear throughout: "There is not one of all these sects—Kabalism, Judaism, and our present Christianity included—but sprung from the two main branches of that one mother-trunk, the once universal religion, which antedated the Vadaic ages—we speak of that prehistoric Buddhism which merged later into Brahmanism" (Blavatsky, *Isis* 2:123). Blavatsky's claim to spiritual authority was that she had received "esoteric Buddhism" through direct transmission from the Mahatmas, who, situated as they were at the planet's spiritual axis mundi, had privileged access to its ancient roots. Prehistoric Buddhism, by which Blavatsky meant Buddhism long before the Buddha named Siddhartha Gautama, had been the foundation for the ancient wisdom religion and, therefore, was the foundation of Theosophy.

However, whatever knowledge Blavatsky had about Buddhism appears to have come less from the Mahatmas than from her reading in the literature of comparative religion. Among the most frequently cited authorities in *Isis Unveiled* are the works of the eminent Buddhologist F. Max Müller. The influence of comparative religion on Theosophy is clear even in the founding tenets, the second of which Sinnett summarized as, "To encourage the study of comparative religions, Philosophy and Science" (Sinnett, *Early* 13). While the advent of comparative religion was significant for the founding of late-Victorian hybrid religions in general, Theosophy adopted the methods as well as the products of that scholarship. Blavatsky took those methods as a working template as well as a justification for the approach she chose in comparatively analyzing ancient and medieval philosophies and sects. Indicative phrases such as this appear throughout *Isis Unveiled:* "Let us begin by once more comparing the myths of the *Bible* with those of the sacred books of other nations, to see which is the original, which copies" (Blavatsky, *Isis* 2:405). Comparative analogy is one of her primary rhetorical strategies, and, though it is weak both logically and historically, Blavatsky uses it to convincing effect. She sets a column of Pythagorean verses next to one of similar New Testament verses, for instance, or a column of Hindu scripture beside analogous Old and New Testament passages. By juxtaposing the mythical/biographical events in the lives of Krishna, Buddha, and Jesus, she suggests, not unpersuasively, a precedent for the latter in the former two and builds an argument about the influence of the ancient wisdom religion on every subsequent world religion.

In the process, *Isis Unveiled* enlists some of the rigor and credibility of the "scientific study of religion." At the same time, it replicates a prejudice of comparative religion and, more generally, of Protestantism in favoring the presumed "purity" of primary sources, such as canonical scripture, over indigenous practices, one outcome of which was to transfer authority over Buddhism from practitioners and their countries to Western scholars and Europe—a form of intellectual imperialism. Theosophy outdid comparative religion in this regard; since its primary source was the Mahatmas and therefore unverifiable, Blavatsky was licensed to make claims like this one: "When we use the term *Buddhists,* we do not mean to imply by it either the exoteric Buddhism instituted by the followers of Gautama-Buddha, nor the modern Buddhistic religion, but the secret philosophy of Sakyamuni, which in its essence is certainly identical with the ancient wisdom-religion of the sanctuary, the pre-Vedic Brahmanism" (Blavatsky, *Isis* 2:142). Indeed, the Buddhism Blavatsky and Sinnett claimed to derive from their arcane sources was not a Buddhism that Müller or the majority of practicing Buddhist would recognize.

While many thousands of Blavatsky's readers credited her historical argument and her alignment of Buddhism with the ancient wisdom religion, those most knowledgeable about the history of religions or about Buddhism challenged her. Müller "acknowledged the Eastern provenance of Blavatsky's doctrines, but was utterly scornful of her scholarship" (Oppenheim 163). He was especially irritated by the fact that Sinnett's *Esoteric Buddhism* had outsold his own erudite works on Buddhism.[36] Denouncing the entire concept of "esoteric Buddhism," he wrote: "If I were asked what Madam Blavatsky's Esoteric Buddhism really is, I should say it was Buddhism misunderstood, distorted, caricatured" (Müller, "Esoteric" 775). F. Legge, writing in 1889, argued that "the system of the Theosophical Society has *not* been handed down from prehistoric times by secret and mysterious means, but has, on the contrary, been copied *en bloc* from the relics of Gnosticism" (Legge 21). In a published rejoinder, Olcott argued as follows: "If, therefore, Theosophy is found identical with the Gnosticism of Marcion [excommunicated for heresy around 144 CE] and his school, it must have the same primal source, viz. India, which is exactly what the founders of the Theosophical Society have affirmed from the first" (Olcott 212). Taking a different angle of attack, Merwin-Marie Snell's "Modern Theosophy in its Relation to Hinduism and Buddhism" (1895) supported Blavatsky's claim about the Indian origins of Theosophy, though to nineteenth-century Hinduism, not prehistoric Buddhism. Snell demonstrates that while Theosophy bears some similarities to certain aspects of Tibetan Buddhism, "nearly all the elements of its religio-philosophical system are distinctly Hindu" (Snell 264). Snell argues that Theosophy became increasingly "Hinduized" after Blavatsky and Olcott moved the headquarters to Adyar and became associated with the Arya Samaj, a Hindu reformist group founded in 1875 favoring Vedic purism and, later, Indian nationalism.[37] Theosophists in India indeed did find it socially and politically efficacious to revise the definition of "esoteric Buddhism" in the direction of Hinduism.[38] But perhaps the most trenchant attack on Theosophy came in Frederika MacDonald's article "Buddhism and Mock Buddhism" (1885). MacDonald systematically rebuts Theosophy's primary misconceptions about Buddhism, accurately noting that the Buddha of canonical scripture "distinctly denies that he has any esoteric doctrine," refers practitioners not to the authority of any controlling clerisy of adepts but rather to the Four Noble Truths and the Noble Eightfold Path alone, and explicitly disavows all mystical and metaphysical speculations, prescribing instead the more modest and difficult "practice [of] self-control and self-culture" (MacDonald 713–14). MacDonald concludes as follows: "We are able to prove *all* other statements concerning the inner meaning and purpose of Gotama Buddha's teaching made through Mr. Sinnett by the Theosophical Society, or (if it be preferred) by the Tibetan Brotherhood, to be one by one baseless and false" (MacDonald 713).

This much was clear in the late nineteenth century, at least to the minority of readers sufficiently informed: Theosophy's esoteric Buddhism was not Buddhism. But this conclusion still leaves open for investigation questions such as the following. What specific elements of Buddhism did Theosophy reject and which did it appropriate and for what apparent reasons? Exactly how did Blavatsky, Olcott, and Sinnett reinterpret those elements and what interests did those reinterpretations serve? What do the answers to these questions teach us not only about Theosophy but about the Victorian assimilation and failed assimilation of Buddhism?

In the first place, Blavatsky and the other founders of Theosophy chose to overlook much of the doctrinal and ethical foundation of Buddhism. The founding teachings of the Buddha were the Four Noble Truths and the Noble Eightfold Path, as delivered in his first sermon, "The Setting into Motion of the Wheel of the Dharma" (and summarized in appendix 2). These are listed and explicated throughout both the Theravada and Mahayana canons, and all denominations of Buddhism observe them, though of course interpretations vary. Along with central concepts like the Dharma, karma, reincarnation, and nirvana, they are part of the historical and doctrinal consensus of Buddhism in general. Blavatsky certainly was aware of them. They were detailed in multiple works of comparative religion that she had read and cited. She had posted at her London headquarters a shorthand version of the Five Precepts, the Buddhist layman's practical ethics derived from the Eightfold Path: "right thought, right feeling, right speech, right action, and right living" (Dixon 49). It is especially telling, then, that in shaping Theosophy she chose for the most part to ignore these foundational teachings. If, as it appears, she relegated them to the list of "exoteric" aspects of Buddhism that therefore were irrelevant to true "esoteric Buddhism," why did she?

Perhaps Blavatsky shared the most common Victorian prejudice against the Four Noble Truths, the first of which, *Dukkha,* states to the effect that living involves suffering.[39] While practicing Buddhists—whether in the nineteenth or the twenty-first century—tend to view this tenet as a relatively neutral statement about the nature of reality, most Victorians considered it the blackest pessimism. At the same time, however, most commentators praised the ethical system prescribed by the Four Noble Truths—namely, the Eightfold Path and the Five Precepts—as exemplary of the popular Victorian ideology of "self-help" (Clausen, "Victorian" 5). They considered it to be a similarly practical and progressive prescription for living an ethically healthy life. The author of an 1899 journal article was representative in mixing admiration with reservation when he wrote: "The perfect man was the sole ideal of the great Buddhistic sage, and Gautama's whole system is devoted to teaching how this ideal is reached. It is thus more a system of ethics than a religion; its foundation resting on four noble truths, as Buddha pronounced them" (Rattigan 307–8). It would seem, then, that Blavatsky was less interested in founding a religion based on the rigors of self-culture or the discipline of day-to-day ethical practice than in building an occult spirituality. While she and others eventually did formulate a practical ethics—for instance, in her book *The Key to Theosophy* (1889)—the impetus for Theosophy remained the vast mysteries and the arcane knowledge, access to which was closely guarded and breathtakingly exciting. Blavatsky was compelled toward secrecy, high drama, contests of will, and battling Christianity, as she conceived it. As Monier Monier-Williams accurately noted in 1889, there are no "mystical teachings" and "no occult, no esoteric system or doctrine" in canonical Buddhism (Monier-Williams, *Buddhism* 224). Also, there is no place in Buddhism for an aspirant more serious than a lay householder outside of the anonymous cloister of a monastery. Thus Blavatsky could not embrace the Buddhism either of comparative religion scholars or of practicing Buddhists. Most elements of scriptural and monastic Buddhism did not truly interest Madame Blavatsky.

However, Blavatsky, Olcott, and Sinnett did enlist the prevalent Victorian conception that the "Law" of the Dharma made Buddhism a "scientific religion." The Dharma is an immensely complex, overarching concept within Buddhism (and, before Buddhism, in ancient Brahmanism). Reflecting its diversity of connotations among Buddhists, Victorians described it variously as "the ethics and philosophy" of Buddhism, the "the law of virtue," "the whole duty of man," the "Laws of Cause and Effect," and the "immutable laws underlying the endless modifications of organic and inorganic life," to take only a few examples (T. W. Rhys Davids, *Origin* 44; *Westminster* 178; T. W. Rhys Davids, *Buddhist* 132; Alabaster 157; Eitel 66). It is this latter connotation—Dharma as the highest natural law governing and connecting everything spiritual and material from the human mind to the galaxy—that appealed to Theosophists. It appealed to other Victorians as well. After all, Enlightenment Deism— followed by Romanticism and then Transcendentalism—already had made a not dissimilar sensibility familiar. By the nineteenth century that sensibility had become part of what one concerned Catholic commentator criticized in an 1875 article as part of "the modern idea": "that the universe, which the celestial sphere does not enclose, is a deity, eternal, immense, unborn, or uncreated, and destined never to pass away" (*Dublin* 16). Understandably, then, Victorians saw an obvious if superficial analogy between the Dharma and the invisible, causal connectedness implicit in all three of the seminal scientific theories of the age: evolutionary theory, Dalton's atomic theory, and the law of conservation of energy.[40]

A critical feature of the Dharma as understood by Victorians was that it did not describe the natural universe as a random machine—as Darwinism seemed to threaten—but rather as a system regulated by its own laws of causal interconnectedness. For humans (or rather for all "sentient beings," to use a common Buddhist phrase), this causality operates as the law of karma, which can be translated as "action/reaction" or "choice/consequence." Because karma naturally and automatically links every action or choice to its consequences, it indicates an inescapable, mutual responsibility linking each being to all other beings. The Dharma and the system of karma therefore describe an inherently ethical universe. As one 1870 journal article put it, the universe is governed by "a law of inevitable moral causation" called "Kam,—i.e., moral necessity," or, as another commentator expressed the same idea in 1905, "the whole universe is under one and the self-same law of causation which is ethical" (*Littell's* 237; Lilly 213). Even Thomas Henry Huxley—eminent scientist publicly known as "Darwin's bulldog"—adopted this understanding in both the title and the content of his *Evolution and Ethics* (1893). Liberal intellectual humanists like Huxley yearned to believe that there was an ethical order to the universe that would continue to operate even in the absence of a creating deity. The founders of Theosophy responded to this generalized Victorian yearning by capitalizing on the connotations of the Dharma in order to offer a model of the universe as naturally just and scientifically spiritual. Blavatsky enlisted Buddhism's "theological dogmas of reincarnation and the law of karma on the grounds that they reconciled the idea of a moral universe with the idea of a universe governed by natural law in a way that could provide a basis for acting morally in an age when the sanctions of Christianity had lost their force" (Bevir 764).

But even the Dharma was not sufficient to the model of the universe that Blavatsky and Sinnett had in mind. They abstracted from it in order to theorize a mystical cosmos, a multi-layered frontier designed for the individual soul's spiritual questing. This cosmology, which to my knowledge is antithetical to Buddhism, is most evident in Sinnett's writing.[41] He summarizes Theosophy's "broad truths" as "the existence of the Masters, the growth of the Ego under the law of Reincarnation, itself subject to Karma, and the stupendous magnitude of a planetary scheme to which we of this Earth belong" (Sinnett, *Early Days* xx). The latter point refers to the theory, which came to be widely accepted by Theosophists, that the earth belongs to a "planetary union" and that individual spiritual evolution occurs between incarnations as a journey upward through ascending spheres, "a *spiral progress* through the worlds," a notion that foreshadows the "gyre" concept of William Butler Yeats, a member of the Theosophical Society until a falling out with Blavatsky sent him to the Hermetic Order of the Golden Dawn (Sinnett, *Esoteric* 77, 85). This combination of astronomy (or perhaps astrology) and spiritualism in effect proliferates a traditional conception of heaven into a multiplex structure through which human spirits travel according to their own merits without the oversight or interference of divine judgment.[42] One intermediate location or spiritual state is "Devachan," "the state between earth-lives into which the human entity, human monad, enters and there rests in bliss and repose" before reincarnating (Purucker 36). The ultimate destination, after sufficient spiritual evolution obviates the need for reincarnation, is union with or absorption into the divine source. Critically, however, the divine is conceived neither as the anthropomorphic Judeo-Christian God nor as the entirely non-anthropomorphic Buddhist Dharma, but rather somewhere in between as an approximation of the Hindu Atman. William Peiris rightly argues that in Anglo-Indian Theosophy "ultimate reality was seen more in Hindu than in Buddhist terms: all beings were regarded as containing an inner *ātman,* or Self, which was a portion of the universal One or *Brahman*" (Peiris 303).

At the same time, and perhaps in a parallel fashion, Theosophical doctrine multiplied the self far beyond the traditional dualism of body and soul.

Following the lead of Spiritualism, Blavatsky first adopted the triune structure of body-soul-Spirit, the latter denoting the "Higher Self" as an atom of the universal Spirit, Atman, or, as it was called, the *Ātma*. She subsequently theorized a sevenfold structure, detailed in *The Key to Theosophy,* composed of a "lower quaternary" and a "higher trinity" (Blavatsky, *Key* 91–92). The former consists of "the four principles which do not reincarnate, but are destined for annihilation": the physical body (*rūpa*), the life-principle (*prāna*), the astral body (*liṅga-śarīra*), and the animal passions (*kāma-rūpa*) (Neufeldt 242). The higher trinity consists of the mind or intelligence (*manas*), the spiritual soul (*buddhi*), and the pure spirit (*ātma*), the latter two of which, along with the most spiritual ideations of the *manas,* continue on as an essential identity through multiple lives until worthy of merging back into the origin of the *Ātma.* Sinnett solidified and simplified this model, and Annie Besant perpetuated it but, especially after Blavatsky's death, developed her own subsidiary theory of the spiritual self as a layering of "sheaths."[43] Writers from Blavatsky to present-day Theosophists have elaborately developed the split-and-multiplied self, theorizing exactly what happens to each component upon earthly demise— which disintegrate, which remain temporarily adrift in *Kāma-loka* (a realm encircling the earth akin to the Spirit World of Spiritualism), which proceed on to Devachan, and how the "spiritual Ego"—the *buddhi-ātma*—reincarnates or achieves ultimate divinity (Blavatsky, *Keys* 94). I am less interested here in the details of such theorizing than in trying to understand from what motives and sources Theosophists derived it and what purposes it may have served.

The most obvious model for Blavatsky's sevenfold self was the Buddhist skandhas (in Pali, *khandhas*), which is indeed the precedent she cites in her writings.[44] The Buddhist model of the mind, which received lengthy attention especially from Caroline Rhys Davids in such works as *Buddhist Psychology* (1914), recognizes no unified, singular identity. Instead, it theorizes the self as "an assemblage of different properties," called the skandhas or The Five Aggregates (T. W. Rhys Davids, *Buddhism* 90). Monier-Monier Williams, writing in 1888, gives this summary of the skandhas: "1. Form (*rūpa*), i.e. the organized body. 2. Sensation (*vedanā*) of pain or pleasure, or of neither, arising from contact of eye, ear, nose, tongue, skin, and mind with external objects. 3. Perceptions (*sañña* = *sañjñā*) of ideas through the same sixfold contact. 4. Aggregate of formations (*samkhāra* = *sanskāra,* i.e. combination of properties or faculties or mental tendencies, fifty-two in number, forming individual character and derived from previous existences...). 5. Consciousness (*viññāna* = *vijñāna*) or thought" (Monier-Williams, *Buddhism* 109).[45] To oversimplify a model of selfhood as complex in its interpretations as any in Western psychology, the skandhas interact and continuously change to produce all of the effects of identity and psychological experience, including the impression within the fifth aggregate, consciousness, that there exists in those effects a continuous, unified personality. Suffice it to say that Theosophy's model of the self was in part inspired by but in fact very little modeled upon the Buddhist skandhas. As in her use of the Dharma, Blavatsky used the skandhas as a justification for her own purposes.

Other cultural currents moved Theosophists, along with other Victorians, to view the self or the soul as manifold and fragmented. In the first place, the foundations of Western metaphysics rest upon a series of models of split subjectivity, including Platonic idealism, Judeo-Christian soul theory, and the Cartesian *cogito*. Thus in one sense Theosophists only were extending a long-standing and pervasive tradition of splitting and multiplying the self. The impetus to amplify that tradition may have come in part from the perception that it was failing. It is as if by the nineteenth century a singular spiritual entity called the soul no longer held sufficient explanatory force to resist the fragmenting pressures of modernization. Some Victorians apparently felt that a more adaptive, sophisticated, and scientific model of the soul was required in order to stand up to the onslaught of materialism and science, which had thrown its efficacy into question. Thus, following the lead of Spiritualism, Theosophy and other late-century hybrid religions, in the process of rescuing what they perceived to be the embattled soul-theory, demoted the traditional Judeo-Christian soul to a component within the larger Spirit.

This demotion may have served a number of purposes. It posited a principle higher than the soul and produced a potentially more powerful champion for spiritualism against materialism. It also served the rhetorical purpose of claiming superiority over the presumably failing institutions of Christianity. In then multiplying the self beyond soul-and-Spirit, Theosophy produced a seemingly more refined, systematic, and technical model of the self, one perhaps that sounded scientific enough to stand up to science. As Sinnett wrote: "In esoteric science, as in microscopy, the application of higher and higher powers will always continue to reveal a growing wealth of detail; and the sketch of an organism that appeared satisfactory enough when its general proportions were first discerned, is betrayed to be almost worse than insufficient when a number of previously unsuspected minutiae are brought to notice" (Sinnett, *Esoteric* 21). Theosophy claimed to apply a higher power of perception and analysis to the human soul.

Furthermore, in a century when the individual subject finally had claimed the logical birthright of the Protestant Reformation to be its own spiritual guide, but then had found itself precariously alone and exposed in a post-Darwinian universe, multiplying the self may have been a method of giving the individual strength in numbers, as it were. Theosophy's multiple subjectivity, in combination with its concomitant cosmology, effectively extended the boundaries of the self to those of the universe. It personalized an otherwise increasingly alien and cold universe by projecting the self throughout it. As

Alex Owen's *The Place of Enchantment: British Occultism and the Culture of the Modern* argues in this regard, the last decades of the century in England saw the birth of "a new spirituality that was intrinsically bound up with the self-conscious exploration of personal interiority and the modern drive towards self-realization" (Owen, *Place* 13). As a result, the "researches of the 1880s and 1890s had the effect of postulating a new and unstable subjectivity that bore only a passing resemblance to the dominant Enlightenment concept of the unified rational subject" (Owen, *Place* 119). If Theosophy's multiple self was in some senses stronger, it also was more fragmented. It was both a symptom of an increased sense of fragmentation in modern, urban, industrial, secular society and an attempt to understand and heal that sensibility by tying it to a theory of a higher and more prolific self.

In a similar vein, John J. Cerullo's *The Secularization of the Soul: Psychical Research in Modern Britain* argues that late-century occultisms, followed by the science they spawned, psychical research, strove to "preserve the soul" apart from the Judeo-Christian tradition in terms amenable to science (Cerullo 11). The resulting "secular soul" was based upon "a vision of the self that incorporated what had been the supernatural qualities of the soul into the worldly persona itself, with the vitalism religion would truly unleash only after death operational in the here and now" (Cerullo xxi, 11). Cerullo considers the impact of these efforts on the advent of modern psychoanalytic theory, signaled especially by Sigmund Freud's *The Interpretation of Dreams* (1900). The pioneers of psychoanalysis effectively supplanted the attempts of Spiritualism and psychical research to preserve an inherently spiritual aspect of subjectivity. What is missing from Cerullo's argument, however, is consideration of Theosophy and other late-century hybrid religions. Prior to and then contemporaneous with psychical research, Theosophy responded to these same pressures, though neither by secularizing nor by reducing the significance of the soul. Even so, Theosophy's splitting and multiplying of the self was a precursor of Freud's well-known multi-component models of consciousness. Freud had been a corresponding member of the Society for Psychical Research, but then his theories scientifically explained away the Spirit World by relocating it from outer space to the interior space of the human psyche, thereby obviating the work of the Society for Psychical Research.[46] Psychoanalysis fully secularized the soul. Though Theosophy had the opposite objective in theorizing a manifold subjectivity, it prepared the way for the hegemony of a materialist theory of split-and-multiplied identity for which it likely served as one of the models. The Theosophical subject can be read as a stage in the emergence of the secular, fragmented subject of modernism.

Theosophy almost entirely avoided several key Buddhist concepts, in particular, nirvana. Nirvana was inconceivable within Theosophy except as a version of the Hindu Atman, as "absorption into the great universal soul" whereby a person's spirit "becomes a *part* of the integral *whole,* but never loses it individuality for all that" (Blavatsky, *Isis* 2:116, 117). Without delving here into the Victorian nirvana debate (the subject of a subsequent chapter), I only will note that the predominant interpretation of nirvana was that it signified nothing more or less than nothingness, total annihilation. This "notion of Nirvana tormented the nineteenth-century mind"; "how could a religion have 'nothingness' or 'annihilation' as its *summum bonum?*" (Godwin 324). Like many Victorians, Blavatsky could not accept the annihilationist interpretation of nirvana. She wrote that "it is useless and unprofitable task to offer to humanity the choice between a future life and annihilation," and that "it is not true that Gautama never taught anything concerning a future life, or that he denied the immortality of the soul"—the first statement being practical advice to anyone building a new religion and the second being highly questionable to anyone familiar with Buddhist scripture (Blavatsky, *Isis 2:* 25, 319). In thousands of pages, she makes very little use of the word "nirvana" and no use of the commentaries on it that were attributed to the Buddha in the sutras. Instead she summarized with an allusion to the famous line from Edwin Arnold's *The Light of Asia,* that "nirvana is the ocean to which all tend" (Blavatsky, *Isis II* 639).

But then the Christian alternative to nirvana as Blavatsky conceived it was equally unacceptable, namely, the belief in divine judgment possibly resulting in eternal damnation. This doctrine, which Blavatsky associated with Christianity generally, but which was a feature especially of evangelical and fundamentalist Protestantism, is perhaps the one with which Theosophists took greatest exception. Blavatsky could not tolerate the idea that a human is created for a single, short lifespan, judged on such small evidence, and consigned on that basis to an eternal and unrepealable state. To her—as in fact to many Victorian Christians with Broad Church or latitudinarian leanings—this seemed the opposite of justice. For this reason, Theosophical writings, while indicating that the ultimate goal of reincarnation is reabsorption into the divine, concentrated not on any end-state so much as on the processes of reincarnation and Devachan as themselves the goal. While in Buddhism, as well as Hinduism, one predominant understanding of reincarnation is as a return to life necessitated by unfinished karmic responsibilities, the Theosophical interpretation emphasized the opportunity it presents as a second chance or fresh start. While neither nirvana nor heaven/hell were tolerable concepts, Devachan offered a much needed respite from the strife of lived existence followed by a promise of continued existence. It evaded both the harshest aspect of life and the harsh reality of death. Devachan, Sinnett writes, is "a life of being paid your earnings, not of laboring for them," a life where one is united with one's loved ones in "companionship with all that the true soul craves for, whether persons, things, or knowledge" (Sinnett, *Esoteric* 129, 128). At the same time, however, Devachan is a state of self-reflection and processing, "the fulfilling of all the unfulfilled spiritual hopes of the past incarnation" (Purucker 36). One goal while there is to ready one's monad or spiritual Ego through spiritual self-improvement for ascending to a more realized state in the next lifetime. Thus Devachan is part of the progressiveness of Theosophy in particular and of Victorian ideology in general. It is progressive, evolutionary, and self-help oriented. It is a very optimistically Victorian afterlife, and it offers the immeasurably valuable benefit of functioning also as a prelife.

Blavatsky and other founders of Theosophy and of other late-Victorian hybrid religions developed models of the afterlife that they thought, whether consciously or not, would be appealing to Victorians in search of an alternative. They wanted this in part, I would speculate, for practical reasons related to attracting followers, but they also wanted this because they saw no alternative but to believe in their model, being unable to brook either the Christian or the Buddhist models as they perceived them. In comparison with the practices of Buddhism (or, for that matter, devout religious practice of any kind), Theosophy placed relatively little emphasis on spiritual or ethical discipline in the current lifetime or on working in the present moment not to acquire additional karmic debt. Theosophical karma and Devachan contain an element of deferral of responsibility; they appear to shift karmic debt forward, as it were, without accruing substantial penalties or interest.[47] Devachan reverses the (reverse) psychology that Victorians perceived in the Buddhist conception of reincarnation; rather than being that which one should work to avoid, it became a reward, a promise of a better next life. On the one hand, Victorian Theosophy may have lacked accountability, whether the accountability of the Buddhist concepts it borrowed or the more familiar accountability of the Victorian moral rectitude drawn from a long Christian history. On the other hand, as Ronald W. Neufeldt argues, it is not difficult to believe that Blavatsky worked as hard as she did to propagate her adaptations of karma and rebirth because she truly believed in the beneficial effects that "the teachings of Theosophy will have on mankind and on nations" (Neufeldt 251). If the Theosophical system lacked the rigor of Buddhist karma and reincarnation, it offered a forgiving and hopeful system meant to inspire spiritual striving and compassion in an age tormented by its own evangelical, imperial, scientific, and market successes.

In largely ignoring the founding tenets and canonical doctrines of Buddhism while at the same time drawing upon the authority Buddhism had gained within Victorian culture, Theosophy may only have been representative of a broader Western response to Buddhism in the nineteenth century. Founding Theosophists enlisted a certain credibility from the Victorian construction of Buddhism. They amplified carefully selected elements of Buddhism that served their purposes in building a new religion. Often those selected elements were those that coincided with elements of Victorian ideology. Thus Theosophists emphasized the self-help aspects of the Buddhist ethical system.

They foregrounded the parallels between the Dharma and Western science, especially evolutionary theory, but, at the same time, they drew upon an understanding of the Dharma within Buddhism that seemed to rescue the universe from the perceived randomness of Darwinism. They centered Theosophy on the doctrines of karma and reincarnation, though they eschewed the most demanding aspects of those doctrines within Buddhism while at the same time using them to critique and remedy the shortcoming they perceived in the doctrines of sin, redemption, and heaven/hell. They similarly used the Buddhist skandhas less for their own meanings than as a vehicle for theorizing a multiform self that could rescue the traditional Judeo-Christian soul, though by demoting, supplanting, and improving upon it. In the process, they provided a model for the fragmented modern subject. And, they articulated and advanced Victorian progressivism in the realm of spirituality. Theosophy would not and could not have taken the form that it did without the Western encounter with Buddhism, but Buddhism then functioned more as a catalyst for the formation of a uniquely Victorian religion.

Postscript

The international Theosophical movement, as well as some other late-Victorian hybrid religions, not only was shaped by Buddhism but then became a vehicle for a certain construction of Buddhism that disseminated throughout Western culture. "Esoteric Buddhism" is virtually unrecognizable as Buddhism, and yet it was this very non-Buddhism that was instrumental in disseminating a popular understanding of and fascination with Buddhism in the West. This may be typical of the history of the Western encounter with Eastern religions: elements of Buddhism enter scholarly, literary, and popular discourses, become embroiled with a complex array of pre-existing issues and ideologies, subtly but profoundly shift the terms in which those issues and ideologies are contested, but remain themselves largely unassimilated. Theosophy failed to assimilate the majority of the foundational teachings of Buddhism, even those it claimed as its own, yet it could not have taken the shape that it did without exposure to the concepts of the Dharma, karma, and reincarnation, or without reaction against certain other Buddhist doctrines. Exposure to these concepts and doctrines altered what was possible. It made perceptible new possibilities for revising or abandoning Christian doctrines and for adapting and combining elements drawn from Natural Theology, the history of Western occultisms, and even scientific naturalism. In hindsight, it also raises the perceptibility of what was utterly inassimilable about Buddhism. It was beyond comprehension for the Theosophists, as for the majority of Victorians, to surrender either the promise of an immortal soul or the primacy of individual spiritual identity, both of which only were intensified within late-Victorian hybrid religions. Those aspects of Buddhism that were most incommensurable, such as karmic responsibility for all of one's actions or reincarnation without continuing identity, are thrown into negative relief in relationship to the dominant ideologies of individual freedom and personal immortality, by which they were occluded.

Those ideologies in part explain why the cooption of Buddhism by Theosophy must be recognized as an example of discursive imperialism, the appropriation of the foreign other by turning it into the self. At the same time, however, I have been most concerned with analyzing the ways in which the other invaded the self, how Buddhism infiltrated and utterly changed Western religious discourse. Indeed, in re-expressing Buddhism, Theosophy and other late-Victorian hybrid religions contributed to a radical reorientation of the West. While co-opting Buddhism and Hinduism, the founders of Theosophy at the same time effected a partial re-centering of the mythic map of the ancient world from Greece, Palestine, and Rome to India. They backed up their rhetoric with action in moving the Society to India, a move that both participated in colonization and also represented a reversal of the imperial impulse. They worked to reverse a founding assumption of "Western civilization," namely, that the flow of civilizing ideas always had been from West to East. After Blavatsky's death, Annie Besant came to India as the new head of the Theosophical Society International. The combination of her experience as a secular activist and her commitment to the egalitarian principles of Theosophy challenged the Christian hegemony of the British Raj and contributed to the cause of Indian nationalism, while of course in other ways simultaneously supporting the Raj and furthering the British colonial mission.[48] The formation of hybrid religions in nineteenth-century Britain performed the double-edged cultural work of colonizing the religious Other while simultaneously subverting the authority of the dominant domestic and colonial religious institutions. They functioned—to extend a metaphor—as mediums channeling the voices of foreign religions. In doing so, they put *both* the domestic and the foreign traditions in the "impossible position" of attempting to translate the self into the other, the other into the self (Bhabha 118).

Chapter 3

Romances of Reincarnation, Karma, and Desire

[T]he great empire of the Christian Religion is being assailed.
—MARIE CORELLI, *A Romance of Two Worlds* (1886)

Departed empire has a metempsychosis, if nothing else has.
—JAMES RUSSELL LOWELL, *Fireside Travels* (1864)

"No subject claims more earnest attention from religious thinkers in the present day than the doctrine" of reincarnation, according to A. P. Sinnett, a recognized late nineteenth-century authority on the subject (Sinnett, "Preface" v). T. E. Slater, in *Transmigration and Karma* (1898) argued that no one can deny "that there is such a law as Karma" and that "it is clearly taught in the Bible" (Slater 29, 30). I doubt reincarnation was the subject foremost on the minds of the majority of late-Victorian religious thinkers, and I feel confident that few Christians of any denomination saw the doctrine of karma as fully consistent with their concepts of sin and redemption, but the statements by Sinnett and Slater accurately reflected an increasing fascination with reincarnation and karma as the turn of the century approached. According to Victorian sources, the doctrine of reincarnation had been introduced into Western intellectual discourse through the writings of Pythagoras (followed by Plato), who had been exposed to Egyptian and Brahmanic sources.[1] After centuries of disregard and suppression in Europe, reincarnation resurfaced as a topic of debate in Britain among eighteenth-century Platonists, who worked to de-Orientalize the doctrine, purging it of those

Hindu and Buddhist features antithetical to Western soul-theory and sub-suming it within Anglican Natural Theology or Deism.[2] But it was only after the encounter with Buddhism in the mid-nineteenth century that reincarna-tion, attended by the doctrine of karma, fully entered popular consciousness in the West, becoming a familiar topic in literature and the periodical press. One primary vehicle for those doctrines was the Theosophical movement, particularly through the writings of H. P. Blavatsky, A. P. Sinnett, and Annie Besant. But interest spread far beyond Theosophical circles as reincarnation and karma infiltrated the discourse of the late Victorian decades and early twentieth century.

Reincarnation and karma entered popular consciousness especially through the works of two of the period's most widely read authors of romance novels, Marie Corelli and H. Rider Haggard. Both Corelli and Haggard published multiple best-selling novels, and Corelli is sometimes noted as the first modern international blockbuster author in English. Over the course of her career, her novels sold on average 100,000 copies a year, nearly seven times more than those by authors like H. G. Wells and Arthur Conan Doyle.[3] Both Corelli and Haggard penned a series of novels in which reincarnation and karma figure prominently, for example, Corelli's *A Romance of Two Worlds* (1886), *Ardath* (1889), *Ziska* (1897), and *The Life Everlasting* (1911) and Haggard's Ayesha series, including *She* (1887), *Ayesha: The Return of She* (1905), and *She and Allen* (1920). As Carolyn Burdett has observed, "Throughout his work, but with increasing intensity, Haggard explored the idea that the dead do indeed live again via the process of reincarnation, an idea contemporaneously being described and espoused by the emerging Theosophical movement" (Bur-dett 217). The same can be said of Corelli's work, as will be shown. My analysis focuses on two novels by each author—Corelli's *A Romance* and *Life Everlast-ing* and Haggard's *She* and *Ayesha*.

The purpose of this chapter is to investigate how each of these authors adapted and reinterpreted reincarnation and karma for their readers, serving as primary conduits for those modified doctrines into their culture. What do their uses of those beliefs teach us about the hopes and fears of late Victori-ans and early modernists in relationship to questions of the afterlife at a time when the traditional notion of heaven had lost some of its surety? But the first question to be asked concerns the sources from which each author derived an understanding of those doctrines. What debates about reincarnation and karma were active in Victorian culture, and what were the prevalent under-standings? Clearly the ongoing encounter with Buddhism, which began in the first half of the century with translation and scholarship, and spread in the second half of the century to the popular and literary presses, was a primary source. But, it was one among a number of other sources, and sorting out exactly which aspects of reincarnation and karma came from direct and indirect exposure to Buddhist doctrine is difficult to determine. The obvious next question is how exactly the novels of Corelli and Haggard represent and use reincarnation and karma in their plots and in the beliefs and ideologies they forward. What are the similarities and differences in this regard between these two authors, and how did the conceptions of each author change between the early novel and the later novel? The third question, then, is this: in what ways are the constructions of reincarnation and karma by Corelli and Haggard consistent with Buddhist doctrines (as available to them in the most authoritative Victorian sources) and in what ways does each author subtly or radically modify Buddhist doctrine? Those modifications are of key significance in understanding the Victorian response to reincarnation and karma, in particular, and to Buddhism in general. How, specifically, did Corelli and Haggard shape those doctrines for their own purposes, and what were those purposes? How did their constructions serve Victorian cultural imperatives concerning spiritual life, the afterlife, and the ongoing contest between Christian, Buddhist, and other alternatives?

The Buddhism of Marie Corelli and H. Rider Haggard

Marie Corelli's *A Romance* and *Life Everlasting* and H. Rider Haggard's *She* and *Ayesha* are permeated with Buddhism, especially the later novel by each author. It is quite possible, however, to read them without dwelling upon the Buddhist content. This certainly is the case for Corelli, who always denied the influence on her work of other belief systems than Christianity. These novels are not "about" Buddhism, but Buddhism is pervasive in the margins and in the background, much as it was coming to be in Western cultures. Each author made use of certain adaptations of reincarnation and karma that in ways were uniquely their own and in other ways highly representative of that culture. These novels could not have been written, and would not have found the large audiences they did, had the way not been so thoroughly prepared by the intensified encounter with Buddhism in the immediately preceding decades.

Corelli's *A Romance* and *Life Everlasting* both focus on a female protagonist who is, as the reader comes to understand, spiritually ill. She at first thinks her illness is physical or psychological. Her lack of health finds expression as a loss of creative force—artistic force and life force—and as an ennui that, the novels show, must affect all who have not yet found their spiritual/romantic soul-mates. It also is a product of the maladies of the age, as Corelli and many of her contemporaries saw them: materialism, science, and atheism—the ungodly trinity of the Victorian era. The novels show their protagonists surrounded by characters who represent these cultural and social ills, that is, until they encounter a spiritual guide who recognizes their adeptness and so leads them out of the modern morass and into the hands of a spiritual master. At the climax of each novel, the master initiates the female protagonist into an ancient, esoteric spiritual tradition. While claiming that this is none other than the original, pure essence of Christianity (as opposed to modern institutional forms of Christianity), the novels prove that tradition to be heavily indebted to Spiritualism, Theosophy, and Buddhism, as well as to scientific naturalism and comparative religious studies. In other words, Corelli's writing constructs a fictional hybrid religion, as defined in the previous chapter. In both *A Romance* and *Life Everlasting,* the protagonist's quest is at one and the same time spiritual and romantic. Spiritual enlightenment is coterminous with finding one's destined and eternal lover—truly a "romance of two worlds." The spiritual progress each protagonist experiences—and progress is a key concept here—relies upon belief in reincarnation and karma.

But the most obvious presence of Buddhism in *A Romance* is as a counterexample to the kind of spirituality that Corelli hopes to exemplify for her readers. Many of her readers recognized elements of Spiritualism and Theosophy in her novels, and some wrote letters to her enquiring about them. She responds to them in the introduction to *A Romance* by vehemently denying any debt to those sources, claiming precedence in "Christ alone" and citing Buddhism as her foil: "Were I to initiate them—into some new or old form of Buddhism—could I show them some poor trickery such as the vanishing of a box in the air, the turning of a red flower to white, or white to red, or any of the optical illusions practised with such skill by ordinary conjurers, I might easily be surrounded by disciples of 'Occultism'—persons who are generally ready, nay, even eager to be deceived" (*Romance* xvii). The first paragraph of the narrative then alludes to Buddhism as a negative example. It sets up as a straw-figure to be knocked down a representative atheist and puts these words in his mouth: "'A candle when lit emits flame; blow out the light, the flame vanishes—where? Would it not be madness to assert the flame immortal? Yet the soul, or vital principle of human existence, is no more than the flame of a candle'" (*Romance* 1). The allusion is to a common metaphor drawn from Buddhist scriptures for entering nirvana. It was quoted frequently in the nineteenth century to summarize, usually in disbelief, that most difficult of Buddhist concepts for Westerners to understand, as in this passage from F. Max Müller: "True wisdom consists in perceiving the nothingness of all things, and in a desire to become nothing, to be blown out, to enter into Nirvâna" (Müller, *Chips* 227–28).[4] The novel characterizes the source of modern religious doubt in terms of Buddhism.

More directly, *A Romance* attacks Buddhism as a threat to Christianity in the following passage quoted within the narrative from the "Electric Creed of

Christianity," which is the esoteric spiritual science into which the protagonist has been initiated:

> All religions, as known to us, are mere types of Christianity....Buddhism, of which there are so many million followers, is itself a type of Christ's teaching; only it lacks the supernatural element. Buddha died a hermit at the age of eighty, as any wise and ascetic man might do to-day. The death and resurrection of Christ were widely different. Anyone can be a Buddha again; anyone can NOT be a Christ. That there are stated to be more followers of Buddhism than of Christianity is no proof of any efficacy in the former or lack of power in the later. Buddhists help to swell that very large class of persons who prefer a flattering picture to a plain original; who, sheep-like by nature, finding themselves all together in one meadow, are too lazy, as well as too indifferent, to seek pastures fresher and fairer. (*Romance* 241–42)

Employing a line of argument familiar from other Victorian commentaries on Buddhism (for instance, Richard Phillips's poem *The Story of Gautama Buddha and his Creed* [1871]), this passage first claims Buddhism, then appeals to the standard West/East dichotomies of active/passive and individual/collective to indict the inertia of the Buddhist masses relative to the action-oriented Protestant individual, and ends by using that conclusion to underwrite colonization of the greener pastures and the sheep around the globe. On the other side of that coin, however, *A Romance* also posits Buddhism as an invading force hostile to the West in general and to Corelli's revitalized Christian mysticism in particular. In scapegoating Buddhism, Corelli's hybrid religion draws upon the very sources it denies, including, in particular, Theosophy, scientific naturalism, and Buddhism (as described in point seven of the definition of "hybrid religion" in chapter 2).

The novels of H. Rider Haggard, as male-centered action-adventure romances of empire, were both antithetical and complementary to Marie Corelli's woman-centered romance novels. Haggard himself, following the popular culture, recognized the logic of being paired with Corelli in this way. In his diary entry of 22 April 1924 he wrote: "Marie Corelli is dead....I never met her but once at a party in 1887, I think....Nearly a generation ago there was a craze for making absurd couplets about well-known people. One of the best of these ran: Why was Rider Haggard? / Because he must Marie Corelli" (Haggard, *Private* 270). He and Corelli had corresponded, and in one letter she "wrote to Rider saying that she had been 'dazzled to my very heart's core by the splendour of *She*'" (Ellis 113). *She* and its first sequel, *Ayesha*, focus largely on the same three characters: Horace Holly, a Cambridge don with knowledge of ancient languages and archaeology; Leo Vincey, his adopted son and, as we learn, both the genetic descendant and the reincarnation of an ancient Egyptian priest named Kallikrates; and Ayesha, the "She" of the title, whom her subjects address as "She Who Must Be Obeyed." The reader, along with Holly and Leo, first encounters Ayesha as a supernaturally powerful white queen ruling in the heart of Africa and then learns that she has preserved her devastating beauty for the two thousand years since she murdered Kallikrates out of jealousy over another woman, Amenartas, Leo's matrilineal forbearer. Both *She* and *Ayesha* are quests by Holly and Leo to find Ayesha, first in vengeance to Africa, then in the second novel in adoration to Tibet, to which Ayesha's spirit has returned and assumed a different body.

The plots of Haggard's two novels focus on travel and exploration, exotic and sublime foreign settings, ancient civilizations and "primitive" religions, and upon combating and defeating all kinds of racial others. However, both ultimately are melodramas, perhaps in line with the nautical and military stage melodramas earlier in the century. They are most concerned with the spiritual and romantic ties between the major characters, which have been sustained over the course of two millennia of multiple lifetimes. Both involve a love triangle between Leo-Kallikrates, Ayesha, and Amenartas, who is doubled in the first novel by the character of Ustane and reincarnated in the second as Atene. The driving emotional tension concerns whether Ayesha ever can expiate her former sins, whether Leo can forgive and then master her, and whether the two can ascend to the spiritual/romantic union for which they are destined as eternal soul-mates. Thus Haggard's novels, though virulently masculine, British, and imperialist, are no less romances than Corelli's novels—"romance" both in the sense of a genre category with a history and formal features, as well as in the colloquial sense of focused on love, sex, and marriage.

Haggard's novels make more explicit use of Buddhism than do Corelli's. Though he professed and his characters profess to be Christians at a most general, non-denominational level (presumably Anglican), Haggard had no qualms about recognizing the merits of Buddhism. This is especially true in *Ayesha* wherein we learn that She has studied the doctrines "of the prophet Buddha," about whom Holly "has spoken to [her] so much" (*Ayesha* 172). Early in the story, hoping to over-winter in a "Thibetian Lamasery," Holly quotes "sayings of Buddha" and chants "a long Buddhist grace" for the benefit of the Lamas (*Ayesha* 5, 17). He claims that he and Leo are "Lamas sure enough . . . who belong to a monastery called the World, where alas! one grows hungry," and the head Lama, Kou-en, remarks, "Their feet are in the Path!" (*Ayesha* 17). Holly and Kou-en subsequently hold discussions about reincarnation and nirvana, and the latter recalls an encounter with Ayesha in one of his previous lives as an initiate monk at that same monastery when She was crossing those mountains at the head of a column of the army of Alexander the Great. Holly comments, "After all, also, as Leo himself had once said, surely we were not the people to mock at the theory of reincarnation, which, by the way, is the first article of faith among nearly one quarter of the human race, and this not the most foolish quarter" (*Ayesha* 22). In choosing to set the novel in Tibet, Haggard was invoking common Victorian projections of Tibet as the ancient seat of spiritual wisdom, ostensibly Buddhist wisdom, but in its Western representation more occult and mystical even than in works like L. Austine Waddell's *Tibetan Buddhism* (1894) (*Ayesha* 5).[5] Haggard was drawing upon the two most influential Victorian sources of the popular conception of Tibetan Buddhism: H. P. Blavatsky's Tibetan "Mahatmas" or "Masters," analyzed in the preceding chapter, and Rudyard Kipling's Tesho Lama in *Kim* (1901), analyzed in the next chapter. Like those authors, Haggard was enlisting Buddhism for his own purposes, but, like them, he did not do so without genuine interest, some knowledge, and respect for Buddhism.

Both Corelli and Haggard made it difficult to determine through which sources they were exposed to Buddhist concepts and doctrines. Certainly each of them would have read Edwin Arnold's ubiquitous poem about the life of the Buddha, *The Light of Asia* (1879), but neither of them cites it. Neither the autobiographical writings by them nor the biographical writings about them reveal the sources they obviously had consulted.

In his late autobiography, for example, Haggard links the Biblical suggestion that Elijah returned to earth as John the Baptist to his belief in the resurrection of Jesus to Buddhist reincarnation, about which he must have read. He wrote that "some of us, already have individually gone through this process of coming into active Being and departing out of Being more than once—perhaps very often," concluding that "like the Buddhists, I am strongly inclined to believe that the Personality which animates each of us is immeasurably ancient, having been forged in many fires, and that, as its past is immeasurable, so will its future be" (*Days* ii.241).[6] In contrast, Corelli, denied throughout her writings the influence of non-Christian sources upon her mystical Christian theology, even though she obviously had sampled these non-Christian sources. Her biographers followed her lead; none gives a hint of when and where she was exposed to Theosophy or Buddhism, tending to support her own contentions about the divinely inspired Christian basis of her spirituality.[7] Yet it is clear that Corelli had read works from comparative religion scholars on Buddhism, certainly those by the Buddhologist F. Max Müller. In a single sentence from the "Postscript" to *A Romance,* she reveals her debt to scientific naturalism (and Deism), comparative religion, and Spiritualism in the process of denying them: "The greater and wider the discoveries of Science, the nearer shall we feel the actual presence of God, and the more certainly shall we know that what we call the 'Miracles' of the New Testament are no 'legends' or 'historical coincidences,' as Professor Max Müller has recently observed, but eternal truths,—the most splendid and positive truth of all being the Resurrection of Christ, which was intended as the lasting symbol and open manifestation of the fact that each one of us holds the eternal germ of Spirit" (*Romance* 356). Both for Corelli and Haggard, as for some other late Victorians, belief in the resurrection of Jesus was a stepping stone to belief in reincarnation.

The debt of both Corelli and Haggard to the Theosophy of Madame Blavatsky deserves special note. Like Blavatsky, each had early experiences with spiritualist phenomena, which then materialized throughout their novels.[8] Despite her many disclaimers, Corelli, "with her adaptation of scientific discoveries, such as electricity or telecommunication for the religious context...and with her lecturing before the Theosophical lodge at Leeds," "situated herself within the creed of a Madame Blavatsky, Annie Besant or Arthur Sinnett" (Kuehn 185). Haggard's attendance of séances at Lady Paulet's, and the fact that Maria Countess of Caithness, a devotee and supporter of Blavatsky, was a member of that circle, "puts the group Haggard frequented at the centre of the new occult and Theosophist movements of the 1870s and 1880s" (Coates 38–39). But the real proof of the influence of Blavatsky on both authors resides in the allusions to her and her work in their novels.

In the first place, the novels of both authors draw heavily on the figure of "*The Goddess*," Ayesha's deity, the primary source of which in Victorian culture was Blavatsky's *Isis Unveiled* (1877) (*Ayesha* 181). Ayesha is a former high-priestess of Isis and a demi-goddess in her own right, and female characters in Corelli's two novels approach that status. The spiritual "Master" in *A Romance,* Heliobas, and Ayesha as the hierophant of an ancient "wisdom religion" from Tibet are both unavoidable allusions to Blavatsky's "Masters" (*Romance* 163). Corelli's characters sometimes clearly echo phrases common in Blavatsky's writings, as when Heliobas says, "The world is not ready for wisdom, and the secrets of science can only be explained to a few" (*Romance* 210). Corelli, whether intentionally or not, wanted to build a new hybrid religion with a spirituality similar to Blavatsky's. This necessitated denying the influence of Blavatsky all the more. Haggard, far from modeling himself on Blavatsky, does in part model Ayesha on the "pseudo-Egyptologist Madame Blavatsky" (Gilbert 133). Ayesha is very much a comparative scholar of religions, like Blavatsky having "explored the religions of her day and refused them one by one" in the process of synthesizing her own hybrid—part Egyptian, part Buddhist, part Spiritualist (*Ayesha* 169). Haggard sets up Ayesha's occultism, in particular, her trafficking with the dead as a negative example of what he saw as a dangerous treading on God's prerogative. *She* and *Ayesha* are punctuated by earnest religious debates between Holly and Ayesha, in which Holly represents an ostensibly Christian but Buddhism-inflected position. I would agree with John Coates's argument that the ultimate focus of those debates is, in effect, "the contradiction in Blavatskyan occultism between the search for power and the quest for spiritual progress," the two alternatives between which Ayesha must choose (Coates 51). Coates concludes: "The reader can detect a coherent pattern in *She* and *Ayesha* in which one aspect of the occult revival, involving the pursuit of power and the artificial prolongation of life is examined and rejected. There is a corresponding movement through the two novels towards the other [Buddhist] side of Blavatsky's confused legacy. Reincarnation and purification by suffering dominate and shape the narrative of *Ayesha*" (Coates 53). My analysis queries and expands upon Coates's latter observation. The immediate point is that Blavatsky undeniably influenced both Corelli and Haggard and that Theosophical texts were an important secondary source for those authors' conceptions of Buddhism, as they were for many thousands of late Victorians.

Victorian Reincarnation: Definitions, Debates, Types

Not only could Victorians who wrote about reincarnation not agree on the definition of it, they were uncertain by which name to call it. Many used interchangeably the terms "metempsychosis," "transmigration," "rebirth," and "reincarnation." The *Cyclopaedia of Biblical, Theological, and Ecclesiastical Literature* of 1886 uses "metempsychosis" and "transmigration" as synonyms for one another. Others recognized significant etymological, historical, or theological differences among these concepts. "Metempsychosis" was the term most often used in discussing the ancient Egyptian variant associated with Osiris, the "myth of the dying god" who returns from death to live again (Cook 37). In his 1898 article, "The Philosophical Aspect of the Idea of Metempsychosis," Robert Cust argued that there were two primary ancient theories of it: "(1) The continuance of this life in another World," in which "the future life was very much as the old one," and "(2) Retribution, in which the future life depended on conduct in the present" (Cust 48–49). The latter of these points to the subsequent emergence in India of the doctrine of karma, which the *New International Encyclopaedia* of 1902–1904 described in these terms: "The Hindu system is an outgrowth from a general belief in transmigration of souls. There is at first no notion of retribution connected with this belief....About the seventh century B.C., however, arose the doctrine of Karma...which turns this belief into a system based on morality" (*New* 170). After the earliest forms of reincarnation, "Later ages struck out new ideas: (1) Absorption of the Soul, and practical destruction of its individuality. (2) The Transmigration of the Soul into a new body. (3) The wandering of the Soul, free from its corporeal covering" (Cust 49). Absorption of the soul is akin to some Hindu conceptions of the Atman; the destruction of individual conscious identity between each rebirth and the assumption of a different body in each points to Buddhist reincarnation; and belief in wandering souls suggests nineteenth-century occultism. With historical precedence, then, interested Victorians debated these and other distinctions between types of reincarnation, defending or decrying one type or another.

One recurring debate about reincarnation centered on the question of the sources from which ancient Grecian thinkers had adopted it, whether it had originated more from Egyptian or from Indian sources. This was a historical question, but the answers said as much about Victorian culture as about ancient history. The majority of Victorian writings that I have consulted emphasized the Egyptian origins, following the pattern set by Clement of Alexandria (c. 150–215), who in the following statement famously identified Egypt as the place of origin of the belief in the immortality of the human soul: "'From Pythagoras Plato derived the immortality of the soul, and he from the Egyptians'" (qtd. in Cook 35–36). A few commentators, especially those with Theosophical leanings, argued against the Egyptian hypothesis, as did John Wier, who in his 1894 article "Forms of Belief in Transmigration" wrote: "At least two centuries before Pythagoras or Pherecydes it appeared in the Brahmana texts of India. . . . If, as very recent investigation seems to disclose, the Egyptian doctrine was of the nature of an immediate reward, that country could not have supplied the pattern" (Wier 566).[9] It is curious that Victorians favored the Egyptian side of this debate in light of the fact that according to some Egyptologists of the time metempsychosis was far from a prominent feature of Egyptian belief. For example, John Wilkinson's *The Manners and Customs of the Ancient Egyptians* (1837), even in its long concluding chapter, "Religious Opinions of the Egyptians," makes absolutely no mention of metempsychosis or transmigration or reincarnation, and the same is true of John Hoare's 1879 article, "The Religion of the Ancient Egyptians." It therefore is especially telling that some subsequent scholarly and popular commentators aligned metempsychosis with Christian resurrection.

In *Egyptian Ideas of the Future Life* (1899), Wallis Budge, Keeper of the Egyptian and Assyrian Antiquities at the British Museum, argued that Osiris was the first "God of Resurrection" (Budge 13). Far from fearing that this might undermine the originality of the crucial Christian claim, Budge saw it as confirmation in advance of the truth of Christ's resurrection, and the editor of the 1959 reprinting concluded anachronistically that thus "the Egyptians were well prepared to absorb the teachings of Christianity" (Budge 7). For a complex set of culturally embedded reasons, late Victorians felt that Egyptian metempsychosis was more compatible with their own Christian history and beliefs than was either the Hindu or the Buddhist doctrine. This partially explains why Blavatsky named her first book *Isis Unveiled* while between the covers drawing more heavily upon Buddhist than Egyptian terms.

Egyptian metempsychosis was preferable in part because much less was known about it. It therefore was more of a blank canvas onto which Victorians could paint their own projections and fantasies, as evidenced in such works as Austen Henry Layard's *Nineveh and Its Remains* (1849), D. G. Rossetti's "The Burden of Nineveh" (1856), and Richard Marsh's *The Beetle* (1897)—not to mention Blavatsky's books, Haggard's novels, and many actual paintings of Cleopatra, mummies, pyramids, etc. This also is to say that Egypt was *not* India, about which perhaps too much was known. India was at once too close and too far away. It was too close economically and politically, especially after the Indian Mutiny of 1857, and it had drawn uncomfortably close linguistically and racially. Around the turn of the eighteenth and nineteenth centuries, philologists had determined the membership of English in the Indo-European language group. By the middle of the nineteenth century, "the term 'Aryan' had gained common currency, not merely to denote the new language group opened up through the discovery of Sanskrit, but as an ethnographic concept" linking European people to a race in ancient northern India (Batchelor 266).[10]

Some Victorians began to ask themselves in concern if the Indians must replace the Greeks as the genetic, cultural, and mythic forefathers of Caucasians. Thomas Henry Huxley joined this debate with his essay "On the Aryan Question and Prehistoric Man" (1890), which attempts to demonstrate that the ancient Aryan conquerors of the northern Indian peninsula had migrated there from Europe and, therefore, that "we" came from "us," not from "them," because "they" came from "us" in the first place. Rider Haggard replicated this move but revised the target from India to Egypt in having Leo trace his exemplary British heritage back through the genetic and cultural lineage of the English people to a blonde Egyptian, Kallikrates, and in portraying Ayesha as a white queen ruling in darkest Africa over a lost civilization called Kôr, in which "the white memories of a forgotten human history" are preserved as mummies (*She* 183).[11] Thus the small debate that pitted Egyptian metempsychosis against Indian reincarnation was embedded in a much broader debate concerning nothing less than the origins of the white race and its European heritage. If not the Greek and Roman origins assumed for two millennia to be the basis of "Western civilization," Egypt apparently was a nearer East than was India.

A primary explanation for why metempsychosis was more appealing to some Victorians than reincarnation was because it lent itself more readily to alignment with the predominant theory of the soul in the West. By that I mean the historical, doctrinal, and, ultimately, popular consensus within Christianity most broadly conceived, as well as the causally related history of ontology, ethics, and metaphysics from Plato to Descartes. To attempt to summarize this immensely complex historical amalgamation of beliefs: Western soul-theory depends first on the claim that something called the soul exists. The soul is separate from the body, a spirit dwelling inside of a body, which in contrast is mutable, if not in fact degraded, vile, the cause of the "sins of the flesh." Soul-theory relies upon a strict body/soul dichotomy. Also, the soul is unique to human beings, not available to other "sentient beings," as expressed in Hinduism and Buddhism. The soul is immortal, eternal, and permanent, an essential "atom"—the term some Victorians used for it—and thus irreducible and unchanging. Part of the soul's immortality is that it comes from the divine or God and returns to the divine, though, importantly, it is not dissolved into the divine, losing its singularity. Rather, each soul is individual and unique and continues to be so eternally.

This belief in the individuality of the soul had significant ramifications for Victorian debates about reincarnation. In the first place, it suggests that each life is unique and singular, not repeatable. A soul is born into a body and lives its single earthly life, upon which the body dies and the soul departs to reside for eternity in one of two places, heaven or hell, according to the judgment and grace of God. In the second place, the individual uniqueness of each soul means that it is tied to personal identity, what some Victorians, prior to Sigmund Freud, called "the Ego." Identity continues after death through consciousness and memory, which is the only practical way that heaven can be a reward or hell a punishment. As T. W. Rhys Davids wrote in his 1896 analysis of Buddhist reincarnation: "For two essential conditions of future life, as held in the West, and indeed wherever the 'soul' theory is in vogue, are the continuation of memory and the consciousness of identity" (Rhys Davids, *History* 87). The issue of memory—remembering and therefore being responsible for past lives—was a recurring motif within Victorian debates about reincarnation. A productive contradiction resulted, however, between two tenets of soul-theory: the body/soul dichotomy and the individualism of the soul. Humans find it challenging to conceive of their individual selfhood entirely divorced from their body. After all, Jesus, like Osiris, arose from the dead initially in his same body—the "rebirth of the body" as well as the "rebirth of the soul"—and the most popular conception of heaven, for obvious practical reasons, is of oneself not only thinking but looking largely like one's self but now in a paradisial state. Hence the question of what exactly continues after death—the soul with identity, the soul without identity, the soul with the body, or karma without identity—was central to Victorian discussions of reincarnation.

Indian reincarnation, whether Hindu or Buddhist, could not be squared so easily with Western soul-theory. Hindu reincarnation was somewhat more assimilable for Westerners. Eighteenth-century Platonists—followed by Romanticists, Transcendentalists, and then adherents of late-century hybrid religions—saw a parallel between the final re-absorption of the soul into the Atman and the Deistic conception of unity with the divinity of the natural universe. Of critical importance was that Hinduism maintained the existence of the soul, its immortality, and its dualistic relationship to the body. At the same time, however, Hinduism and Buddhism posited multiple lifetimes through reincarnation, and this presented a series of troubling issues that were debated among those Victorians interested in the subject. For the sake of convenience, I will treat these issues as follows: the problem of heaven/hell, the problem of karma, the problem of identity/memory, and the problem of progression/retrogression, though they in fact were not entirely separable within Victorian discourse.

Reincarnation, accompanied by the doctrine of karma, appears to challenge God's prerogative of judgment in the first place by delaying any final determination until after many lifetimes (if in fact God—or Brahm, Vishnu, Shiva—even exercises a final judgment). While Hindu reincarnation could be thought to retain the carrot of something akin to heaven, it seemed to do away with the stick of hell, replacing it with inescapable return to another earthly life—not such a terrible option, a Westerner might think. This made what I will call the moral economy of karma and reincarnation more appealing to some Victorians than the economy of sin and redemption. As Haggard's Ayesha puts it when Leo suggests that "our faith" requires hell as incentive and punishment: " 'Nay,...there is not hell, save that which from life to life we fashion for ourselves within the circle of this little star. Leo Vincey, I tell thee that hell is here—aye *here!*' as she struck her hand upon her breast" (*Ayesha* 115).

The nineteenth century witnessed a widespread turning away from Calvinistic theology, even within evangelical churches and chapels. The idea of eternal damnation increasingly became untenable as unjust to humankind and unworthy of a loving God. Blavatsky did not mince her words on the subject: "And now I advise you to compare our Theosophic views upon Karma, the law of Retribution, and say whether they are not both more philosophical and just than this cruel and idiotic dogma which makes of 'God' a senseless fiend; the tenet, namely, that the 'elect only' will be saved, and the rest doomed to eternal perdition!" (Blavatsky, *Key* 215). Both Corelli and Haggard, though professed Christians, concurred. As Corelli's protagonist insists in *Life Everlasting,* "the idea of Eternal Punishment is absurd" (*Life* 222). While for the majority of practicing Christians the problem of heaven/hell would have excluded reincarnation from consideration, for some indeterminate minority it made karma and reincarnation more appealing as an alternative ethical system.

The problem of karma itself was yet more complex and troubling. Karma directly supplants the hand of Providence and effectively obviates the necessity of faith. As E. D. Walker succinctly defined it in *Reincarnation: A Study of Forgotten Truth* (1888), "the doctrine of Karma is that we have made ourselves what we are by former actions," and T. W. Rhys Davids observed that according to it "no exterior power can destroy the fruit of a man's deeds, that they must work out their full effect to the pleasant or the bitter end" (Walker 285; Rhys Davids, *Buddhism* 103–4). Victorian karma emphasized the other side of the historical dichotomy within Protestantism between faith and works. It therefore appeared to some to reinforce certain of their key ideologies, namely, self-help, ethical responsibility for one's choices and actions, and the individual freedom and right to reap the rewards of one's own work/works. Proponents of karma were quick to reference Saint Paul's injunction, which Bertha Vyver, Maria Corelli's partner, cites in her biography of Corelli: "In *Ziska* she deals definitely with the law of Karma, and, giving as her two chief characters a re-incarnated man and woman, works out the hypothesis to its logical conclusion that, 'as we sow, so do we reap'" (Vyver 265). The "law of karma," as Victorians knew it, also appeared to promise something that many longed for as an alternative both to the unpredictability of God's judgment and the random-ness of Darwinian selection: a justly ordered universe. Blavatsky summarized the point: "For Karma in its effects is an unfailing redresser of human injustice, and of all the failures of nature; a stern adjuster of wrongs; a retributive law which rewards and punished with equal impartiality"; it is "that unseen and unknown law *which adjusts wisely, intelligently and equitably* each effect to its cause, tracing the latter back to its producer" (Blavatsky, *Key* 198, 201). But these potentially attractive attributes of karma could not outweigh the fact that it appeared to negate the essential singularity of the human soul by denying the continuance of individual identity and its memory.

The problem of identity/memory was the largest concern that Victorian commentators upon the subject had about karma and reincarnation. Even if they might entertain the idea of the dissolution of the soul into the manifold divine after the spiritual progress of many lifetimes, they could not accept the loss of conscious selfhood between reincarnations. They understood that in Buddhist reincarnation, in particular, the "personal connection between the individual who died and the individual re-born is by no means viewed as a physical or psychic identity, but simply as a moral and personal relation of cause and effect," "cause-effect" being one translation of "karma" (Eitel 74). T. W. Rhys Davids summarized the situation bluntly: "In no case is there, there-fore, any future life in the Christian sense. At a man's death, nothing survives but the effect of his actions; and the good that he has done, though it lives after him, will rebound, not to his own benefit, as we should call it, but to the benefit of generations yet unborn, between himself and whom there will be no consciousness of identity in any shape or way" (Rhys Davids, *Lectures* 108–9). Some Victorians challenged the fairness of holding a person responsible for ac-tions in a previous life that one could not remember. But what disturbed them at root was the idea that their identity might not be eternal, as promised by Western soul-theory, since "people naturally think...their own self is so impor-tant that it cannot possibly ever cease to be, and they are constantly concerning themselves with the ways and means of making that little self of their own happy and comfortable for ever" (Rhys Davids, *History* 82).

Those interested in the subject therefore fixed on the issue of memory as the index of continuing conscious identity. Some commentators appealed to this issue in rejecting especially Buddhist reincarnation. T. E. Slater argued that it was "*unphilosophical*," because "The human soul stores up its knowledge in memory; it never loses an atom of the information which it has once acquired"; how is it possible then "that the soul, having such marvelous powers of recollection, never remembers anything of former births?" (Slater 22). Some others, especially those concerned with merging reincarnation into a revised Christianity, simply posited a version that retained identity and memory, as here: "Reincarnation demonstrates that the personal ego, which permanently maintains its identity amid the constant changes of the bodily casement and the mental consciousness, must continue its individuality" (Walker 276). Yet others acknowledged rare exceptions of people remembering former lifetimes (the Buddha and the Dalai Lama were discussed as examples) or suggested that all instances of déjà vu were lingering traces of past lives. Annie Besant, in the section of her book *Reincarnation* (1893) titled "The Proofs of Reincarnation," included these points as minor justifications among a list of fourteen proofs. William Knight in "The Doctrine of Metempsychosis" (1878) suggested that "If the soul has pre-existed, what we could...anticipate are only some faint traces of recollections, surviving in the crypts of memory" (one thinks of the crypts of Kôr) (Knight 430). And Mortimer Collins's novel *Transmigration* (1883) tells the story of a man who dies, sojourns in a celestial spirit-world (where he flirts with an "Irish poetess, a flame half red half green"), and returns to earth as a newborn with complete memory of his former life (M. Collins 114). The protagonist explains: "I leant that almost all the spirits coming from earth, or any other star passed through the water of Lethe, and forgot altogether what had previously occurred to them. None were excepted, save those who heartily believed in the doctrine of metempsychosis; I, being such a believer (the only one during more than a century), was to be rewarded by a return to earth, with my memory of previous events perfectly clear" (M. Collins 113). E. D. Walker's conclusion on this subject is especially telling, since it proposes to answer the identity/memory problem by referring it to the progression/retrogression problem. Walker writes, "The strongest objection to reincarnation, our ignorance of past lives, is met by the fact permeating all nature and experience, that progress depends upon forgetfulness" (Walker 305).

One form that Victorian progressivism took was as belief in progressive spiritual evolution. Commentators on karma and reincarnation agreed that it was a system of ethical self-development, which to some seemed only a short step from the idea of progressive spiritual evolution. A few objected to that idea on the grounds that it implied a primitive, perhaps animalistic, origin for the human soul, which Western soul-theory promises is eternal and unchanging, but most who wrote about the subject agreed with E. W. Keely, who in the 1898 article "Christianity and Reincarnation" wrote: "If we accept physical evolution why must we not also accept spiritual evolution?...As there must have been a succession of improved forms, in an ascending scale, to bring man to his present perfectness of form, so must there have been a succession of incarnations, to make the soul that knows God, a fit soul for its improved temple" (Keely 235). Keely, similar to nearly all others writing on the subject after Blavatsky, was influenced by the Theosophical model of karma and reincarnation. That model, as outlined in the preceding chapter, was more Lamarckian and Social Darwinist than Darwinian, but it succeeded in enlisting scientific progressivism to support the notion of upward spiritual evolution through multiple lifetimes. Blavatsky and her disciples argued for continuing *spiritual* individuality and unified *spiritual* identity in the absence of conscious, personal memory and identity. One of those disciples, Francesca Arundale, summarized as follows: "The process of human interior growth, of that which I have elsewhere spoken of as the Evolution of the Higher Self, is a process of infusing the permanent consciousness—which *is* the Higher Self...—the individuality of the man, the continuous individuality—with *capacities,* not with specific recollections of events" (Arundale xxi). Another follower, William Burnet Tuthill, in "Development Through Reincarnation" (1896), wrote that "this development of the soul to its limit in God is the sublime teleology of the universe," and that such a process requires "countless ages of accumulation" (Tuthill 256).

Arundale and Tuthill's statements represent the basic logic underlying the Theosophical argument: (1) as demonstrated both by ancient spiritual wisdom and by modern science, the natural universe and the human soul were created for the purpose of evolution toward spiritual perfection and union with the divine source; (2) such evolution only could occur over a very long timeframe and is not conceivable within a single human lifetime; therefore, (3) reincarnation must be a divine/natural law of the universe.[12] Many Victorians, whether Theosophists or not, whether attracted to reincarnation or not, were quite ready to answer Darwinian evolution with some form of progressive spiritual evolution. Belief in progress, "the primary dogma of the Victorian period" that was itself "almost a substitute religion," offered a consoling promise of a rosy future for Britons, not only as a people, a nation, and an empire but spiritually too (Buckley 41, 42).

But some Victorians—not least among them Thomas Carlyle, Matthew Arnold, and Thomas Henry Huxley—noted the complementary dark side of progressivism. It was expressed, for instance, in the Darwinian observation that a species or, by popular extension, a nation or a race might fail to adapt and thus perish. It surfaced toward the end of the century in debates about "degeneration," which in the process of celebrating the superiority of Caucasian peoples and nations revealed a horror (Kurtz's word in Joseph Conrad's *Heart of Darkness*) of being overwhelmed by the masses of "inferior" races or classes, or, worse, of degenerating back toward the dark-skinned origins of the species.

Hindu and Buddhist doctrines of reincarnation appeared to offer a corollary: "karmic debt" resulting in spiritual devolution. The flashpoint on this subject was the thought of being reborn as an animal, such as a pig or worm. This violated Western soul-theory by denying the privileged status of human beings within God's creation: that humans were "created in His image." As a result, nearly all who advocated reincarnation and karma denied the Hindu or Buddhist element.

Jerome A. Anderson, in *Reincarnation, A Study of the Human Soul In its Relation to Re-Birth, Evolution, Post-Mortem States, the Compound Nature of Man, Hypnotism, etc.* (1896), wrote that "reincarnation is quite distinct from metempsychosis, when this is understood to mean the return of the soul to earth through human or animal bodies," because the soul can never "retrograde into an animal condition" (Anderson 66). The second of Annie Besant's proofs of reincarnation was that it explains why the human's "persistent intellectual and moral Ego, learning by experience, developing through millenniums," can evolve morally while animals cannot, "why a man progresses while animals remain stationary" (Besant, *Reincarnation* 72). Besant also offered as her fourteenth proof that the "rise and decay of races is best explained on the hypothesis of reincarnation," accompanied by the notion of collectively shared karma, what Blavatsky had analyzed as "Distributive Karma" (Besant, *Reincarnation* 88; Blavatsky, *Key* 203). The degree of racism in this aspect of Theosophical reincarnation is not transparent; Theosophists did not identify Anglo-Saxons as the most spiritually evolved, and the potential for racial degeneration could apply to them. Chi-ming Yang argues in this regard that in eighteenth-century England "reasoning animals and reasoning Easterners—from Egypt to China—thus seem to be the two sources of anxiety for theorists of transmigration; the two represent a hybridity against which exemplary Western rationality, that of Pythagoras, and of human uniqueness, must be defended" (Yang 23). This may be borne out in the continued trend in the nineteenth century to de-Orientalize reincarnation and karma by forcing them into alignment with Western soul-theory. As Victorians imposed their progressivism upon reincarnation, they tended to suppress its degenerative or devolutionary elements.

The least compatible element of karma and reincarnation with Western soul-theory was the belief unique to Buddhism that the soul is not what continues from reincarnation to reincarnation because in the first place no such thing as a soul exists. Within canonical Buddhism, belief in the soul is a delusion counter-productive to spiritual practice that results from clinging to individual identity or selfhood. The scholar Ernest J. Eitel outlined the distinction between Hindu and Buddhist doctrine on this point:

> In the place of Brahma, the fountain source and goal of Brahmanic metempsychosis, he [Buddha] substituted therefore the idea of Karma, i.e. merit and

demerit. Again, whilst the Brahmans believed each human soul to originate in and to be part and parcel of Brahm, Buddha avoided the term soul entirely and taught, that about the primitive origin of each human being nothing further could be said but this: that each living being, after the dissolution of its previous embodiment, comes again into mundane existence and is endowed with a new body, in accordance with its moral merit or demerit accumulated in a previous form of existence. (Eitel, *Buddhism* 73)

Also writing in the 1880s, T. W. Rhys Davids wanted to be very clear about what Buddhist reincarnation was not. Observing that no mention is made in the Pali canon of "transmigration of souls," he concludes that he has "no hesitation in maintaining therefore, that Gotama did not teach" that doctrine (Rhys Davids, *Lectures* 91). What he did teach, "would be better summarized, if we wish to retain the word transmigration, as the transmigration of character," but "it would be more accurate to drop the word transmigration altogether when speaking of Buddhism, and to call its doctrine the doctrine of Karma," since "Gotama held that after the death of any being, whether human or not, there survived nothing at all but the being's 'Karma,' the result, that is, of its mental and bodily actions" (Rhys Davids, *Lectures* 91–92). Victorians who wrote about reincarnation and karma had a clear understanding of Buddhist doctrine on this point, and the large majority of them rejected it. Buddhism, the primary source of these concepts within nineteenth-century discourse, the source that finally brought them into common usage, offered the version of reincarnation with which Victorians least could agree.

Returning finally to the question of definitions, I propose the following distinctions. They emerge less from any dictionary than from my reading of British culture, but they unavoidably also reflect the demands of convenience for a consist terminology, even at the risk of oversimplification. I do not offer myself as an expert either on ancient Egyptian religion or on Hinduism of any period; I therefore proffer these definitions as partial and provisional, if reasonably accurate to the context of nineteenth-century Britain. These, then, are the types of "reincarnation"—most broadly understood—that I have observed in Victorian discourse:

- *Metempsychosis.* Often used as a synonym to "transmigration" but with special reference to ancient Egyptian doctrine. It may imply rebirth both of body and of soul. Conscious identity continues intact. It is non-progressive in that its primary concern is neither ethical development nor spiritual evolution.
- *Hindu reincarnation.* A soul-based system according to which after many different bodily reincarnations a soul sheds mundane attachments and is reabsorbed into the divine. Whether conscious identity and memory are retained between lifetimes, they are dissolved back into the Atman upon the attainment

of moksha, or salvation. A soul may progress or retrogressive on the merits of its karma.

- *Buddhist reincarnation.* A non-soul-based system involving multiple reincarnations between which one's karma continues but in the absence of identity or memory or of anything like a soul. Progression or retrogression may occur on the merits of karma.

- *Transmigration*—Often used synonymously with other terms, this is a catchall term signifying any form of out-of-body travel. It may mean travel from and return to the current body; travel by a spirit following death, whether to the spiritualist Summerland, another planet, or anyplace other than the traditional heaven; or migration of one's soul to another body (as in possession). Identity and memory must remain, and this may limit ethical development and spiritual evolution.

- *Resurrection.* The rising from earthly death of a deity or an elected soul to fully assume divine status. Christian proponents of reincarnation argued that "the birth of Christ is the proof of reincarnation" and that for all humans "there will be many resurrections and not one, which is the transmigration of souls" (Keely 237; Howard 143). It implies the "re-rising" of the original physical body, as in the case of Lazarus, but is associated with spiritual ascension to heaven, as believers expect to do at the Last Judgment. It is an historically specialized variant of metempsychosis.

- *Immortality.* The eternal spiritual life attributed to the traditional Judeo-Christian heaven or hell, but also involving transmigration, through which the soul quits the body, travels to one of those locations, and resides there. Conscious identity and memory continue intact. It is not progressive in the sense used elsewhere: faith supersedes merit or works, and a soul has no opportunity following death to improve itself, remaining either blissfully or tormentedly fixed for eternity.

- *Demi-immortality.* Perpetual earthly life in which the same body continues to live indefinitely, usually without aging. The "demi-immortal Oriental" became a common figure in the nineteenth century. The vampire (zombie, mummy) is an unholy version in which the body continues without the soul. Retained identity and memory are key. Wisdom may accrue, but not spiritual evolution: the soul is stuck with itself.

- *Inheritance.* In a figurative sense reinforced by Victorians, genetic reincarnation, the passing down from generation to generation of blood, property, and aspects of identity, often involving the "sins of the father" or the privileges of primogeniture and often assumed to be naturally fated or divinely sanctioned. Theorists of reincarnation drew genetic inheritance into that debate by frequently comparing and contrasting the two.[13]

I will use these definitions in the following analysis.

Reincarnation and Karma in Novels by Marie Corelli and H. Rider Haggard

The novels of Corelli and Haggard each portray multiple forms of reincarnation, and it is not always easy to keep them straight. Each author's earlier novel makes sometimes indirect but unmistakable allusions to Hindu and/ or Buddhist reincarnation and karma, but their later novels make explicit and unapologetic use of those doctrines, both in plot and in theme. In the case of Corelli, this may represent a surprising reversal. In her *Life Everlasting,* the protagonist is given a vision of what could only be her karmic record: "I saw more plainly than I have ever seen anything in visible Nature, a slowly moving, slowly passing panorama of scenes and episodes that presented themselves in marvelous outline and colouring....I realized to the full that an eternal record of every life is written...and that not a word, not a thought, not an action is forgotten!" (*Life* 172). She then takes a transmigratory journey back through some of her own past lives during which she views a filmic series of scenes of herself and Santoris, her soul-mate, struggling unsuccessfully to realize their immortal love in ancient Egypt, in early-Christian Rome, in Renaissance Florence, and so forth chronologically. She later says, "the soul pictures, presented to me were only a few selected out of thousands which equally concerned us, and which were stored up among eternal records" (*Life* 207). In each, she "recognized *my own face in hers!*—and in his *the face of Santoris!*" (*Life* 173). Because bodies as well as souls have been reborn, this is more metempsychosis than reincarnation. The same is true in Haggard's novels in the case of the reincarnation of Kallikrates as Leo Vincey, since the two share not similar but identical physical bodies. As Ayesha pulls the sheet in a magician's gesture from the perfectly preserved mummy of Kallikrates, she turns toward Leo saying, "Kallikrates is dead, and is born again!" (*She* 240). Leo's metempsychosis is further complicated by the fact that he also is the lineal descendent of Kallikrates. Thus three types of reincarnation are combined in him: metempsychosis, inheritance, and a modified Hindu or Buddhist reincarnation. In both Haggard and Corelli, the presentations of karma and of multiple rebirths with spiritual progress between them clearly draws upon Indian reincarnation. The novels of both authors mix-and-match Buddhist terms with Hindu concepts with Egyptian metempsychosis with various types of transmigration.

Among a number of unexpected similarities between the novels of these two very different authors are the terms they use to deny the existence of death by referring to reincarnation. Corelli's protagonist in *A Romance* has come to learn that "There is no death," a claim remarkably similar to Ayesha's statement in Haggard's *She* that "There is no such thing as Death, though there be a thing called Change" (*Romance* 215; *She* 149). This thread is picked up again in Corelli's *Life Everlasting* when Aselzion, the Master, tells the protagonist that "there is no Death, but only Change" and later that "Death is an impossibility in the scheme of Life—what is called by that name is merely a shifting and re-investiture of imperishable atoms" (*Life* 251, 316). This does not describe a single life and a single death, accountable before God, but a series of lives at different stages of evolution accountable to one's own soul. Thus for Santoris in *Life Everlasting,* "each individual life is a perpetual success of progressive changes, and he holds that a change *is* never and *can* never be made till the person concerned has prepared the next 'costume' or mortal presentment of immortal being, according to voluntary choice and liking" (*Life* 140). "Change" is a coded term for the progressive transition between lifetimes (and, perhaps, between worlds). In *A Romance,* Heliobas speculates that if he fails in his current life to reach the same spiritual plateau as his beloved sister Zara, then "I might begin over again in some other form, and so reach the goal" (*Romance* 216). This is reincarnation, though not Buddhist reincarnation, since the implication throughout is of continuous memory and identity between lives.

This denial of death correlates with a downplaying of heaven/hell and even of God's role as creator and judge. One might expect that heavenly immortality would figure prominently in works in which characters profess themselves to be Christians, but even the word "Christian" is used infrequently in Haggard's novels, and Corelli makes heavier use of it in her prefaces than do her characters in the novel. Though the life of Jesus is offered as an exemplar in *A Romance* and by Holly in *She,* that too fades by the writing of *Life Everlasting* and *Ayesha.* Both authors de-emphasize heaven/hell, or those terms, especially Corelli, who strenuously argues against the Calvinistic "Gospel of…Fear" and its hell in favor of the universal "Law of Love," according to which a benevolent Creator would not condemn His creations (*Romance* xxiv, 31). Though he periodically defends Christian ethics (sometimes merged with Buddhist ethics) to Ayesha, Holly's hope of heaven is itself very nebulous, for, as he comments, it too may "prove but a kindly mockery given to hold us from despair" and humans at death may "be gently lowered into the abysses of eternal sleep" (*She* 119).[14] The corollary of heaven in Corelli's *A Romance* is called the "Electric Circle," the celestial/spiritual hub of the universe overseen by the "Central Intelligence" (*Romance* 203, 236). Both Haggard and Corelli use multiple euphemisms to revise the traditional "God," for example "the Power that made you" or "O Divine Power of Love and Life"—"power" being a key term for both (*She* 12; *Life* 330). Death, God, and heaven have not been removed, but they have been decentered to accommodate other alternatives.

In *A Romance,* when the protagonist takes her culminating "transmigration" into interstellar space to the "Electric Circle," she herself is placed in the role of the creator of a populated planet, witnesses the people's slide into unfaithfulness, and is ordered by a "Great Voice" to choose between destroying them or "suffer[ing] the loss of heavenly joy and peace, in order to rescue thy perishing creation" (*Romance* 172, 195). She assumes the self-sacrificing role of Jesus, oversteps the judgment of God-the-Father, and effectively replaces Him with a more thoroughly anthropomorphized and now feminized Christ-figure, herself. She also encounters spiritual beings floating in space who are "expiating sins of their own in thus striving to save others—the oftener they succeed, the nearer they approach to Heaven"—a concept very loosely parallel to karma (*Romance* 183). The backstage stand-in for death/heaven/God is made clear in this passage in *Life Everlasting* from the creed of the occult Christian order into which the protagonist has proved herself worthy for admittance: "We know that from the Past, stretching back into infinity, we have ourselves made the Present,—and according to Divine law we also know that from this Present, stretching forward into infinity, we shall ourselves evolve all that is yet To Come. There is no power, no deity, no chance, no 'fortuitous concurrence of atoms' in what is simply a figure of the Universal Mathematics. Nothing can be 'forgiven' under the eternal law of Compensation [karma],— nothing need be 'prayed for'" (*Life* 330). Reincarnation and karma have all but occluded God and heaven/hell.

Nevertheless, the types of reincarnation that are most apparent in the novels of Corelli and Haggard are transmigration and demi-immortality. Transmigratory soul-travel is the central spiritual initiation in each of the Corelli novels. In Haggard's *Ayesha,* we learn late in the story that Ayesha's soul had not "reincarnated in Central Asia—as a female Grand Lama," as Holly and Leo first thought, but rather that a "transference of her spirit from the caves of Kôr to this temple" in Tibet had occurred so that she might take possession of the dying body of the one-hundred-and-eight-year-old high-priestess, whose position she then assumes (*Ayesha* 14, 135). After Leo passes the test of the "loathly lady" by choosing Ayesha in a withered body over the young and beautiful Atene, Ayesha prays to "Thou inevitable Law that art named Nature...the goddess of all climes and ages" for the return of her "immortal loveliness" (*Ayesha* 127, 128). Following dramatic lighting effects, her preternaturally young and beautiful body is restored to her through what appears to be a form of resurrection. As we find, her body is not quite mortal, but, then, it has not been for two thousand years. Ayesha is a case of the demi-immortal Oriental, a figure that will reappear in Guy Boothby's *Dr. Nikola* (1896), James Hilton's *Lost Horizons* (1933), and a range of twentieth-century texts, especially films in what I call the martial-arts-Buddhism subgenre. She is less reincarnated—though she has reincarnated prior to her current "last, long life"—than perpetually incarnated (*Ayesha* 121). This was the result of her having been led by the Goddess Isis to the "womb of the Earth" and there having bathed in the phallic fire of the "Fountain and Heart of Life," "the bright Spirit of the Globe" (*She* 286, 287).[15]

This fiery fountain of youth has its corollary in the novels of Marie Corelli. In *A Romance,* it is electricity, by which each individual's "electric Germ of the Soul" is plugged into the divine-universal energy source, the "Electric Circle" (*Romance* 249). In *Life Everlasting,* Corelli has kept pace with science by shifting her metaphor to atomic radiation, the recently recognized "Eternal Spirit of Energy...throughout *all* Nature" (*Life* 35). The human "Spirit, called the Soul" is "an exhaustless supply of 'radium'" (*Life* 376). Corelli even uses radioactive half-life as a metaphor for the "*change of form*" the spirit undergoes upon the death of one body, continuing into a new life (though she might not have liked this comparison if she had known about the future problems of radioactive waste disposal) (*Life* 20). In Corelli's novels, as in Haggard's, contact with the naturally supernatural Power grants demi-immortality. Santoris explains his preternatural youthfulness—a topic of fascination to all the other characters (and apparently to the aging author)—by saying, "The soul is always young,—and I live in the Spirit of youth, not in the Matter of age" (*Life* 127). Spiritual health naturally leads to physical health, and any human who accesses genuine spiritual energy can be demi-immortal, "can himself be Divine, in the Desire and Perpetuation of Life" (*Life* 372). Thus Corelli, like Haggard, foregrounds two types of reincarnation in particular: transmigration and demi-immortality. The broader point to be made is that in doing so both authors invoke, respectively, "the spirit of Nature" and the "Spirit of Life or Nature"—represented by radium and the "fire of life"—as a feminized, natural-theological or transcendentalist alternative to the traditional patriarchal God (*Life* 17; *Ayesha* 103). The portrayal in these novels of other types of reincarnation therefore participates in a Deistic worldview, and this in turn is the foundation for forwarding Hindu and/or Buddhist karma and reincarnation as the "natural law" of an ethically ordered universe.

In line with other Victorian interpreters of karma and reincarnation, Corelli, and Haggard to a lesser degree, saw this ethically ordered universe as a progressive system. In Corelli's electrical and then radiational theology, the divine spark, "the germ of a soul or spirit," "is placed there to be either cultivated or neglected as suits the *will* of man"; it is "indestructible; yet, if neglected, it remains always a germ; and, at the death of the body it inhabits, goes elsewhere to seek another chance of development" in another lifetime and in another physical form (*Romance* 114). Corelli departs from the interpretation preferred by many Theosophists and by Victorians in general: she recognizes and endorses the possibility of spiritual retrogression. She writes in her "Prologue" to *Life Everlasting* that "a faulty Soul, an imperfect individual Spirit, is likewise compelled to return to school and resume the study of the lessons it has failed to put into practice" (*Life* 34–35). Her system posits this doctrine: "Eternal Punishment is merely a form of speech for what is really Eternal Retrogression. For there is a Forward, so there must be a Backward. The electric Germ of the

Soul—delicate, fiery, and imperishable as it is—can be forced by its companion Will to take refuge in a lower form of material existence, dependent on the body it first inhabits" (*Romance* 249). Corelli theorized her own version of hell as karmic devolution, which, she threatens, could lead all the way down to lower life forms.

However, Corelli's account is not Hindu karma and reincarnation, and it is even farther from Buddhism. In the first place, Corelli remains wedded to the faith side of the traditional Protestant faith/works dialectic. One of her key terms, "will," ultimately refers to faith, as she explains in her 1896 "Preface" to *A Romance:* "To ensure Progression the Will must be guided by faith in Christ,—and Christ only; equally to ensure Retrogression, the Will is centered on SELF,—and rapidly works degradation on the whole Spiritual Germ" (*Romance* x). There is Christ, and there is self, and this leaves no place for community or society or accountability for one's actions and intentions in relationship to others, the latter being closer to a common understanding of karma. In the second place, the punishment that Corelli attaches to spiritual retrogression is tied to continuation between lifetimes of individual consciousness and personal identity as signaled by memory. In Corelli, there is one thing that the reincarnating soul "can never escape from—*Memory*," for "Eternal Retrogression means that the hopelessly tainted electric germ recoils further and further from the Pure Centre whence it sprang, *always bearing within itself* the knowledge of *what it was once* and *what is might have been*" (*Romance* 250). The self becomes its own hell, or its own heaven. This doctrine is enacted in the protagonist's journey back through her past lives in *Life Everlasting,* in which "each individual Spirit preserves its individuality and, to a certain extent, its memory" (*Life* 395). Corelli revised reincarnation and karma to accommodate her very Western and Protestant investment in redemption through faith and in the sanctity of individual identity.

Related themes appear in Haggard's novels, to which the issue of memory is central. Ayesha repeatedly characterizes herself with phrases like "memory haunts me"; she languishes, because for her "life cannot bring forgetfulness!" (*She* 156, 165). Not only has she committed acts worthy of remorse and "karmic debt"—the murder of her lover Kallikrates foremost among them—but she has lived in a state of suspended memories for two millennia. This would be Corelli's "Eternal Retrogression," except that there have been no reincarnations, no "change," and that is the problem. It is as if Ayesha's willful choice to live perpetually without aging, death, or reincarnation has stymied her spiritual growth by disallowing the development for which only multiple lives might provide adequate opportunity for progress. Her soul has been stuck in time, forced to relive without revising. Her demi-immortality stands in the way of the spiritual progress that Haggard, like Corelli, saw as the potential of reincarnation and karma. Perhaps this is why Haggard, at the end of *She,* chose to regress Ayesha so dramatically. In showing Leo that it will be harmless to him, she steps for a second time into the "fire of life" and in a moment is withered to her actual age. Holly's servant Job screams, "*Look!—look!—look!* She's shrivelling up! she's turning into a monkey!*" (S 293). If she will not progress through death and rebirth, then she must devolve into that Darwinian form that many Victorians most feared to find swinging in their family trees. While Corelli concentrates on examples of spiritual progress, acknowledging spiritual retrogression as a cautionary tale, Haggard focuses on spiritual stagnation and the consequences of a failure to progress.

At the end of *Ayesha*, Ayesha does appear to progress, or at least to be rewarded with the promise of eternal union with Leo in an after-death state, but it also seems as if Haggard purposefully muddies the waters concerning her spiritual condition. Early in that novel, the Buddhist monk, Kou-en, speaking to Holly about his quest to find Ayesha, passes a judgment upon her that the text supports: "Doubtless you will find her there as you expect, and doubtless her *khama,* or identity, is the same as that which in some earlier life of hers once brought me to sin [in desiring and worshipping her, as she has the power to make any man do]. Only be not mistaken, she is no immortal; nothing is immortal. She is but a being held back by her own pride, her own greatness if you will, upon the path towards nirvana. That pride will be humbled, as already it has been humbled" (*Ayesha* 29). Ayesha had mocked not only Kou-en but Buddhism as lesser than her power. Readers of *She* know that she has been humbled, and readers of *Ayesha* witness her choice to humble herself to Leo and to moderate her lust for global political and religious conquest. As critics have observed, Ayesha's feminine power poses a threat to (white, British) masculinity, and her potential for conquest poses a threat to Queen Victoria, the British Empire, and the world, all of which she promises to conquer.[16] The text is clear: Ayesha's dangerous powers and desires demand domestication. Her love for a highly masculine and thoroughly British man, Leo, is the only force on the planet capable of doing that. Yet, even after Leo takes her "sins upon [his] head" and "redeem[s]" her with his love, figuratively converting her pagan Goddess worship to his masculine Christianity, she persists in serving the "mighty Motherhood...of Nature" (*Ayesha* 142, 143, 195). What is worse from the perspective of Haggard, who in his youth had "burned his fingers at that game" of Spiritualism, Ayesha holds communion with the spirits of the dead (Haggard, *Cloak* 16).

The dilemma that Haggard set for himself was how to redeem and reward Ayesha, while still showing that her dabbling in realms of power—spiritual and political—beyond the proper sphere of woman and of mortal is dangerous to moral order and to spiritual evolution. For this purpose he turns in closing to Buddhism. The last word spoken in the novel is given to Kou-en, who says, "Yes...doubtless you are all winning merit ["good karma"]; but, if I may venture to say so, you are winning it very slowly, especially the woman" (*Ayesha* 198). Ayesha finally "is assessed by the standard of actual Buddhism," and there is "a toughness in this Buddhist coda to the novel" (Coates 53). Ayesha has not, as she thinks, entirely slipped her responsibility for her karmic debt. Haggard could not send Ayesha to heaven, and, despite mixed professions of faith by himself and by his characters, he did not trust Christian doctrine to provide sufficient correction and guidance. Though he remained skeptical about Buddhism as well, he ultimately turned to karma and reincarnation as the source of ethical order in the universe and the adjudicator of spiritual progress.

Especially in their later novels, *Ayesha* and *Life Everlasting,* Haggard and Corelli turned to karma and reincarnation. They explored an array of types of reincarnation, reflecting and constructing the Victorian fascination with and confusion about this topic. But they each settled ultimately on their own adaptations of the Victorian understanding of Hindu reincarnation and Buddhist karma. They significantly reinterpreted those doctrines in order to maintain certain ideological commitments. They each worked, though quite differently, for at least passing compatibility with the spirit of Christianity as they very liberally interpreted it. Each insisted on key tenets of Western soul-theory and Protestant individualism, in particular, the continuation of identity and, therefore, memory between reincarnations and in the final state. Corelli decried all non-Christian religion, while at the same time working to incorporate elements of Spiritualism, Theosophy, Hinduism, and Buddhism into her own fictional hybrid religion. Haggard himself, as well as characters in his novels, preached religious tolerance, but he struggled to understand the similarities and contradictions between his tacit Anglicanism, his attraction to the occult, and his belief in reincarnation and karma.

Though Haggard was more comfortable in acknowledging the Buddhist origins of those doctrines, Corelli was more successful than Haggard at squaring them with Christian faith, though Christian faith had to be significantly modified for this purpose as well. Perhaps one explanation for this difference is that Corelli felt much more comfortable then did Haggard with the feminine aspects of the divine, to which both were deeply attracted. Corelli may well have thought it blasphemous to speak in reverence of "the Goddess," but she worked in her writing to feminize God-the-Father and to portray a woman's religious perspective, though her definitions of femininity and womanhood would have matched neither those of the New Woman nor those of conservative Victorian propriety. Haggard's novels sometimes appear to endorse the Goddess, redefined in a Deistic sense as "universal motherhood" and "Nature," but at the same time he was terrified of female spiritual power and ultimately aligned it with the occult as too divergent from order and authority, both religious and social. Finally, though Buddhism was the most recent and available source to Corelli and Haggard on karma and reincarnation, the source with which they were most familiar, its version of those doctrines was the one least assimilable by them and by Victorians in general.

The Economy of Sin/Redemption versus the Economy of Karma/Reincarnation

One of the strongest associations that Victorians made between Christianity and Buddhism was that both Jesus and the Buddha taught love, compassion, and forgiveness. After that important similarity, however, the two religions hardly could be more different. Speaking at the broadest level about what I defined in the introduction to this book as the "historical and doctrinal consensus of Christianity," it is a religion of the soul that subscribes to a strict body/soul dichotomy and relies upon the concept of sin ("fallenenss"), which is associated especially with the body. It is based ethically on the Ten Commandments and other teachings of the Bible but places greatest emphasis—varying from denomination to denomination—upon the necessity of faith, whether in the God of the Old Testament, Christ of the New Testament, the Trinity, or a Unity. Faith is the primary means of seeking divine forgiveness of sin, through which the individual soul may receive "redemption" and "life everlasting" in heaven. Summarized at a similarly broad level, the canonical Buddhism to which Victorians were exposed views the concept of the soul as a self-delusion; obviates the body/soul dichotomy; has no true corollary to the concept of sin; posits no creating or judging deity and therefore no redemption; describes lived reality in terms of the cycle of karma and reincarnation; offers no eternal heaven but rather the liberation/annihilation of nirvana; and describes the road to attaining nirvana through the founding teachings of the Buddha, the Four Noble Truths, and the Noble Eightfold Path (as outlined in appendix 2). The moral economy of sin/redemption and that of karma/reincarnation are fundamentally and nearly irreconcilably different one from the other.

A second point concerns the place of suffering and desire in the two religions. To recall the story of the life of the Buddha, Siddhartha Gautama was born a prince whose every desire was satisfied; he denounced the pleasures of his wealth and position to take up the begging bowl and spent six years in extreme asceticism, attempting to eradicate desire through disciplined meditation and bodily mortification. When this failed to bring him enlightenment, he conceived of the way of the Middle Path, avoiding both the extremes of self-denial and the extremes of self-indulgence. Soon afterward he sat under the Bodhi Tree until he attained enlightenment, and his realization became the basis of his first sermon, which contains the revelation of the Four Noble Truths. Summarized briefly, they are: (1) *Dukkha,* suffering exists, to live is to suffer; (2) *Samudaya,* the origin of suffering is desire for perpetually fulfilled desire, desire for permanence, which means clinging to the self and the soul, or, in postmodern terms, the unsatisfiable longing for presence; (3) *Nirodha,* the cessation of suffering is possible by adhering to the path of non-attachment and non-aversion, equanimity, and openness; (4) *Magga,* that path is the Middle Way, as detailed in the Noble Eightfold Path, in which neither gratification nor mortification is either craved or feared.

Understanding the nature of human desire and suffering is a foundational concern of Buddhism (which is one reason why some chose to think of it more as a psychology than a religion). In contrast, in nearly all forms of Christianity, human suffering is ascribed in part to human fallenness—"original sin"—and ultimately is inexplicable except as "God's will" and as his means of instruction, to which the appropriate response is deepened faith. According to this logic, "Man's suffering…means that God is seeking man's good"; it should be understood as "a Divine discipline, designed to bring us out of evil…; a means of training for perfection"; and "the proof of God's love" (Slater 17, 18). Human fallenenss is tied also to the body/soul dichotomy, in that the "desires of the flesh" are a source of sin, perhaps the original source in Eve's willful desire. The body and its desires always threaten to become sinful, and they must be disciplined or corrected in order to permit the soul to be worthy of redemption. The explanations for and responses to suffering and desire within the economy of sin/redemption differ profoundly from those within the economy of karma/reincarnation.

A third point concerns one of the oldest and most persistent stereotypes about the Orient in general, about Indians especially, and perhaps particularly about Buddhists: they are passive, tradition-bound, fatalistic, ruled by the masses, and thus ultimately nihilistic, in contract to Westerners, who are active, progressive, optimistic, individualistic, self-determining, and guided by certain faith in future redemption. Victorians replicated and reinforced these stereotypes, even if a few questioned them. Thus, for example, Ernest J. Eitel, in his 1884 work on Buddhism, wrote: The Buddhist "counts death—if he may rest after that—a blessing. To suffer, to suffer even the fiercest tortures of hell…is not half as frightful an idea to him as to be forced to act, to labour, to work for aeons" (Eitel 76). The respected Sanskrit scholar Monier Monier-Williams concurred: "According to Christianity:—Work the works of God while it is day. According to Buddhism:—Beware of action, as causing re-birth, and aim at inaction, indifference, and apathy, as the highest of all states" (Monier-Williams, *Buddhism* 560). "Action," or "action/reaction," is one way to translate the word "karma"; it is the total of what remains as a result of a sentient being's "mental and bodily actions" (Rhys Davids, *Lectures* 91–92). Because Buddhists hope to avoid the generation of karmic debt, Victorians concluded that theirs must be a religion of passivity rather than activeness in the face of suffering and thus naturally leads to senseless annihilation rather than to heavenly reward.

To summarize, from one predominant Victorian point of view, Buddhists utterly failed to recognize the urgency and rewards of faith in God; they settled for "intellectual enlightenment" rather than genuine faith (Monier-Williams, *Buddhism* 544). As atheists, they denied the existence of the soul, which put them on the materialist side of the pervasive spiritualism/materialism dichotomy, the side of the body. Logically, then, like all Orientals, they might have a tendency toward and aptitude for the pleasures of the body, or so one popular imperialist fantasy runs. However, Buddhists, even more than other Orientals, were too passive, too "languid," to actively seek their ambitions and desires. They lacked will ("will" being one of Corelli's key words). They were indolent when they should have worked, and they sought surrender—in the spiritual as well as military sense—when "we" would have fought. These familiar dualisms—body/soul, faith/works, active/passive—inform the following analysis of how Marie Corelli and H. Rider Haggard struggled with issues of suffering and desire. In that struggle, each author juxtaposed the economy of sin/redemption to the economy of karma/reincarnation and could not resolve the contradictions between the two.

The Suffering of Desire and the Desire for Suffering

Love and desire, sex and death—these are the perennial preoccupations of romance fiction, as they are of the novels of Haggard and Corelli, though with a superadded spiritual dimension. Another striking parallel between the novels of these two authors is that they similarly invoke a universal "law of love." In Corelli's *A Romance,* "The Universe is upheld solely by the Law of Love," and in *Life Everlasting* the "Force behind the Universe is Love" (*Romance* 31; *Life* 371). In Corelli, romantic love between two people, in order to be more than animal passion, must be a spiritual love originating from that universal, divine Love. The plots of Haggard's two novels are driven by the love between Leo/Kallikrates and Ayesha, and Leo professes himself a believer that "Love is the law of life" (*Ayesha* 29).[17] Though Corelli's law of love does not have exactly the same referent as does Haggard's, both authors take Buddhism as one foil against which to define that law. In *A Romance,* the opposite of the "law of love" is the "Law of Universal Necessity." It signifies materialism and atheism and alludes to a combination of the Darwinian "law of natural selection" and the Buddhist "law of the Dharma" (*Romance* 2). Cellini asks: "Who portioned out this Law of Necessity? What brutal Code compels us to be born, to live, to suffer, and to die without recompense or reason? Why should this Universe be an ever-circling Wheel of Torture"—as in the title of the Buddha's first sermon, the "Setting into Motion of the Wheel of the Dharma" (*Romance* 65). He characterizes this antithesis to the "law of love" in terms of "eternal nothingness," a reference to one Victorian understanding of nirvana (*Romance* 65). In Haggard's *Ayesha,* She mocks Kou-en and his Buddhism in similar terms: "So your Path is renunciation and your nirvana a most excellent Nothingness which some would think it scare worth while to strive so hard to reach. Now I will show you a more joyous way, and a goddess more worthy of your worship....The way of Love and Life...that makes all the world to be, that made *you,* O seeker of Nirvana, and the goddess called Nature" (*Ayesha* 22–23). But here is the first of a series of related, unresolved contradictions that I will identity: both Corelli and Haggard tie their "law of love" to the "law of karma," the doctrine undergirding the naturally just and presumably loving universe they theorize; yet, they derived karma in part from the very Buddhism that supposedly also opposes the "law of love." The "law of love," through its associations with Buddhism, is a conflicted concept in the novels of Corelli and Haggard.

As one might predict, desire is a primary source of that conflict. Corelli and Haggard confront the dilemmas of desire and suffering in a number of strikingly similar ways. Each portrays characters—Zara and Leo, respectively—who are romantically engaged with quasi-deities or demi-immortals and who die in a rapture as a result of physical contact with them. Both authors insist on the separation between "spiritual desire" and physical desire, while indistinguishably intertwining the two (*Romance* 55). Both dwell upon the bodily features of extremely sensual women who deny—if not loathe—sexuality: Zara in *A Romance* and both Ayesha and Atene in *Ayesha.* Both situate their main characters between two choices, surrender to desire and transcendence of desire, and then show that neither choice is acceptable or achievable. In Corelli it seems clear that the "animal passions of the mere *man*"—in this case, Prince Ivan's passion for Zara—are "to be met with pity and forbearance," approaching disgust (*Romance* 295, 297). Yet, Zara, whose tempting lips and "rounded bosom" figure as prominently in this novel as Ayesha's do in Haggard's novels, and who, like Ayesha, has received demi-immortal youth charged with sexual magnetism, shares nightly embraces with a "beautiful and all-powerful angelic spirit": her destined soul-mate who jealously guards her against the touch of mortal man (*Romance* 167). Spirits apparently are as passionate and sensual as those with bodies.[18] To complicate the issue further, Corelli develops a theory of desire that aligns it to will, and, therefore, to faith. "We are the arbiters of our own fate....Our WILL is positively unfettered....We must ourselves desire to love and obey—*desire it above all things in the world*" (*Romance* 337). Indeed, desire demonstrates the existence of a blissful afterlife, according to an especially tautological version of the Deist "argument from design": "The mere fact of *the existence of a desire* clearly indicates and *equally existing capacity* for the *gratification* of that desire; therefore, I ask, would the *wish* for a future state of being, which is secretly felt by every one of us, have been permitted to find a place in our nature, *if there were no possible means of granting it?"* (*Romance* 336). It would seem, then, that gratification and denial of desire are equally to be desired. Desire is all, *and,* because both unsatisfiable and potentially sinful, it is the cause of all suffering.

Haggard makes this dilemma even more explicit and certainly more male-oriented. Leo and Ayesha suffer one of the most protracted cases of unquenched desire in literature, as Haggard chronicles two thousand years of delayed consummation. As Richard Pearson argues: "The narrative trajectory of Haggard's romances is usually towards this fulfillment of the male desire, towards orgasm and the preparation for the possession of desire. And yet the narrative always in the end thwarts this desire and leaves the male protagonist in a state of unsatisfied frustration and prolonged repetition of desire" (Pearson 228). Near the end of *Ayesha,* after Leo has redeemed Ayesha, physically as well as spiritually, with his love, he presses for the complete union of the marriage bed. But there is a catch, and it is the same one that Zara experiences in *A Romance:* "Man and spirit cannot mate" (*Ayesha* 133). The body/soul dichotomy must be strictly observed. Therefore, the driving tension of the plot is the suffering of a desire that must not be satisfied. Corelli creates a similar dynamic in *Life Everlasting,* in which the protagonist and her lover, Santoris, have been struggling through many lifetimes to realize their union. The text focalizes a desire in order to bar its fulfillment for reasons to which it repeatedly refers but refuses to answer.[19] We are told only that "It may be thousands of years before such a meeting is consummated" (*Life* 170). In Haggard's novel, Leo finally is prepared to give up everything—even co-rulership of the world with Ayesha as his warlord queen, even the demi-immortality that is guaranteed him when they revisit the "fire of life"—for just one night of connubial bliss with "the splendours of [her] breast" (*Ayesha* 187). Against Ayesha's warning, Holly performs a hasty, generic ceremony: the bride and groom embrace in both "flesh and spirit," and Leo is "withered in Ayesha's kiss" (*Ayesha* 189). Sex with spirits is at once irresistibly desirable and fatal. These novels fan desire—that of the characters and, therefore, that of the readers—to a feverish pitch only to demonstrate that it must never be gratified, not in this world.

This contradiction is restated in Haggard's prequel written fifteen years after *Ayesha.* In *She and Allan,* Ayesha says to Allan: "Hast never heard that there is but one morsel more bitter to the taste than desire denied, namely, desire fulfilled? Believe me that there can be no happiness for man until he attains a land where all desire is dead" (*She and Allan* 276). Allan says, "That is what the Buddha preached, Ayesha," to which she responds: "Aye, I remember the doctrines of that wise man well, who without doubt had found a key to the gate of Truth, one key only, for mark thou, Allan, there are many. Yet, man being man must know desires, since without them, robbed of ambitions, strivings, hopes, fears, aye and of life itself, the race must die, which is not the will of the Lord of Life" (*She and Allan* 276).[20] The Buddha was correct in theory, but he was unacceptably passive for Westerners. British spirituality, like British economic and foreign policy, must be progressive and active, if not in fact manly and "muscular," in the sense of Victorian "muscular Christianity." The "Law of Love and Life," underwritten by the natural order of the universe that Corelli's protagonist honors, and Ayesha worships as the "Spirit of Life or Nature," demands the active pursuit of desire, even though—or especially because—desire must lead to suffering.

In fact, this makes perfect sense within the moral economy of sin/redemption. The apparent contradiction of the dual imperative to pursue desire actively while with equal vigor suppressing it serves a particular logic. In short, to the extent that suppression intensifies desire, it might double the pleasure, as Freud and Foucault might have pointed out. This effectively translates within the economy of sin/redemption into increasing sin—as pleasure/suffering—in order to increase redemption. Though simplistic, it is not inaccurate to say that sin must precede redemption just as redemption requires sin. It follows that the greater the sin, the greater the redemption and, therefore, the greater the glory and grace of God. Within this paradigm, the proof of God's existence depends absolutely upon human fallenness and the divine redemption it necessitates and justifies. Desire and suffering evidence the former and require the latter. Thus desire and suffering are equally central to the economy of sin/redemption as to the Four Noble Truths of Buddhism, but for diametrically opposed reasons. As Monier-Williams summarized the point in 1889, while the Buddha urged his follows to overcome suffering by overcoming desire, Christ "told them to glory in their suffering—nay, to expect the perfection of their characters through suffering"; while Buddhism strives for "annihilation of the suffering body," Christianity undertakes the "glorification of the suffering body," making the body of Christ on the cross into a sacred fetish (Monier-Williams, *Buddhism* 545). Within the economy of karma/reincarnation, one objective is to reduce human suffering by way of understanding and controlling desire. Within the economy of sin/redemption, desire, sustained and heightened by the perpetual deferral of gratification, is good because it leads to suffering (as a form of pleasure), and suffering is good because it is the means to and the proof of salvation.

Corelli and Haggard complicated the already immensely complex set of paradoxes within the economy of sin/redemption not only by juxtaposing it to the economy of karma/reincarnation but by working to reconcile the two. The attempt at reconciliation required them to work both with and against predominant Victorian assumptions about Buddhism, such as its assumed passivity, and criticisms of its doctrines, such as their materialism and perceived emphasis on works rather than faith. Thus the phrase "acquiring merit," most familiar to Victorians from Tibetan Buddhism, came to signify selfish materialism. As Ernest Eitel argued: "For the theory of a man's destiny, being entirely determined by the stock of merits and demerits accumulated in previous forms of existence, constitutes Buddhism a system of fatalism; whilst the idea of improving one's future prospect by works of supererogation, converts morality into a vast scheme of profit and loss" (Eitel 83–84). Monier-Williams objected to the Chinese Buddhist "determination of storing up merit—like capital at a bank," while William H. Rattigan wrote approvingly that Buddhism teaches "that we be tolerant of others, that we never think or say that our own religion is the best, that we do not esteem one's self better than others, that we practice reverence and humility, dwell free from hatred in the midst of those who hate us, and that we do not love the wealth of the world but accumulate a merit balance in the bank of *Karma,* or good works" (Monier-Williams, *Buddhism* 546; Rattigan 309). This shared terminology—"profit and loss," "capital," "bank"—points to Max Weber's thesis in *The Protestant Ethic and the Spirit of Capitalism* (1930), which concerns the parallel historical development in Europe of Protestantism and capitalism and the resulting ideological interpenetration of the two. With that in mind, Rattigan's "do not love the wealth of the world" points further to what I believe was the most insoluble contradiction that the economy of karma/reincarnation highlighted within the economy of sin/redemption. Here is one way of stating that contradiction: the body of material banking and the soul of spiritual banking had to be in the same instant mutually reinforcing *and* utterly dissevered one from the other.

One must not confuse body with soul or works with faith, which is precisely what some Victorians perceived that Buddhism had done. The most appealing feature of Buddhism to Victorians was the rigorousness of its ethical system, but this also meant that Buddhism emphasized works over faith. As W. S. Lilly wrote in 1905 on the topic of karma: "To say that what a man sows here he shall reap hereafter, falls far short of this tremendous doctrine. His works *are* himself: he *is* what he has sown" (Lilly 204). While this collapses the necessary differences of body/soul and works/faith, it also points to the *ethical activeness* of Buddhism. It points out that the economy of karma/reincarnation is less flexible and forgiving than the economy of sin/redemption. At the risk of overextending the economic metaphor, according to the economy of sin/redemption, human beings accrue the debt of sin upon birth and are extended credit toward that debt by divine grace (Christ's sacrifice), but, when the bill comes due, one can appeal to God's mercy for redemption and the debt will be forgiven. In theory, however heinous one's deeds may have been, a deathbed confession or a genuine profession of faith will guarantee admission into heaven. Some Victorians made this very criticism, as in this passage from Francesca Arundale in 1890: "Western systems of religious teaching lead men to believe that eternal bliss or eternal misery is the result of one life upon earth—that deeds of hatred and cruelty may be blotted out by repentance and faith at the last moment before death, and that a life of evil may bring the same result to the individual as a life spent in the exercise of unselfish devotion to others, the evil acts of a whole life being shorn of their consequences by the belief of an hour" (Arundale 35).[21] In contrast, karma, as understood by the majority of Victorians who wrote about it, never is forgotten or forgiven; it *must* be relived until fully confronted, expiated, and understood, at which point its effects cease. Few envied this level of accountability: karma/reincarnation was perhaps too demanding. It placed faith in danger of appearing as a convenient out. It implied that faith, however passionately desiring and suffering for salvation, may be passive in comparison to the system of karma and reincarnation. It was not that Buddhism—the presumed exemplar of Oriental apathy and fatalism—was too passive; rather, it was *too active* in its ethical standards and spiritual practice.

And here is where the traditional dualisms upon which both Western soul-theory and British imperial assumptions about East and West begin to unravel. By drawing the economy of sin/redemption into comparison with the economy of karma/reincarnation, Victorians like Haggard and Corelli drew attention to a contradiction between the essential dichotomies of faith/works and active/passive such that faith appeared relatively passive and works the more appropriate sphere for spiritual activeness. To raise this contradiction was to raise for critical scrutiny the implicit historical contract that had emerged over the course of centuries in northern Europe between Protestantism and capitalism. To simplify for the sake of argument, that contract was that the former would mind things spiritual, the soul, and leave the latter largely free—as in laissez-faire—to mind things material: the body, the economy, the empire, and works. But then the European encounter with Buddhism imported a new threat that might expose and collapse that contract. The moral economy of karma/reincarnation made explicit a claim that what Western culture increasingly had sublimated as capitalism became the dominant ideology: that banking in the material realm of economics might pose an obstacle to banking on redemption. If the pursuit of desire and the resulting accrual of material credit might produce karmic debt, then a positive entry on the worldly side might necessitate a negative entry on the spiritual side. This was all but inadmissible, the Biblical camel and needle's eye notwithstanding. Spiritual progressivism was fine and good, but only as long as it did not pose a serious threat to the progress of "the market" that in the nineteenth century began to assume the abstract autonomy by which it would come to be invoked as a natural or God-given force. Thus Buddhism had gotten things exactly reversed: it wrong-headedly prescribed banking in the spiritual sphere while wrong-headedly proscribing against banking in the material sphere. Its spiritual banking must be wrong, because material banking had to be right. It was not that Buddhism was too materialistic, as many Victorians charged; Buddhism was not materialistic enough.

The economy of karma/reincarnation also foregrounded the discomforting question, which concerned Christians across denominations long had raised, that perhaps Christian institutions were not active enough in regulating those aspects of industrialism and commercialism that were antithetical to the principles of compassion, charity, and equality before God. As I have shown in the previous chapter, a central concern of the age was the perceived encroachment of materialism upon spiritualism. No one was more concerned than those Christians in evangelical churches and chapels who throughout the century were instrumental in effecting social reforms (for example, anti-slavery, "poor laws," child labor, temperance, suffrage, etc.). Nevertheless, by the nineteenth century Protestantism had nearly completed the historical accommodation of itself to coexistence within capitalism, an accommodation that effectively made it into the ideological underpinning of capitalism and capitalism into an essential complement to it.

Marie Corelli, throughout her writings, protested against this very condition of modern society as she saw it. She repeatedly casts as one of the primary nemeses of spirituality the "magnificent institution of free trade, which has resulted in a vulgar competition of all countries and all classes to see which can most quickly jostle the other out of existence" (*Romance* 62).[22] Corelli herself might have pointed out that the major Christian "holy day" was well on its way to becoming synonymous with the most important seasonal "holiday" in the annual cycle of capital exchange. This accommodation depended upon keeping up the traditional dualisms of soul/body, faith/works, and redemption/sin. It was that split that made it possible for a society increasingly defined by laissez-faire and consumer capitalism to maintain, and be maintained by, a Christian based culture. It made it possible—nay, inevitable—that Scrooge repent and be saved. It made it possible for the active pursuit of desire to be justified by redemption in the end. It made it possible for the disproportionate suffering of a class, gender, race, or nation to be rationalized as "God's will" to be compensated not on earth but in heaven. To the extent that it might open this arrangement to scrutiny, Buddhism and its economy of karma/reincarnation hardly could have posed more of a threat to the established order of Church and State.

The preceding argument also offers an answer to the question of why many Victorians persisted in casting Buddhism as the epitome of passivity. In order to sustain this stereotype, they chose to emphasize certain unassimilable elements of Buddhism, such as nirvana, and chose in the main to overlook the foundational teachings of the Buddha, who in canonical scripture says relatively little about nirvana. Perhaps some were stopped by the first of the Four Noble Truths—that to live involves suffering—which instantly appeared too pessimistic for their progressive optimism, or by the second, which seemed to them to suggest that all desire, whether fervent spiritual desire or the desire for wealth and progress, had to be squelched. What they ignored in particular was the Buddhist response to the natural condition of suffering and desire offered in the third and fourth Noble Truths, which prescribe the Middle Way, and in the Noble Eightfold Path, which teaches how to live that Middle Way. T. W. Rhys Davids, as well as other scholars, understood the centrality to Buddhist teaching of the Middle Way, as he summarized it in this passage: "The discourse [of the first sermon] laid stress on the necessity of adhering to the 'Middle Path'; that is to say, in being free, on the one hand, from 'devotion to the enervating pleasures of sense which are degrading, vulgar, sensual, vain and profitless'; and on the other, from any trust in the efficacy of the mortifications practiced by Hindu ascetics, 'which are painful, vain, and useless'" (Rhys Davids, *Buddhism* 47).[23] The Middle Way, according to sources available to Victorians, prescribes avoiding the extremes of desire and suppression of desire in order to avoid the extremes of suffering; it does not prescribe passivity in the face of suffering—quite the contrary—nor the denial of all desire.[24] As I have shown, it was in fact the economy of sin/redemption that stressed the opposite of any middle path by prescribing the intensification of both extremes at once: actively pursued desire combined with mortification of desire. I therefore suggest that it was not the perceived passivity (fatalism, pessimism, nihilism, etc.) of Buddhism that was most threatening to Victorians, though this was the convenient answer they frequently gave. It went deeper than that.

What made the economy of karma/reincarnation most threatening was that it offered to obviate the foundational dualisms of body/soul, works/faith, and active/passive upon which much within Western culture and society—its metaphysics, its religions, its social philosophies—relied for historical validation and ongoing justification. Two and a half millennia before postmodern theory, Buddhism had deconstructed in advance the Judeo-Christian, Platonic, and Cartesian dualisms as counterproductive to spiritual growth, precisely because they increase the extremes of desire and suffering. Buddhism offered a third term, a Middle Way. But to perceive it as such might be to perceive the polarities upon which Western thought depended as possibly unnecessary and perhaps unethical. This would mean perceiving the twin imperatives of sin and redemption, consuming desire and expiating desire, worldly accumulation and spiritual purification, the work week and one weekend morning, not as essential or natural but as artificial oppositions that served specific socially constructed and ideologically maintained interests.

Because Buddhism discursively threatened those interests, it was naturally necessary to read it as the opposite of the values of the institutions invested in those interests, which included both the institutions of the economic powerbase and the institutions of the spiritual powerbase.[25] Thus once it entered Victorian culture, Buddhism necessarily came to function as a straw-figure drawing fire that might otherwise hit those institutions of materiality that operated under the rubric of "the market" or those of spirituality that operated within church and chapel. Neither could its Middle Way be acknowledged nor could it be cast in the opposite direction from passivity as the ethical activism some Victorians recognized it to be. To do the latter would risk highlighting the inability of the economy of sin/redemption to curb the un-Christian aspects of. the economy of capital. In a sense, Buddhism was necessary as an evil other, less because of any radical differences from certain ethics of Christianity than because of its very similarities to those aspects of Christian doctrine and practice that stood in direct opposition to capitalist ideology, but had not succeeded in standing up to that ideology. In the second place, to dwell upon the ethical activism of Buddhism might be to draw fire upon those arenas of British, masculine, worldly activism that had to be kept above serious challenge at all cost, namely, "the market" and its two great sources of wealth: the battlefield and the Empire. By throwing into question the foundational Western dualisms, the economy of karma and reincarnation indirectly threatened the most powerful interests and institutions in Victorian England. By speaking as it did about suffering and desire, Buddhism threatened the foundation of Western thought, and therefore Western society, at its very roots.

Conclusion

The novels of Marie Corelli and H. Rider Haggard portrayed reincarnation and karma almost as variously as the array of sources that were available to them. They drew quite selectively upon Christian theology and mythology, but also upon Natural Theology, Spiritualism, Egyptian occultism, Theosophical synthesis, Hindu concepts, and Buddhist doctrines (not to mention Swedenborgianism, Mesmerism, astrology, etc.). With these they interwove elements drawn from the pervasive secular discourses of scientific naturalism, progressivism, and Darwinism to produce pseudo-scientific and progressive-evolutionary models of reincarnation and karma. On the basis of a survey of Victorian literary, scholarly, and periodical literatures, I have identified eight variants of "reincarnation" that were in circulation in the discourse of the time: metempsychosis, Hindu reincarnation, Buddhist reincarnation, transmigration, resurrection, immortality, demi-immortality, and inheritance. The novels of Haggard and Corelli represent all of these types in varying degrees. It is telling that while both authors dwelt with greatest fascination upon metempsychosis, transmigration, and demi-immortality, their primary sources for understanding reincarnation and karma were Hinduism, as co-opted by Deist and Theosophical thought, and Buddhism, which was the most widely circulated and debated source of these doctrines in late-Victorian Britain.

Haggard and Corelli mixed and matched these religious and secular elements to create their own unique theories about the ethics and operation of karma and reincarnation. At the same time, their theories shared similarities that were equally significant. Both authors were influenced by Theosophy and by its adaptations of Hindu and Buddhist elements. However, in opposition to Madame Blavatsky, who strove to create a hybrid religion to replace what she perceived as a degenerated Christianity, Corelli enlisted karma/reincarnation to fashion a new—one might say "New Age"—Christianity, one both more occult and more scientific. In this she was influenced by the nineteenth-century shift away from Calvinistic theology toward "incarnation theology," a "shift of emphasis from the death of Christ to the life of Christ—from a theology centred on the Atonement to one centred on the Incarnation—and a shift from the wrath and judgement of God to the love and Fatherhood of God" (Parsons, "Dissenters" 109). For Haggard as well as Corelli, the resurrection of Jesus modeled and justified the doctrine of reincarnation. Corelli strove to reconcile her mystical Christian spiritualism with karma/reincarnation, but this required deforming both Western and Eastern traditions virtually beyond recognition by practitioners. Haggard apparently saw neither a necessary opposition between his belief in karma/reincarnation and his Anglican practice nor the necessity of reconciling the two; these diverse elements coexist in his novels in dialogue with one another without full resolution. Holly, Leo, Ayesha, and Kou-en all speak what the text presents as spiritual truths, sometimes Christian, sometimes Buddhist, sometimes an indeterminate combination. I believe that Ayesha, despite her trafficking with spirits, which Haggard could not endorse, speaks for her author's own latitudinarian and humanistic beliefs when she says that "all great Faiths are the same, changed a little to suit the needs of passing times and peoples" and that "in mercy it is given to us to redeem one another" (*Ayesha* 141, 143). Even so, Haggard's writings no less than Corelli's juxtaposed the economy of sin/redemption to the economy of karma/reincarnation in such a way that the all but irreconcilable differences between the two could not be left unaddressed.

Those differences generated a series of debates within late-Victorian culture, debates by which Haggard and Corelli were instructed and to which their novels contributed, directly and indirectly. The overarching debate, which was implicit in all others, concerned the relationship between Western soul-theory and the doctrines of karma and reincarnation. Thus Victorians were more attracted to Egyptian metempsychosis than either Hindu or Buddhist reincarnation, because the former appeared more likely to retain their own conception of the soul, its eternal individuality and remembered identity. The Egypt-versus-India debate linked to a broader question about the genetic and cultural origins of the Caucasian race and the British people.

Another recurring debate concerned the question of what exactly is passed on from lifetime to lifetime in reincarnation, whether it be the soul with continuing identity, the soul without identity, the body as well as the soul, or only a karmic record without soul, identity, or memory. The latter of these was considered horrifying, if not also blasphemous. A number of debates focused on the nature of karma/reincarnation as an ethical system: whether it might be compatible with or antithetical to the ethics of heaven/hell and sin/redemption. Some Victorians were attracted to what they saw as the ethical rigorousness and evenhandedness of karma/reincarnation and its compatibility with their ideologies of self-help, individual responsibility for one's own soul, and a spiritual progressivism to match material progressivism. But then there were insurmountable problems. Buddhist karma/reincarnation threatened to supplant the authority of God and to obviate Western soul-theory. That was inconceivable, almost literally so, since it was exterior to what the history of Western theology and metaphysics had made thinkable. Karma/reincarnation also appeared to privilege works over faith, which made it antithetical especially to evangelical Protestant Christianities, and it held the possibility not only of spiritual evolution but of spiritual retrogression, perhaps even to lower life-forms. Darwinism lurked in the background. As Victorians imposed their progressivism upon reincarnation, so they tended to deny its de-evolutionary potential, though both Corelli and Haggard enlisted that potential as a cautionary tale. Both authors joined in these and other debates sparked by the penetration of Western consciousness by karma and reincarnation.

Through this process, Haggard and Corelli synthesized a karma/reincarnation that still retained the core of Western soul-theory. While drawing upon Hindu and Buddhist elements, they fashioned a reincarnation that preserved the soul—its individualism and conscious identity—and a karma that though clearly tied more to works somehow remained loyal to the Protestant emphasis on faith. Neither could achieve this synthesis, however, without encountering serious contradictions. The situation was made yet more complex by the fact that the contradictions between the ethical economy of karma/reincarnation and that of sin/redemption happened to resonate with the historical contradictions between the latter and the material economy of "the market." Those contradictions had become embedded and partially sublimated within Western culture as a result of the necessity of accommodating the two primary ideological systems of Protestantism and capitalism. The encounter with karma/reincarnation stirred up fundamental and deeply troubling contradictions that long had existed within Western culture and society.

Whether they intended to or not, both Corelli and Haggard drew attention to those contradictions and generated new ones by juxtaposing karma/reincarnation to sin/redemption. For instance, they each theorized a universal, Deistic "law of love" that was based in part on the "law of karma," which was perceived as orderly and equitable, but at the same time was defined in opposition to the mechanical and merciless "law of the Dharma," of which the doctrines of karma and reincarnation were definitive. Both authors similarly addressed the immensely complex issue of the relationship between human desire and human suffering in a way that demonstrated the essentialness of active desire and, simultaneously, the essentialness of actively suppressing desire. This contradiction expressed the conflicting ideological imperatives to equally legitimate the material desire and activism of financial banking *and* the spiritual desire and activism of faith. But doing this required keeping the two spheres separated. That separation was signified by the slash in the middle of the root dualisms of body/soul, works/faith, and active/passive. Not to maintain that slash would be to imperil the foundations of "Western Civilization." The threat that karma and reincarnation posed was of dissolving that slash into a Middle Way, which ultimately was inconceivable. Karma and reincarnation nevertheless raised the disturbing possibilities that faith might be passive in the face of material activism, that material banking might be antithetical to spiritual activism, and that spiritual activism might be more beneficial for the individual and for society if conceived not through the ethics of sin/redemption but through those of karma/reincarnation. While it therefore was essential for Victorians to perceive the economy of karma/reincarnation as fatalistically passive in the face of human suffering, I have attempted to show that the real threat it posed was of appearing too spiritually and ethically active.

Marie Corelli and H. Rider Haggard struggled mightily, personally and in their writings, to confront and represent these debates and contradictions. Their works—more than their faith, I cannot resist saying—provide a vital record of issues, questions, and concerns about spirituality and the afterlife that were definitive of late-Victorian and early-Modernist culture in Europe. They could not resolve those debates and contradictions. Analysis of their partial successes and failures in attempting to do so provides a key to understanding which elements of Western belief—both religious and secular—were so sacred that they could not be assailed and which elements of Buddhism were so threatening to those that they could not be assimilated.

Chapter 4

Buddhism and the Empire of the Self in Kipling's Kim

And whoso will, from Pride release,
Contemning neither creed nor priest,
May feel the Soul of all the East
About him at Kamakura.
—RUDYARD KIPLING, "Buddha at Kamakura" (1892)

The world that exists is the result of the *non*-existence of any
independent self-established substance. *This emptiness
of self-existence ... is what the world is full of,
a fullness sometimes called the Void.*
—NOLAN PLINY JACOBSON, *Understanding Buddhism* (1986)

The Critical Polarization over Kim

Criticism of Rudyard Kipling's *Kim* (1901) has a history of polarization that is familiar to Kipling scholars, though not all scholarship has participated in this debate. The divide is between these two camps, oversimplified here for the sake of argument: (1) those who celebrate the novel's accomplishment in portraying Indian peoples and Eastern religions with an evenhandedness and sympathy that transcends its author's well-known prejudices, and (2) those who focus on the implicit racism of the novel, its assumption of British superiority, and its polemic to the effect that wise Indians must recognize the God-given rightness of British colonial rule.[1] A few scholars, among them Alan Sandison and Zohreh T. Sullivan, have suggested that both positions are supportable and limited; each is necessary, neither sufficient. Ian Baucom goes so far as to argue that "selecting either *one* of these interpretations amounts to an act more of censorship than of reading" (Baucom 99).[2] Even so, the critical polarization persists to the extent that virtually no treatment of *Kim*, including the present one, now can avoid addressing it.

The critical polarization, which of course I have had to simplify, emerges most clearly in relation to two central interpretive questions: (1) how to read the character of the Teshoo Lama, and (2) how to read the ending of the novel, which amounts to how to read the character of Kim. Those who adhere to the first position read the Lama as a sage scholar of Buddhism, a devout pilgrim, and the most significant of Kim's father figures. They argue that the Lama's search is equally if not more important for plot and for theme than Colonel Creighton's Great Game of espionage, noting that the novel ends with the Lama's sacrifice of nirvana in order to return and guide Kim and gives him the closing words: "Just is the Wheel! Certain is our deliverance. Come!" (289). Those who adhere to the second position read the Lama at best as a well-intentioned but childlike old man and at worst as an infantile dupe, a pawn in the Game whose "naiveté suggests an atrophied absence of adulthood" and whose "absence of anxiety must be similarly read as an expression of complicity in...the imperial enterprise" (Suleri 117, 120). They build upon Edward Said's paradigm-shifting argument that the contest for Kim's allegiance between Creighton's Game and the Lama's Way is in fact no contest at all because the latter is simply subsumed within and reduced to the former.[3] In reading the ending of the novel, these critics focus on Kim's penultimate crisis of identity and interpret the moment when he feels "the wheels of his being lock up anew on the world without" as confirmation of his vocation in the "active" world of the British Secret Service and necessary rejection of the "passive" world of Buddhist renunciation (282). Prior to Said, Irving Howe attempted to maintain a balance by concluding that "the parallel lines" of the Great Game and The Way "*cannot* meet," for they are "two ways of apprehending human existence, each of which is shown to have its own irreducible claims" (Howe 334). This balancing act, no less than the criticism on both sides of the divide, utterly solidifies the dichotomy.

What interests me is the persistence of this polarization. The too ready explanation is, "It's in the novel—don't you see that the novel itself juxtaposes The Game and The Way?" But I question whether the text makes an exclusive choice between the two either necessary or obviated by either side. Why has the assumption of a dualism—whether agonistic, one-sided, or irreducible—been virtually automatic in Western criticism? An overarching agenda would be to argue that this polarization, regardless of the position taken, is symptomatic of a culture-specific critical blindness. My goal is to build a rationale for a Middle Way of reading *Kim,* one that gives the text itself credit for drawing upon and embodying the Buddhist concepts it represents.

An indication of the critical blindness to which I refer is the fact that few if any interpretations of *Kim* have given substantial attention to the Buddhism present in the novel.[4] Certainly many critics have analyzed the character of the Lama; many have noted the novel's use of Buddhist concepts such as "the Way" and "the Wheel," though without seriously querying those concepts. The level of this attention has gone very little beyond that of the explanatory endnotes in scholarly editions of the novel. Here is a text saturated with Buddhist figures and terms in which at least one if not both of the main characters is a Buddhist, yet no one has demonstrated much interest in questions such as the following. From what sources did Kipling derive his understanding of Buddhism, and how informed and limited was that understanding? What were the range of reasons that influenced his choice of Buddhism rather than Hinduism or Islam, aside from the frequently noted motive of evading the historical violence between these two religions?[5] Most importantly, how exactly does the novel portray Buddhism and how accurate is that portrayal? What do the inaccuracies tell us about the reasons behind that particular construction of Buddhism? How is that portrayal informed by the history of Buddhism in India, which only recently had been "discovered," and by the history of archaeological study of Buddhist sites and artifacts in India during the nineteenth century? How might critical understanding of the novel be informed by those same histories? What would it mean to read *Kim* from a perspective informed by knowledge of Buddhism, in contrast to the Christian, Hindu, and Muslim perspectives that are evident enough between the lines of certain studies of the novel?

In order to put the failure to ask these questions into perspective, consider what the past hundred years of criticism of John Milton's *Paradise Lost* would look like if no one had inquired about the history of the Reformation and Restoration nor analyzed the specific ways in which Milton's epic is faithful to and departs from the Bible. Or consider Nathaniel Hawthorne scholarship that labels certain figures in *The Scarlet Letter* simply as representative of "Protestant Christianity," failing to reflect upon the origins of the beliefs cited by the characters or upon the history of Puritanism in New England. I suggest that just such an omission has occurred in the history of scholarship on *Kim.* Thus, the primary purpose of this chapter is to remedy that omission by seeking answers to the questions noted above. In the process, an explanation for this massive critical lacunae will emerge. It will emerge from consideration of Kim's much-analyzed identity crisis, first as understood within the framework of the Western metaphysics that has predetermined the critical polarization, and then from the perspective of Buddhist philosophy, which suggests a quite different reading.

Kipling's Religions

In order to situate the representation of Buddhism in *Kim*, some consideration of Kipling's religious background and of the general role of religion in the novel is warranted. Given the plethora of religious affiliations and figures in *Kim*, it is surprising that the topic of Kipling and religion has received relatively little attention. It is not surprising, given the history of the Indian subcontinent, that the novel should open by juxtaposing the warring forces of Hinduism, represented by Chota Lal, and Islam, represented by Abdullah, the two separated by and subjugated to the third term of which Kim is representative.

What does Kim represent? This is another version of the perennial, polarizing question. Certainly Kim knows he is of Anglo-Irish descent and assumes the ability to exploit that advantage, though he also knows much more about himself that exceeds that singular heritage. W. B. Parker, in an 1898 essay, observed that Kipling's religion was essentially "a matter of clan and family, of company and regiment," an "exclusively masculine" "religion of action" in a post-Darwinian universe where struggle and suffering are assumed to be central to the natural order of which mankind is organically a part (Parker 666, 667). This is empire-as-religion. Writing more recently, Andrew Lycett recounts that Henry James, after enthusiastically reading *Kim*, encouraged Kipling in a letter to continue to avoid "the base humbug" of politics and instead to "ask the Lama" for guidance in his choice of subject matter (Lycett 332). Lycett concludes, however, that Kipling's real "guru" was Cecil Rhodes, that figurehead of empire in Africa whom Kipling revered and whom Lycett observes was "much more demanding than any Tibetan lama" (Lycett 333). Scholars on one side of the critical divide might argue that Kim ultimately subscribes to his author's religion of empire. Though this perspective is partially accurate, it provides a very limited understanding both of Kipling and of Kim.

Kipling's religion, like that of his protagonist, was too heterodox and syncretistic to be reduced to any single belief. Both of his grandfathers were Methodist ministers, the influence of which appears to emerge contradictorily in his distaste for evangelical Protestantism and, on the other hand, in an Old Testament and perhaps Manichean worldview that predisposed him favorably to the Muslim conception of the deity, as he understood it. He opens his late autobiographical work, *Something of Myself* (1937), with this non-ironic benediction: "Therefore, ascribing all good fortune to Allah the Dispenser of Events, I begin" (*Something* 355). Whatever Kipling's religion was, it was not orthodox Christianity of any denomination, and his sometimes evangelical vision for the British Empire was not underwritten by and cloaked in evangelical zeal for saving the pagans.[6] As Sandra Kemp points out, his heterodox religious views produced critical controversy from the beginning of his career. Some readers of his poem "Recessional" (1897), for instance, recognized a discomforting implication about "the potential abuse of power in the Empire by means of a Christianity too closely interwoven with commerce and imperialism," and this contributed to charges that Kipling's religion was really "muscular Paganism" (Kemp, *Hidden* 82, 83).

After all, Kipling, like Kim, had a wide diversity of "pagan" influences. He spent his earliest years in India, of which he recalled, "Meeta, my Hindu bearer, would sometimes go into little Hindu temples, where, being below the age of caste, I held his hand and looked at the dimly-seen, friendly Gods" (Kipling, *Something* 355). In 1871, the Kiplings shipped the six-year-old Rudyard and his sister, Alice, back to England, where they spent six years under the unhappily strict Methodist tutelage of Captain and Mrs. Holloway at Southsea until liberated, as the young Kipling saw it, by the return of their mother to England in 1877. They took up residence in Kensington, of which Kipling recalls that "the Mother" got his sister and himself "season-tickets for the old South Kensington Museum which was across the road": "From the big Buddha with the little door in his back, to the towering dull-gilt ancient coaches and carven chariots in long dark corridors...we roved at will" (Kipling, *Something* 366–67). There Kipling must have studied the stone bas-reliefs salvaged (or plundered) from the Amaravati Stupa in northern India, which illustrated scenes from the time of the Buddha and were on display during Kiplings' stay.[7] This likely was his first exposure to Buddhism. After schooling, Kipling returned to India in 1882 to work as the editor of the *Civil and Military Gazette* in Lahore, where his father, Lockwood Kipling, was the Principal of the Mayo College of Art and Curator of the Lahore Museum. This was the "Wonder House" as described in *Kim:* "In the entrance-hall stood the larger figures of the Greco-Buddhist sculptures....There were hundreds of pieces, friezes of figures in relief, fragments of the statues and slabs crowded the figures that had encrusted the brick walls of the Buddhist *stupas* and *viharas* of the North Country and now, dug up and labeled, made the pride of the Museum" (6). Kipling later wrote that he painted the Wonder House directly from his memory of "the Lahore Museum of which I had once been Deputy Curator for six weeks—unpaid but immensely important" (*Something* 454). There "his father had told him a good deal about the early traditions of Buddha Gautama's sayings and travels in India" (Mason 183). There, also, it is likely that he witnessed at least one visit from a Tibetan Lama on pilgrimage, with obvious relevance for the writing of *Kim.*[8] Thus Kipling, by the time he was a young man, had significant exposure not only to Hindu, Christian, and Muslim cultures but also to Buddhism. Though he was "far indeed from being a Buddhist,...that he felt...an appreciation of what he believed to be Buddhism can hardly be doubted" (Mason 184). He was perhaps no farther from being a Buddhist than he was from being a Catholic or a Muslim, the two religions his writings most often portray sympathetically.

Kipling's syncretism was not limited to major world religions. Mixed with them were elements of Freemasonry, Spiritualism, Theosophy, and occultisms peripheral to Hinduism and Islam, all of which appear in his writings. In 1885, Kipling was drafted by the Lahore Freemason lodge—Hope and Perseverance, no. 782 E C—to which his father belonged. Thus Kim's Masonic heritage from *his* father is one part of the genuinely prophetic trajectory in *Kim*, leading him to Creighton, another Mason. In addition, Kipling had spent part of five summers in the 1880s with his family at Simla in the Himalayan foothills and there was exposed to nearly every religious hybrid that the interfacing of East and West produced in the nineteenth century. As Andrew Lycett describes the scene, "These seekers after enlightenment ranged from the saddhus and fakirs of the hills, the prototypes of the lama in *Kim*, to Westerners like the enigmatic A. M. Jacobs...who featured later as Lurgan Sahib" (Lycett 111). Among the most celebrated figures to visit Simla was Madame Helene Blavatsky, famed spiritualist and co-founder of the Theosophical Society, the headquarters of which she moved to Adyar, India, in 1879. Blavatsky claimed that she had received the spiritual authority underpinning Theosophy directly from the "Brothers," "Masters," or "Mahatmas," as they variously were called, first during a pilgrimage in Tibet and then through telekinetic transmissions, the famous Mahatma letters. Blavatsky and Kipling were perhaps the two most important sources at the turn of the century for a growing European fascination with Tibet, "one of the last great sacred places of Victorian Romanticism," so much so that "references both to Blavatsky's mahatmas and Kipling's lama abounded in Tibetan travel writing at the time" (Bishop 2, 143).[9] My point is not that Kipling subscribed unreservedly to any one of these various religions or quasi-religions but that he did *not* subscribe to any one of them to the exclusion of the others nor deny the legitimacy of any of them. In his life and in his writing, he gave each its due, even, I would argue, Hinduism, though it is true that his fiction tends to be more critical of Brahmins than of other religious figures.[10] He sampled from a wide range of beliefs and doctrines in building an unsystematic hybrid matrix of religions, both for himself and for his most well-known character.

Thus Kipling created Kim as a character who is able to embrace and move between a variety of religious positions. He was careful to give Kim a father-figure of every religious stripe: a Buddhist Lama, a Muslim in Mahbub Ali, and a hybridized Hindu in Hurree Babu. Kim's lesser father figures are Lurgan Sahib, an occultist, and Father Victor, from the church of "Bibi Miriam," the Virgin Mary (117). He places Kim at the intersection of at least five religions or spiritual practices, six if one argues that Creighton's faith in the imperialist mission of the British Secret Service is an ideological belief system functioning in certain ways like a religion.[11] There is one very telling exception, however, and that is Anglicanism. One might expect Kipling as a champion of British imperialism to embrace the official religion of the Empire. Yet Mr. Bennett, the Anglican Chaplain in *Kim*, is the only utterly unsympathetic religious figure, an anti-father-figure who disdains the Lama "with the triple-ringed uninterest of the creed that lumps nine-tenths of the world under the title 'heathen'" (88). Why is this? In the first place, Kipling held strong opinions against the cultural violence and political strife generated by dogmatic or overzealous missionaries in India and Southeast Asia. From Kipling's perspective, such disregard was a sign of irresponsible ignorance that soured cross-cultural relations and made the job of governing more difficult. As Colonel Creighton tells Kim: "Therefore, do not at any time be led to contemn the black men. I have known boys newly entered into the service of the Government who feigned not to understand the talk or the customs of the black men. Their pay was cut for ignorance. There is no sin so great as ignorance" (119). In a letter of 16 October 1895, Kipling criticized those who followed "a doctrine of salvation imperfectly understood by themselves and a code of ethics foreign to the climate and instincts of those races whose most cherished customs they outrage and whose gods they insult" (qtd. in Islam 33). Part of Kipling's paternalistic guardianship of India was a belief in the responsibility of knowledgeable Anglo-Indians to protect "Mother India" from the wrong sorts of Europeans.[12] As David Gilmour suggests, "In Kipling's eyes the real enemies of British India were British: zealous and misguided missionaries (secular as well as religious) and interfering politicians in England" (Gilmour 80).[13] In contrast, the character of Strickland, the District Superintendent of Police, who makes two appearances in *Kim* and features earlier in *Plain Tales from the Hills* (1888), is representative of the appropriately informed and empathetic Anglo-Indian. One of the more glaring expressions of Kipling's Orientalism is that he puts into the mouth of Indian characters, such as the old Rassaldar or the Mahratta spy on the train, endorsements of British occupation in the form of praise for such exemplary Anglo-Indians, as when Gobind Sahai, the Sahiba from Kulu, says of Strickland: "These be the sort to oversee justice. They know the land and the customs of the land. The others, all new from Europe...are worse than the pestilence" (76). As Parama Roy argues, through Kipling's positioning of them, the "Anglo-Indian..., because he is an (almost) unhyphenated Indian, becomes the native of the Indian nation," a discursive displacement that obviously served colonial interests (Roy 87). Nevertheless, the complexity and ambivalence of Kipling's views are indicated by his refusal to endorse Anglican or even Christian occupation of Indian religions and in his creation of Kim as a hybrid religious figure.

Kipling was an Orientalist in the nineteenth-century sense, as well as the postmodern sense derived from it. Historians Fred Reid and David Washbrook argue that "Kipling's political ideas show strong affinities with those contained in what might be termed 'the official mind' of the I.C.S.," the "Indian Civil Service, a small elite corps of a few hundred men who held exclusively the highest posts in the government" (Reid 18). They disdained tampering from London and disruption by missionaries, while at the same time remaining wary of the growing number of Western-educated Hindus who presumed to know how to rule themselves. They, like Kipling, saw the role of the colonial government as "protective and conservative rather than active and interventionist" (Reid 20). They conceived of themselves, however accurately or not, as respecting and preserving indigenous cultures and religions. This mindset similarly characterized a growing body of Orientalist translators, philologists, archeologists, archivists, and curators (for example, Lockwood Kipling) who were working in India at that time to find and preserve ancient Buddhist manuscripts, artifacts, and sites.[14]

Victorian Orientalists defined their position in opposition to that of the "Anglicists." Prior to the 1830s, the British Raj aligned itself with the ruling Hindu order, if generally for mercenary reasons and through systematic violence to Indian peoples, and thus attempted an uneven policy of noninterference with indigenous Hindu culture, as long as it operated under British oversight. Anglican, but also Nonconformist, missionaries and associated interests in London saw this policy not as noninterference but rather as the opposite: government interference with their freedom to intervene in indigenous cultures to recruit converts. They wanted an open market of religions in India.

This debate culminated in Thomas Babington Macaulay's infamously racist *Minute on Indian Education* of 1835, which marked a victory for those Anglicists who wanted to "educate" the pagans. Anglicist policies eventually backfired. Later in the century, they gave Indian nationalists a target that begged opposition. The Orientalist position "that Hindus had a great civilization whose achievements could be compared to the highest ones of classical antiquity" and therefore deserved to be studied with a similar respect and rigor contributed to a revival of Hindu pride, the formation of the Arya Samaj in 1875, and the associated move toward Indian nationalism (van der Veer 114). Thus Kipling, however unintentionally, participated in the nineteenth-century Orientalist "discourse on 'Eastern spirituality'" that subsequently was "reappropriated by the Indian religious movements" fueling Indian nationalism (van der Veer 69).[15]

While Kipling's Orientalism unavoidably was an appropriation of Indian culture and religion for colonialist purposes, it also was a genuine expression of respect for and celebration of that culture and those religions. Though justifiably condemned by postcolonial scholars for its masking of cultural violence with paternalistic sympathy, nineteenth-century Orientalism nevertheless was sympathetic toward its construction of India, concerned about the damage that Western encroachment brought (while being part of that same encroachment), and open-minded toward difference in comparison with the alternative Anglicist position. The ambivalence of this situation is the primary source of the ongoing polarization of critical positions on *Kim,* either side of which tends to oversimplify a very complex history and a very complex novel.

Kim's Hybrid Buddhism and Religious Tolerance in Kim

The preceding consideration of Kipling's religious syncretism lays the foundation for understanding that of his protagonist. Kim is a hybrid figure in the sense theorized by Homi Bhabha, or as employed by Ian Baucom in analyzing him as "something of a monster: a putatively white but performatively Asiatic hybrid," or as Kipling himself signaled when he has the French spy describe Hurree Chunder Moorkerjee, the Babu, in these terms: "He represents *in petto* India in transition—the monstrous hybridism of East and West" (Baucom 98; *Kim* 239).[16] As an educated Hindu who professes agnosticism, fearfully believes in the occult, worships Herbert Spencer, spies for the Raj but has ties to the Arya Samaj, the Babu is hybrid in more ways than one.[17] His character points to the Western-educated Hindu reformists who organized the Indian National Congress in 1885 and led the nation out from under British colonial rule in 1947, eleven years after Kipling's death. It is Kim, however, who is the figure of hybrid religion in the novel. Kim's hybridity in term of national and racial cultures is multiplied in the sphere of religion. It is not only that Kim dresses as a low-caste Hindu one day and then changes the color of his turban from red to blue and accompanies Mahbub Ali the next day as a Muslim servant. He is a mimic, but he is not merely a mimic, because he also is a seeker of his own identity and his place in the world; his character is distinguished from the majority of other Bildungsroman protagonists by the fact that his search does not ultimately concern parentage or family, and certainly not romance or marriage, but rather is focused to a degree rare outside of allegory on his religious identity. "What am I," Kim asks Mahbub Ali, "Mussalman, Hindu, Jain, or Buddhist?" (143). Is Kim confused, undecided, or a nascent pilgrim attempting to discern his religious affiliation in a world of multiple, shifting religious positions? He is in the first place a boy, and he will move through confusion and indecision toward religious vocation in the course of the novel. But his religion will never be singular or exclusive. It will reflect a mixing of cultures characterized on nearly every page of the novel by collision, overlapping, and interpenetration of diverse religious positions.

Within this context, a crisis of identity would seem inevitable. Kim's much-analyzed identity crisis reaches its first climax in the liminal space of adolescence and in transition between two worlds, the world of St. Xavier's, where he has just completed his training as a sahib, and the Lama's world of Buddhist pilgrimage, which he is on his way to rejoin as a *chela*.[18] In a wonderfully bizarre rite of passage, Kim is taken by Mahbub Ali to "the Bird-Cage," a house of prostitution, where Haneefa, the blind seer of this novel, puts him in a trance, "charms" him with "*Jadoo*" magic for the "full protection of the Road," strips him of his clothes and his identity as a sahib, and changes his race with dye, despite the resistance to Eastern occultism of his "White blood" (177–79). In an orgiastic ceremony, which the Babu, who is there making ethnographical notes from a safe distance, calls "ventriloquial necromanciss," Haneefa invokes "Zulbazan, Son of Eblis, who lives in bazaars," "Dulhan, invisible about mosques," and "Musboot, Lord of lies and panic," among other devils and spirits. She then endows Kim with "*the keys of the Secret Things*," a phrase Kipling either borrowed from Theosophy or else from the same sources as Madame Blavatsky (179). But Kim's rite of passage does not end there. Hurree Babu then initiates him for espionage purposes into a secret society of a syncretic religious nature, making him a "Son of the Charm" (183). These events culminate in the crisis of identity and Kim's famous question, "Who is Kim—Kim—Kim?" (185). Lingering then in a trance-like state, he almost grasps an answer but falls out of the reverie with a shake of his head, upon which he is approached by yet another seer, "a long-haired Hindu *bairagi* (holy man)," who says, "I also have lost it.... It is one of the Gates to the Way.... Thou wast wondering there in thy spirit what manner of thing thy soul might be. The seizure came of a sudden. I know." (185–86). The old man then asks, "Of what faith art thou?" And this is the reply: " 'I too am a seeker,' said Kim, using one of the lama's pet words. 'Though'—he forgot his Northern dress for the moment—'though Allah alone knoweth what I seek' " (186). The old man does not comment on the fact that Kim has confused Buddhist and Muslim religious signs but only answers, "Go in hope, little brother.... It is a long road to the feet of the One," adding an ascetic Hindu blessing to the mix.

Kim now has completed his crucial transition. He is now truly on the "long road," which is both the road of the Great Game and the Way of the Lama's pilgrimage. This multi-stage rite-of-passage has immediate effect: Kim has come of age. He is recognized as a holy man a second time by a Jat with a sick child—"the very respect the Jat paid him proved that he was a man"—and proceeds to rejoin his master the Lama as a more devout *chela* than perhaps he knows he is (187). It is as if only such a passage through the most diverse elements of Eastern occultism and religion would be powerful enough to cleanse Kim sufficiently of his whiteness and his Western, Catholic training and prepare him for his new role. In the process, he is guided by a Muslim, a Westernized Babu agnostic who invokes Herbert Spencer but believes in the occult, and a Hindu ascetic. Kim has become a repository for an array of religious influences without discounting any one of them.

But Kim's deepest if still non-exclusive religious commitment is to Buddhism. It begins as a commitment to the Lama, which grows over the course of the story from curiosity and self-serving possessiveness to admiration, love, and finally devotion. One exemplary moment occurs during Kim and Mahbub Ali's lengthiest conversation when the latter, who is not above showing his jealousy of the Lama's influence over Kim, asks, "Is it necessary to the comfort of thy heart to see that lama?" Kim responds: "It is one part of my bond. . . . If I do not see him, and if he is taken from me, I will go out of that *madrissah* [school] in Nucklao and, and—once gone, who is to find me again?" (144). Here he reverses the threat of his own cultural hybridity—the very quality that makes him a useful tool to the British Raj for espionage—by saying, in effect, "Don't forget, I can use that very tool just as well against you." More than testifying to his love for the Lama, Kim makes it clear that his participation in the Great Game, rather than being the true calling for which the Buddhist pilgrimage is merely a cover, is instead contingent upon his freedom to follow the Lama's Way. However, the Lama's Way is only "one part" or Kim's bond, the other part of course being the Great Game. Recognizing this, however, need not precipitate an absolute dichotomy. Kim himself, following the Lama, disclaims dichotomies. For example, after the Lama is injured by one sahib, the Russian spy, he remarks to Kim that it is strange to be tended so faithfully by "a [-nother] Sahib," and Kim responds: "Thou has said there is neither black nor white. Why plague me with this talk, Holy One? Let me rub the other foot. It vexes me. I am *not* a Sahib. I am thy *chela*" (270). At this moment, Kim is not a sahib; yet, the reader knows he also is a sahib. Though Zohreh Sullivan ultimately argues that *Kim* privileges the Great Game over Buddhism, she leaves the other interpretive pole open in these terms: "Kim as orphaned In-dianized hybrid is both produced and initially despised by the [Anglo-Indian] system; so that an alternative reading might allow us to read the very existence of his love for the lama as an alternative to the system's denial of such possibil-ity" (Sullivan 150). Even Sullivan's evenhandedness misses the point, however, and it does so by failing to take the religious themes of the novel seriously and, therefore, to analyze sufficiently its Buddhist content.

Scholars on both sides of the critical polarization have analyzed the relation-ship between Kim and the Lama primarily in terms of the mutual love between the two.[19] Some celebrate the redeeming quality of this love as the ultimate moral of the novel; others argue that this focus on love "in scenes with the lama is used to counter and sacramentalize the insidiousness of the negotiation with power" (Sullivan 166). Both miss the point. It is not the novel but rather some of its readers who have been unable to permit the ambiguity that the text itself accommodates: Kim's love and devotion are genuine, *and* he is in part an instrument of power. Placing primary emphasis on love, whether in defending or attacking Kim's or the text's motives, obscures something else. Love has functioned within *Kim* criticism as a means of evading the issue of the spiritual foundation of the relationship.[20] This evasion is perhaps predetermined by the

Romantic heritage of Western literature and criticism, but love is not a concept sufficient to describe the level of devotion Kim approaches by the end of the novel.

To offer one example from the middle of the story, after he emerges from his rite of passage and heals the Jat's child with a combination of Western medicine and the weight of the Lama's imprimatur, Kim finds himself alone for the first time in years in the presence of his master. The Lama commends Kim's wise treatment of the Jat, and this exchange follows: " 'I was made wise by thee, Holy One,' said Kim, . . . forgetting St. Xavier's; forgetting his white blood; forgetting even the Great Game as he stooped, Mohammedan fashion, to touch his master's feet in the dust of the Jain temple" (189). There is no textual irony here, and more is involved than either gratitude or love, namely, religious devotion. The shift in Kim's motivation for following the Lama away from interpersonal and instrumental reasons to those befitting the religious seeker he becomes is telegraphed early in the story during a conversation with the Hindu Rassaldar. The old soldier asks, "But why should one whose Star leads him to war follow a holy man?"—the very question underlying the critical polarization. Kim answers: "But he *is* a holy man. . . . In truth, and in talk and in act, holy. He is not like the others" (51). In a sense, then, it does not matter which religion the Lama follows; what matters is that his religious practice is genuine, his piety sincere. Genuine spiritual practice, as much or more than personal love, is what Kim seeks. Buddhism is the vehicle Kipling chose for this message.

This message is key to understanding Kipling's attitude concerning religion: he despised hypocrisy, whether of a Methodist who preaches the compassion of Christ while damning all unbelievers to eternal torment or of a Hindu who uses false piety to extort donations. Corinne McCutchan argues that Kim's periodic mockery of religious figures, most frequently Brahmins, is not intended as an condemnation of any one faith but is rather an indictment of religious poseurs and hypocrites within all faiths, "not only those of India, that substitute mechanical observance for vital piety" (McCutchan 139). McCutchan concludes that between "the lama's Buddhist teaching and Kim's ecumenical practice Kipling reaches toward a vision of Eastern piety as both theologically profound and humanly practicable" (McCutchan 140). I concur. This message is, finally, what Kipling was trying to accomplish with his creation of Kim as a hybridized religious figure: to present the possibility of religious piety, genuine devotion and practice, without religious intolerance or violence.

Thus in answering Kim's question, "What am I?", Mahbub Ali becomes a perhaps unlikely mouthpiece for one of the novel's central messages: "The matter of creeds is like horseflesh. The wise man knows horses are good—that there is a profit to be made from all; and for myself . . . I could believe the same of Faiths. . . . Therefore I say in my heart the Faiths are like horses. Each has merit in its own country" (143–44). As one scholar argues, this "appeal for moderation and tolerance, such as Kipling himself had learned over the years, is the dominant theme of *Kim*" (Rao 132). The novel suggests that all faiths are equal within their respective contexts and, further, that perhaps context should if not dictate one's faith then provide the terminology—God, Allah, Brahma, nirvana—that one uses to describe religious faith and practice within that context. Though this attitude must be blasphemous to any religious fundamentalist, it was not so to Kipling nor to Kim, which, the novel suggests, need not make him less capable of genuine religious experience. Kim indeed shows reverence for at least two religions, Islam and Buddhism. Islam is his religious base prior to encountering the Lama, so much so that even after embracing his role as a *chela* he periodically mixes his religions. When he says, unmindfully, "Allah be merciful," Hurree Babu responds, "When next you are under thee emotions please do not use the Mohammedan terms with the Tibet dress" (281). One's religious expression should be harmonious with one's cultural context. It follows that Kipling's purpose was not to place Buddhism above other religions. Rather, Buddhism provided a suitable vehicle for the dual message of genuine piety combined with religious tolerance, the only such vehicle Kipling perceived in an India torn by religious conflict. Kipling chose Buddhism because it was the only world religion without a history characterized substantially by violent suppression of other faiths.[21] Among world religions, only within Buddhism does tolerance of other religions pose no threat to one's own beliefs.

Gauri Viswanathan, among others, argues that British colonial interests used discourses of religious tolerance and then secularization to undermine Indian religious traditions and, in connection with them, Indian nationalist movements. "Tolerance" indeed was the thin edge of one wedge by which those on the Anglicist side of the early-nineteenth-century debate with the Orientalists effectively made Anglican evangelicalism part of British colonial policy in India. But Kipling was not an Anglicist, and his tolerance was not identical to their "tolerance," though I recognize that it may have contributed nevertheless to some of the outcomes that Viswanathan describes. The distinction between the religious tolerance represented in and by *Kim* and that of nineteenth-century Anglicists is worth maintaining. It is a distinction that leaves open the potential long-term, global benefits of a form of religious tolerance that strives truly to respect difference. Tolerance that respects difference does not use the rhetoric of tolerance as a disguise for imposing one's own religion on others (or, equally familiar from history, of forcing other nations to open their markets for exploitation). Recognizing this distinction opens the possibility of reading the message of religious tolerance in *Kim* without then reducing it either to "love" or to nothing more than a cover for imperial violence. If one is able to resist the reductionism of the dualistic thinking that equally characterizes both sides of the critical polarization, then one is reading if not like a Buddhist then perhaps at least with adequate attention to the Buddhist content of this novel.

Buddhist Pilgrimages and Archaeological Narratives

The Jain Temple where Kim reunites with the Lama after St. Xavier's is located in Benares, just outside of which is the Deer Park in Sarnath where the Buddha delivered his first sermon, the "Setting into Motion of the Wheel of the Dharma." Southeast of Benares is Bodh-Gaya (or Buddha-Gaya), where the Buddha sat under the Bodhi tree and attained enlightenment. Due north is Kapilavastu country, the seat of the Sakya clan into which Siddhartha Gautama, or Sakyamuni, was born in 563 BCE; Lumbini, just over the modern border in Nepal, where his mother, Mayadevi, gave birth to him; Sravasti, where he and his disciples gathered for each of 45 years during the rainy season; and Kushinagar, where in 483 BCE he entered Paranirvana, the state those who already have attained nirvana enter at death.[22] *Kim* is set squarely in the historical Buddhist holy land. For centuries before and after the beginning of the common era, the modern-day borders of India with Nepal, Pakistan, and Afghanistan were populated with thousands of practicing Buddhists and covered with hundreds of temples, monasteries, shrines, and monuments. For a complex range of historical reasons—including persecution by Brahmins, invading waves of Muslims, and absorption into modern Hinduism—Buddhism began declining in the land of its birth starting around the third century CE. By that time, it had migrated north through Tibet and China and south to Ceylon and Burma, and by the twelfth century, when it was extinct in India, it was the most widely practiced religion throughout Asia. By the eighteenth century, however, the physical traces of Buddhism's existence in India had been erased, demolished in persecutions, dismantled for building materials, and covered over by meters of accumulating soil. No living Indian knew where the ancient sites of Kapilavastu or Kushinagar were. Only after the British invasion and occupation of India were the origins of Buddhism rediscovered, unearthed, cataloged, and either restored or carted off to museums. The common but erroneous theory among the few interested Europeans in the eighteenth century was that Buddhism had been a primitive predecessor of Hinduism. Military engineers and East India Company surveyors, represented in *Kim* by Colonel Creighton, were the first Orientalist scholars and amateur archaeologists to rediscover many of the ancient sites of Buddhism. Charles Allen's history of these events, *The Search for the Buddha: The Men Who Discovered India's Lost Religion,* states the case most bluntly: "The European discovery of Buddhism and the subsequent resurgence of Buddhism in South Asia arose directly out of their [the Orientalist scholars'] activities" (Allen 5). The curator of the Wonder House of Lahore, though a partisan of British occupation and Western science, is not bragging falsely when he tells the Lama "of the labours of European scholars, who...have identified the Holy Places of Buddhism" (8). As part of its appropriation of India, the British Empire served Buddhism by recovering its historical roots, which were well on their way to being lost forever.

Clearly Kipling had read with great interest not only best-selling archaeo-logical fictions like Sir Austen Layard's *Nineveh and Its Remains* (1849) and his friend Rider Haggard's *She* (1887) but also accounts of the textual and archaeological detective work in India of such figures as Sir William Jones, "the father of oriental studies" and founder of the Asiatic Society of Ben-gal, and James Pinsep, who in 1837 "broke the code" of the Asoka Brahmi stone inscriptions found scattered throughout northern India, which opened up the history of the Buddhist Emperor Asoka (ruled 268–233 BCE) and pro-vided the key to decipher subsequently discovered Asokan pillars (Allen 69, 182). Most of the significant finds of ancient sites tied to events in the life of the Buddha occurred in the last half of the nineteenth century, spanning the period when Kipling was there covering such events himself.

To take one example, during the summer of 1875, the assistant to Colonel Alexander Cunningham, who served as the Director and then Director-General of the Archaeological Survey of India, was dispatched to make reconnaissance diggings near the small village of Nagarkhas north of Benares. Digging down to a depth of ten feet, an assistant, Archibald Carlleyle, struck a carved stone surface that he continued to unearth and that turned out to be nothing less than a reclining statue of Buddha 30 feet long and 12 feet wide lying on a decorated platform bed inside of a collapsed temple (Allen 235). The size and traditional posture of the figure identified this as the likely site of the Buddha's Paranirvana, Kushinagar. Cunningham already had made important discoveries, including the relic caskets of two of the Buddha's chief disciples, Sariputa and Maha Mogalana, at the Great Tope at Sanchi in 1851—"the first 'modern' archaeological dig in India"—and in 1863 he found the ancient city of Sravasti, which provided a fixed point from which to locate other sites (Allen 216, 223). Far from immune to the romantic aspects of the archaeological treasure hunt, Kipling enlisted some of that romance in the character not only of the Curator but especially of the Lama. The Lama experiences awe when he encounters statues found by those archaeol-ogists on display in the Lahore Wonder House.[23] The Lama's search for the River of the Arrow might be read as a re-Orientalized transposition of the archaeologi-cal mission narrative. After all, one connotation of "Teshoo Lama" in Tibet is "Learned One," and the Curator recognizes the Lama as a brother scholar, "no mere bead-telling mendicant, but a scholar of parts" (Hopkirk 40; *Kim* 1.8). In place of the Western archaeologist, Kipling has substituted the Buddhist pilgrim come to recover his religion's heritage. This represents both an erasure of Euro-pean intervention and a desire to return to Buddhists their own history.

From another perspective, however, Colonel Cunningham was less the his-torical model for the character of the Lama than the Lama, or, rather, Buddhist pilgrims like him were the model for Cunningham. The treasure maps that Cunningham followed in order to make his discoveries were the pilgrimage narratives written by two Chinese Buddhists: Fa Hian, who traveled overland to Gandhara in 400 CE, recorded his visits to the primary holy sites in the life of the Buddha, with locations and distances, and then sailed to China by way of Ceylon in 414; Huan Tsang, who followed a similar course starting in 626 CE but who was more of a scholar than Fa Hian, stayed longer in India, and provided more detailed descriptions, including notation of changes since the time of Fa Hian.[24] In 1837, Jean Pièrre Abe Rémusat, founder of the Société Asiatique de Paris, published a translation from the Chinese of Fa Hian's narrative, *Foe Koue Ki*, of which Cunningham acquired a copy in 1843. An English translation titled *The Pilgrimage of Fa Hian from the French Edition of the Foe Koue Ki of MM. Remusat, Klaproth and Landresse* appeared in 1848 from the Baptist Mission Press in Calcutta, and in 1853 and 1857 a two-volume French translation by Stanislas Julien of Huan Tsang's pilgrimage narrative became available, *Voyages des Pèlerins Bouddhistes*.

The importance of these documents to archaeological finds in India of Buddhist holy sites cannot be overestimated. In turn, they were important sources for Kipling's writing of *Kim*. The Lama "had heard of the travels of the Chinese pilgrims, Fo-Hian and Hwen-Thiang, and was anxious to know if there was any translation of their record," and, with these translations in hand, he "drew in his breath as he turned helplessly over the pages of Beal and Stanislas Julien" (8). Beal is Samuel Beal, author of a number of works with which it is likely that Kipling was familiar, in particular *Travels of Fah-Hian and Sung-Yun, Buddhist Pilgrims, from China to India (400 A.D. and 518 A.D.) Translated from the Chinese* (1869).[25] Kipling's Teshoo Lama was inspired by and partially modeled upon Chinese Buddhist pilgrims of the fifth and seventh centuries, though it is likely that Kipling first was inspired both by contemporary Tibetan travel narratives and by narratives of European archaeologists who followed in the footsteps of those Chinese pilgrims.

One of the more curious aspects of the novel from a Buddhist perspective is why the Lama's pilgrimage is focused on the River of the Arrow, or the "arrow well" as it is more commonly known. The Lama's initially stated purpose, "to see the Four Holy Places before I die"—Limbini Grove, Bodh-Gaya, the Deer Park at Sarnath, and Kushinagar—would be the expected pilgrimage (5). To then place so much significance on the arrow well simply does not make sense from a Buddhist perspective. In the first place, the event of Siddhartha shooting the arrow is a minor one in his early life; it occurred before he began his religious quest and attained Buddhahood. In a number of ancient accounts that I have consulted, little mention is made of the arrow and no mention is made of the arrow well. Depending on which Beal Kipling intended the Lama to look through, he might have found this account:

> Outside the south gate of the city [Kapilavastu], on the left of the road, is a *stûpa;* it was here the royal prince contended with the Sakyas in athletic sports

(*arts*) and pierced with his arrows the iron targets. From this 30 li south-east is a small *stûpa*.... Here it was, during the athletic contest, that the arrow of the prince, after penetrating the targets, fell and buried itself up to the feather in the ground, causing a clear spring of water to flow forth. Common tradition has called this the *arrow fountain (Sarakûpa)*; persons who are sick by drinking the water of this spring are mostly restored to health. (Beal, *Si-Yu-Ki* V.2, 23–24)

In Beal's *Romantic Legend of Sakya Buddha* (1875), the most widely read of his works, the greater portion of the description of the competitions between the rivals for the hand of Yoshodhara is focused on contests in the "art of writing" and the "art of calculating and arithmetic" (Beal, *Romantic* 85–87). The "competition in martial exercises" is recounted in less detail at the end of the sequence and concludes thusly: "the prince shot his arrow right through the seven [trees], and where his arrow entered the ground beyond the seventh, it penetrated down to the very bottom of the earth...and there sprung up through the hole it made a spring of water, which is called to this day the 'Arrow Well'" (Beal, *Romantic* 90).

Further, as these excerpts demonstrate, no mention is made of the well washing away sins, as Kipling has the Lama proclaim throughout the novel. Indeed, "sin" does not exist in Buddhism in any Christian sense. There is no God to sin against or by whom to be redeemed; there was no original fall from grace for which to expiate. Kipling knew this. His narrator understands the difference when the bazaar letter-writer translates the Lama's phrase "to acquire merit" as "to 'Almighty God'" (106–7). According to the ethical system detailed in the canonical literatures of the major schools of Buddhism, humans, as a result of ignorance, desire, and avarice, commit immoral or, to use a Mahayana term, "unskillful" actions; these actions remain as part of one's karmic record; an accumulation of these actions leads to rebirth and continued suffering, though not so much as punishment as an unavoidable outcome, until one transcends the attachments and aversions that lock one into this cycle of samsara. A summary of this sort cannot but grossly oversimplify a system that complexly integrates cosmology and ethics, especially since there are as many schools or sects of Buddhism as there are denominations of Christianity and significant differences of interpretation exist between them. Suffice it to say for the moment that Kipling is accurate at least in attributing the phrase "to acquire merit" to his Lama, since it is much more common among Tibetan Buddhists than among other Mahayana or any Theravada Buddhists. To some Westerners, the phrase has suggested a simplistic accounting scheme of karma by which, for instance, a past murder can be cancelled out by saving someone else's life. This is closer to some Christian, in particular Catholic, understandings of sin/redemption than it is to karma. Father Victor is quite sympathetic to the Lama's search for, as he puts it, "A river that washes away sin!" (89). Kipling, as I believe he knew, was closer to the Buddhist expression when the Lama says to Kim "when we come to my River thou wilt be freed from all illusion" than he is when he more frequently says that the river will make them "free from all sin" (212, 289). Karma cannot be washed away in this manner; it cannot be expiated by a moment of confession or repentance and so forgiven and redeemed, as sin can be within Christian tradition (though of course very differently within different denominations). Kipling chose here and in other ways to Christianize the Lama. Whether he did this out of ignorance, or because he disagreed with a more Buddhist conception, or for the sake of reader accessibility and approval, which I believe most likely, or some combination thereof, we cannot know.

This still leaves unanswered the question of why Kipling focuses the Lama on such an un-Buddhist search. One possible answer is precisely to Christianize Buddhism. The metaphor of "wells of salvation," from Isaiah 12.3, or "a spring of water welling up to eternal life," from John 4.14, is familiar from the Bible.[26] Another possibility is that a combination of Kipling's own ideology and interests and the thematic concerns of *Kim* in particular drew him to perhaps the only moment in the story of Gautama's life that directly involves military prowess. An archery contest seems more in keeping with Zam-Zammah and Kim's Red Bull of war than would, say, a grove of meditation. This possibility adds support to the side of the critical polarization that argues that the Lama's search is subsumed into Kim's search.[27]

Alternately, an explanation might lie once again in Kipling's awareness of contemporary archaeological narratives. One of the most dramatic and publicized stories concerned the race between Dr. L. Austine Waddell, a British physician who spent substantial spare time researching Buddhist sites in India and monasteries in Tibet, and Dr. Alois Führer, a Viennese archaeologist working for the British Survey, to locate the last remaining unfound holy sites from the life of the Buddha, Limbini and Kapilavastu. Both were working from Huan Tsang's narrative. To make a long story short, Waddell did the painstaking detective work to correctly identify the sites in 1896 but was unable to document his findings sufficiently before Führer, who used Waddell's own research, mislocated what he believed to be those sites and rushed into print in both India and Europe. He falsified his research in order to hide his use of Waddell's work and claimed sole credit for one of the greatest archaeological finds of the end of the century.[28] An acrimonious series of exchanges in the public press followed. The Royal Asiatic Society was involved in this scandal up until 1899, while Kipling was writing *Kim*. It is unlikely that Kipling failed to notice these events, and it is highly likely that he was familiar with Waddell's several well-known books on Tibetan "Lamaism." Waddell's *Tibetan Buddhism* (1894), for instance, while often giving an unsympathetic portrayal of Tibetan monks, applies Christian terminology such as "sin" to Tibetan doctrines and details the lineage of the "Tashi-lhunpo monastery," "Tashi" being synonymous with "Teshoo" (Waddell, *Tibetan* 231).[29]

With all of this in mind, it appears significant that Kipling's Lama's search for the River of the Arrow is in effect a search for Kapilavastu, the object of the Waddell/Führer contest. Huan Tsang had used the location of the "Arrow Spring" in order to locate Limbini from Kapilavastu (Allen 271). Thus Kipling's choice to focus the Lama's search on the River of the Arrow may have been shaped by a combination of ancient Chinese pilgrimage narratives and contemporary European archaeology narratives as a re-Orientalized re-reenactment of the search for the birthplace and first home of the Buddha, truly the spring of Buddhism.

Kipling's Law and the Law of the Dharma

The most obviously Buddhist concepts in *Kim* are "the Law," "the Wheel," and "the Way." The former refers to the Dharma, which Victorian scholars often translated as "Law" and of which the "law of karma" is part; the second refers to the Wheel of Life, as portrayed in the Lama's drawings of it, which is a representation of the doctrine sometimes translated as "dependent origina-tion"; and the latter refers to the Middle Way, a foundational tenet derived from the Four Noble Truths in the Buddha's first sermon, though Kipling often uses "the Way" colloquially to indicate the path of Buddhist practice in general. These figures point to three foundational doctrines within Buddhism at the broadest level. The Dharma and the Middle Way appear throughout the can-ons of both major schools, Theravada and Mahayana, portions of which were available to Victorians in translation, especially the Theravada canon translated from the Pali. The Wheel was most familiar to Victorians through the colorful depictions of it brought back from Tibet by travelers and anthropologists (and governmental intelligence gatherers), Tibetan or Vajrayana Buddhism being a culturally and historically unique branching from Mahayana. Though of course interpretations of these concepts vary significantly across schools and, within schools, across the many denominations of Buddhism, the ubiquity of them in Buddhist literature and the multiplicity of summaries and commentary on them by Victorians permit discussion of them at a summary level. My purpose here is to unpack Kipling's representation and understanding of these concepts and, where possible, to identify Kipling's sources for them. I will use as a base-line of comparison what might be called "consensus definitions," which I draw as much as possible from trends in Victorian usage and, in places, from defini-tions that since the Victorian period have become more or less standardized in the West (which I realize opens those definitions to challenge and, certainly, to refinement).

To start, the Lama in *Kim* appears at times to mix and match the Law, the Wheel, and the Way, and this overlapping use may suggest less an understanding on Kipling's part of the nature of their connectedness than a lack of understanding of significant distinctions. As Sandra Kemp comments, "Kipling makes no distinction between Dharma (Law) as 'the way things are' and Dharma as 'the Way'—a journey along an eightfold path to Nirvana...through a cycle of existences" (Kemp, *Kipling's* 26). However, Kipling would not be alone in this confusion, given the fact that each of these concepts is as difficult to define as the most challenging within Western theology or philosophy. Each has multiple connotations that are woven throughout a body of scripture in two major canons that are more voluminous than the canons of Judaism, Christianity, and Islam combined. This complexity, and the resulting Victorian confusion, is reflected in Sir Edwin Arnold's *The Light of Asia. Being The Life and Teaching of Gautama, Prince of India and Founder of Buddhism* (1879), which Kipling read and which was a primary influence on his writing of *Kim,* in particular his characterization of the Teshoo Lama.[30] The final section of that poem consists largely of a monologue by the Buddha summarizing the principle tenets and doctrines of Buddhism, including a paean to the all-encompassing justness of the Dharma. Arnold's Buddha summarizes aspects of the Dharma drawn clearly from Arnold's study of works in comparative religion, but at the same time he Christianizes and anthropomorphizes the Dharma in ways not supportable by Buddhist doctrine as found in the canonical scripture.[31] Given Kipling's debt to Arnold, it is not surprising that his Lama similarly weaves together the Wheel, the Way, and the Law, reinterpreting them in ways also found in Arnold.

To take one example, after Kim's diversion of the Lama's search for the River of the Arrow into the foothills of the Himalayas has crescendoed in a violent encounter with the Russian and French agents, the Lama is struck on the forehead and in one moment of passion nearly commits an extremely unskillful action by not immediately checking the protective wishes of the Spiti hillmen to shoot the two spies. This lapse motivates him to "meditate upon the Cause of Things" and to recognize that "Just and perfect is the Wheel," recognizing that he has invited violence and suffering by his own previous actions and by allowing his own desires to lead him away from his search (260). When Kim tries to claim some responsibility, as the reader knows he should, the Lama says: "No! It was because I was upon the Way—tuned as are *sinen* (cymbals) to the purpose of the Law. I departed from that ordinance. The tune was broken: followed the punishment" (261). The Lama is not being naïve here, as some critics have argued, though it is true that he is unaware that Kim designed to lead him into the mountains. According to one Buddhist understanding of karma, even if the Lama knew of Kim's designs, he still would claim responsibility for his own actions, his own karma, in precisely the same way. Also, his mixing of Wheel and Way and Law, if muddled, is not unfaithful to Buddhist scripture or practice at a very general level. Kipling's knowledge of Buddhism was not deep, but it was neither misguided nor entirely uninformed.

Considered separately, the Law of the Dharma is an immensely complex doctrine for which there is no single definition and manifold interpretations. In common usage among practicing Buddhists it has connotations that range from "the natural order of the universe" to, most simply, "the teachings of the Buddha." At the most general level, it might be expressed as "true understanding of the nature of reality," the most comprehensive natural law of cause and effect (karma) governing the universe. To be enlightened, to attain nirvana, is fully to comprehend the Dharma, the way things really are. This is achieved not by faith, in a Christian sense, but through knowledge, "Right Understanding," the first of the Noble Eightfold Path, the primary tenets of Buddhist ethics. This knowledge is at once practical, philosophical, ethical, and scientific. According to the Dharma, the fundamental, inescapable nature of reality—from the level of galaxies to the level of microorganisms, from global ecology to personal relationships—is interconnectedness, the mutual dependence of all phenomena through causes and effects. As W. S. Lilly wrote in his 1905 essay, "The Message of Buddhism to the Western World," "The truth is there is really one sole dogma of Buddhism—that the whole universe is under one and the self-same law of causation which is ethical" (Lilly 209). For many Victorians, Buddhist thought appeared to fill the fearful gap between Darwinian evolutionary theory and a Judeo-Christian moral universe in jeopardy from that theory. Lilly thus continues in this way, addressing his contemporaries: "You have grasped the fundamental fact that law rules everywhere throughout the phenomenal universe, whose secrets you have so largely explored. That is well, too. The religion of the Buddha is not in conflict with modern science" (Lilly 213). The perceived compatibility of Buddhism with science, Darwinian science in particular, but, at the same time, its reassurance that the universe, rather than being governed by "random selection," is ordered by immutable law that is unswervingly just, resonated strongly with the post-Darwinian British sensibility.[32]

At the same time, however, the Dharma rests equally on an understanding that everything and everybody is impermanent, a doctrine profoundly threatening to certain cherished Western beliefs. This foundational doctrine is articulated especially in one of the traditional teachings especially within Mahayana Buddhism called "The Three Marks of Existence," summarized here: (1) *duhkha* (in Pali, *dukkha*), which translates as "suffering" or "unsatisfactoriness" and is synonymous with the First Noble Truth; (2) *anitya* (in Pali, *annica*), "impermanence," which states that all things are conditioned by change, nothing is constant or universal; and, (3) *anatman* (in Pali, *anatta*), which means "no soul" or "not self," the doctrine that autonomous, continuous, and eternal selfhood, as in the Western conception of the soul or the Hindu *Atman,* is an illusion.[33] These concepts express the aspects of Buddhism that were and are most threatening to Westerners and that therefore generated vehement charges by Victorians of pessimism, fatalism, nihilism, and sheer absurdity. A few, such as I. Salzer, writing from Calcutta in 1890, celebrated their understanding that "Gautama Buddha's doctrine of continuous Change, or tendency towards Change within the Universe, is the only doctrine as yet known that includes all the elementary processes of this world, both physical and mental; it is the highest generalisation yet proclaimed by man" (Salzer 8). Even if one were capable of conceiving this universalization of the doctrine of impermanence, one would be left with the very real dilemma it poses for lived human experience. That dilemma, put most simply, is this: "The incongruity between the permanent happiness we seek and the impermanence of the things in the world whose possession and avoidance we think will bring happiness results in a life of craving that is often frustrated and always at risk" (Gowans 133). Because the reality of impermanence is not merely distasteful but terrifying, Buddhist doctrine, as represented in the translations of canonical scripture made in the nineteenth century, suggests that human beings tend to choose to live in denial rather than face reality. As the second Noble Truth indicates, and as the Wheel of Life depicts, humans often cling to illusions: the illusion that one can escape suffering by consuming one's desires, the illusion that what one loves is permanent, and the illusion that one possesses a socially autonomous self that corresponds on the spiritual plane to an eternal soul.

Kipling's Lama expresses some understanding of the Dharma's doctrines of interconnectedness and impermanence. He recognizes the effects of clinging to illusions, as here: "But those who follow the Way must permit not the fire of any desire or attachment, for that is all Illusion.... Now I am sorrowful because thou [Kim] art taken away and my River is far from me. It is the Law which I have broken!" (92). The Lama strayed from the Dharma by forgetting that attachment to Kim, or to anyone, unavoidably produces suffering as the pain of separation or loss (though part of Kipling's motive throughout the novel is to show that one must risk loving, regardless of this suffering). Elsewhere, the Lama uses "Law" in a more colloquial sense. Since the Four Noble Truths and the Noble Eightfold Path from the Buddha's first sermon express the Dharma, describing the implications of that natural order for human existence and prescribing on that basis a plan for living harmoniously within it, "Dharma" and "Law" most simply mean "duty" or "the Buddha's teachings." Thus when the Lama says such things as "I bowed before the Excellent Law," he simply is saying, "I follow the teachings of the Buddha" or "I observe the duties of a Buddhist monk" (13). Here again the Lama's usage is at least not inconsistent with Buddhist practice (most generally conceived without reference to school or denomination).

However, there is one instance where Kipling's use of "Law" clearly is inconsistent with Tibetan Buddhism. In speaking to the curator in the Wonder House, the Lama offers several reasons for his pilgrimage to India, one of which is this: "For...years it was in my mind that the Old Law was not well followed [in Tibet]; being overlaid, as thou knowest, with devildom, charms and idolatry" (9). "Old Law" refers to Theravada, the original school of Buddhism as preserved in the Pali canon, the predominant form of Buddhism in Southeast Asia. The "Reformed Law" is Mahayana, the northern Buddhism of the Sanskrit canon of which Tibetan Buddhism was a variant. It is not credible that a Tibetan Monk would denigrate Mahayana, "The Greater Vehicle," relative to Theravada, which Mahayanists dubbed "Hinayana," "The Lesser Vehicle," following the schism that formed Mahayana beginning around 100 CE. Kipling's choice to put these words into the mouth of the Lama marks a telling moment of self-consciousness in the text about its representation of Buddhism. After all, Kipling could have chosen to make the Lama a Theravada Buddhist from Ceylon (Sri Lanka) or Burma (Myanmar), for instance. Clearly he had a range of other reasons for making the Lama Tibetan, including the proximity of Tibet to India and his personal knowledge of the territory and peoples along the border northeast of Simla. Also, in creating the character of Kim, he drew upon a news story of his day concerning Sergeant Tim Doolan, whose son with a Tibetan woman was arrested in Darjeeling with identifying "papers sewn up in a leather case of Tibetan workmanship...suspended from his neck" (Hopkins 103).[34] Of course, he also drew heavily upon the contemporary intrigue of the Great Game. Kipling had arrived in India just a decade after the "classic age of Tibetan exploration" was inaugurated by the forays into the Himalayas of Colonel Nikolai Prejevalsky of the Imperial Russian Army, which sparked a "renewal of the 'Great Game' with Russia after 1875" (Bishop 145). By the time of Kipling's stay in India, Tibet had become "a cherished prize in the Great Game played by Britain and Russia," both of which "often sent [hired Indian] spies, sometimes disguised as Buddhist pilgrims, into Tibet on map-making missions" (Lopez, *Prisoners* 5). Colonel Creighton is modeled on Captain Thomas Montgomerie, who in the 1860s and1870s was assigned the mapping of parts of Afghanistan and Tibet, and the character of Mahbub Ali shows signs of Kipling's familiarity with espionage along the border in the 1890s (Kling 304; Parry 311). The reasons for choosing Tibet are clear, but why then have the Lama effectively slander his own Tibetan Buddhism?

Kipling's decisions first to make his Lama Tibetan and then to have him deny the roots of his Mahayana (more specifically, Vajrayana) tradition resonate with two specific contradictory positions within the discourse surrounding Buddhism in late-Victorian Britain. On the one hand, Kipling capitalized on a growing fascination with Tibet, which *Kim* then helped perpetuate. As Peter Bishop documents, from Madame Blavatsky's Tibetan "Masters" in the

1870s to James Hilton's Shangri-La in *Lost Horizon* (1933), Tibet grew in the imperial and popular imagination from a place of strategic interest and a mysteriously unexplored "Absence on the Map" to the seat of the Aryan race—"the long-lost 'ancestors'" of white Europeans—and the "storehouse of ancient wisdom"(Bishop 102, 121, 182).[35] Tibet became, and perhaps remains to this day, the imagined spiritual utopian counterpart of modern, Western, industrial, secular society.

On the other hand, Kipling's use of Tibet flew in the face of a countervailing treatment of Mahayana as opposed to Theravada Buddhism within the field of comparative religion and an unsympathetic conception of "Lamaism" within popular culture. The first wave of European translations of Buddhist texts in the early decades of the nineteenth century focused on Mahayana manuscripts in Sanskrit, but as the comparative study of religions became increasingly institutionalized, scholars in England came to favor the more ancient Theravada canon in Pali as being closer to the source. By the time the Rhys Davidses founded the Pali Text Society at Oxford in 1881, the European textual colonization of Buddhism had been founded on the belief that Theravada was "true Buddhism," while Mahayana, and its Tibetan variant in particular, was bastardized through hybridization with indigenous myths and practices. Europeans traveled to Tibet hoping to find their fabricated ideal of the guru on the mountaintop and were disappointment by what they perceived to be dirty heathens chanting nonsense to demon-gods.

Waddell's several books on Tibetan Buddhism confirmed and helped create the view that "Lamaism is only thinly and imperfectly varnished over with Buddhist symbolism, beneath which the sinister growth of poly-demonist superstition darkly appears" (Waddell, *Tibetan* xi).[36] What is more, Lamaism, with its hierarchical structure, robes, and chanting, became synonymous with "Popery" at a time of anti-Catholic sentiment in England, marked by the Murphy riots of the late 1860s to early 1870s.[37] Donald S. Lopez, Jr. summarizes the contradiction between this conception of Tibetan Buddhism and the simultaneous idealization of Tibet: "Thus, Lamaism may be portrayed in the West as the most authentic and the most degenerate form of Buddhism, Tibetan monks may be portrayed as saintly and rapacious, Tibetan artists may be portrayed as inspired mystics and mindless automatons, Tibetan peasants may be portrayed as pristine and filthy" (Lopez, *Prisoners* 10).

Recognizing these opposed late-Victorian responses to Tibet explains the contradiction in *Kim* surrounding the Lama's statements about the "Old Law" and the "Reformed Law." It is not, I suggest, that Kipling did not understand the unlikelihood of a Tibetan Lama denigrating his own tradition; rather, Kipling was aware of the contradictory constructions of Tibet and its Buddhism prevalent at the time and incorporated that contradiction into his novel. He therefore chose to make his Lama Tibetan but then to make him more sympathetic to the contemporary reader by having him break from Tibetan Lamaism.

One last comment on Kipling's understanding of the Dharma as law: Shamsul Islam's *Kipling's Law* (1975) argued that Kipling built a conception of "the law" throughout his writings as consisting of three components: "moral values, the Imperial Idea and the doctrine of disinterested suffering and positive action" (Islam 9). No reader of Kipling can be surprised by the observation that he was in specific ways a moral and political conservative who believed in a stoic but non-fatalistic and action-oriented attitude toward the demands of duty, as he conceived it. His model of the "Law"—natural and moral—as "impersonal, stern and cruel" may be a distant analogue to karmic law within the Dharma (Islam 92). Andrew Lycett observes that in the process of writing *Kim,* which spanned seven years between when he started a story about Kim o'Rishti in 1894 and the publication of the novel, Kipling "acknowledges something [to himself] he had known but...had rejected while in India: the similarity between Indian philosophy and his own metaphysical interests— between the Buddhist concept of dharma (the law) and his own developing ideas of a corpus of received wisdom, also known as 'the law', that is necessary for the health of a community" (Lycett 331). Kipling may have seen in his limited understanding of karmic law a parallel to his own code of social conduct and personal responsibility, his own "Old Law" of duties and consequences.

The Wheel and The Way

The first verse of the *Dhammapada,* a compilation of epigrammatic teachings attributed to the Buddha and perhaps the most widely translated Buddhist text, runs as follows: "Mind is the forerunner of all actions. / All deeds are led by mind, created by mind. / If one speaks or acts with a corrupt mind, suffering follows, / As the wheel follows the hoof of an ox pulling a cart"(*Dhammapada* 1). In a figurative sense, Kipling's Lama's "Wheel of Things" or "Wheel of Life" is this wheel, and Kim's Red Bull is this ox (41, 210).[38] In his 1892 essay on a Tibetan painting of the Wheel, Waddell noted that "Buddha himself is reported to have been the author of the original figure which, in order to illustrate his oft repeated dogma of the Causes of Existence...he drew in diagrammatic form with grains of rice from a stalk-in-ear which he had plucked while teaching his disciples in a rice-field" (Waddell, "Pictorial Wheel" 135–36).[39]

In his book of two years later, *Tibetan Buddhism,* Waddell observes that while the Wheel is "the chief corner-stone of Buddhism," "scarcely any two European scholars are agreed upon the exact nature and signification of some of its chief links" (Waddell, *Tibetan* 106). Compare, then, Kipling's presentation of the Wheel when the Lama first begins to teach Kim about it, saying,

"Sahibs have not *all* this world's wisdom." The narrator continues: "Men say that the Bodhisat Himself first drew it with grains of rice upon dust, to teach His disciples the cause of things....Few can translate the picture-parable; there are not twenty in all the world who can draw it surely without a copy; of those who can both draw and expound are but three" (192). It again appears likely that Kipling had read Waddell, and it is clear that he shared Waddell's respect for the teaching represented by the Wheel, as well as for the mastery of it on the part of the Lama. As Kim says about the Lama's painting, "This is a marvel beyond marvels," and the narrator later instructs us that "All Tibet is full of cheap reproductions of the Wheel; but the lama was an artist" (192, 241).

Some Victorian Orientalists, including Waddell in his earlier writings, were more fascinated by those elements of the Wheel culturally rooted in Tibet or China than original to India, in particular, the giant fanged demon, Yama, the Lord of Death, who often appears holding the Wheel, and the scenes between the spokes of the Wheel of the six realms of existence into which sentient beings might be reborn, depending on their karma.[40] In Tibetan renderings, each realm is teeming with colorful figures of demons, animals, and people, some segments as fantastically grotesque as paintings by Hieronymus Bosch. They attract attention, both from Westerners unfamiliar with the underlying teachings and from uneducated Buddhists, represented in *Kim* by the Spiti hillmen, whom the Lama controls with a threat after being struck by the Russian: "*I* say there shall be no killing—I who was Abbot of Such-zen. Is it any lust of thine to be re-born as a rat, or a snake under the eaves—a worm in the belly of the most mean beast?" (244). However, the aspect of the Wheel that is most important in terms of centrality to the teachings shared by Mahayana and Theravada alike appears on the less spectacularly figured outer rim. Depicted there are the twelve segments of the chain of dependent origination, a doctrine the Buddha purportedly formulated on the night he attained enlightenment. Thus it is appropriate that the Lama is concerned especially with these images after the Russian rips his painting of the Wheel, as Kipling's narrator describes it: "Kim stared at the brutally disfigured chart. From left to right diagonally the rent ran—from the Eleventh House where Desire gives birth to the Child (as it is drawn by Tibetans)—across the human and animal worlds, to the Fifth House—the empty House of the Senses. The logic was unanswerable" (262). The eleventh and fifth "houses" refer to two of the twelve links in the chain of dependent origination, and the Lama apparently knows precisely how to interpret the rip joining those two.[41] The fact that in the course of the novel he never mentions Yama nor dwells on the fantastical demons within the typical Tibetan Wheel suggests that he may be informed by an Orientalist prejudice on his author's part against these Tibetan elements, but also perhaps that Kipling had enough of an understanding of the importance of the doctrine of dependent origination not to undercut it by emphasizing other more sensational aspects of the Lama's Wheel.

The doctrine of dependent origination (*Paticca-samuppāda* in Pali), also sometimes translated as "conditioned genesis" or "interdependent co-arising," is considered by some experts, ancient and modern, to be "the foundation of all of Buddhist study and practice" (Nhat Hanh, *Heart* 221).[42] It integrates and illustrates the Four Noble Truths, the Three Marks of Existence, the doctrine of karma, and the doctrine of reincarnation. Simply put, it is a model of reality in its entirety—it describes the chain of causes and effects that govern all existence. This chain is represented pictorially on the outer rim of the Wheel by a series of images representing the twelve links in the chain of dependent origination (see appendix 2 for details). The model, as illustrated by the Lama's paintings, describes twelve stages or stations of human life in a cycle of rebirth and death that has no beginning point and no end short of enlightenment. In attaining enlightenment, one steps outside of this cycle, which is why in some renderings a figure of the Buddha stands outside the Wheel in the upper right-hand corner, showing the way out.

I will not attempt here a thorough enough exegesis of the Wheel or of the doctrine of dependent origination to convey the dynamic reality that students of Buddhism see in this densely symbolic picture. Suffice it to say that the Wheel is a model of the operation of karma depicting the processes of cause and effect by which human desire, ignorance, and avarice lead to a potentially endless cycle of rebirth, suffering, and death from lifetime to lifetime. The essential meaning of the Wheel, the dynamic reality that any static representation can only hope to suggest, is the infinitely complex flow of causes and effects that conditions absolutely everything in the universe. The meaning is in the movement, the impermanence, the becoming. A taste of this meaning may be suggested by a short excerpt from one of the Buddha's many teachings on dependent origination, as here in the *Mahātaṇhāsankhaya Sutta*:

> So, bhikkhus [monks], with ignorance as condition, formations...[of volitions or actions come to be]; with formations as conditions, consciousness; with consciousness as condition, mentality-materiality; with mentality-materiality as condition, the sixfold base [of the senses]; with the sixfold base as condition, contact [between the senses and the perceived world]; with contact as condition, feelings; with feeling as condition, craving; with craving as condition, clinging; with clinging as condition, being; with being as condition, birth; with birth as condition, ageing and death, sorrow, lamentation, pain, grief, and despair come to be. Such is the origin of this whole mass of suffering. (*Middle* 353)

This sort of "if-then" or "because of" formulation is common throughout canonical Buddhist scripture in describing dependent origination.

When Kipling's Lama says such things as, "We must think of the Cause of Things," he is referencing the doctrines of dependent origination and karma (245). A central feature of these doctrines is the mutual conditionality of all events and phenomena. As Major-General Dawsonne M. Strong, writing from India in 1899, put it, it is the "connectiveness of everything with everything" (Strong 77). Every effect has causes; every cause produces effects; every cause is the effect of other causes, and every effect is the cause of other effects. There are no self-originating, autonomous occurrences or beings and no first-causes. The result is what might now be described as an ecological worldview in which all systems are understood to be interconnected and mutually dependent (hence the mutual attraction of environmentalists and Buddhists as demonstrated by the growing body of literature that combines the two). Thus *Kim* portrays the Lama as representatively Buddhist whenever he directs himself and Kim to consider the causes and the effects of their choices and actions beyond those that are most immediately evident. The first obvious occurrence of this takes place the morning after the Lama has first shown Kim a painting of the Wheel and is awakened by the father of the child whom Kim has healed. He lectures Kim as follows: "The thing [the healing] was done. A Cause was put out into the world, and, old or young, sick or sound, knowing or unknowing, who can rein in the effect of that Cause? Does the Wheel hang still if a child spin it—or a drunkard?" (194).

A more significant example occurs after the climatic encounter with the Russian and French spies. Kim's response to that encounter is Mahbub Ali's: if they shoot at you, shoot back; action, not understanding, is what matters. The Lama's response is, "We must think of the Cause of Things" (245). The next day, he tells Kim, "Had I been passionless, the evil blow would have done only bodily evil—a scar, or a bruise—which is illusion" (252). Several days of deep reflection later, he reports that he has "seen the Cause of Things" and recounts a story from when he was close to Kim's age, took part in a pen-case duel between competing monasteries, and was struck on the forehead precisely where the Russian just had struck him again (259). Two interpretations suggest themselves. The first is that the Lama is appealing to a simplemindedly deterministic model of karma, according to which a bad action subsequently will be punished by an analogous payback that links cause to effect with linear directness. This is indeed a prevalent understanding of karma in the West—for instance as "instant karma"—and it may be that Kipling's understanding was little deeper than this. The alternative is based on a more thorough understanding of dependent origination, one that recognizes that the Buddha "depict[ed] the world of experience as one in which typically processes causally interact with one another in complex ways: for a given effect, there are multiple causes, and for a given cause, there are multiple effects" (Gowans 130–31). The text suggests at least some of this understanding on the Lama's part. His explanation of the "Cause of Things" includes multiple causes: a recognition that it is he who chose to come to the mountains, that he had come by neglecting his search for the River of the Arrow, that he had passionately celebrated his vigor as a mountaineer, becoming "strong to do evil and to forget," that he had sought to recapture something of his youth, in part out of a fear of the loss of prowess that aging brings, and that his lack of mindfulness about these desires, intentions, and fears conditioned his crossing of the Russian's karmic path, all of which led to a blow like a wake-up call (259). It is interesting to read the Lama's conclusion—"Who can read the Cause of an act is half-way to Freedom!"—also as a prescriptive wake up call from the text to its readers: be mindful of the complexity of causes and effects in this novel, as in the hybrid world of colonial India, as in life in general (261).

The Wheel, like Buddhist teachings generally, is diagnostic and prescriptive; "the paradigm chosen [by the Buddha] to represent the authority along the way was the physician and not the priest" (Santina 150). The malady is every-day suffering, the diagnosis is the conditionality and causality portrayed by the Wheel, and the prescription is to practice preventative medicine by breaking that cycle at any of the twelve points. A Buddhist might note, for example, that one can choose to remedy ignorance by gaining understanding of the Four Noble Truths, or one can prevent the automatic reflexes of grasping and clinging that lead to addictive behaviors, for instance, by practicing mindful observance of those impulses before acting upon them. This emphasis on thinking before acting, contemplating causes and effects, is central to Buddhism. Buddhist practice depends upon intention and mindfulness, contemplation and meditation. These activities, however, were not active enough for the ideologies underpinning nineteenth-century British progressivism, market capitalism, "muscular Christianity," or imperial conquest, all of which were more apt to urge, "Don't just sit there, do something!" The perceived passivity of Buddhism, and the "indolent Orient" in general, not only discomposed but threatened Victorian sensibility. It made Kipling, despite his sympathy for Buddhism, squirm in his seat to get cracking, seize the day, and live life to the hilt.[43] Thus one finds in *Kim* a struggle to resolve contradictory responses to the Lama's practice of dispassionate contemplation, which the text worries throughout by juxtaposing it to Kim's lusty embrace of teeming, sensual Indian life, described repeatedly as "the world." The novel draws upon the terms of this debate as they existed within the discourse surrounding Buddhism in Victorian Britain, namely: the active, masculine, progressive, optimistic West versus the passive, feminine, tradition-bound, pessimistic East. But these terms happen to be appropriate in a way that destabilizes this rigid dichotomy and its slant. They point also to karma as "action/reaction" and to the continuously available choice between creating more actions that perpetuate suffering and refraining from doing so, which is the diagnosis and prescription of the Wheel. For the Teshoo Lama, as for Buddhists in general, to choose not to act is itself an action.

To take one example of the discourse of active/passive in *Kim,* Kim looses two "Act[s] upon the world" by curing the Jat's child and then saving the life of the Mahratta on the train (209). The Lama approves of the first action, because it was done out of compassion "solely to acquire merit," but disapproves of the second action, because it appeared to him to be the use of a "spell," the "prideful workings" of which inflamed in Kim a passionate thrill of power, which indeed it did (209). Thus the novel portrays neither the Lama nor Buddhism as being opposed to all actions. He sees the former Mahratta, whom Kim has transformed into a Saddhu, arrested by the police (without knowing that this is the Mahratta's purpose), and he is concerned that this has "loosed an Act upon the world," by which he means negative ramifications for others and a karmic debt for Kim. Though he is ignorant of the Western techniques of espionage used by Kim, he is not naïve: he recognizes covert methods and prideful attachment, which his Buddhism tells him are misguided. Soon after, the Lama commends Kim to cure other poor people if he is given the opportunity, but to "by no means work charms" or repeat his display with the Mahratta (212). Kim asks him, "Then all Doing is evil?" This means to ask, "Is the Great Game contrary to Buddhism?" and the Lama answers, "To abstain from action is well—except to acquire merit." Kim then trots out the Western ideology he has been taught in order to see what the Lama thinks of it: "At the Gates of Learning [St. Xavier's school] we were taught that to abstain from action was unbefitting a Sahib. And I am a Sahib." The Lama's response is telling: "Friend of all the World, . . . I am an old man—pleased with shows as are children. To those who follow the Way there is neither black nor white, Hind or Bhotiyal. We be all souls seeking escape. No matter what thy wisdom learned among Sahibs, when we come to my River thou wilt be freed from all illusion" (212).

Once again, two readings of this exchange suggest themselves. The first, from one side of the critical polarization, is that the Lama is a childishly passive old man, a dupe who is too simple to catch on that Kim's action has saved a man's life and served the cause of the Great Game and, therefore, that the novel portrays Buddhism as merely a cat's paw of the British Empire. The reading on the other side of the critical divide typically has been to state, in effect, "But the Lama really loves Kim, and Kim reveres and loves the Lama, and the novel portrays Buddhism with genuine respect," which though true does not answer the charge of the first reading. Between (or perhaps outside of) these two readings is one that recognizes that the Lama's ignorance of Kim's engagement in the Great Game need not be equated either with imbecility or complicity, nor, more importantly, does it negate the Lama's message. The Lama's typically Mahayana message is that action is skilful if it is compassionate but unattached and unskillful if it comes from ignorance, clinging, or passion (these are "The Three Fires," represented by the pig, the cock, and the snake in the hub of the Wheel). This suggests that the Lama's personal ignorance actually underscores his Buddhist message, since if he did understand that Kim had saved the life of a fellow human being, he would consider Kim's action to have "acquired merit," though he still would hold that Kim must work on his prideful attachment to that action.

Those who feel that a strict dichotomy in the novel between the Great Game and the Lama's Way is the only possible basis for interpretation, and those who think that the former "acts" upon the "passive" other, are at risk of reifying the dualistic thinking and one-sided logic of the sahibs at St. Xavier's.[44] This represents a failure to hear the Lama's point, which is that it does not matter whether one is a sahib or an Indian or a Tibetan, whether one saves a life in service of the Great Game or whether one saves a life for some other reason, as long as one is mindful of one's intentions and of the effects (karma) that will be produced by one's actions. Illusion is to act without understanding that one acts out of ignorance, clinging, or passion. This is illustrated by Kim's pride and by the sahibs' claim to mastery through action, or any claim to mastery, including a Buddhist one, because these are considered to be "shows" to entertain children and old men. Some critics will insist that this reading turns a blind eye to the fact that Kim's action, however well intentioned, serves the Empire, which it does, and therefore demonstrates an utter complicity with it, which it does not. This latter view again exactly misses the Lama's point by clinging to the sahib's dualistic thinking. From one Buddhist perspective, dichotomies such as British and Indian, West and East, Great Game and Buddhist Way are illusory to the extent that one believes they are categorical rather than co-dependently arising, as the Wheel instructs. In other words, the Lama's perspective is a meta-view that is an order of magnitude broader than the level of such dualisms. From this perspective, it is as possible to practice as a Buddhist while working for the British Empire as it is to be a good Buddhist while working for Indian nationalism. What matters is that one strive to think non-dualistically, to bring an awareness of causes and effects to one's actions, and therefore to act only on the basis of these reflections as disinterestedly and compassionately as possible for all concerned.

The ending of the novel does not require Kim to make an either/or choice between the Great Game and the Buddhist Way, between Mahbub Ali and the Lama. Their conversation occurs after the Lama has found the River, or rather, in a characteristically Buddhist way, after the River has found him once he was ready to see it. He effectively had predicted this when he said, "if need be, the River will open at our feet" (197). Mahbub, who is concerned that the Lama's "cleansing" of Kim's "sins" in the River will make him too holy to act any longer as a spy, probes Kim's future vocation. Uncharacteristically for a nineteenth-century Tibetan monk with a *chela,* the Lama does not expect Kim to become a monk (which may reflect a consciousness on the part of the author of the fact that the idea of a European Buddhist monk was almost unthinkable in the nineteenth century). Rather, he expects Kim to "go forth as a teacher," with "teacher" holding multiple connotations. Mahbub sees his opening and says: "Certainly he must go forth as a teacher. He is somewhat urgently needed as a scribe by the State, for instance" (285). The Lama, who after all has "acquired merit" by paying for an education to prepare Kim for that sort of service, concurs with Mahbub in these terms: "Let him be a teacher; let him be a scribe—what matter? He will have attained Freedom at the end. The rest is illusion." Again, some critics will be inclined to read this strictly as the Lama's unknowing capitulation, but a reading from a perspective informed by Buddhism must recognize that the Lama's response would be precisely the same even if he knew that Kim was a spy. The point is that it does not matter what Kim does as long as he does not violate the basic moral tenets of Buddhism and strives to act mindfully and compassionately. The ending of the novel is, therefore, indeterminate in a specific way, because it suggests that Kim will continue as the Lama's *chela* even after the Lama's death, that he will continue to play the Great Game, and that he will not feel compelled to construct a dichotomy or to see an irreconcilable contradiction between his Buddhism and his espionage work. This indeterminacy *is* the Middle Way in and of this novel. The Buddha formulated the Middle Way as lying between the indulgence in sensual pleasures that he experienced in his youth as Prince Siddhartha and the extreme asceticism and bodily mortification that he practiced for six years prior to realizing that this too did not lead to ultimate truth. At the most basic level, the Middle Way is the Buddha's prescription for overcoming suffering, a prescription issued as the fourth of the Four Noble Truths and detailed in the Noble Eightfold Path. At the very broad conceptual level represented in *Kim,* the "Middle Way" signifies non-dualistic thinking (and perhaps a partial corollary to the "third term" of deconstructionist theory). As the Lama says to Kim, "There is neither high nor low in the Middle Way" (20). The Middle Way is neither the wheel of the road, with reference to the Great Game, nor the Wheel of Buddhism, nor is it *not* these. It always is the path between any two sides in any dualism, even if one of those is an ostensibly Buddhist side. By definition it cannot be one side of any dichotomy; thus, contrary to the most common Victorian assumption, it is not dichotomous to what the novel calls "the world." Especially for non-monastic lay practitioners such as Kim, the Middle Way does not preclude active engagement in the cultural, social, and political worlds. According to the *Devadaha Sutta,* one engaged in "fruitful" striving and exertion "does not give up the pleasure that accords with *Dhamma,* yet he is not infatuated with that pleasure" (*Middle* 833). In the latter part of the novel, on the road with the Lama, Kim is practicing the Middle Way.[45] By refusing to force Kim to one side of any dichotomy, *Kim* enacts the Middle Way.

Finally, the representation in *Kim* of the Wheel and the Middle Way is notable for several things that it does not include. While partially reproducing the Victorian stereotype about Buddhist passivity, *Kim* does not solidify the active/passive dichotomy but rather throws it into question. The Lama approves actions that "acquire merit" and do not generate karmic debt. The text does chide the Lama throughout for his resistance to his attachment to Kim, as when he says such things as "...not because I was led by any affection towards thee—that is no part of the Way," the purpose of which is to communicate to the reader via dramatic irony how much he does in fact love Kim (121). Kipling cannot help but correct what he understood as a tendency in Buddhism toward unhealthy dispassionateness. But the novel does not underwrite the popular view, legitimated in the contemporary writings of prestigious scholars like Ernest J. Eitel and Monier Monier-Williams, that a strong dichotomy naturally exists and that the Orient suffers from an utter lack of practical activeness and ethical activism.[46] If anything, the novel characterizes the Lama as more active in a masculine way than his Buddhism might predict. However, his final act in the novel—returning from the brink of nirvana in order to guide Kim—rather than demonstrating a breakdown of a presumed Buddhist commitment to non-action, as has been argued by Zohreh Sullivan, is in fact prescribed by Mahayana doctrine and illustrates the *bodhisattva* ideal that in part distinguishes Mahayana from Theravada, as well as further demonstrating that a simple dichotomy of active/passive applies neither to Buddhism nor to *Kim*.[47]

Similarly, while the novel appeals to a clichéd conception of karma as "acquiring merit," it refrains from taking the typical next step within Victorian discourse, which was to cast it as a doctrine of sheer determinism. As Eitel, a reputed expert, wrote in 1884, "For the theory of a man's destiny, being entirely determined by the stock of merits and demerits accumulated in previous forms of existence, constitutes Buddhism a system of fatalism" (Eitel 83). There is a strain of fatalism in *Kim*, but it issues not from the Lama but from the patriarchal inheritance of Kim's "father's prophecy" of the Red Bull, which the Brahmin outside Umballa confirms with his astrological prediction that Kim, who was born in "the House of the Bull" (Taurus?), will find within three days his Bull under "the sign of War," which indeed comes true (16, 40). The Lama in fact countermands this fate, at least in part. For him, the Red Bull is simply the headstrong ego that must be disciplined, the ox pulling the wheel of dependent origination, akin to the "Red Mist of anger," because "All Desire is red—and evil" (42, 93). As a Buddhist he opposes all killing, and thus, though he is willing to pay to have Kim trained at St. Xavier to be a sahib, he directs Kim specifically not to become a soldier, because "these men follow desire and come to emptiness" (93). In the place of determinism, the Lama inserts choice, not a choice that erases preexisting conditions but one that is capable of altering their direction. Many Victorians, like Eitel, held the misconception that karma means an entirely predetermined fate that obviates the efficacy of the will and the exercise of moral choice. In contrast, karma, accurately understood on the basis of the sutras (or *suttas,* in Pali), places more, not less, emphasis on responsibility for one's actions to the future and thus on the importance of moral choice in every moment of existence. Thus Lilly observed in 1905: "It is curious that while so emphatically repudiating the existence of a soul, he [the Buddha] teaches the extremist individualism. He held that every man is wholly responsible for what he is and for what he does, and must work out his own salvation, without reference to any Gods, great or small" (Lilly 205).[48] As Douglas A. Fox has more recently put the same point: "Yet this idea [karma] is no naïve determinism, because the individual still possesses the power to adopt a moral or an immoral response to the circumstances which *karma* presents to him, and that response becomes influential for the next karmic moment. This limited power in us is not quite what is usually meant by 'free will,' for a really 'free' will would be outside the realm of karmic conditioning, a conception that introduces a note of chaos into what is, in fact, a very orderly development" (Fox 116). Whether Kipling understood this or not, he at least chose not to reproduce a predominant stereotype of his age concerning karma. The novel therefore leaves Kim with the indeterminacy of continuous choice, not the unconditioned choice of absolute "free will," nor the surety that a fixed identity guarantees, but with the uncertainty and excitement of becoming.

Western Metaphysics Compared to Buddhist Psychology

Questions of choice and identity constitute the pivotal crisis in *Kim* and in ways that distinguish this novel from most other examples of the Bildungsroman. Kim's identity is exceptionally splintered between multiple racial, national, and religious positions. The novel furthermore resists the closure of a final synthesis, refusing to end with one of the repertoire of events that signals finalization of the search for identity, most often marriage. The crisis begins to come to a head after Kim has been taken from the Lama to St. Xavier's and first feels the pressure to remake himself as a full-fledged sahib. He holds the following conversation with himself: "But I am to pray to Bibi Miriam, and I am a Sahib....No; I am Kim. This is the great world, and I am only Kim. Who is Kim?" (117). This question then haunts the rest of the novel. Kim "considered his own identity, a thing he had never done before, till his head swam" (118). No definitive answer ever emerges, and it is the open-ended nature of Kim's identity crisis that has been the occasion for the critical polarization over who Kim is. While he is well aware of his genetic heritage, and Kipling lends his character a strain of his own racial essentialism, having him play the race card of his "white blood" whenever it is a useful move, Kim never does nor ever can become a genuine sahib, anymore than he can be a genuine Indian. He never is able to believe that he is possessed of a singular, fixed, essential identity.

This is to say that Kim is not able to realize himself as the subject of Western, Christian, middle-class civil society. Kim is no Robinson Crusoe. His sense of self is not predicated upon the twin ideologies of Protestant individual faith and capitalist individual self-interest. These two individualisms, which, as Max Weber tells the familiar story, developed as parallel strands in Early Modern Europe, converged between the seventeenth and eighteenth centuries in the form of the bourgeois civil subject to become the foundation of the individualism upon which rests the dominant ideologies in modern Western society. I oversimplify an immensely complex history in order to make two points. First, Western individualism is historically constructed and unique to the West. The apparent obviousness of this statement nevertheless still does not prevent Westerners, even those most attuned to issues of difference within the postcolonial world, from assuming their model of identity is universal. As the Anthropologist Clifford Geertz points out, " 'The Western conception of the person as a bounded, unique, more or less integrated motivational and cognitive universe; a dynamic center of awareness, emotion, judgement, and action organized into a distinctive whole and set contrastively both against other such wholes and against a social and natural background is, however incorrigible it may seem to us, a rather peculiar idea within the context of the world's cultures' " (Geertz 30–31, qtd. in Collins 2). Secondly, the Western metaphysics of identity is profoundly conflicted, and in ways that will prove significant for understanding Kim's crisis of identity. This conflict emerged historically from the process through which the Judeo-Christian conception of the soul was incorporated into the Renaissance humanist conception of the socially autonomous individual self. According to the Christian model, informed by Platonic idealism, the self is split as a body/soul, the body half of which is merely mechanical and thus corruptible, while the soul, created by and answerable only to God, is essential and eternal, continuous after death as a self-aware consciousness. René Descartes translated this model into the split consciousness of the "*Cogito ergo sum,*" but with a world-shifting difference: the individual now became, in effect, self-creating, ultimately autonomous both from God and from society.[49] Thus liberated, the individual self, as prefigured by Protestant individualized faith and realized in the "self-made man" (gender intended) of emerging modern capitalism, became the defining social atom, the essential unity. The resulting peculiarly Western ideology of identity posits the self as both split and unified, both subject to God and self-determining.

This baseline definition of Western selfhood, which if unavoidably reductionistic remains serviceable, is necessary in order to understand how truly different the Buddhist philosophy of self is. And, this understanding is required in order to consider which model of identity is most efficacious in explaining Kim's identity crisis. Rudyard Kipling, champion of the British Empire, certainly did not transcend the Western paradigm of identity that underwrites invasion and occupation of the other, but *Kim* does. Works of art can exceed their creators, and Kipling succeeded in creating a character in Kim whose identity is at least in part from outside of the Western paradigm. The character of Kim represents "a point of view and a personality almost at the furthest possible remove from Kipling himself"(Kinkead-Weekes 441). Indeed, the model of identity represented by Kim may be more thoroughly understand through a definition of selfhood from outside the Western paradigm, specifically from the perspective of Buddhist psychology. Kipling was aware of the Buddhist doctrines of *anatman* (no-self) and reincarnation, and it is likely that he had encountered the theory of the Five Aggregates (the components of identity within Buddhist psychology, defined below) in his reading in comparative religion. However, I do not rest my argument on author intention or degree of familiarity with Buddhism; rather, the real test is which model of identity—the dominant Western paradigm or the Buddhist paradigm—has greater explanatory power in this case and thus provides the most complete and convincing reading of the character of Kim.

Some two thousand four hundred years before Sigmund Freud, Gautama Buddha formulated a model of human psychology that is as systematic and complex as any since then. Caroline Rhys Davids wrote *Buddhist Psychology*—contemporaneously with Freud—to disprove the Western assumption that "the observation and analysis of the mind began with the Pre-Socratics" (C. Rhys Davids, *Psychology* viii). She observes that Buddhism is based upon a unique psychology of non-essentialized identity, which she summarizes as follows: "And thus, by learning habitually to break up the complex web of conscious experience, the Buddhist sought to gain a dual vantage-point: control over sense and impulse on the one hand, and, on the other, insight into the compound and conditioned nature of that which *seemed* to be a unitary Ego, or subject of conscious experience" (67). Following Rhys Davids by a century, Nolan Jacobson argues that "Buddhism, indeed, is the deepest and most persistent reflection upon the nature of our concrete individualized experience ever to make its appearance anywhere on earth" (Jacobson 134). It is extremely phenomenological and practical, having originated from such questions as "What produces suffering?" and "How can one overcome suffering?" These questions issue directly from the Buddha's first sermon as The Four Noble Truths. It is only to be expected that Victorian progressivism viewed the First Noble Truth, *Dukkha*, which states that human life unavoidably entails suffering, as sheer pessimism, since "pessimism itself was the dark side of the general facade of optimism that the nineteenth century had erected" (Almond 83). But from one common Buddhist perspective, acknowledgment of the existence of suffering is merely a factual statement about reality (Dharma), neither pessimistic nor optimistic, though perhaps hopeful to the extent that an accurate diagnosis is the first step to a successful cure. *Dukkha* also names the first of the Three

Marks of Existence (outlined above), the second of which, *anitya* or impermanence, informs the second Noble Truth's statement about the origins of suffering in desire for permanence. Suffering occurs because people grow attached
to situations that are familiar, secure, or pleasurable, and, since impermanence
is a universal condition, these desirable situations invariably change. The thing
to which human beings cling most tenaciously and least reflexively is their own
self-conceptions, their sense of the permanence of their self, their own centrality to their perception of the world, and their own privileging of self over other.
Thus clinging to identity is in particular an obstacle to enlightenment. The first
of the ten "fetters" or "defilements" is "Belief in personality" (Snelling 66).
The "thirst" that is the cause of all suffering "has as its centre the false idea of
self arising out of ignorance" (Rahula, *What* 30). The "false idea" is that one
possesses a self in the first place and, then, that this self is constant, unified,
self-determining in its freedom from preexisting conditions, unitary and autonomous in its separateness from others, and eternal in the afterlife. In other
words, *the dominant paradigm of personal identity in the West is exemplary
of the misconception of self that Buddhism sees as the primary cause of human
suffering.*[50] As T. W. Rhys Davids summarized the situation, "the peoples of
the West have inherited a belief in spirits inside there bodies, and in other
spirits, good and evil, outside themselves, and to those spirits they attribute an
individuality without change, a being without becoming, a beginning without
end," while Buddhism denies this "great soul-theory" and instead understands
the self as a process of becoming without being (T. Rhys Davids, *History* 80;
Lectures 28).[51] One characteristically epigrammatic expression of *anatman,* the
no-self doctrine attributed to the Buddha, is his statement that all conceptions
of self should be addressed with, "This is not mine, this I am not, this is not
my self" (*Middle* 123). One of the fuller discourses on this doctrine appears in
the *Alagaddūpama Sutta,* one conclusion of which is: "Since a self and what
belongs to a self [as in "mine"] are not apprehended as true and established,
then this standpoint for views, namely, 'The self and the world are the same:
after death I shall be permanent, everlasting, eternal, not subject to change;
I shall endure as long as eternity'—would it not be an utterly and completely
foolish teaching?" (*Middle* 232). While the *bhikkhus* answer "yes," as expected,
the vast majority of Victorians would have answered vehemently in the negative. Westerners in the nineteenth century found the doctrine of *anatman*
utterly unassimilable, and understandably so, since "eternalism," the belief in
the immortal soul as a consciousness that continues intact after death, is the
center-post of Western theology and ontology, while according to Buddhism
that very belief is a form of ignorance that results from clinging to what is by
the nature of reality impermanent.[52]

Victorians horrified by such notions as these concentrated their rebuttals
on what they perceived as logical contradictions within the Buddhist theory

of identity. The least sophisticated of these rebuttals might be called the Cartesian or tautological conundrum, which can be expressed as, "If I don't have a self, then who is thinking this question?" For a Westerner, this reads like a joke, the humor of which derives from the implicit assumption that all listeners must share the Cartesian paradigm of selfhood according to which any fool knows that thinking constitutes identity thus defined. The humor comes from a form of "nonsense," as defined by Susan Stewart, that throws unquestionable ideology into question. Within Buddhist philosophy, however, the action of thinking is a process among others and does not necessitate the positing of a permanent or unified self, nor prove its existence: "In other words, there is no thinker behind the thought. Thought itself is the thinker. If you remove the thought, there is no thinker to be found. Here we cannot fail to notice how this Buddhist view is diametrically opposed to the Cartesian *cogito ergo sum*" (Rahula, *What* 26). Stated by James Giles in terms perhaps more familiar to Western philosophy:

> I must exist, reasoned Descartes, because even when I doubt that I exist there is still an I that is doing the doubting. But Descartes has become led astray by his own language; for there is no need for the 'I' in 'I think' or 'I doubt' to refer to anything. What Descartes was aware of, as both Hume and Buddha would agree, was just thinking, not an I who was doing the thinking. Consequently Descartes might just have as well said (and should have said if his concern was with ultimate rather than conventional truth) 'there is thinking, therefore there are thoughts'. And such a deduction, if one may call it that, does not suffice to prove the existence of an I. (Giles, *No Self* 132)[53]

In Buddhism, "I," in effect, is a verb, a process of becoming inseparable from all other processes in the universe.

Buddhism does not fail to recognize, however, that at a practical level individual human beings exist and that given the limitations of language it is unavoidable and desirable in everyday life to refer to oneself and to others using words such as "I" and "you." In the *Buhudhātuka Sutta*, for example, Ananda asks the Buddha to help him understand the difference between the "skilled" understanding of the *bhikkhu* and common understanding, and this is part of the reply: "He [the *bhikkhu*] understands: 'It is impossible, it cannot happen that a person possessing right view could treat anything as self—there is no such possibility.' And he understands: 'It is possible that an ordinary person might treat something as self—there is such a possibility'" (*Middle* 928). In ignorance or denial of this distinction, some Victorian critics quoted passages in which the Buddha uses personal pronouns and then claimed a logical inconsistency in regards to the concept of *anatman*. Christopher Gowans provides a thoughtful rejoinder to this perennial misunderstanding with his theory of "substance-selves" and "process-selves." The former is recognizable as what I have called the Western paradigm of identity, namely, that the self "is a single, unified substance . . . *ontologically distinct* from other substances" and believed to possess "a set of essential, unchanging properties" (Gowans 69, 70). Without doing justice to the rigor of Gowans's philosophy, the present point is served by one of his summary conclusions: "When the Buddha speaks of the absence of any self he should be understood as meaning (in part) the absence of any substance-self. On the other hand, when he appears to presuppose selves in the doctrines of *kamma* [karma] and rebirth, and more generally seems to refer to selves, he should be understood as referring to the dependent reality of process-selves" (Gowans 72). Gowans also makes the suggestive point that it is typical that "a process-self has false self-awareness" (not unlike "false consciousness" in the Marxist sense) and therefore "mistakenly believes it is aware of itself as a substance-self" (Gowans 71). It is this very error that Buddhist psychology attempts to describe and remedy. That task is made all the more difficult by the fact that the limitations of language perpetuate the misunderstanding. As Giles argues in this regard, the use within Buddhism of the Pali word "*ahamkara*" to mean both "the utterance 'I'" and "I-make" illustrates the linguistic process by which identity reifies itself and suggests "not only that the language of the self leads to the fabrication of a self but also that a fabricated self leads to a misconstrual of the language of the self" (Giles, "No-Self" 197). Thus in a sense that Descartes did not intend, "I think, therefore 'I' think I exist," and this licenses a perpetual, self-interested confusion of language with reality, a condition that some varieties of poststructuralist theory describe as inescapable but out of which Buddhist philosophy describes a path.

Perhaps the singularly most vexing conundrum in Buddhism for those Victorians who cared to think about it was stated in 1890 by Helen Graham McKerlie as "If there is no personal soul, what is to benefit by the good or evil actions committed?" and again by W. S. Lilly in 1905 as "What is it then, which transmigrates?" (McKerlie 213: Lilly 204). If there is no personal soul, no eternal identity, then how does Buddhism describe the entity that is reborn? A number of Victorian Buddhologists enlisted the concept of "character," separated from personality and consciousness, to describe what is passed on as karma from lifetime to lifetime.[54] In the second place, if the person experiencing rebirth is not the same person as he/she was in the previous life, then how is it fair to expect that new person to bear the karmic burden of the previous lifetime(s)? This issue provided some of those predisposed to champion Christianity relative to Buddhism with sufficient grounds for damning the latter utterly. Writing in 1915, Frank Ballard, on the basis of the premises that good and evil must be defined by divine judgment and that "an individual without a self is a contradiction in terms," concluded that "Karma is both non-moral—in assuming a mechanical consequence which makes no distinction between good or ill; and at the same time immoral—in visiting the consequences of one being upon another being who is in no way responsible for them" (Ballard 131–32). His views were representative of the majority, but even some among the more informed and sympathetic minority also baulked at the concept of selfless reincarnation.

Even McKerlie baulked at the idea of *anatman* and so strained in her defense of Buddhism to bend it toward a Transcendentalist or Theosophical belief in a "Supreme Essence" to which one's own essence is rejoined at death (McKerlie 208). The Theosophical Society itself responded to *anatman* not by fleeing back to the Christian body/soul dichotomy but rather by one-upping it with an even more multi-level nesting of selves. Annie Besant, the head of the international Society after Madame Blavatsky's death, wrote such works as *The Self and Its Sheaths* (1895) to theorize identity as layers within layers of "sheaths," the kernel of which was, in effect, the Hindu *Atman*.[55] Even so knowledgeable a scholar as Caroline Rhys Davids began in her later writings (and especially after the death of her husband, who would not have agreed) to "assert condemnation of the dogma called *Anatta* [*anatman*] as being no teaching of the first Buddhists" (C. Rhys Davids, *Wayfarer's* 1137). Her "attempts to turn the Buddha into an advocate of an Upanishadic style self" may have made Buddhism more assimilable to Victorian culture, but they only diminished her scholarly credibility (Santina 149).[56] It would appear, then, that the most difficult nut for Westerners to crack was the notion that one's karmic responsibility continues as a trajectory of becoming, while one's conscious being is impermanent and thus ceases to exist at the end of the present life. After all, who wants to trade in the limited liability of redeemable sins and the promise of eternal bliss for what appears as inescapable responsibility for one's actions and guaranteed erasure of one's cherished self? Henry Alabaster, in his widely read work *The Wheel of the Law* (1871), compared karma and reincarnation to the line in mathematics: it can have infinite length with a thickness of zero and so is all but unimaginable to the average person (Alabaster xl).

The conundrum of "who is reborn?" is partially addressed by returning to the basics of the Buddhist psychology of self. In place of the soul of Christianity or the "enlightened self-interest" of civil society or the ego-based identity of Western psychology, Buddhist psychology theorizes the Five Aggregates or *skandhas* (in Pali, *khandhas*), as follows: (1) the aggregate of matter, including the body as its five material senses: eyes, ears, nose, tongue, and the body/mind complex; (2) the aggregate of sensations or feelings, of which there are three types: pleasant, unpleasant, and neutral; (3) the aggregate of perceptions, the recognition and processing of sensations and feelings; (4) the aggregate of mental formations, a primary basis for karmic formations, which includes intentions, the will or volition, and the idea of self, what in Western psychology might include "emotions," "attachments," "projections," etc.; and, (5) the aggregate of consciousness, a sort of base awareness, perhaps a partial corollary to the "unconscious." Of course, these cursory definitions can be little more evocative than would be a one-sentence definition of the Freudian "preconscious," for instance. For the purposes at the moment, the salient point is that each *skandha* describes forms of energy, rather than matter, in a process of becoming, and, though the five directly interact and influence one another, they never constitute a discrete unified self.[57] Thus the non-existence of an essential self partially obviates the question of who or what is reborn. There is no self to be passed on, though there are the effects of one's intentions and actions in the present life, one's karma, the consequences of which continue to have ramifications even after the present life has ended in a way analogous to the Law of Conservation of Energy: no energy is created or destroyed.

The concept of the *skandhas* is exemplified by a story familiar to Victorian readers like Kipling of the first-century CE Buddhist monk Nagasena, a missionary to the Indo-Greek court of King Milinda (or Menandros, or Menander) in Bactria, now northern Afghanistan.[58] Over the course of many dialogues recorded in the *Malindapahna,* Milinda cross-examined Nagasena on the very same questions that vexed Victorians, such as: how can one accept reincarnation without also affirming the existence of a self who reincarnates? One day the King thought he could trap Nagasena by asking him his name, but the monk answered that his name was merely a convention, a sound or written sign, which did not prove a permanent identity. He continued in Socratic style by asking the King how he traveled to court that day; the King answered that he had come in a chariot. Nagasena asked if the chariot was the pole, the wheels, the body, the yoke, and so on through all the parts, to which the King each time answered "no," and if all of these parts were removed would the chariot exist, to which the King answered "no." Nagasena then asserted that the chariot, as an essential entity distinct from all other entities, does not exist.[59] Nagasena was not naïve or stupid; he understood that a chariot exists at a practical level as a means of conveyance. As Charles C. Everett attempted to explain in 1882, "The lack of a permanent identity of the individual extending from one life to another, or from one moment to another, did not affect the Buddhist's sense of personality" as a practical, everyday conveyance (Everett 432). Though conventionally useful, the chariot is not the ultimate reality; it's interdependent origination is the ultimate reality. Thus Everett goes on to describe how the goal of enlightenment might be understood in relation to the no-self doctrine: "If, however it [identity] is momentarily produced, the result of a process, it may be supposed possible to find a method by which this process may be stopped, and the I may cease to be, simply because it is no longer produced. We may thus understand the great theoretical importance of the lack of any personal identity, even though this did not affect at all the sense of the relationship of the individual to his past and his future" (Everett 432).

In a related dialogue with King Milinda, Nagasena employs the well-known metaphor for karma and reincarnation of a flame that is passed from candle to candle as each previous candle burns out. Is the flame the same flame or a different flame? As Hermann Oldenberg, one of the most eminent Buddhologists in nineteenth-century Europe, translated the answer from the *Milindapahna:* "'Without beginning, without end, the circle completes itself: therefore it is neither the same being nor another being, which presents itself last to the consciousness'" (Oldenberg 262).

Kim's Identity Crisis and the Empire of Criticism

How might the preceding overview of Buddhist psychology inform our understanding of Kim's identity crisis? Specifically, what is the difference between reading the novel with the assumption that it conforms to the dominant Western paradigm of identity and reading the novel with the possibility in mind that it may be drawing upon a Buddhist understanding of selfhood? If one assumes the Western paradigm, as indeed critics on both sides of the critical polarization have, then one will be predisposed to assume that Kim has an essential self, which even if richly ambivalent and conflicted must "mature" in the course of the novel and thus resolve into a singular, permanent, fixed identity possessing clear allegiance either to the Game or the Way. The expectation of this is of course reinforced by the tradition of the Bildungsroman, itself a product of and producer of the Western metaphysics in question. If, however, one removes this assumption and reads through the lens of *anatman,* then it becomes possible to perceive a quite different reading, one invited by the text itself, namely, that Kim's identity—the narrative's construction of his character and representation of his experience of his own selfhood—is not fixed but rather is inherently impermanent. If one reads Kim's character in relation to the Five Aggregates, then it becomes possible to perceive it as just that: an aggregation of elements in a process of becoming, which though functioning as a conventional personality cannot be reduced to a unified identity. This opens possibilities for reading Kim's character that tend to remain unrealized when reading from within the traditional Western paradigm, which typically describes such characters only negatively as "inconsistent" or "not unified." For one thing, Kim's struggle to resolve the potential inconsistencies between his commitments to the Great Game and the Buddhist Way then can be read as an enactment of what Buddhism always has understood as the natural attempt by a "process self" to reify itself into a "substance self," to use Gowans's terms. From this perspective, Kim's identity crisis and failure to realize an essential self indeed demonstrate the Buddhist point: there is no substance self there to be realized. The more one attempts to force it into being the more self-destructive one becomes—hence Kim's illness at the penultimate moment. On the other hand, if one can realize the non-existence of a substance self, then one approaches enlightenment, as I will argue Kim does. Kim's participation in both the Great Game and the Buddhist Way need no longer be viewed as a contradiction or as a one-sided contest or as a split that must eventually be unified by a choice in one direction or the other.

I do not mean to imply that the critic therefore is freed from the responsibility of analyzing this conflict, but rather that the Buddhist reading that I am attempting to imagine opens the possibility for understanding it more fully in the complexity that the text itself offers. As a foundation for this understanding, consider the interpretative options made available if one reads *Kim*'s representation of British imperialism from the perspective of the Western paradigm as opposed to the Buddhist one. Western imperialism is discursively founded on a dualistic logic of us/them, which in turn has as its base a definition of identity according to which the "I" or "we" must create, validate, or protect itself through confrontation with and victory over a chosen other. This is of course among the oldest and most frequently repeated stories in Western literature, and to summarize its traditional features in this way is only to repeat what postcolonial theorists have articulated since Edward Said's *Orientalism* (1978). The imperial self/race/nation therefore must define itself as the carrier of authentic identity, genuine humanness, while "they" must be defined as ontologically other, not quite human like "us," and so expendable if not indeed utterly evil.

Furthermore, the history of Western imperialism is inseparable from the history of Christianity. After all, the rise of the early Church from the declining Roman Empire provided the conditions out of which the image of the compassionate Jesus was transformed into the Medieval conception of Christ as the "Knight" of the "Lord." This discourse justified the launching of the Crusades, provided England with the Arthurian mythology of nationhood that underwrote the Empire, and continues to lend divine sanction to each generation of "Christian soldiers." Monier Monier-Williams triumphantly summed this up in 1889 when he wrote: "According to Christianity:—Fight and overcome the world. According to Buddhism:—Shun the world, and withdraw from it" (Monier-Williams 559). No fan of Buddhism, he meant this as condemnation of a religion that he perceived as posing a threat to Christianity in spite of the clichéd Oriental passivity he attributed to it.

A more even-handed statement might be this: imperialism defines the self by conquering the other; Buddhism dissolves that distinction by conquering the self. Thus the discursive foundation of Western imperialism rests upon its paradigm of the self. According to that model, every European male is a Robinson Crusoe whose natural penchant for adventure evidences providential sanction for carving out a little England in the heart of the colonized other.

Identity thus becomes manifest destiny. If one returns with this in mind to the function of the critic, then one can see that the model of identity a critic reproduces carries embedded in it assumptions about self and other that directly impinge upon his or her reading of imperialism. Therefore, if one reads imperialism in *Kim* either consciously applying or unreflexively assuming the dominant Western model of identity, then one opens oneself to the risk of blindly reproducing the understanding of imperialism that issues from that very model of identity. Criticism of *Kim* of which this is true would be expected to find in the novel a clear dichotomy between the poles of the Great Game and the Buddhist Way based upon a strong self/other dualism that necessitates Kim to choose one way or the other at the end of the novel.

In contrast, the Buddhist reading that I am imagining would challenge the dualisms of body/soul and self/other in the novel. It would do this in the first place because they are based upon illusory distinctions and a misguided understanding of self and, in the second place, because the text itself makes this reading available by restraining the authoritative, monological voice and so refusing to force a resolution of these dichotomies.[60] The natural bridge joining self/other to Great Game/Buddhist Way—the very bridge that "hails" a dualistic reading within Western discourse—must then also come into question.[61] Though no one would question that these dichotomies are represented in the novel, nor that Kipling himself held a highly interested and biased position on these issues, one still can find in the text the basis for a non-dualistic reading of them, which is invited by and implicit in the Buddhist influence on the novel. In order to perceive this reading, however, one must resist the pressure from one side of the critical polarization to discount the aspects of the novel that clearly champion British colonial rule of India and, in the other direction, resist the pressure to read a phrase like "non-dualistic thinking" as merely another cover for soft imperialism that duplicates Kipling's own sympathetic paternalism toward India.[62] Achieving this perspective is vexed, to say the least, since the dualisms cannot but appear natural within the context of Western discourse and since critics on both sides will be attracted by their respective high moral grounds: the critic on one side celebrates the novel's transcendence of the *body* of the Empire; the critic on the other side savors the satisfaction of outing Kim's, and therefore Kipling's, complicity in the evil Empire—his betrayal of the *soul* of the Indian people's right to liberty and self-determination. A Buddhist reading would have to resist both of these poles and work to read the dependently arising interconnectedness between them, resisting in particular the side of the dualism that appears to champion Buddhism itself, since from a Buddhist perspective even a Buddhist dogma is a trapdoor into dualistic thinking.[63]

For example, in a dialogue with Vacchagotta about the nature of the self, the Buddha chooses, as he does in other key instances in the sutras, to remain silent, confirming neither that "I have no self" nor that "I have a self."[64] When later asked by Ananda why he remained silent, the Buddha explains that Vacchagotta was not ready to comprehend *anatman* and so would have clung to the dualism of self/not-self rather than understanding the teaching, which is that both views and all dualisms "are fetters, both arising out of the false idea 'I AM'" (Rahula, *What* 66). The Buddhist paradigm of self is based on both-and-neither logic, while the Western paradigm of identity is based on the dualistic logic of either/or, self/other. The dialogue then takes up the related dualism of "eternalism," as in the eternal soul and heaven, versus "annihilationism." Annihilationism, according to the Buddha, is an inverse form of clinging to self and thus is not synonymous with *anatman*.[65] Most Victorians failed to understand this, and many who opposed Buddhism therefore did so with the claim that it was nothing but a philosophy of nothingness, sheer nihilism. Like Vacchagotta, they were not ready to grasp Buddhist logic.

One corner post of Western logic, the Aristotelian logic of identity ($A = A$) and non-contradiction ($A \neq B$), "asserts itself through confrontation, in accordance with the principle of the excluded middle" (Faure 48). Thus if eternalism ceases to be an option, as in the so-called death of God, then the only alternative is annihilationism, the terror of nihilism with which Buddhism became synonymous for many caught up in the Victorian crisis-of-faith. But Buddhism resides in the excluded middle, the Middle Way. The Buddhist logic exemplified by its use throughout the sutras is the logic of the tetralemma. At the most basic level, tetralemma logic describes these alternatives: "A; B; both A and B; neither A nor B" (Faure 36). Douglas A. Fox summarizes the positions within that logic as follows: "1. Being, or Affirmation 2. Non-being, or Negation 3. Both Being and Non-being...4. Neither Being nor Non-being" (Fox 89).[66] Buddhism uses the tetralemma as a heuristic to exemplify the range of logical traps of dualistic thinking. The point is not to force a choice between the four lemmas but rather to explode the illusion of ultimate separation between them; the point is to step outside of the clinging to identity and confrontation of opposites that is definitive of Western metaphysics. In terms of reading *Kim*, the tetralemma invites non-dualistic readings that permit all of the following positions, simultaneously: 1. Kim serves the Middle Way (or the Great Game); 2. Kim does not serve the Middle Way (or the Great Game); 3. Kim both serves and does not serve the Middle Way (or the Great Game); 4. Kim neither serves nor does not serve the Middle Way (or the Great Game). From the perspective of Aristotelian logic, this is "nonsense," again recalling Susan Stewart. The third lemma in particular—both A and B, both the Middle Way and the Great Game—is impossible, inconceivable, unassimilable. But it is precisely this alternative that *Kim* makes available to readers, if they are able to perceive it.

Few critics of Kipling have been able to perceive it. There are two primary reasons for this. In the first place, Western and Western-educated critics have, understandably and perhaps unavoidably, reproduced the dominant ideology of Western metaphysics, unreflectively projected it onto the novel, and thus have found mirrored in the text their own assumptions about the nature of self and the nature of imperialism, which have in turn predetermined dualistic readings. This applies equally to those on both sides of the critical polarization. In the second place, criticism has neglected the Buddhism in this novel, treating it as either transparent or negligible. As Corinne McCutchan has argued for a different but related purpose, "that Kipling might have modeled his book on Eastern art and narrative is never considered" (McCutchan 132). This culture-specific critical lacuna is in part a result of that same reproduction of Western metaphysics, which invites the assumption that it is not necessary to consider any other model of subjectivity either because no other genuine alternative can exist or none other is worthy of consideration. This is a form of critical imperialism, the invasion and occupation of another's domain of knowledge without adequate attention to the differences that define that domain. The critic most vulnerable to this charge is he or she who attacks Kipling and *Kim* for undeniable imperialist tendencies while in that very action reproducing the attitudes of Western imperialism, first by discounting the Buddhist content of the novel and secondly by projecting a dualistic logic that issues as much or more from the critic's discursive foundation as from this text. This is to enact the very blindness to one's own imperialist assumptions that one is in effect accusing *Kim* of failing to see in itself.[67]

As a range of postcolonial theorists have demonstrated with convincing force and insight, there is more at stake in how one reads and writes about literature than intellectual chit-chat or academic careerism. The obscene violence and injustice of imperial conquest does not occur independently of the discourses used to describe it. By the same token, the discourses used to describe it can perpetuate that violence or create potential alternatives. To reproduce the dualistic thinking of imperialism, even in literary criticism, may be to perpetuate imperial violence. Thus, while I would argue that the non-dualistic reading of *Kim* that I am building is warranted alone on the basis that it provides a more complete reading of this text instead of condescending to it, I also am aware that a Buddhist reading, whether of novels or of social conditions, carries with it the potential for imagining a way out of the dualistic impasse. The effects of that impasse are demonstrated to us in the early twenty first century on nearly a daily basis by the examples of suicide bombers who claim God's imprimatur and state-funded terrorism that calls itself "freedom fighting" or "peace keeping." At that point, no one is right, and, as Mohandas Gandhi, a student of Buddhism, understood, only a view that recognizes the interconnectedness of all parties involved can lead to a peaceful solution. The Buddhist term for this is dependent origination, according to which it is impossible for me to do violence to you without also doing violence to myself, not in some airy-fairy mystical sense but in a very real, ecological sense that can have both immediate and long-term effects.

A more familiar expression for this might be the concept of process thinking (contrasted to product thinking), as reflected in Gowans's theory of "process-selves" and "substance-selves," or as described here by Jacobson: "Buddhism has the distinction of having formulated the first process philosophy. It anticipated by over two thousands years the efforts of a whole series of philosophers of the West—Bergson, Dewey, Darwin, Fechner, James, Hartshorne, Whitehead, and Peirce—to construe the world as events in their novel, emerging forms of togetherness. Reality is in transition; process is more basic than being.... The original discovery of the Buddha is that reality is a social process, no element of which is either separate, independent, or of a self-established nature" (Jacobson 48–49).

If one understands that "reality is a social process" constructed by the entire history of causes shared by all of the participants, then one cannot interpret an act of aggression by any one party as the inexplicable madness of an isolated act of an individual, racial, religious, or national other that must therefore be revenged. Rather, one must interpret such an act as causally connected to one's own karma, meaning to the history of the actions and intentions of the individual, racial, religious, and national self. We must learn to read history non-dualistically. To force a dualistic reading, whether of *Kim* or of current world events, is to perpetuate the violence of imperialism and war. To recognize the non-dualistic reading that *Kim* itself makes available is, in part, to cultivate the seeds of non-dualistic solutions to real-world ethnic and religious conflicts.

These seeds exist in *Kim,* in spite of and contrary to some of Kipling's own prejudices. They exist not only in the Buddhist elements that are obvious to any reader but also as a more subtle influence of Buddhist thought on the writing of the novel, a grounding in Buddhist sensibility that shows through the text. For example, and to give *Kim* the last word, I return in closing to the perennial question about how to read Kim's final struggle to resolve his identity at the ending of the novel. That moment is set up by a liminal passage from the mountains back to the plains. The Lama is injured and lectures Kim on the illusory nature of the body, but then Kim grows ill as the Lama "live[s] upon his strength—eating him," eucharistically (273). The depth of the love between the two is openly acknowledged and, what is more, "Kim really becomes a *chela*...and begins to deserve the comparison with Ananda, living the role he acted so long" (Kinkead-Weekes 438).[68] This liminal passage culminates in the Lama's finding of the River and, likewise, Kim's parallel epiphany, his finding of...of what? That is the question. Kim first finds that "his soul was out of gear with its surroundings—a cog-wheel unconnected with any machinery" (282). In the subsequent paragraph, however, his soul will reaffirm its commitment to the body, the physical, material "world" of "Mother Earth." In one of the most balanced readings of this passage, Mark Kinkead-Weekes affirms the ascendancy neither of the Great Game nor of the Buddhist Way, arguing that, "as the 'gear' imagery makes clear, this is commitment not to the Game, with which we are no longer concerned, but at a far more fundamental level, to the Wheel of earthly and human life, against the [Buddhist] view which holds that all these things are illusion, and one must keep oneself apart from them" (Kinkead-Weekes 439).

But even this reading fails to take account of something else that occurs in the gap during Kim's apparent swing between soul and body. Again comes the failed attempt to assert identity, and again it is followed by the unanswerable question: "I am Kim. I am Kim. And what is Kim?" The "what," not "who," here is critical. In the next moment, which is the moment that most begs interpretation, "He did not want to cry,—had never felt less like crying in his life,—but of a sudden easy, stupid tears trickled down his nose." Something very significant has happened here, an insight, a realization, a change. The idealized Buddhist reader that I have come to imagine sitting behind me as I write this would simply nod and smile at this moment in the novel. "There," he or she would say, "is a moment of enlightenment, a little opening onto ultimate reality." Kim has found the "what" of the "who." He has realized that it does not matter who he is, since there is no separate "Kim" to be, no self. He has dissolved the body/soul dualism, seen through it into non-dualistic thinking. In that moment, Kim and the novel as a whole finally dissolve the dualism of the Great Game and the Buddhist Way.

From a perspective informed by Buddhism, what happens next then makes perfect sense. Buddhism, as the most practical of religions, focuses practitioners on being mindful of each present moment of existence, not being distracted either by second thoughts about the past or cravings for the future. Present reality is the only door to ultimate reality. Thus when Kim sees that the elements of the material world around him "were all real and true—solidly planted upon the feet—perfectly comprehensible—clay of his clay, neither more nor less," he is not disclaiming Buddhist spirituality, as some critics have argued, but rather recognizing the givenness of each material moment and expressing a gratitude that is consistent with a Buddhist understanding of being fully in the present. It is in this same way that King Malinda's chariot, in its immediate physicality, is also an image of impermanence. When Kim then looks out, the first thing he sees is "an empty bullock-cart on a little knoll half a mile away, with a young banian tree—a look-out, as it were" (282–83). A Buddhist reading would recognize an allusion here to the Malinda story, as well as to the opening verse of the *Dhammapada,* which was available to Kipling in multiple translations: "Mind is the forerunner of all actions. / All deeds are led by mind, created by mind. / If one speaks or acts with a corrupt mind, suffering follows, / As the wheel follows the hoof of an ox pulling a cart"(*Dhammapada* 1). Kim's cart is empty and still. Thus in the next sentence Kim appreciates the "good clean dust—no new herbage that, living, is half-way to death already, but the hopeful dust that holds the seed of all life" (283). This is more than familiar mother-earth imagery; the phrase "half-way to death already" and, more than that, the tone of the text at this point carry with them a Buddhism-inflected awareness of the cycle of samsara. Rather than replicating the expected celebration of rebirth, this passage recognizes the suffering that rebirth brings and a desire to step out of that cycle. Finally, and most tellingly, this enigmatic paragraph draws toward closing with this sentence: "The many-rooted tree above him, and even the dead man-handled wood beside, knew what he sought, as he himself did not know." Not merely the organic world, but the very dust, the atoms of cellulose in the firewood, all particles of the universe, are aligned with Kim's new search, one set to commence as the novel closes, one utterly different from the search with which he started the novel. In most Western discourse, this level of integration and connectedness typically is dismissed either as a form of irrational mysticism or as a Romantic fantasia, a fit of pathetic fallacy.[69] From a Buddhist perspective, Kim simply is experiencing the Dharma as expressed in the doctrine of dependent origination—the Lama's Wheel—which is to experience the reality of what is.

Concfusion:
The Afterfife of Nirvana

Damn heaven. Damn holiness. Damn Nirvana. Damn *it all*.
—D. H. LAWRENCE (1921)

There is no thing that is Nirvana; there is only the word "Nirvana."
—HERMANN HESSE, *Siddhartha* (1922)

And, nothing himself, beholds
Nothing that is not there and the nothing that is.
—WALLACE STEVENS, "The Snow Man" (1923)

The Victorian Nirvana Debate

Nirvana is everywhere, and in more senses than one. I recently heard the word used three times within a day: once by a radio DJ to indicate the state induced by a particular group's music (not the group Nirvana), once in an advertisement for a health-and-beauty spa, and once by my teenage daughter parodying valley-girl-speak on the telephone. How many nirvanas must there be in the air of twenty-first-century Western culture? All of this "nirvana talk" started with the Victorians, and thus began in terms of a more earnest set of debates (Whitlark 17). Indeed, one of the most sustained and contentious debates about Buddhism throughout the nineteenth century concerned the meaning of nirvana. Thus Charles C. Everett, writing in 1882, observed that "the most important controversies" surrounding Buddhism concerned "the great questions in regard to Nirvana" (Everett 421).[1] Nirvana is an especially telling boundary marker at the interface between Buddhism and the Victorians because of the specific ways they did and, more tellingly, did not assimilate it. The nineteenth-century nirvana debate was split between two predominant interpretations, for which I will use the terms attributed in the sutras to the Buddha more than twenty-four hundred years before the Victorians: annihilationism versus eternalism.[2] Each of these two strands directly influenced a cultural movement that emerged in the nineteenth century. The afterlife of nirvana—a phrase I use with verbal irony and historical sincerity—consists of the ramifications of the Victorian nirvana debate as they have continued to reverberate throughout Western cultures over the past hundred years.

If one picks up the threads of the nirvana debate at the middle of the nineteenth century, one encounters warnings about the vexed nature of the subject, such as this one drawn from the Reverend Spence Hardy's *Manual of Buddhism* (1853), a semischolarly guide for missionaries, as summarized here by a subsequent commentator:

> If anyone hopes to arrive at a full understanding of this subject [nirvana], let them be well forewarned of its impossibility. Mr. Hardy states that there are forty-four Buddhist sects, each holding different views of the future [after death]. 1–16. Those who hold a future state of conscious existence.... 17–24. Those who hold a future state of unconscious existence. 25–32. Those who hold a state between consciousness and unconsciousness. 33–39. Those who hold that death, at once, or ultimately, is annihilation. 40–44. Those who reason on the mode in which perfect happiness is to be obtained [in the current life]. (Hauser 301)

Westerners always have struggled against their own desire to mystify nirvana even beyond the considerable difficulty of it as a concept. Mystification is invited by the fact that the Buddha offered no singular definitive description of it; he strategically refused to do so.[3] The sutras record many passing references to nirvana, such as the following from the *Makhādeva Sutta,* though the sum of these references does not constitute a unified definition: "But there is this kind of good practice that has been instituted by me now, which leads to complete disenchantment, to dispassion, to cessation, to peace, to direct knowledge, to enlightenment, to Nibbāna" (nirvana in Pali) (*Middle* 696–97).[4] The sutras also show the Buddha on a number of occasions being pestered by disciples for an unambiguous definition, and in each instance he turned the question back upon the questioner in a way that makes his message plain: obsessing on metaphysical issues like those concerning the creation and the afterlife is a distraction from genuine practice. Indeed, the Victorian debate about Buddhism as a "cult of nothingness" represents a fascination with that subject that likely exceeded the level of concern with it among practicing Buddhists. It is no surprise that the debate tells us less about Buddhists than about the

Victorians, that "in the many pages from the nineteenth century that dealt with Buddhism, Asia, and the cult of nothingness, the only thing at issue was really...European identity" (Droit 161). In the nineteenth century, European identity became tied, peripherally but significantly, to understanding nirvana.

Resisting the attraction of an utterly mystified nirvana, which found ample expression in Romantic poems and then Romance novels, the scholarly contributors to the nirvana debate struggled to demystify it. They labored to determine exactly what, according to this doctrine, happens after death. From early in the century, the debate became polarized. In 1827, Henry Thomas Colebrooke, in the first European monograph based on Sanskrit texts, characterized nirvana either as annihilation *or* as eternally happy but apathetic bliss, and "the question has remained for Western Europeans substantially as Colebrooke framed it" (Welbon 27).[5] The earliest Orientalist scholars established this polarity but left the question open. However, the most influential Buddhologist of the first half of the century, Eugène Burnouf (along with his student Jules Barthélemy Saint-Hilaire) then weighed in heavily on the side of nirvana as annihilation. Citing the etymology of the word as "extinguish" or "extinction," their dark assessment provided the authority behind what became the predominant philosophical and popular understanding of nirvana in the West. Their definition came to serve the argument made by some defenders of Christianity that Buddhism was "a system of cold Atheism and barren Nihilism," a religion based absurdly on the worship of nothingness (Eitel 97). F. Max Müller, another eminent student of Burnouf's, imported the annihilationist thesis into British comparative religion. In *Chips from a German Workshop* (1867), he wrote: "True wisdom consists in perceiving the nothingness of all things, and in a desire to become nothing, to be blown out, to enter into Nirvāna. Emancipation is obtained by total extinction, not by absorption in Brahman, or by a recovery of the soul's true estate" (Müller, *Chips* 227–28). He actively argued against the other predominant understanding of nirvana as eternalism, rebutting those who strove to assimilate Buddhism to Christian culture by remaking nirvana as a version of heaven or, if not quite that, as "absorption" into the divine essence, ostensibly of God but similarly of the Transcendentalist's Over-soul or the spiritualist's Spirit World. At the same time, he defended Buddhism against his own conclusion by developing an argument, which then was replicated as a common claim by Orientalist scholars, for the greater purity or authenticity of the textualized Buddhism of the West over the "degraded" indigenous Buddhism of actual practitioners in Tibet or Ceylon (now Sri Lanka).[6]

The generation of comparative religion scholars that followed Müller, armed with a much larger body of translated scripture, developed a more sophisticated understanding of nirvana. Hermann Oldenberg countered the annihilationists in his influential *Buddha: His Life, His Doctrine, His Order*

(1882), arguing as follows: "Entry into nothingness for nothingness' sake is not at all the object of aspiration which has been set before the Buddhist. The goal to which he pressed was...solely deliverance from the sorrowful world of origination and decease" (Oldenberg 265). He likewise refused the eternalist position, turning to language worthy of Wallace Stevens: "The longing of the heart that craves the eternal has not nothing, and yet the thought has not a something, which it might firmly grasp" (Oldenberg 284). T. W. Rhys Davids subsequently argued for a third understanding of nirvana, which, unlike either annihilationism or eternalism, has clear support in the sutras, namely that the "victory to be gained by the destruction of ignorance is, in Gotama's view, a victory which can be gained and enjoyed in this life, and in this life only" as a result of "the Buddhist system of self-culture and self-control" (Rhys Davids, *History* 108).[7] He attempted to follow the Buddha's example by removing nirvana from metaphysical debate, theorizing it as an ethical state achievable in the current life, as exemplified by the Theravada Arahant and, differently, by the Mahayana Bodhisattva ideal.[8] Oldenberg and Rhys Davids had arrived at the more accurate understanding that neither the annihilationist nor the eternalist position is supported by Buddhist scripture, but it was too late. Both philosophical and popular conceptions of nirvana already have been determined by this polarization.

A primary reason for the polarized response was that the nirvana debate had been drawn into and made to serve one of the most pervasive and disruptive cultural schisms in modern European discourse, that between spiritualism and materialism, most broadly conceived. Having analyzed this schism at length in a previous chapter, I only will point out that Victorians aligned Buddhism with the latter. Undeniably atheistic and perceived to be compatible with Darwin's science, Buddhism appeared to heap Eastern materialism upon Western materialism. The Victorians thus were predisposed to read nirvana as further grounds for their deepest fear: the extinction of the human soul. These concerns partly determined the annihilationist side of the nirvana debate.

This predominant interpretation was cemented by Arthur Schopenhauer, whose philosophy came to be known in the popular conception of many Victorians—however little they may have known about his work or about Eastern philosophy—as "European Buddhism" (Shanks 127). Schopenhauer claimed, near the end of his career, that "'Buddha, Eckhart, and I, we basically teach the same things'" (Schopenhauer, qtd. in Dumoulin 468). Though he published the first edition of his major work, *Die Welt als Wille und Vorstellung* (*The World as Will and Representation*) (1818), before sufficient translations were available in Europe for him to have known very much about Buddhism, he revised and expanded it in 1844 with a "supplement" of six hundred pages that makes frequent reference to Buddhism. By that time, he had read, among other contemporary texts on Buddhism, Burnouf's *L'introduction à L'historie du Buddhisme Indien (Legends of Indian Buddhism)* (1844), a primary source of the annihilationist interpretation of nirvana, which Friedrich Nietzsche and Richard Wagner would also read somewhat later.[9] Though Schopenhauer's well-known philosophical pessimism originated from his own life and thought, he became convinced that his "critical thinking had led him to the same conclusions that centuries before Indian and Buddhist teachers had intuited through allegory and mystical insight" (Batchelor 257). Thus his work is littered with passages such as the following:

> As a rule, the death of every good person is peaceful and gentle; but to die willingly, to die gladly, to die cheerfully, is the prerogative of the resigned, of him who gives up and denies the will-to-live. For he alone wishes to die *actually* and not merely *apparently,* and consequently needs and desires no continuance of his person. He willingly gives up the existence that we know; what comes to him instead of it is in our eyes *nothing,* because our existence in reference to that one is *nothing.* The Buddhist faith calls that existence *Nirvāṇa,* that is to say, extinction. (Schopenhauer 2:508)

My concern is neither primarily with the content of Schopenhauer's philosophy nor with the extent of its debt to Buddhism, but rather with the historical effects of its influence. First, after Schopenhauer, the popular conception that had been predisposed by the materialism-spiritualism divide became fixed on the idea that Buddhism was a "cult of nothingness" and nirvana sheer nihilism.[10] The establishment of this concept required that "an atheistic, nihilistic, and provocative [European] philosopher claim the Buddha as an ancestor, if not as a precursor" (Droit 92). Second, the union of Schopenhauer's pessimism with the annihilationist interpretation of nirvana was an essential basis for the philosophical nihilism that would be articulated by Nietzsche, a disciple of Schopenhauer's, and spread into other forms of Western philosophical nihilism through Nietzsche's far-reaching influence. For the moment I will leave this point with Roger-Pol Droit's summary observation, which his book demonstrates in relation to Schopenhauer, Hegel, Nietzsche, and Heidegger: "This is a primary fact: when they spoke of the Buddha, nineteenth-century philosophers were dealing with nothing: regularly, explicitly. 'Buddhism' and 'worshipping nothingness' became synonymous, or equivalent, in their writings" (Droit 20).

During the same decades of the mid nineteenth century, those on the other side of the nirvana debate built arguments in defense of the eternalist interpretation of it. Some found it inconceivable that nirvana would not be similar to familiar conceptions of immortality in heaven. When John Stuart Mill observed sensationally that, given the large number of Buddhists on the planet, perhaps "not annihilation but immortality may be the burdensome idea," the Reverend M. L. Gordon responded with an argument that became common as a defense of the eternalist interpretation of nirvana: "'This longing after immortality', is one of the ineradicable instincts of the human soul" (Mill, qtd. in Gordon 527; Gordon 535). Human nature innately longs for immortality; therefore, the Buddha surely formulated nirvana as such and, regardless of what latter-day Buddhist metaphysicians may have theorized regarding it, the masses of practicing Buddhists surely bank on some sort of blissful eternity, just like "us."[11]

Other defenders of eternalist nirvana used terms effectively shared with Spiritualism's conception of the Spirit World. Though it is unlikely that Buddhist nirvana could have influenced the emergence of Spiritualism in upstate New York in the 1840s, it is likely that the Hindu concept of Atman—which is part of the definition of nirvana as its foil—did exert influence via New England Transcendentalism. Like Schopenhauer and many other intellectuals, Ralph Waldo Emerson had read translations of the *Avaita Vedānta* and *Bhagavad Gītā,* and he filtered into his formulation of the Over-Soul the Atman, understood as the universal Self or Godhead from which individual selves issue and back to which they return at death.[12] Spiritualists constructed the Spirit World along similar lines as an eternal spiritual limbo considered ecologically part of the natural universe but parallel to and in contact with the material world. Some saw parallels between this eternalism and eternalist nirvana.

But the amalgamation of various blissful eternities with eternalist nirvana only became explicit with the formation of late-Victorian hybrid religions, and most clearly in Theosophy. Madame Blavatsky—who started as a spiritualist medium, who was adamantly both anti-materialist and anti-Christian, who received Buddhist vows in Ceylon in 1880, and who claimed that "prehistoric Buddhism" was the Ur-religion from which Theosophy had issued—integrated the eternalist interpretation of nirvana into Theosophy. In *Isis Unveiled* (1877) she made ample use of the scholarship of comparative religion, frequently referencing Max Müller's work, but took exception with his annihilationist reading of nirvana, arguing instead for an Atman-like "absorption into the great universal soul" (Blavatsky, *Isis* 2:116). The appropriation and mixing of elements of Spiritualism and Buddhism is obvious in such statements by Blavatsky as this: "Nirvana means the certitude of personal immortality in *Spirit,* not in *Soul,*" soul being a limited Christian concept and only an atom of the larger Spirit (Blavatsky, *Isis* 2:320). "Spirit" had become the Soul (in upper case), sans Christianity and inflected by Buddhism. In sum, a range of non-Christian eternalist concepts circulating in Victorian discourse amalgamated (or perhaps blurred) into an Oversoul-Spirit-World-eternalist-nirvana matrix and were disseminated throughout that culture, filling any gaps created by doubt about the promise of heaven and the threat of hell.

As I have indicated and will argue further, the annihilationist side of the Victorian nirvana debate was an important source for modern Western philosophical and popular nihilism, and the eternalist side, in conjunction with a broad range of other sources, provided part of the foundation from which the New Age movement of the mid-twentieth century emerged. Both forks of the debate contributed to far-reaching cultural events and discourses.

What Nirvana Is Not

What is nirvana? The Buddha of the sutras suggests that the answer may come only with enlightenment and that the way to enlightenment may consist, in part, of not fixating upon such metaphysical questions but rather focusing upon spiritual practice and ethical living. The sutras provide a somewhat clearer understanding of what nirvana is *not*, and that understanding reveals the contradictions inherent in the polarized Victorian response to nirvana. Nirvana is neither eternalism nor annihilationism. At the very least, both the eternalist and the annihilationist stances represent misinterpretations. Neither side could have been supported by a careful reading of Buddhist scriptures available to late-Victorian commentators on the subject. In canonical Buddhism, there is no final heaven in which enlightened souls might reside in eternal bliss, and, what is more, there are no eternal souls to reside anywhere.[13] There is no eternalism in any Judeo-Christian sense.

The annihilationist position is more difficult to dispel, because in very particular ways, and in part due to the limitations of language (to which the Buddha made reference), nirvana cannot but appear in the sutras as a kind of nothingness, though, critically, *not* the nothingness of Western nihilism. Christopher W. Gowans, in *Philosophy of the Buddha*, summarizes one stage of his painstaking analysis of scriptural representations of nirvana in this way: "It is evident from these passages... that *Nibbāna* is something real. Therefore, the contention that *Nibbāna* is simply nothingness, and hence that in this respect Buddhism is ultimately nihilistic, is mistaken. The terminology of absence—*Nibbāna* as not earth, not born, and so on—is intended to show that *Nibbāna* is completely beyond the conditioned world, not that it is nothing at all" (Gowans 150). And Droit opens his history of nirvana in Western discourse unequivocally: "Let us say it straight out: Buddhism is not a religion that worships nothingness" (Droit 1). Yet, neither the availability of a more accurate understanding of nirvana in translated scripture nor the fact that the most eminent Buddhologists of the latter part of the century disclaimed eternalism and annihilationism prevented philosophical adaptation and popular conception from casting nirvana primarily as nihilism.

Why? I have offered one partial answer in terms of the pervasive cultural schism between spiritualism and materialism. Buddhism was atheistic, which meant non-eternalistic, and so materialistic; therefore, it must be nihilistic, because if one does not believe in God, heaven, and the soul, then the only alternative must be belief in utter nothingness. This dualistic way of thinking excludes consideration of a great many other alternatives. It is those that are of most significance in understanding why Westerners cast nirvana primarily as nihilism. Limiting nirvana to nihilism contained its potential to undermine the dualistic thinking of soul/body, faith/works, active/passive, and self/other, upon which the dominant power structures within Western, Judeo-Christian, capitalist societies depended. Channeling nirvana into nihilism directly served specific cultural urgencies and social interests that existed in the West long before Buddhism entered.

Thus the Victorian polarized response to nirvana, far from being a naïve or nonchalant misinterpretation, was a deeply invested denial. Nirvana was, as Müller once labeled it, a form of madness, but the madness was not, as he intended, among Buddhists; it was the madness of Westerners confronted with concepts and doctrines so utterly incommensurable with their most cherished ideals that they could not be assimilated. Foremost among those ideals, the one most critically threatened, was that of individualism. I use the term "individualism" as an unavoidable general catchall for a range of individualisms: the spiritual individualism of the essential soul and the eternal individualism of heaven; the doctrinal individualism of Protestantism; the humanistic individualism of Enlightenment self-interest; the self-governing individualism of civil society; the self-divided but self-creating individualism of Cartesian philosophy; the self-regulating individualism of Adam Smith's capitalist state; the self-made man[14] of the Victorian self-help movement, which came to flourish especially within American ideology; the existentially isolated individualism of modernism; and the "self-maximizing individual of competitive 'hedonic' consumer society" (Gagnier 321). These individualisms, if distinct, are causally related within Western history. The nexus they form is part of the fascia of the body of Western culture and society, the elastic and connective web of tissue encasing the muscles, bones, and organs of postindustrial modernity. It was nothing less than this, then, that nirvana discursively threatened.

The threat derived in part from the fact that nirvana, similarly to karma and reincarnation, assumes anatman, the "no self" doctrine. Having treated anatman in previous chapters, I will summarize here only a few points relevant to its relation to nirvana. According to the Four Noble Truths and the Three Marks of Existence (listed in appendix 2), if one clings to the illusion of the ontologically distinct self—akin but not identical to "Being" as defined throughout Western philosophy—then one suffers and causes others to suffer, thus producing the karmic debt that will be reborn as another suffering self. If, to the contrary, one can realize that the naturally attractive idea of self—"me, my, mine"—is an illusion, then there is no self to be reborn. This *is* nirvana, whether in the present lifetime or thereafter.

Such an understanding of nirvana also recognizes the nonseparateness—the non-individualism, in effect—of one's self from the social and natural worlds. One translation of the Buddhist term for this is "dependent origination," the connectedness of one's self with all other selves in an unavoidably mutually interdependent process of becoming. This selfless ecological unity is the ultimate nature of reality, which is one translation of "Dharma." According to the Dharma, the "world that exists is the result of the *non*-existence of any independent self-established substance," and this emptiness of self-existence *"is what the world is full of, a fullness sometimes called the Void"* (Jacobson 52).[15] This "void"—also referred to as sunyata by some Mahayana Buddhists—is the emptiness of self that *is* nirvana. For Buddhists, such emptiness is the highest form of fullness or wholeness. Full-emptiness is liberation, a liberation that comes only *from* self, not *for* a self. Understood in this way, nirvana is a neatly auto-deconstructing paradox: there is no self not to be reborn. Nirvana is the not-nothingness.

Guy Richard Welbon's *The Buddhist Nirvāna and its Western Interpreters* aptly captures this paradox and the Western blindness to it. Welbon analyzes Müller's failure to understand nirvana, noting that he had dismissed the "absolute annihilation of all modes of existence for an individual personality as a myth ... grounded in the ambiguity of the very word *nirvāṇa*" (Welbon 126). Welbon argues that there was "a measure of irony in this of which Müller was presumably never aware," because while for him, "nirvana-as-annihilation is a myth: a name without a reality that corresponds to it," for the Buddhist " 'self' is a myth: a name, a convention to which no thing corresponds" (Welbon 126). Thus from "remarkably similar attitudes regarding the weaknesses of language, Müller and the Buddhists reinforce two radically different conclusions," and "one cannot suppose that this paradox would surprise a Buddhist" (Welbon 126). Müller, like virtually all Victorians, could not assimilate the idea that the self as essential Being is a myth. To do so would require transcending the very conception of selfhood that is the basis of the Judeo-Christian soul, the focus of Western ontology since before the Greeks, and the core of the central ideology of individualism. For the Victorians—for most Westerners then and now—no-self can mean only utter annihilation, because if there is no individual autonomous self, there can be no world. The doctrines of nirvana and anatman threw into question the ideal of the individual, autonomous self, the self-made man, the traditionally masculine loner of the battlefield and the boardroom, upon which depended the primary institutions of market and empire that constituted the social order of modern Western society.[16] "Buddhist nihilism," as Müller labeled nirvana in the title of his widely read 1872 work, hardly could have posed more of a threat.

Nirvana is not individualism; it is not progress, not survival of the fittest, not market competition, not a promise of endless consumption, not imperial conquest, and not a rationale for the superiority of any religion, nation, or race. It must be nothing. But, as such, it served a number of vital functions first within Victorian culture and then in the modernism of the early twentieth century. In the first place, it exemplified the not, the most extreme example of the not us. At a deeper level, and more significantly, it also was the doppelgänger, the necessary twin, to the indigenous Western nihilism that observers including Thomas Carlyle, Matthew Arnold, and Thomas Henry Huxley noted as the complementary dark side of Victorian progressivism. If progress was the promise of endlessly fulfilled expectation, horizonless advancement, and the superiority of Western commerce and Christian reward, then Western nihilism was the shadowing doubt behind that promise and the active response to it. As progress was the promise of future fullness or completeness, Western nihilism was an expression of the accompanying emptiness or hollowness, as T. S. Eliot named it in his 1925 poem "The Hollow Men." Anthony Giddens summarizes the basis of modernism in familiar terms as the "break with providential views of history, the dissolution of foundationalism, together with the emergence of counterfactual future-oriented thought and the 'emptying out' of progress by continuous change" (Giddens 51). Some part of this "'emptying out' of progress" was linked to and expressed through the Victorian nirvana debate. Modern hollowness was the "I want" that never can be filled, however much wealth, technological advancement, and military superiority one amasses. But to admit that hollowness would be to open our individualism and our progress to doubt. Thus Buddhist nihilism came to fulfill an essential function, which was as a straw figure for nascent Western nihilism, a target other than our own, drawing the fire that otherwise might land too near to home. Buddhist nihilism was a necessary not.

To briefly consider one Victorian example, as early as 1875 an article by an unidentified author in the *Dublin Review* titled "Modern Society and the Sacred Heart" lamented the rise of "the Modern Idea." The author identifies the Modern Idea with the writings of men such as Auguste Comte, John Stuart Mill, Friedrich Strauss, and Charles Darwin. He writes, "What we know is that for the infinite, these men mistook the finite, and brought the spiritual down to the level of matter" (*Dublin* 15). The Modern Idea is materialistic, scientific, and atheistic, just like Buddhism; it is "paralleled with the overpowering imaginations of those Oriental mystics to whom we owe Buddhism" (*Dublin* 13). However, one should not confuse the Modern Idea with the "affinities with Buddhism, however startling and undeniable they may be" (*Dublin* 17). Though "Buddhism agrees with the moderns in considering this visible universe as the only reality, and as neither beginning nor ending ever;

[and though] it is further consistent with Hegel in alternately declaring that nothing is," the critical difference is this: "The Eastern withdraws himself into contemplation, subdues every movement of passion, and longs vehemently for one only consummation, that the semblance of life, which he has, may be taken from him, and pain may cease with annihilation. The Western cannot learn this hopeless asceticism; he believes that the cycle of things is an evolution from mere potentiality to some large perfection; he *worships progress,* and looks out for the means of advancing society and mankind in its onward path" (*Dublin* 17–18, my emphasis). The author proceeds to juxtapose his solution, Christian eternalism combined with Victorian progressivism, to the stereotyped annihilationism of nirvana. But, to his credit, he was insightful enough both to see the parallels between Buddhist nihilism and Victorian progressive materialism and *not* to confuse the two. He recognized the Western hollowness at the heart of progressive individualism, which, as his thesis now appears prescient in predicting, was on its way to becoming the basis for the disillusionment of the "modern existential condition." He understood, as many Victorians did not, the difference between the emptiness of nirvana and the hollowness that was uniquely a product of the history of European scientific, industrial, and economic progress.

The majority of Victorians who considered the question at all instead found it much more serviceable simply to scapegoat Buddhist nihilism in the act of denying the possibility of Western nihilism. In this sense, the appearance of Buddhism at midcentury proved to be convenient, as was the Darwinian revolution with which it was associated: the middle classes could blame these for the decline of spirituality rather than recognizing the engine of their own progress as the cause. That engine was the league formed between corporate and state interests in industrialism, finance or the stock market, and colonial expansionism. I will refer to this league hereafter as "corporate-state capitalism." It posed a much greater threat to spirituality than scientific materialism ever had; however, it was too powerful to become a target of sustained criticism (despite the best efforts of late-century socialists). Capital had become the ultimate materialism and, by the end of the century, held sway over the old materialism, which had consisted of unbelief and science. Even so, Darwin and the atheists, including the Buddhist atheists, would go on serving as the necessary scapegoats. Only in this way could the modern partnership of Protestant Christianity and capitalism be kept from appearing as the giving away of the bride of spiritualism to the bridegroom of materialism. For the Victorians, to recognize capital as the new materialistic Satan might mean to give up on progress and to face their own hollowness. Better to bank on progress, redirect criticism to, among other things, Buddhist nihilism, and leave facing that hollowness to modernism.

Nietzsche and the Self-Made Man

Friedrich Nietzsche, though he died in 1900, was perhaps the first modernist, and his diagnosis as well as prescription for the modern hollowness, the dark side of progress, was nihilism, which, though European, owes its formation in part to the Victorian nirvana debate. His writings replicated the polarization of that debate and fashioned, in response to perceived Buddhist nihilism, a new, uniquely Western and positive nihilism. The "Preface" to the collection of Nietzsche's notes published posthumously in 1901 as *The Will to Power* (1883–1888) states Nietzsche's purpose clearly: "I describe what is coming, what can no longer come differently: *the advent of nihilism*" (*Will*, Preface §2.3).[17] I will not pretend to give a full consideration here of the meaning of nihilism in Nietzsche's writing, a task I leave to professional philosophers; rather, I make two summary observations that the philosophers whom I have consulted support.[18] First, nihilism for Nietzsche, as later for Martin Heidegger, meant the logical culmination and endpoint of Western metaphysics and Christianity, the point of the failure of those systems to support their own truth claims. "What does nihilism mean? *That the highest values devaluate themselves.* The aim is lacking; 'why'? finds no answer" (Nietzsche, *Will* §2.9). As Richard Beardsworth neatly puts it, this "marks the historical coming-to-be of metaphysics *as* the (historical) event of nihilism" (Beardsworth 37). Second, nihilism in Nietzsche describes the nature of one's response to that historical fact. He drew a strong distinction between two types of response to the demise of traditional metaphysical and Christian ideals: "*passive* nihilism" and "*active* nihilism" (*Will* §22.17).

Nietzsche's passive nihilism has been summarized variously as the symptom of the loss of traditional values and ideals, a form of denial of that loss, and the resulting degeneration of will in the face of the suffering of life, now unjustified by either deity or reason. It was for Nietzsche the modern malaise, "the sort of modernity that made us ill,—we sickened on lazy peace, cowardly compromise, the whole virtuous dirtiness of the modern Yea and Nay" (an allusion to Thomas Carlyle) (*Antichrist* 1:42). Nietzsche's diagnosis set the stage for existentialist philosophy and the modern existential condition. From the writing of *Thus Spoke Zarathustra* (1883) forward, Nietzsche relied on two primary examples of passive nihilism. First and foremost is the faith and morality of Christianity, of which his entire oeuvre is a critique, culminating in the last book he wrote, *The Antichrist* (published in 1895). "Nothing is more unhealthy, amid all our unhealthy modernism, than Christian pity," which is "the technic of nihilism" that hollows out the "the self-preservative instincts of sound life" and replaces them with "the *rottenness* of man" (*Antichrist* 7:48-9, 5:45, 6:46). Christianity is "the greatest of all imaginable corruptions" (62:180).

Nietzsche's second recurrent example of passive nihilism is "the weary nihilism that no longer attacks; its most famous form, Buddhism; a passive nihilism, a sign of weakness" (*Will* §23.18). Nietzsche took his understanding of Buddhism in part from Schopenhauer and then from reading major works of comparative religion by Burnouf, Oldenberg, and others.[19] He, like many at the time, aligned Schopenhauerian pessimism with Buddhism, as here: "The will to nothingness has the upper hand over the will to life—and the overall aim is, in Christian, Buddhist, Schopenhauerian terms: 'better *not* to be than to be'" (*Will* §685.364). And yet, for Nietzsche Buddhism was far superior to Christianity: "Buddhism is a hundred times as realistic as Christianity....[I]t is the product of long centuries of philosophical speculation. The concept, 'god,' was already disposed of before it appeared. Buddhism is the only genuinely *positive* religion to be encountered in history" (*Antichrist* 20:69). Beyond a begrudging sympathy toward Buddhism, Nietzsche's philosophy also resonates in limited ways with elements of its doctrine. His emphasis on confronting suffering bears comparison to Buddhism's Four Noble Truths, the first of which states, in short, that to live unavoidably entails suffering. While according to Nietzsche Christian morality is merely a form of denial of this truth, his "authentic Dionysian wisdom," characterized by "the joyful acceptance of whatever amount of suffering may prove to be the price of a life lived to the full," is not incompatible with the Buddhist emphasis on non-avoidance and mindful transformation of suffering (Shanks 130). But, even if Nietzsche was partially sympathetic to Buddhism, he could not excuse its emphasis on compassion, surrender, and self-abnegation. Buddhism remained an enervating threat to the will to power; the "probability of a new Buddhism" arising in Europe was "the greatest danger" (*Will* §69.45 n. 39). Thus Nietzsche largely followed the predominant Victorian interpretation of Buddhism and its nirvana by casting them as ultimately passive and therefore antithetical to the series of related tenets he championed throughout his writings.

One of those tenets was active nihilism, the curative counterpart to the "values of *décadence,* of [passive] *nihilism,* [that] now prevail under the holiest names" (*Antichrist* 6:46). In short, active nihilism smashes the old idols, casts aside the twin crutches of supernatural God and metaphysical Truth. It is honest and brave enough to "behold the world in its painful, amoral immanence," and, by force of will, acts in that world despite these conditions (Conway 125). Active nihilism is "a sign of increased power of the spirit," "a sign of the strength" of the will to power (*Will* §22.17).[20] It affirms life as a moment-to-moment process of individual self-creation, of becoming, despite the suffering that is an unavoidable condition of living. Active nihilism can be related back to Nietzsche's earliest major work, *The Birth of Tragedy* (1872), in which he similarly used Buddhism as a foil, writing that "tragedy should save us from Buddhism" (Nietzsche, qtd. in Droit 20).

Indeed, Nietzsche's signature concepts—active nihilism, the will to power, the *Übermensch,* the Dionysian, eternal recurrence—are developed and linked across multiple works.[21] The Übermensch (the overman or superman), which is traceable forward from *Thus Spoke Zarathustra,* might be thought of at once as the hero of Nietzschean tragedy, the embodiment of the will to power, the most active of active nihilists, and the human as his own suffering god—truly the ultimate self-made, as opposed to divinely made, man. Nietzsche himself "insisted on the close relationship of both concepts" of the *Übermensch* and eternal recurrence, though the two might appear to be antithetical (Kaufmann 276). Eternal recurrence effectively subjects the *Übermensch* to a natural universe beyond his powers, one characterized by an infinitely "'eternal recurrence of the same' and the affirmation of the self-destroying and self-creating cycles of energy" (Beardsworth 39). Nietzsche dramatized eternal recurrence in *The Gay Science* (1882) in this way: "This life, as you now live it and have lived it, you will have to live once more and innumerable times more; and there will be nothing new in it, but every pain and every joy and every thought and sigh...and even this moment and I myself" (Nietzsche, qtd. in Kaufmann 280). Eternal recurrence might be understood as the greatest test of the active nihilist's will to power, because it requires him to embrace his life, including all of its suffering, with such fierceness that he would choose to relive it infinitely: "This new man affirms not God but himself, Man, creative will, who, in the face of decay and decline, wills his own existence again and again for all eternity" (Ratschow 64).

Thus, though active nihilism is defined in opposition to Buddhism, the eternal recurrence that is the condition that necessitates active nihilism bears some striking similarities to certain Buddhist doctrines, in particular karma and reincarnation. Walter Kaufmann concludes that in formulating eternal recurrence Nietzsche "returns to the visions of Pythagoras, Heraclitus, the Stoics, and the Buddhists" (Kaufmann 286). Bret W. Davis observes that previous scholars have "suggested that Nietzsche may have first conceived of the idea of 'die ewige Wiederkehr des Gleichen' [the eternal recurrence of the same] when reading Hermann Oldenberg's *Buddha* in 1881" (Davis 93). Eternal recurrence, as a cosmology in which the "Übermensch would also realize how inextricably his own being was involved in the totality of the cosmos," is unmistakably similar to the doctrine of dependent origination (Kaufmann 276). But the strongest parallel is between eternal recurrence and the doctrines of karma and reincarnation. The similarity is at the least analogical and may represent direct influence (mediated through Nietzsche's sources), though here is not the place to substantiate the latter possibility.

But then there also is a crucial difference between eternal recurrence and reincarnation. While reincarnation is rebirth without continuous identity, eternal recurrence implies continuous identity without rebirth—eternal *non-reincarnation* (which I have discussed in terms of the figure of the demi-immortal Asian, an example of the Western failure to assimilate reincarnation).

This same logic, however, draws a comparison between eternal recurrence and nirvana, only to the extent that both provide an escape from the eternal cycle of rebirth. This same observation led Guy Richard Welbon to argue that "there is no basic conflict between Nietzsche and Buddhism on several important issues" and that "Nietzsche was more profoundly Buddhist—and not in some hybrid European transformation, but rather in an authentic sense—than either Schopenhauer or Wagner" (Welbon 189, 187–88). However, again there is a definitive opposition between eternal recurrence and nirvana that I already have analyzed in relationship to anatman: in nirvana there is no self; in eternal recurrence there is, in one limited sense, nothing but self, replayed for eternity.

This apparent emphasis on the individual autonomous self is the link between the Nietzschean *Übermensch* and the middle-class Victorian ideology of the self-made man. The two might seem to be diametrically opposed, and certainly they were, though perhaps as one stands opposite one's reflection in a mirror. Certainly the Victorian middle class only could have viewed both Buddhist nihilism and Nietzsche's "death of God" as the grossest assaults upon its values and ideals. Certainly Nietzsche's nihilism was a brutal critique of those very values and ideals. But each championed forms of individualism that were complementary by their very opposition.

The most well-known statement of the doctrine of self-help was Samuel Smiles's *Self Help* (London, 1859). It famously opens in this way: "'Heaven helps those who help themselves' is a well-tried maxim, embodying in a small compass the results of vast human experience. The spirit of self-help is the root of all genuine growth in the individual; and, exhibited in the lives of many, it constitutes the true source of national vigour and strength" (Smiles 2). Here, and throughout the book, God is linked first and foremost to individualism—the heritage of Protestantism—that is linked to "national vigour" and that in turn requires both individual and market freedom from state regulation. God and free-market economics are united through individualism, as Max Weber and many others have argued. The body of *Self Help* consists of a series of exemplary biographical summaries of the rise of "great, but especially of good men" (Smiles 4). Smiles emphasizes that "great men of science, literature, and art—apostles of great thoughts and lords of the great heart—have belonged to no exclusive class nor rank in life," that some "of God's greatest apostles have come from 'the ranks'": "Take, for instance, the remarkable fact, that from the barber's shop came Jeremy Taylor, the most poetical of divines; Sir Richard Arkwright, the inventor of the spinning-jenny and founder of the cotton manufacture; Lord Tenterden, one of the most distinguished of Lord Chief Justices; and Turner, the greatest among landscape painters" (Smiles 4). The story to which Smiles gave definitive articulation was well on its way to becoming one of the founding myths of corporate-state capitalism and, in particular, of "the American dream"—the ideology of the self-made man, the man who, entirely by his own will, "pulls himself up by the bootstraps" through individual hard work justified by individualized faith in himself.

If Nietzsche scorned such idealisms, he theorized a form of individual self-creation through active nihilism that was not merely the opposite of Victorian self-help. Each was the necessary evil twin to the other in opposition to which each defined itself. Maintaining the foundational dualisms of soul/body and faith/works, Smiles's model is self-made only in terms of character, society, and economics, leaving the spiritual realm to God, who happens to underwrite the former. Nietzsche exploded the distinction between material and spiritual self-creation. His active nihilist is self-made ontologically, ultimately, even at the cost of being isolated within society and left alone in a universe of alienation. Thus, while the individualism of the active nihilist exceeds that of the self-made man, the two still share a core doctrine of self-creation independent from outside determination, whether social or divine. Understood in this way, nihilistic individualism might suddenly appear as Protestant individualism freed from the religious and ethical strictures of Protestantism. After all, the distinction between the Nietzschean *Übermensch* and the modern head-of-state who claims justification from God or Allah for his (or her) military invasion of another nation for its natural resources might come down only to this: the former refuses to justify self-maximization with ideals, while the latter forces ideals to justify self-maximization. If by opposite means, both negate the same ideals. As Buddhist nihilism served as a dark twin to Western progressivism, so Nietzsche's active nihilism might be considered as the necessary other to the progressive individualism of the Victorian self-help movement.[22]

In the nineteenth century, "nihilism emerges as a psychologically necessary affect of the decline of belief in God," and thus from "1870 to 1940, the experience of nothingness swept through the educated class of Europe" (Pearson and Morgan ix; Novak 2). Nihilism signaled the beginning of the end of Christian and Enlightenment idealisms, according to which humanity occupied the privileged center of creation, its science would explain and control the natural universe, and its science of "political economy" would solve all social ills. Nietzsche's nihilism is widely credited as the source of the modern "nihilistic problematic," the early twentieth century's "culture of nihilism," as it subsequently was expressed and refined in the diverse philosophical and creative writings of the modernists (Goudsblom 43; Beardsworth 38). The existentialist nihilism of modernism appears through the lens of hindsight as a predictable outcome of the conditions of the nineteenth century that this chapter and this book have detailed. Nietzsche was prophetic to the extent that modernist culture did in part fulfill the promise—or threat—of his nihilism.

The Hollowness of the Modern Existential Condition

The Victorian nirvana debate, in particular its annihilationist side, was one source for the emergence of Western nihilism, and that nihilism, still bearing the marks of Buddhism, contributed significantly to the shaping of European modernism. Bits of Buddhism are scattered throughout modernist literature, most notably in works by Joseph Conrad, T. S. Eliot, Hermann Hesse, and, to a lesser degree, W. B. Yeats, D. H. Lawrence, and E. M. Forster, among others. But these clear signs of Buddhism are much less significant for tracing the residual impact of the Victorian nirvana debate than is the ubiquity within modernism of a range of forms and expressions of nihilism, whether directly by that name or as "the void," "nothingness, "emptiness," or "hollowness." These echo throughout the literature of the period like the "terrifying echo" of the "ou-boum" in the Marabar "Buddhist Cave" (or Jain cave) in Forster's *A Passage to India* (1924) (Forster 162, 164, 247). They are the signature of modernism's sensibility of human alienation within a universe divested of spiritual order, its focus on the fragmentation of subjectivity, and its recourse to an existentialist individualism that persisted in appearing hollow at the core. That hollowness is one of the defining subjects of modernist literature: the failure of its own media—language, and art more generally—to represent adequately the realities of modern life. Modernism "is distinguished by this incessant thematization of its fundamental disengagement from strict designation—by its ongoing encounter with the presence of its own nothingness" (Kevin Bell 9). Some modernist authors directly thematized nihilism, notably Samuel Becket, Albert Camus, Franz Kafka, and Thomas Mann.[23] For others nihilism was more understated and ambivalent; the British writers who belong to this category are most relevant to my purposes.

Well-known examples include the wounded and hollowed-out (non-)heroes of literary modernism, such figures as Conrad's protagonist in *Lord Jim* (1900)—perhaps all of Conrad's protagonists—and Eliot's Fisher King in "The Waste Land" (1922). Conrad and Eliot, like many other intellectuals and artists, had read Buddhist and Hindu scripture, works of comparative religion on Buddhism, Nietzsche's philosophy, and, certainly in the case of Conrad, the manifestos of Russian and European nihilistic anarchism.[24] Thus Conrad's Mr. Kurtz in *Heart of Darkness* (1901), having ventured too close to the empty center of non-meaning and having recognized the failure of human progress to remedy it, was hollowed out by that contact and that knowledge: "It echoed loudly within him because he was hollow at the core" (Conrad, *Heart* 74). Eliot then gave his poem "The Hollow Men" an epigraph from Conrad's novel that he had intended to use for "The Waste Land": "Mistah Kurtz—he dead." Eliot's work uses the "notion of spiritual hollowness" "to bring a devastating castigation of his own age" (Gillis 464). That critique, which became one of the features of modernism, was refined in the writings of Lawrence, who loathed "the ultimate nothingness of the egoist," the modern self-centered producers and consumers of mass culture, as "vitally below par, hollow" (Lawrence, *Phoenix* 193, 210).

Both Conrad and Lawrence became more explicit in their later writings about the correlation between this modern hollowness and nihilism. Conrad's *The Secret Agent* (1907), for example, characterizes the double agent, Adolf Verloc, as a "moral nihilist," which generally describes the characters and society portrayed in the novel (Conrad, *Secret* 12). Karl Yundt, the "Perfect Anarchist," who moves among the citizens of London with an explosive device in his pocket, clearly is modeled on one interpretation of the Nietzschean *Übermensch*. As an active nihilist, he disdains "the weak," "the multitude" of unreflecting consumers who passively buy whatever is fed to them as ideology and as products (Conrad, *Secret* 303). Echoing Kurtz's infamous exclamation, "Exterminate all the brutes!" Yundt concludes: "Exterminate, exterminate! That is the only way of progress" (Conrad, *Heart* 66; Conrad, *Secret* 303). These and characters from many other works of the period provided the template for the modern existential condition. Their hollowness was inherited in part from Buddhist nihilism, reconstructed as Western nihilism, and that nihilism was at once the opposite and the necessary complement of progress.

Progress, civilization—"humanizing, improving, instructing"—this was "the idea" that Kurtz and perhaps even Marlow had intended to bring to the savages of the dark places of the earth (Conrad, *Heart* 21, 48). Kurtz, followed by Marlow, comes to understand that he and all humans are savage, that progress and civilization are a thin veneer and a rationalization for "aggravated murder on a great scale," the "conquest of the earth, which mostly means the taking it away from those who have a different complexion or slightly flatter noses than ourselves" (*Heart* 21). Kurtz "represents the (dis)illusion of progress, the false rational principle which both Eliot and Conrad believe lies at the 'heart of darkness' of the modern world" (McConnell 147). He is transformed by this realization into another representation of Conrad's understanding of the *Übermensch;* he possesses the will to power to hold a tribe in thrall, to post human heads on stakes, to explode all ideals. Kurtz represents Nietzsche's active nihilism at its apocalyptic extreme as "a part of that virulent materialism that runs through Occidental civilisation in perpetual, absolute opposition, destroying idols, pronouncing the end of ideals, renouncing states, smashing superstitions" in the process of building a "new world order" (Albert 8). Kurtz began the novel as the most representative modern, Western, Christian, free-trading, self-made man; Conrad's point is that he ends the novel under the same designation. No mere madman, Kurtz is the fullest realization at its extreme of the West's corporate-state capitalism and imperialism and continues to the end to be the "representative Western self" (Brown 17).

Marlow, to the contrary, struggles to retain the ideals of humanitarianism and compassion for weakness that the *Übermensch* explodes, ideals that Nietzsche associated with Christianity and with Buddhism. It makes perfect sense, then, that the novel should open with Marlow sitting on the deck of the Nellie in the position recognized as that of "the teaching Buddha"—"lifting one arm from the elbow, the palm of the hand outwards, so that, with his legs folded before him, he had the pose of a Buddha preaching in European clothes and without a lotus-flower" (Caracciolo, "Typologies" 69; Conrad, *Heart* 21). The last sentence of the novel replicates this image: "Marlow ceased, and sat apart, distinct and silent, in the pose of a meditating Buddha" (*Heart* 95). Yet Marlow does not transcend Kurtz. Rather, he retains his ideals only through a lie; his lie to Kurtz's Intended about Kurtz's last words (not her name but rather "The horror! The horror!") is but a token of the big lie. He, along with the reader, is left in the utterly untenable position of maintaining negated ideals. This is the modern existential condition: trapped midway between the brutal truth of the *Übermensch* about self-interest and acquisitiveness and the lie that modernist literature detects behind the promise of progress and civilization. Marlow is weak, passive before the lie. He is the Buddha of Nietzsche's passive nihilism and the eternalist side of the Victorian nirvana debate. Kurtz is the active nihilist, self-made, though his self-fashioning comes up against greater forces that destroy him. While he has freed himself of "restraint," he cannot celebrate his will to power or exercise it with impunity. His destruction is mandated less by his personal excesses than by the absolute necessity of the lie to the political and economic interest behind the "Western civilization" he thought he represented. Therefore he is hollowed out by the lie, as Marlow nearly is. Kurtz and Marlow embody the two sides of the Victorian nirvana debate, annihilationism and eternalism, reconstructed as Nietzsche's active nihilism and passive nihilism. The modern existential condition is that of being suspended between the two.

I am far from the first either to note the bits of Buddhism in modernist culture or to note the prevalence of nihilistic themes and figures in its literature. I may however be the first to observe that all of these bits and themes and figures are linked by a common debt to the Victorian nirvana debate and its shaping of Western nihilism. To the extent that nihilism and the modern existential condition are defining components of modernism, that massive cultural paradigm shift was itself shaped at least in small part by the Victorian nirvana debate.

The author who above all others placed nihilism at the center of modern existentialist thought, Jean-Paul Sartre, must have received the influenced of the Victorian nirvana debate, if only second hand from two of his philosophical fathers, Nietzsche and Heidegger. Sartre's formulation in *Being and Nothingness* (1943) of the freedom of the modern existential individual draws significantly upon the nirvana-inflected nihilisms of his predecessors. Two of Sartre's central concepts, "nothingness" and "nihilation," bear comparison not only to Nietzsche's active nihilism but to Victorian nirvana. Hazel D. Barnes, in her translator's introduction to *Being and Nothingness,* implies this by comparing and contrasting Sartre's nothingness to Buddhism, noting that "the goal of Buddhism is part of Sartre's human data," his source material (Barnes xxviii). I believe that Sartre's existentialism is, among many other things, an expression of the Western failure to assimilate the Buddhist understanding of nirvana, a topic for further research.

Nihilism and Individualism in D. H. Lawrence

The writings of D. H. Lawrence, both fiction and nonfiction, were a subtle conduit both for Nietzsche's thought and for the polarized Victorian construction of nirvana into modernism. Early in his career, Lawrence studied works of comparative religion on Buddhism and the writings of Nietzsche.[25] His close readings in adolescence of Edwin Arnold's *The Light of Asia;* his long-term friendship with Earl and Achsha Brewster, who lived in Ceylon and practiced Buddhism; his collected correspondence with them, which frequently mentions Buddhism; his decision in 1922 to travel to Ceylon, in part to investigate Buddhism at close range; his subsequent disillusionment about and then, later, partial re-embracing of Buddhist nirvana, as I will show; and the appearance of Buddhist elements throughout his mature fiction all evidence an engagement with Buddhism that spanned the entirety of his writing life.

Lawrence's fascination with Buddhism was paralleled by his fascination with Nietzsche (as well as with Freud). Indeed, as Gerald Doherty's *Oriental Lawrence* argues, his reading in Nietzsche and Schopenhauer, which was encouraged by his German wife Frieda, was one of the primary sources of his knowledge about and attitude toward Buddhism, along with his reading of theosophical texts and his cultural exposure to "the common lore about Buddhism, which English colonists propagated through semi-popular books and tracts" (Doherty, *Oriental* 16). As Kingsley Widmer concludes, "in essential ways, Lawrence had thus become an English Nietzsche" (Widmer 121). I contend that at the same time he became an English Buddhist. I do not mean that he professed or practiced Buddhism; he certainly did not. I mean that his primary failure to assimilate Buddhism, his limited but still significant incorporation of certain Buddhist concepts, and his fierce struggle to rationalize nirvana and anatman to his conceptions of individualism and desire are representative of the modernist relationship to Buddhism.

Lawrence had at first an essentially Nietzschean response to nirvana, which is to say that he replicated Nietzsche's categories of active nihilism and passive nihilism. His relationship to Nietzsche and to Buddhism, and his prediction of philosophical existentialism, is captured in miniature in a passage from his letter to Earl Brewster from Sicily written 2 January 1922: "More and more I feel that meditation and the inner life are not my aim, but some sort of action and strenuousness and pain and frustration and struggling through. All the things you don't believe in, I do. And the goal is not that men should become serene as Buddha or as gods, but that the unfleshed gods should become men in battle. God made man is the goal" (Lawrence, qtd. in Brewster 43). Here, clearly, is Nietzsche's opposition between the active nihilist's embracing of suffering—the *Übermensch*'s audacity and courage to become his own God— and the passive nihilist's withdrawal from life into contemplation and nirvana. Earlier that year, Lawrence had written from Baden-Baden: "I *believe* in wrath and gnashing of teeth and crunching of coward's bones. I believe in fear and in pain and in oh, such a lot of sorrow. As for your white nirvana, my boy: paint stripes on it, and see how it looks. I'll bet it has a tiger's hungry sides and buzzing, disagreeable tail" (Lawrence, qtd. in Brewster 22–23). "White Nirvana" points to passive nihilism (and, perhaps, to race), and Lawrence testifies here, as in many other places, to active nihilism, which it seems appropriate to label "black Nirvana."

Here I will range lightly through Lawrence's works in order to suggest overarching patterns. Nietzschean and Buddhist nihilisms are scattered throughout Lawrence's writings, from *Sons and Lovers* (1913) to *Lady Chatterley's Lover* (1928). In the last pages of *Sons and Lovers,* for example, Paul Morel, devoid of religious faith, following the death of his mother and the failure of his attempts to establish a lasting partnership with any other woman, approaches "annihilation": "The real agony was that he had nowhere to go, nothing to do, nothing to say, and *was* nothing himself" (Lawrence, *Sons* 456). At the penultimate moment, he is at risk of sliding into passive nihilism—literally suicide—but does not: "On every side the immense dark silence seemed pressing him, so tiny a speck, into extinction, and yet, almost nothing, he could not be extinct" (*Sons* 464). Like Conrad's Marlow after experiencing the heart of darkness, he was "at the core a nothingness, and yet not nothing"—this is the modern existential condition (*Sons* 464). There the novel ends. Lawrence, in this early work, had not yet formulated an alternative between passive and active nihilism. For Lawrence, passive or white nihilism is the denial of life and is, therefore, opposed to his famous vitalism, his belief in the divine origin and generative effect of genuine human desire.

By the time of *Women in Love* (1920), Lawrence had become more explicit about the basis of passive nihilism in Buddhist nirvana and about the existence of multiple, competing nihilisms. I would not be the first to read the contest of will between Gerald Crich and Gudrun Brangwen as a contest between active nihilism and passive nihilism. Gudrun is the most apparent Buddha-figure in the novel: "Gudrun had waded out to a gravelly shoal, and was seated like a Buddhist" (Lawrence, *Women* 122). She is the figure of passive nihilism, the will to resist desire, to withhold love, to deny life (literally by closing her womb), which the novel will show has the power to annihilate Gerald's masculine, active nihilism. In Lawrence's world, the passive nihilist is either female or a man who has become feminized by the enervating forces that Lawrence saw as the threat posed by modern industrial society to the essentially sexual root of human vitality. One example is Michaelis in *Lady Chatterley's Lover,* who, Lady Chatterley observes, exhibits "that momentary but revealed immobility, an immobility, a timelessness which the Buddha aims at... something old, old and acquiescent in the race! Aeons of acquiescence in a race destiny, instead of our individual resistance" (Lawrence, *Lady* 23). Lawrence's potential racism aside, here the opposite to passive nihilism is a form of individualism that is theorized throughout his fiction, to which I will return. For him, as for Nietzsche, passive nihilism is antithetical to individualism and progress.

This is not to say that Lawrence therefore follows Nietzsche in championing active nihilism—far from it. Gerald, and later Sir Clifford Chatterley, are typical representatives of active nihilism, which Lawrence associates throughout his work with the modern captains of industry and commerce—the self-made man, as discussed above.[26] They are as much a threat to authentic selfhood and vital sexuality as is passive nihilism. They intellectualize, mechanize, standardize, and dehumanize, negating all individualism but their own; they exercise mastery over Nature and natural desire, as Gerald does over his horse. They are the *Übermenschen,* those with the will to power, as Gerald puts it to himself: "The will of man was the determining factor. Man was the arch-god of earth. His mind was obedient to serve his will. Man's will was the absolute, the only absolute" (Lawrence, *Women* 241). The lover in *Lady Chatterley's Lover,* Mellors, puts it this way, with reference both to the British middle class and to Clifford Chatterley's industry: "Tin people! It's all a steady sort of bolshevism—just killing off the human thing, and worshipping the mechanical thing. Money, money, money! All the modern lot get their real kick out of killing the old human feeling out of man, making mincemeat of the old Adam and the old Eve" (Lawrence, *Lady* 217). This "money-deadness" is the sign of the nothingness of value at the heart of modern society, just as ivory was in Conrad's *Heart of Darkness,* and Lawrence seats Gerald in the same boat with Kurtz, separated by degree but not by kind (*Lady* 261). This, then, is Lawrence's response to Nietzsche's active nihilism, with Gerald as the "the bad-Nietzschean" (Widmer 119). Lawrence enacts Nietzsche's greatest fear in portraying the demise of active nihilism at the hands of passive nihilism: It is Gudrun, not Gerald, who in the end, in the snowy wasteland, feels "*übermenschlich*—more than human"; she has conquered and usurped masculine, active power (Lawrence, *Women* 410). White nirvana, the "icy will of annihilation that killed Gerald Crich," is strengthened by contact with a depersonalized nothingness that ultimately overcomes the active, black nirvana of any egoistic will to power (Widmer 120).

Individualism and self are concepts that recur throughout Lawrence's work and therefore throughout the criticism of it.[27] The subject is vexed by the fact that Lawrence had a very complex and strongly divided understanding of these concepts. He recognized, for instance, the powerful individual will of the *Übermensch* but saw its limitations. He opens the essay, "Blessed Are the Powerful," with the provocatively Nietzschean claim that "The reign of love is passing, and the reign of power is coming again," but he then clarifies his difference from the popular understanding of Nietzsche: "We have a confused idea, that *will* and power are somehow identical. We think we can have a will-to-power. A will-to-power seems to work out as bullying. And bullying is something despicable and detestable" (Lawrence, *Reflections* 145). Lawrence wanted individual will without power over others, self without destroying the other, desire without lust or greed. He likewise recognized the individualism of Protestant faith, which he compares to the nirvana he assumed Buddhists seek: "'Alone I did it!' is the proud assertion of the gentleman who attains Nirvana. And 'Alone I did it!' says the Christian whose soul is saved. They are the religions of overweening individualism, resulting, of course, in our disastrous modern egoism of the individual" (Lawrence, *Phoenix* 188). "Egoism" is a term that Lawrence often couples with "mechanical," "greed," and "money." He also recognized the "cult of Individualism, Liberty, Freedom, and so forth," which he understood was the essential ideology of modern consumer-based civil society. Within that construction of "individual freedom," "consumer choice" takes the place of any potentially more authentic liberty from hegemonic social control. Lawrence writes: "Individualism! read the advertisements!...'No man could lack individuality in Poppem's pyjamas.' Poor devil! If he was left to his own skin, where would he be!" (Lawrence, *Reflections* 189). This is the individualism both of "bolshevism" and of corporate-state capitalism: the proscribed, mass individualism of the revolutionary mob as of majority public opinion, "the innumerable myrmidons of nothingness" (Lawrence, *Phoenix* 685). Lawrence was a great champion of individualism, but none of the above kinds. What, then, was his individualism?

The characters of Rupert Birkin in *Women in Love*, Rowdon Lilly in *Aaron's Rod* (1922), and Mellors in *Chatterley* give clues to Lawrence's ideas of individualism (and both Lilly and Mellors are figured in terms of the Buddha). Here is an excerpt from Lilly's first major lecture on individualism to Aaron:

> I think a man may come into possession of his own soul at last—as the Buddhists teach—but without ceasing to love, or even to hate....I'm learning to possess my soul in patience and in peace, and I know it. And it isn't a negative

Nirvana either. And if Tanny [his wife] possesses her own soul in patience and peace as well—and if in this we understand each other at last—then there we are, together and apart at the same time, and free of each other, and eternally inseparable. I have my Nirvana—and I have it all to myself. But more than that. It coincides with her Nirvana. (Lawrence, *Aaron* 104)

When Aaron fails to understand, Lilly clarifies: "You learn to be quite alone, and possess your own soul in isolation—and at the same time, to be perfectly *with* someone else—that's all I ask" (*Aaron* 105). This is individualism *as* unity with the other, nirvana *as* desire fulfilled, not denied. This is what Rupert, Lilly, and Mellors prescribe and struggle to enact with their romantic partners. This is what Lilly, sounding very much like the Lawrence of "Blessed Are the Powerful," summarizes at the closing of *Aaron's Rod:* "We've exhausted our love-urge, for the moment....We've got to accept the power motive, accept it in deep responsibility, do you understand me? It is a great life motive....It is a vast dark source of life and strength in us now, waiting either to issue into true action, or to burst into cataclysm....The will-to-power—but not in Nietzsche's sense. Not intellectual power. Not mental power. Not conscious will-power. Not even wisdom. But dark, living, fructifying power" (297). Lawrence had rewritten Nietzsche.

This "dark, living, fructifying power" is experienced first and foremost by humans through the un-self-conscious and so total sexual union of two entirely independent individuals. While Paul Morel and Miriam Leivers fail to achieve this in *Sons and Lovers,* fifteen years later in *Lady Chatterley's Lover* Mellors and Connie do. They surrender their selves without losing their souls, their essential, separate individuality. As Rupert describes that state to Ursula in *Women in Love,* "It is death to one self—but it is the coming into being of another" (and Ursula sometimes misinterprets as passive nihilism what Rupert is asking for, as when she says, "What you want me to serve, is nothing, mere nothing") (Lawrence, *Women* 42, 260).[28] This is the basis for Lawrence's reinterpreted nirvana. It issues from his distinction between "false desire"—egoistic and intellectualized and, therefore, possessive, greedy, and mechanical—and "true desire," which was for Lawrence the most sacred realization of what it means to be human, the physical *and* spiritual root of life—his vitalism (Lawrence, *Phoenix* 715; Doherty, *Oriental* 6). This conception of desire is in certain ways compatible with the treatment of it within Buddhism as signaled by the Four Noble Truths. His false desire is effectively the Buddhist *trishna,* "thirst," or *tanha,* "grasping" or "craving," ultimately for psychic completeness, which is the primary cause of human suffering. For Lawrence, true desire comes with the overthrowing of false desire and the willingness to embrace the suffering that true desire may exact. If achieved, true desire has the potential to generate a "nirvanic state" to the extent that it supersedes common orgasmic release or postcoital bliss but rather entails simultaneous surrender and realization of the self as both in and apart from the other (Doherty, *Oriental* 6). Mellors and Connie achieve this state, which the text signals in this way: "And softly, he laid his hand on her mound of Venus, on the soft brown maidenhair, and himself sat still and naked on the bed, his face motionless in physical abstraction, almost like the face of Buddha" (Lawrence, *Lady* 212). No longer solely a negative figure of passive nihilism, the Buddha now has a potentially positive character.

Lawrence eventually arrived at resolution, if partial, to the primary problems that occupy his writing: individualism without egoism and union with the other without denial of the self. Solving those problems required transcending the foundational Western dualistic thinking of body/soul, physical/spiritual, and self/other. In this, Lawrence was closest to Buddhism. And so his theory of individualism bears comparison to the Buddhist concept of anatman. According to that doctrine, the self, rather than being an essential, unified, and eternally fixed "substance-self," as it is in Western soul-theory and in the dominant paradigms of individualism, is a process of becoming, a "process-self," as Christopher Gowans defines it in *Philosophy of the Buddha*. As Lawrence writes in this regard: "*Be Thyself!* is the grand cry of individualism. But individualism makes the mistake of considering an individual as a fixed entity....Even the Nirvanists consider man as a fixed entity, a changeless ego, which is capable of nothing, ultimately, but remerging into the infinite" (Lawrence, *Reflections* 185). This passage demonstrates that Lawrence, having followed Nietzsche and subscribed to his culture's stereotype about Buddhist passivity, failed on the surface to comprehend nirvana and that he absorbed enough Buddhism, and was on his own grounds opposed enough to the least-Buddhist aspects of Western individualism, that he arrived at conclusions about the self compatible with Buddhism.[29] Lawrence struggled to embrace the freedom and responsibility of creating one's self as a continuous process of becoming. In the context of his relentless critique of his society, Lawrence's individualism frequently exhibits the isolation and alienation of the existentialist individual. At the same time, however, the defining moment for the Lawrencian individual is not in utter isolation but rather through dissolution of egoism in relationship to the other. Transcending the little isolated ego is, for Lawrence, the means to realizing individualism, which is a reasonably Buddhist perspective.

Thus Lawrence's (in)famous "obsession with sex" was not limited to concern with sexual union between two isolated but equally strong and open individuals. It was about the individual realizing his or her unity with the vital source of all life, which was for Lawrence the basis of spiritual connectedness. The Buddhist term for this is dependent origination, the unavoidable interdependence of one's self with all others and with the natural universe. Lawrence worked to reduce this understanding to what he intended as its most primal form—vitalism—but his writings demonstrate a more sophisticated conception. In the essay "A Propos of 'Lady Chatterley's Lover,'" for example, he critiques the "world of our little consciousness, which we know in our pettifogging *apartness*" and which is "how we know the world when we know it apart from ourselves, in the mean separateness of everything" (Lawrence, *Lady* 331). He continues: "But the two great ways of knowing, for man, are knowing in terms of apartness, which is mental, rational, scientific, and knowing in terms of togetherness, which is religious and poetic. The Christian religion lost, in Protestantism finally [and Protestant individualism], the togetherness with the universe, the togetherness of the body, the sex, the emotions, the passions, with the earth and sun and stars" (*Lady* 331). Despite Lawrence's tendency to follow Nietzsche in pairing Buddhism with Christianity as similarly life-denying idealisms, here he effectively points to the Buddhist doctrine of dependent origination.

Lawrence came to the position near the end of his life that "while 'Buddhistic inaction and meditation' must be repudiated, 'Buddhistic peace' must be sought after" (Doherty, *Oriental* 58). In his essay "The Reality of Peace," he approaches a Buddhist position when he writes that the "condition of freedom" is the understanding that "I fear neither love nor hate nor death nor pain nor abhorrence," when "I am absolved from desire and made perfect," when "I balance for a space in pure adjustment and pure understanding" (Lawrence, *Phoenix* 677, 680). Some Mahayana Buddhists call this freedom and balance "equanimity," as in one translation of a popular Tibetan prayer, "may all beings come to rest in the great equanimity that is free from attachment and aversion." He likewise sounds Buddhist (with a touch of Hinduism) when he answers his own question—"Where, then, is there peace?"—by saying that "there is peace in that perfect consummation when duality and polarity is transcended into absorption," when the duality of soul/body, the polarity of self/other, that defines Western individualism is transcended (*Phoenix* 693). And he concludes by imagining, in effect, his own nirvana in terms that are familiar to any reader of his novels because of the pervasiveness of flower imagery in them: "There is a new heaven on the earth, there is new heaven and new earth, the heaven and earth of the perfect rose" (*Phoenix* 693).

One might call this Lawrence's "red Nirvana"—after the rose and after the focalization on desire.[30] Lawrence began his career under the influence of Nietzsche's distinction between passive nihilism and active nihilism, and so he replicated the categories of the Victorian nirvana debate, as modified by Nietzsche. While he categorically rejected what he perceived as the asceticism and quietism of passive nihilism, with which he tended to associate Buddhism in general, he ultimately sought a transcendence recognizable as partially Buddhist. While he prized individual self-creation and responsibility, he could not endorse the individualism of the active nihilist, the self-made *Übermensch*, which he perceived as egoistic, power-obsessed, and mechanism-and-money fixated. Lawrence could accept neither white nirvana nor black nirvana, and yet, rather than be satisfied with dismissing them, as most would have done, he was determined to confront the contradictions and to find a position of his own between them. Thus one finds throughout his writings a sustained and fierce struggle to resolve the dualism of soul/body and self/other that is expressed in part by the juxtaposition of characters who represent passive nihilism and active nihilism. Lawrence felt it necessary to resolve the polarities of the Victorian nirvana debate in order to achieve his goal of understanding human desire and its potentially contradictory relationship to individualism, on one hand, and to the originary vitalism of life, on the other. Thus Lawrence "nihilated" himself (to borrow a term from Sartre's *Being and Nothingness*) into the anti-individual individualist, the anti-nihilism nihilist, and the anti-nirvana advocate for nirvana. He posited red nirvana as a not-nirvana, which is about as close to the Buddhist understanding as a modernist possibly could have come.[31]

Final Reflections

The nineteenth-century encounter with nirvana and anatman was a traumatic one for Western culture for the reason that it was a direct and profoundly disturbing challenge to the core identity of the West: the essential individual and its eternal soul. It therefore was inassimilable. Instead, two interpretations developed, eternalism and annihilationism, both of which represented failures to assimilate and therefore involved projection, denial, and scapegoating. The annihilationist side of the nirvana debate contributed to the development of Western nihilism and, thereafter, to modern existentialism. The Victorian nirvana debate certainly did not "cause" nihilism; the elements of it were present in suspension in Western culture long before the nineteenth century. But the exposure to Buddhism acted as an essential catalyst that ignited a reaction from which much of the Buddhism then precipitated out, as it nearly had by the time Sartre took up nihilism.

At the prelude to modernism, the perceived passive nihilism of nirvana required the response of an active nihilism that would defend Western individualism against the annihilation of anatman by strengthening it into an *Übermensch*. The Victorian corollary was the super-self-made-man: a myth—supported by such figures as Cecil Rhodes, Teddy Roosevelt, and Henry Ford—that underwrote the promise of similar opportunity for the self-made everyman. However, as the story often has been told, Victorian progressive optimism passed through decadence and then, with World War I, into grimness, and the woundedness of the paradigmatic modern individual increased relative to his powers of self-creation, the result of which was the modern existential condition. The super-self-made-man had acquired a shadow, become wounded and hollow at the core. That woundedness—the source of existential dread or nausea, as Sartre named it in his novel *Nausea* (1938)—was in part a symptom of the uniquely European hollowness at the heart of progressive individualism and in part a symptom of the sustained effort required to repress its ultimate other, the not-self of anatman.

As anatman was a foil for modern Western individualism, so it made perfect sense that denial of self as personality came to be aligned with totalitarian repression of individual freedom, as represented in Franz Kafka's *The Trial* (1914–1915) or George Orwell's *Nineteen Eighty-Four* (1949), and as projected onto the "atheistic and nihilistic" Communism of the Soviet Union (which is not to suggest that repressive regimes do not exist or that the Soviet regime was not one of them). The cultural response was to cling all the more fiercely to the increasingly embattled and isolated "individual freedom." I have tried to suggest that this occurred both in popular culture and in the modernist nihilism of existential philosophy, the most sophisticated and convincing argument for the absolute value of individual freedom. The modern existential condition *is* the afterlife of nirvana.

My critique might seem to suggest that I am opposed if not to individualism and freedom then at least to existentialism. Not so. Unlike Sartre, who wrote from a modern Europe wedged between Communism and Nazism, I write from within a society where "individual freedom" has become the ubiquitous public representative of the dominant ideology. It is the slogan used to sell cars and to sell wars. Its hegemony has become the potential instrument of repression in a sense quite different from repression by force, to recall Michel Foucault. Though Søren Kierkegaard's passionate individualism, Nietzsche's active nihilism, and Sartre's existentialist freedom were radical philosophies of their times, their basic principles have become primary ingredients of mainstream Western culture, certainly in North America.[32] This has occurred *not* because they were like the Molotov-cocktail-throwing, Russian-revolutionary, atheistic nihilism that became one predominant association for "nihilism" starting in the nineteenth century.[33] On the contrary, they have become pervasive because they are in specific ways the logical outcomes of the convergent historical trajectories of Protestant individualism, Enlightenment rationalism, and laissez-faire capitalism. Thus I agree with those like Justin Clemens and Chris Feik who argue that "nihilism designates the status of the *era* in which *we* are now living" and Jean Baudrillard who writes that "today's nihilism...is indissolubly that of the system" (Clemens and Feik 20; Baudrillard 159).[34] It is not difficult to see how one popular conception of existentialist freedom, as in "realize the potential of yourself by following your desires," might be appropriated and instrumentalized as, for example, "Be all that you can be" or

"Just do it!"—advertisements for the U.S. Army and Nike athletic wear, respectively. At the same time, I am only following the prescription of existentialist freedom and of American democratic freedom at its best by exercising my individual freedom to choose whether or not I choose "individual freedom" as it has come to be defined in my culture and society. I am willing to nihilate "freedom" with which I do not agree in order to imagine freedom that I believe is more authentic.

Throughout this book, I have pointed out the limitations of certain Western conceptions of individualism, human will, and self-definition. Theories of individualism considered to be within the enclosure of dominant Western ideology—for example, Protestant individualism or the self-made man—as well as theories critical of those—Nietzsche's will to power or existentialist freedom—share a common limitation from a Buddhist perspective: They tacitly assume or actively defend the isolation and autonomy of the individual, whether from nature, God, or society. Whether for Nietzsche, Lawrence, or, I would argue, Sartre, freedom means separation and isolation. Individualism thus defined produces an atomized society, a society of separate individuals each working for his or her own benefit without any necessary regard for or obligation to the greater good of the community, the society, or the planet (which is not to deny that many individuals do choose to act charitably and responsibly). Such a social order comes with benefits for certain institutionalized interests. It has the greatest potential of any system for maximizing individual consumption; at the same time, it has a natural inhibitory effect on the formation of organized opposition by citizens to the interests that similarly benefit from that consumption. Thus, to take a single example, greenhouse gases are produced as a direct result of individual and corporate pursuits of self-interest, where no one is held accountable for resulting ecological disasters. Indeed, any such collective responsibility must be censured heavily, because it would constitute direct violation of "individual freedom," which is precisely why certain interests have made "regulation" into a dirty word. "Individual freedom" is the highest principle of twenty-first-century U.S. society for more reasons than the oft-repeated one of defending the rights of individuals. The economic and political stakes could not be higher, and the highest stakeholders are the most powerful organizations on earth. This is why what Buddhism and nirvana represent has been considered so threatening by so many in the West.

At the same time, the ethical system of Buddhism—the Four Noble Truths, the Five Precepts, the Noble Eightfold Path—was the feature that most appealed to Victorians. Here was an ethics that did not depend on a supernatural source, did not involve sin and damnation, yet made each individual fully responsible for his or her moral choices. Its justification was largely practical—"you will live a happier life while creating a healthier society by following these guidelines"— and its approach was less prohibitive than prescriptive of a process of living ethically.[35] Buddhism is founded on a belief in the unavoidable interconnected-ness of all sentient beings, not in some abstract ethereal sense but grounded in social and global reality. Nothing and no one is independently self-originating; everything and every individual is conditioned by mutual interdependence within a society, a natural planet, and an ordered universe. Every action and intention of mine is causally related to—but not predetermined by—past ac-tions and intentions of mine and of many other beings and is causally related to consequences for me and for many others in the future (most directly, my chil-dren). This ethics directly challenges—and offers an alternative to—the indi-vidualized faith of Protestantism, the progressive individualism of the self-made man, and the individual isolationism of the modern existential condition.

According to Buddhist ethics, while I must be responsible for my own karma, it is not possible for me to act "just for myself." It is not possible to be "individually responsible" in the sense that I only have to think about my own freedom and the consequences of my actions and intentions only for myself in the immediate future. According to Buddhism, that is not merely self-centered and shortsighted; it is dangerously ignorant of the way the real world actu-ally operates and therefore threatens the well-being—not to say the contin-ued existence—of the social and natural worlds. To "*canonize self-concern is the very opposite of rationality*" to the extent that rational choice may mean choosing long-term, sustainable, and collective well-being over immediate, in-dividual self-realization or pleasure (Jacobson 59). Does this worldview limit individual freedom? It most certainly does question the wisdom of absolute "individual freedom," the freedom to be absolutely nothing but an isolated and therefore alienated self in a universe perceived as largely hostile to that self, an empty nothingness. The Buddhist alternative is to seek non-individual and therefore genuine freedom by de-essentializing personality in order to re-alize oneself as naturally part of absolutely everything and everybody in the world—a full nothingness. Buddhism imagines a type of freedom that domi-nant Western culture has as yet been unable to imagine.

And this returns us, finally, to the other half of the Victorian nirvana debate, the eternalist interpretation of nirvana. My portrayal in the preceding para-graphs of the Buddhist alternative partakes of that discourse, unavoidably so. Writing from within my cultural time and place, I cannot help but appeal not only to Buddhism, as I understand it, but at the same time to uniquely West-ern, correlative concepts derived from Romanticism, American Transcenden-talism, the hybrid religions of the late nineteenth century, and the synthesis of these and other sources within the New Age movement. For that matter, the modern New Age movement effectively began in the second half of the nineteenth century with the confluence of the spiritualism movement and the European encounter with Buddhism, though its clear emergence was not until the hybrid religions of the 1870s–1890s.

Robert Bellah and other sociologists describe the existence of an American "civil religion," an amalgamation of non-denominational and folkloric Judeo-Christianity with elements of cultural mythology, such as the "Promised Land" of America and the "Chosen People" spreading the message of democracy (Bellah, qtd. in Swenson 297). Civil religion is ritually celebrated on holidays such as Thanksgiving and the unabashedly militaristic nationalism of the Fourth of July, Veterans Day, and Memorial Day. I theorize that the Victorian encounter with Buddhism fed into what has become a Western "un-civil religion," a non-nationalistic, globally oriented, and egalitarian ethical and spiritual ethos. According to that ethos, human beings belong to a larger unity with all other beings in the natural universe, which is not the same thing as the old deistic universe designed with humankind privileged at its center. This, then, is the second half of the afterlife of the Victorian nirvana debate, the half that issued from the eternalist interpretation of nirvana.

Most alternative, occult, New Age, Green, and pro-peace subcultures participate in and contribute to this shared ethos. I would speculate that a large number of average Western middle-class citizens, especially those not active in one of the traditional world religions, also unreflectively subscribe to this worldview. I may as well go further here at the end of this book in suggesting that the early twenty-first-century American cultural and political landscape appears to be divided very roughly between the individualistic, patriotic, national-identity politics of American civil religion and the ecological, tolerance-and-equality-based ethos of un-civil religion. This meta-level cultural division, though certainly not determined by the nineteenth-century encounter with Buddhism, corresponds to the two forks of the Victorian nirvana debate and may in small part be correlated with the annihilationist and the eternalist interpretations of nirvana.

After Victorian fascination with Buddhism peaked in the 1890s, it partially submerged within Western culture until the resurgence of interest that began in the mid twentieth century. All the while, beneath the surface, Buddhism was being refashioned for Western consumption. I am inclined to think that it was precisely during this period that Buddhism cemented its significance as a permanent influence on both Western philosophy and popular culture in the West. Buddhism also continued to surface periodically in various stages of assimilation and distortion in novels such as Herman Hesse's *Siddhartha* (1922), Somerset Maugham's *The Narrow Corner* (1932), James Hilton's *Lost Horizons* (1933), Aldous Huxley's *The Doors of Perception* (1954), Jack Kerouac's *The Dharma Bums* (1958), Robert Pirsig's *Zen and the Art of Motorcycle Maintenance* (1974), and, now, in films like *Little Buddha* (1993). Films in the recently popular martial-arts-Buddhism subgenre—for example, *The Matrix* (1999), *Crouching Tiger, Hidden Dragon* (2000), and *The Last Samurai* (2003)—demonstrate just how intensely Western culture is struggling not yet to resolve but to rationalize the contradictions between its individualism and progressivism and the selflessness of anatman and organic unity of dependent origination. I doubt that either most of the hippies of the 1960s or the majority of the thousands of Westerners practicing meditation as I write understand Buddhism much more thoroughly than did some late Victorians. However, they did and do recognize, as Victorians perhaps did not, that Buddhism is inherently revolutionary, not only in relationship to the institutions of Christianity but also in relationship to the more powerful institutions of corporate-state capitalism. Figures such as The Dalai Lama and Thich Nhat Hanh have become internationally renowned not only as great teachers and spiritual masters but as social and political activists. The "engaged Buddhism" movement is reversing the Victorian stereotype of Buddhist passivity.[36] After 150 years of gradual infiltration, Europe and the United States are perhaps marginally more prepared now to receive Buddhism. The religion sections of bookstores overflow with material on Buddhism, and the number of Buddhists in the West increases every year.[37] The cultural forms of novels, poems, and cinema continue to feed this process, as they first began to do in the late-Victorian decades. The cultural counter-invasion of the West by Buddhism is ongoing.

Appendix 1

Selective Chronology of Events in the European Encounter with Buddhism

The following chronology is highly selective, representing a very small percentage of pertinent events, translations, and publications. Furthermore, it is Anglo-centric. Particularly for the eighteenth and nineteenth centuries, I have selected works and events that in my opinion had a significant impact on the reception of and response to Buddhism in England. Thus substantial and important work in other languages, especially French and German, is only marginally represented here. A more complete chronology can be found in Droit (191–259). In building this chronology, I consulted, in addition to Droit, Almond, Bachelor, Fields, Marshall, Rawlinson, Schwab, and Welbon.

BCE

6th c.	Greek colonies established in the northwest of the Indian peninsula during the lifetime of Siddhartha Gautama, the Buddha.
327–325	Alexander the Great occupies Bactria on the northern border of current-day India.
291	Megesthenes, Greek ambassador to the court of Chandragupta, writes *Indika*.
268–233	Rule of Asoka, Buddhist emperor who dispatched missionaries westward.
ca. 200	Clement of Alexandria, *Stromata*, perhaps the first Western writing that mentions "Boutta."

150–135   Reign of King Milinda (Menander I) of Bactria, author of the *Milindapanha,* dialogues with the Buddhist monk Nagasena.

CE

1245   John of Plano Carpini, Franciscan missionary, perhaps the first European to travel as far east as Mongolia.

1255   Willem van Ruusbroec (William of Rubrock), Franciscan Friar, provides the first substantial documentation of a European encounter with Buddhism.

1293   Marco Polo hears the life story of "Sagamoni Borcan" while in Sri Lanka.

1549   St. Francis Xavier, Jesuit missionary, encounters Zen Buddhism in Japan.

1681   Robert Knox, *An Historical Relation of the Island Ceylon in the East Indies.*

1691   La Loubere, envoy of Louis XIV, *Description du royaume de Siam.*

1716   Ippolito Desideri, a Portuguese Jesuit, establishes a mission in Tibet.

1727   Englebert Kaempfer, *History of Japan Together with a Description of the Kingdom of Siam,* first book in English to describe Zen Buddhism.

1767   John Zephaniah Holwell, *Interesting Historical Events relative to the Provinces of Bengal and the Empire of Indostan,* "The Religious Tenets of the Gentoos."

1768   Alexander Dow, *History of Hindustan.*

1784   Sir William Jones presides over the first meeting of the Royal Asiatick Society of Bengal. Sir Charles Wilkins publishes the *Bhagavad Gita,* the first complete Sanskrit text translated into English.

1787   F. Galdwin, *Dictionary of the Religious Ceremonies of the Eastern Nations.*

1788   First issue of William Jones's *Asiatick Researches* published.

1799   Francis Buchanan, "On the Religion and Literature of Burma," in *Asiatick Researches,* later a source for Schopenhauer and Hegel.

1800   Samuel Turner, *An Account of an Embassy to the Court of the Teshoo Lama in Tibet.*

1808   Robert Watson Frazer, *A Literary History of India.*

1815   Rev. W. A. Ward, *A View of the History, Literature, and Mythology of the Hindoos* (Serampore).
       Léonard de Chézy occupies the first Sanskrit Chair in Europe at the Collège de France.

1817   Robert Tytler, *Inquiry into the Origin and Principles of Budaic Sabism* (Calcutta). Michel-Jean-François Ozeray, *Recherches sur Buddou ou Bouddou.*

1823–27   A. W. Schlegel, *Indische Bibliothek,* discusses the "*Boudhomanes.*"

1825–27   Henry Thomas Colebrooke, five monographs in *Transactions of the Royal Asiatic Society* give the first overview in English of the systems of thought in India, including Jainism and Buddhism.

1826   Brian H. Hodgson, *Notices of the Languages, Literature and Religion of Nepal and Tibet.*

1827   William Francklin, *Researches on the Tenets and Doctrines of the Jeynes and Buddhists Conjectured to be the Brahmans of Ancient India.*

            Hegel, *Encyclopédie des sciences philosophiques en abrégé* defines the basis of Buddhism as "nothingness."

1828   Brian Houghton Hodgson, *Sketch of Buddhism.*

1829   Edward Upham, *The History and Doctrine of Buddhism.*

1834   Alexander Csomo de Körös, *A Dictionary, Tibetan and English.*

1836   George Turnour, *The First Twenty Chapters of the Mahawanso: and a Prefatory Essay on Pali Buddhistical Literature.* Jean-Pierre Abel-Rémusat, *Foé Koué Ki, ou Relation des royaumes bouddiques,* translation of medieval Chinese pilgrimage narratives that help locate the ancient holy sites of Buddhism (trans. in English in 1839).

1837   Henry T. Prinsep and James Prinsep begin publishing translations of the inscriptions on Asokan columns, which locate the ancient holy sites of Buddhism.

1841   Philippe Edouard Foucaux, translation into French of the Tibetan *Lalita Vistara,* a primary source on the life of the Buddha. Sir Alexander Cunningham, begins publishing archaeological reports of the ruins of the ancient holy sites of Buddhism.

1842   Ralph Waldo Emerson publishes excerpts of Charles Wilkins's *Heetopades of Veeshnoo Sarma* in *Dial.*

1843   Wilkins's translation of the *Bhagavad Gita* first arrives in Cambridge, MA; Emerson confuses it with Buddhism, which he will criticize as nihilistic.

1844   Eugène Burnouf, *Introduction à l'historie du Buddhisme indien.* Henry David Thoreau publishes in *Dial* part of the *Lotus Sutra* excerpted from Burnouf.

            Arthur Schopenhauer, *The Will as World and Representation,* is an expansion of the 1818 edition and includes many references to Buddhism.

1848   Sir Alexander Cunningham, *Verification of the Itinerary of the Chinese Pilgrim, Hwan Thsang* verifies locations in the pilgrimage narrative translated by Abel-Rémusat.

1851	Henry T. Prinsep and James Prinsep, *Tibet, Tartary, and Mongolia: Their Social and Political Condition and the Religion of Boodh.*
1853	R. Spence Hardy, *Manual of Buddhism in Its Modern Development.*
1854	Thoreau's *Walden* comments upon the "*Bhagavat Geeta*" and Buddhism.
1855	Jules Barthélemy Saint-Hilaire, *Du Bouddhisme.* Michael Viggo Fausböll, *Dhammapadam.*
1859	Paul A. Bigandet, *The Life, or Legend of Gaudama, the Buddha of the Burmese.*
1860	Jules Barthélemy Saint-Hilaire, *Le Bouddha et sa religion.*
1862	F. Max Müller, *Buddhism.*
1867	F. Max Müller, *Chips from a German Workshop.*
1871	Henry Alabaster, *The Wheel of the Law.* Richard Phillips, *The Story of Gautama Buddha and his Creed: an Epic.*
1872	F. Max Müller, *Lectures on the Science of Religion.*
1875	Samuel Beal, *The Romantic Legend of Sākya Buddha.* Robert Caesar Childers, *A Dictionary of the Pāli Language.*
1877	T. W. Rhys Davids, *Buddhism.*
1879	Sir Edwin Arnold, *The Light of Asia.*
1880	T. W. Rhys Davids, *Buddhist Birth Stories, or Jataka Tales.* Madame Helene Blavatsky receives Buddhist vows in Ceylon, linking Theosophy to Buddhism.
1881	T. W. Rhys Davids and C. A. F. Rhys Davids found the Pali Text Society at Oxford. T. W. Rhys Davids, *Lectures on the Origin and Growth of Religion as Illustrated by some Points in the History of Indian Buddhism.* F. Max Müller, *Buddhist Nihilism.*
1882	Hermann Oldenberg, *Buddha; His Life, His Doctrine, His Order.*
1884	Ernest J. Eitel, *Buddhism: Its Historical, Theoretical and Popular Aspects.*
1883	A. P. Sinnett, *Esoteric Buddhism,* rewrites Buddhism as Theosophy.
1885	Samuel H. Kellogg, *The Light of Asia and the Light of the World.*
1889	Monier Monier-Williams, *Buddhism, in its Connexion with Brahmanism & Hinduism, and in its Contrast with Christianity.*
1893	Thomas H. Huxley, *Evolution and Ethics* makes significant use of Müller's scholarship and Buddhist thought.
1895	The Buddhist Society founded in London.
1901	Charles Bennett takes vows as Ananda Metteyya, the first British Buddhist monk.

Appendix 2

Summary of Selected Buddhist Tenets

Reflecting the Buddhist penchant for enumeration, this appendix consists largely of a series of lists: the Four Noble Truths, the Noble Eightfold Path, the Five Precepts, the Three Marks of Existence, the Five Aggregates (or skand-has), and the Twelve Stages of Dependent Origination. These are itemized and explicated throughout both the Theravada and Mahayana canons. Many sources available to Victorians summarized these tenets. Any current introduction or handbook to Buddhism includes them.

The Four Noble Truths

Among the Victorian sources that summarize this foundational teaching from the first sermon of the Buddha are Ambereley 311; Bloomfield 322; Eitel 86; Hardy 496; Monier-Williams, *Buddhism* 43; T. W. Rhys Davids, *Buddhism* 48, 106–7.

Here is Rhys Davids's clearest summary:

1. *Suffering or sorrow*. Birth is sorrowful; growth, decay, illness, death, all are sorrowful; separation from objects we love, hating what cannot be avoided, and craving for what cannot be obtained, are sorrowful; briefly, such states of mind as co-exist with the consciousness of individuality, with the sense of separate existence, are states of suffering and sorrow.

2. *The cause of suffering.* The action of the outside world on the senses excites a craving thirst for something to satisfy them, or a delight in the objects presenting themselves, either of which is accompanied by a lust of life. These are the causes of sorrow.
3. *The cessation of sorrow.* The complete conquest over and destruction of this eager thirst, this lust of life, is that by which sorrow ceases.
4. *The path leading to the cessation of sorrow* is the Noble Eightfold Path briefly summed up in the above description of a virtuous life.
   (T. W. Rhys Davids, *Buddhism* 48)

More recent introductions to the Four Noble Truths can be found in Erricker, *Buddhism* 35–59; Nhat Hanh, *The Heart of the Buddha's Teaching*, 3–46; Rahula, *What the Buddha Taught*, 15–50; Smith, *Radiant Mind: Essential Buddhist Teachings and Texts*, 65–102; Snelling, *The Buddhist Handbook*, 43–46. These and many other sources of a similar sort also cover the other sets of tenets included in this appendix; thus, I will not cite them again here.

Cross-referencing between Victorian and recent sources suggests the following summary for the Four Noble Truths: (1) *Dukkha*, suffering is a natural and unavoidable part of the human experience; (2) *Samudaya*, the origin of suffering is "thirst," craving, or clinging to that which is by nature impermanent, whether that be one's pleasures/pains or one's self-conception; (3) *Nirodha*, the cessation of suffering is possible if one can relinquish that craving for permanence and achieve non-attachment and non-aversion; (4) *Magga*, the way to do that is to practice the Middle Way and to live according to the tenets of the Noble Eightfold Path.

The Noble Eightfold Path

Victorian sources also treat the Noble Eightfold Path (Bloomfield 322; Lilly 201; *Quarterly Review* 337; T. W. Rhys Davids, *Buddhism* 108–9; T. W. Rhys Davids, *History* 89). Here is the relevant excerpt from Rhys Davids's translation of the Buddha's first sermon:

Right Aspirations (high, and worthy of the intelligent, worthy man)—
Right Speech (kindly, open, truthful)—
Right Conduct (peaceful, honest, pure)—
Right Livelihood (bringing hurt or danger to no living thing)—
Right Effort (in self-training and in self-control)—
Right Mindfulness (the active, watchful mind)—
Right Rapture (in deep meditation on the realities of life).
(T. W. Rhys Davids, *History* 89)

Many ancient and modern commentaries offer exegeses and interpretations of the tenets of the Noble Eightfold Path. Often the eight are grouped as follows: the first three concerning ethical conduct, the second three concerning mental discipline, and the remaining two concerning wisdom. The sources I have consulted—Victorian in combination with contemporary—suggest the following summary of the Noble Eightfold Path:

1. Right Understanding or Right View—understanding the true nature of reality, a summary of which is provided by the Four Noble Truths.
2. Right Thoughts (or Aspiration)—cultivating thoughts of selflessness, compassion, and non-violence.
3. Right Speech—refraining from falsehood, slander, harsh words, frivolous talk (gossip), or using the power of language to mislead or harm others.
4. Right Action—acting only in ways that do not harm oneself or others, the most harmful actions being murder, stealing, and sexual violence or misconduct.
5. Right Livelihood—making one's living in a way that does not harm others, society, or the world, in particular refraining from making or selling weapons, intoxicants, or poisons.
6. Right Effort—to prevent unwholesome states of mind from arising, to rid oneself of them, to cultivate new wholesome states of mind, and to perfect those already present.
7. Right Mindfulness (or Awareness)—of one's deeds, words, and thoughts so that one is present in each moment.
8. Right Concentration—the discipline of training the mind through the practice of meditation.

The Five Precepts

The Five Precepts, which apply both to lay and monastic Buddhists, as well as an extended list for monks and nuns, constitute the practical rules for day-to-day ethical living. They are less prohibitions or commandments (though they partially overlap with the Ten Commandments) than "the minimum essential 'prescription' for treating the human condition, and an antidote to the three poisons: greed, aversion or hatred, and ignorance or delusion" (Erricker 6–7).

Here is a poetic and somewhat Christianized expression of them spoken by the character of the Buddha in Sir Edwin Arnold's *The Light of Asia:*

1. "Kill not—for Pity's sake—and lest ye slay / the meanest thing upon its upward way."
2. "Give freely and receive, but take from none / By greed, or force, or fraud, what is his own."

3. "Bear not false witness, slander not, nor lie; / Truth is the speech of inward purity."
4. "Shun drugs and drinks which work the wit abuse; / Clear minds, clean bodies, need no Soma juice."
5. "Touch not thy neighbour's wife, neither commit / Sins of the flesh unlawful and unfit."
(Arnold 227)

The Zen Master, scholar, and author, Thich Nhat Hanh, has written a version of the Five Precepts adapted especially to address the conditions and concerns of postmodern Westerners. To give a single example, here is his modernized translation of the second precept, which taken in its most reduced form might be "don't steal": "*Aware of the suffering caused by exploitation, social injustice, stealing, and oppression,* we are committed to cultivating loving kindness and learning ways to work for the well-being of people, animals, plants, and minerals. We will practice generosity by sharing our time, energy, and material resources with those who are in need. We are determined not to steal and not to possess anything that should belong to others. We will respect the property of others, but will try to prevent others from profiting from human suffering or the suffering of other beings" (Nhat Hanh, *Interbeing* 21).

The Three Marks of Existence

These are "fundamental doctrines which are to be understood as underlying all Buddhist statements" (T. W. Rhys Davids, *History* 88). They provide the philosophical foundation work upon which rest many of the other tenets listed in this appendix. In one of Rhys Davids's summaries, they are "the three doctrines of Aniccam, Dukkham, and Anattam, that is to say, of The Impermanence of every Individual, The Sorrow inherent in Individuality, The Non-reality of any abiding Principle" (T. W. Rhys Davids, *History* 88).

Both Victorian and contemporary sources suggest the following summary:

1. *Duhkha* (in Pali, *dukkha*), which translates as "suffering" or "unsatisfactoriness" and is synonymous with the First Noble Truth.
2. *Anitya* (in Pali, *annica*), "impermanence," which states that all things are conditioned by change, nothing is constant or universal.
3. *Anatman* (in Pali, *anatta*), "no soul" or "not self," the doctrine that autonomous, continuous, and eternal selfhood, as in the Western conception of the soul or the Hindu *Atman*, is a counter-productive and often harmful illusion.

The Five Aggregates

The Five Aggregates, also referred to as the *skandhas* (in Pali, *khandas*), are in effect the Buddhist response to the following question. If, as the doctrine of *anatman* teaches, there is no essential, unified self, then what constitutes the psychological and practical experience of personhood? How does the individual's psychology, which tends to assume itself as a unified identity, operate? As Walpola Rahula observes in this regard, "what we call 'I,' or 'being,' is only a combination of physical and mental aggregates, which are working together interdependently in a flux of momentary change within the law of cause and effect" (Rahula, *What* 66).

Rev. Spence Hardy summarized them in *A Manual of Buddhism* in 1853: "The elements of sentient existence are called khandas, of which there are five constituents....1. The organized body,...or the whole of being, apart from the mental processes. 2. Sensations....3. Perception....4. Discrimination.... 5. Consciousness" (Hardy 388). "Sensations" includes what might be called feelings or emotions, and "discrimination" more often is referred to as the aggregate of "mental formations," which includes volition or will as well as the conditions or complexes posited by modern psychoanalytic theory. Here is a slightly fuller summary based on the combination of Victorian and recent sources:

1. The aggregate of matter, including the body as its five material senses: eyes, ears, nose, tongue, and the body/mind complex.
2. The aggregate of sensations or feelings, of which there are three types: pleasant, unpleasant, and neutral.
3. The aggregate of perceptions, the recognition and processing of sensations and feelings.
4. The aggregate of mental formations, a primary basis for karmic formations, which includes intentions, the will or volition, and the idea of self, what in Western psychology might include "emotions," "attachments," "projections," etc.
5. The aggregate of consciousness, a sort of base awareness, perhaps a partial corollary to the "unconscious."

The Twelve Stages of Dependent Origination as Shown in The Wheel of Life

The doctrine of dependent origination (*Paticca-samuppāda* in Pali), also sometimes translated as "conditioned genesis" or "interdependent co-arising," is nothing less than a model of reality in its entirety, which is to say that it is the

Dharma. It describes the chain of causes and effects that govern all existence. This chain is represented pictorially by the Wheel of Becoming or the Wheel of Life (*Bhavachakra*). The outer rim of The Wheel consists of twelve pictures, and these depict the twelve links or stages in the cycle of dependent origination. The most widely read Victorian summaries of The Wheel were those written by L. Austine Waddell about the Tibetan Wheel. T. W. Rhys Davids also dedicated a chapter in *The History and Literature of Buddhism* to dependent origination and The Wheel within Theravada. These in combination with modern sources suggest the following summary:

Pictorial Representation	*Very Rudimentary Interpretation*
1. A blind person with a stick	ignorance as the root cause of suffering.
2. A potter making pots	volitional actions creating karmic formations.
3. A monkey clinging	consciousness, psychological awareness of self.
4. A boat with passengers	body/mind. The body is the boat carrying the one who steers. The mind is one's purposeful individuality.
5. An empty house	the empty house of the senses: the five senses plus the mind (as empty windows and door).
6. A person with an arrow	contact between the senses and the perceived sticking in his/her eye—world—the resulting feelings blind one to reality.
7. An embracing couple	sense-impressions create feelings and attachments.
8. A person drinking	thirst or desire. The Second Noble Truth.
9. A person picking fruit	grasping, clinging, attachment to earthly things.
10. A pregnant woman	becoming, coming into existence, rebirth.
11. A woman giving birth	birth as the beginning of a new cycle of samsara.
12. An old man carrying his life	as a result of birth, decay, and death; for to live burdens or a corpse, himself—involves suffering—the First Noble Truth

Note that there is no standardized interpretation of The Wheel and that the pictorial representations and the sequencing of them vary between, for instance, the ancient Ajanta fresco, the Tibetan Wheel, and later Japanese illustrations as analyzed by Rhys Davids *History,* 101–8.

Notes

Introduction

1. As this ordering of languages suggestions, the first serious Western engagements with Buddhism began not in England but in other European countries, in particular France and Germany, but, as I subsequently discuss, the center of Buddhist studies shifted to England by mid century. For key events, dates, and people, see appendix 1.

2. As here with my use of "Siddhartha Gautama" instead of the Pali "Siddhatta Gotama," I have chosen to standardize throughout this book on the Sanskrit rather than the Pali terminology. This does not reflect a preference but rather a practical recognition that a greater number of Westerners are more familiar with "Dharma" than "Dhamma," "karma" than "kamma," and "Nirvana" than "Nibbana," for instance.

3. Victorian authors who commented upon Christian missionaries in Buddhist territory include Alabaster and Eitel. Among twentieth-century studies, see Jacobson, Jensen, and Prothero, *The White Buddhist.*

4. My primary source for places and dates concerning the Stupa at Amaravati and Colonel Colin MacKenzie is Robert Knox, *Amaravati: Buddhist Sculpture from the Great Stupa,* especially 18–20. I also draw in this paragraph on Charles Allen, *The Search for the Buddha: The men who discovered India's lost religion,* and the argument here about the role of Europeans in preserving the ancient history of Buddhism is developed further in chapter 4.

5. On Olcott and the Ceylonese Buddhist revival, see Godwin, 321–22, and, as the best general source, Prothero, *The White Buddhist.*

6. Sources on the earliest contacts between Greeks and Buddhists along the northwestern border of current-day India include Bachelor, 7 and 26; Clarke, 37; Dejong; and Fields, 13).

7. The earliest contacts between European missionaries and Buddhist nations starting in the thirteenth century have been documented and discussed in (Almond, 7; Bachelor, 229; Dejong; Droit, 15; Jacobson, 150; Jensen, 42; Welbon, 11).

8. For an introduction to the influence of exposure to Eastern religions and philosophies on the American Transcendentalists see Dejong; Godwin 309; Schwab, 200; and Fields, 60). The best sourcebook I have found on the impact of Eastern thought on the United States is Tweed and Prothero.

9. My primary source on the 1851 census is McLeod, *Religion and Society in England, 1850–1914,* in particular, the first chapter, "Patterns of Religious Belonging."

10. My primary sources for facts about the history of Nonconformity in Britain are McLeod, *Religion and Society in England, 1850–1914,* and Parsons, "From Dissenters to Free Churchman: The Transitions of Victorian Nonconformity."

11. These trends did not apply to Catholicism, which almost alone resisted pluralism, maintaining unity of doctrine and church, and did so while reestablishing bishops in England for the first time in centuries in 1850 and while the number of Catholics increased to the end of the century as the number of Anglicans declined. Catholic commentators, though not theologically pluralistic, generally tended to be intellectually curious and thorough in their treatments of Buddhism.

12. This claim is supported by the fact that a search of the PCI (Periodicals Content Index) database for articles published with "Buddha" or "Buddhism" in the title reveals this pattern: 3 in the period 1840–1850; 0 in 1851–1860; 13 in 1861–1870; 74 in 1871–1880; 148 in 1881–1890; 367 in 1891–1900; 287 in 1901–1910; and 243 in 1911–1920.

13. See for example Green, "Christianity and Buddhism," in the *Proceedings of the Literary and Philosophical Society of Liverpool* in 1890; Monier-Williams, "Buddhism and Christianity," which appeared in the *Evangelistic Repository* in 1891; and Max Müller, "Christianity and Buddhism," in *The New Review* of 1891.

14. Other articles that discuss the presumed similarities between the histories of Protestantism and Buddhism include Clarke, "Buddhism: or, the Protestantism of the East," in *Atlantic Monthly* in 1869; Bode, "Women Leaders of the Buddhist Reformation," in *Journal of the Royal Asiatic Society of Great Britain and Ireland* in 1893; and, Rattigan, "Three Great Asiatic Reformers: A Study and a Contrast" in the *London Quarterly Review* in 1899.

15. The following articles are representative of a body of others that recounted the life of the Buddha: Kellogg, "Kingdom of, Life of, and Legend of Buddha," in *Bibliotheca Sacra* in 1882; McKerlie, "Western Buddhism," in *Asiatic Quarterly Review* in 1890; and, Lilly, "The Message of Buddhism to the Western World," in *The Fortnightly Review* in 1905. A number of other articles focused on the Jataka, a collection of folkloric tales about the past lives, birth, and childhood of the Buddha, one example of which is Cowell, "Jataka: or stories of the Buddha's former births," which appeared in *Westminster Review* in 1896.

16. On Mill and Buddhism, see the works by Gordon and Salzer. On Arnold and Buddhism, see *Littell's Living Age* and Whitlark, "Matthew Arnold and Buddhism."

17. Other articles that discuss Buddhist ethics included, for example, Bloomfield, "Essentials of Buddhist Doctrine and Ethics," from the *International Journal of Ethics* in 1891; Foley, "The psychological basis of Buddhist ethics," from the *Journal of the Royal Asiatic Society of Great Britain and Ireland* in 1894; and, Rattigan (cited above).

18. For example, the traditional Christian parable of Saint Josaphat appears to be derived at least in part from the story of the Buddha. As T. W. Rhys Davids wrote, "Gotama the Buddha, under the name of St. Josaphat, is now officially recognized and honoured and worshipped throughout the whole of Catholic Christendom as a Christian Saint!" (T. W. Rhys Davids, *Buddhist* xli). For twentieth-century support, see Clarke, 39; De Jong, 60; and Welbon, 5.

1. The Life of the Buddha in Victorian Britain

1. On Arnold's influence on Kipling, see Caracciolo and Whitlark. For a discussion of the influence of Orientalist writings on Yeats, Eliot, and others, see Clarke, 101, as well as Eliot's own response to Arnold in *On Poetry and Poets.*

2. The four rebuttals to *The Light of Asia* were Collins, Flanders, Kellogg, and Wilkinson. For a discussion of them, see Clausen "The Light of Asia", 31–36. At least two other Americans wrote book-length verse narratives of the life of the Buddha following the success of *The Light of Asia;* see Niles and Root.

3. The threshold event in the translation of Buddhist scriptures came in the 1830s after Brian Houghton Hodgson, under the auspices of the East India Company, collected ancient Sanskrit manuscripts and delivered them to the Royal Asiatic Society in London, where they initially were disregarded, and to the *Société Asiatique* in Paris, where Eugène Burnouf used them to write his ground-breaking work, *L'introduction à L'historie du Buddhisme Indien* (1844).

4. For examples of Victorian scholars and commentators who drew an equals sign between Buddhism and Darwinism see *Dublin Review,* 19; Eitel, 63–66; Lilly, 213; *Literary Digest,* 162; and T. W. Rhys Davids, *Lectures,* 94.

5. See for example Dall's "Legend of Buddha and Life of Christ," published in the *Unitarian Review* in 1882, or Johnston's "Christ and Buddha; resemblances and contrasts," from the *Methodist Review* in 1898.

6. See for example Carpenter's essay "The Obligations of the New Testament to Buddhism" which appeared in *Nineteenth Century* in 1880, or E. J. Dillon's "Ecclesiastes and Buddhism" in *Contemporary Review in 1894.* Ernest de Bunsen, *The Angel-Messiah of Buddhists, Essenes, and Christians,* argued that "the remarkable parallels in the most ancient records of the lives of Gautama-Buddha and of Jesus require explanation" (Bunsen vii-viii).

7. Clausen has done the laborious and valuable foundation work of comparing *The Light of Asia* to the primary sources upon which Arnold relied and then annotating the poem, identifying specific passages where Arnold drew on each source. See Clausen, "The Light of Asia," 210–89. Among other sources that he identifies are Hardy's *A Manual of Buddhism* and Rogers's translation of *Buddhaghosha's Parables.* Naravane argues additionally for the influence on the poem of the *Lalitavistara,* "a Sanskrit text of the Mahayana school" (24).

8. The primary source on this point is Almond.

9. *The Light of Asia* was both praised for its accuracy and criticized for its inaccuracy. Rhys Davids commented that the poem "'has caught with commendable accuracy and sympathy the spirit of the ancient faith'" (Rhys Davids, qtd. in Clausen, "Sir" 184). Müller, took the opposite stance: "And we must premise that the reader who would study Buddha in the Vinaya [the *Vinaya Pitaka,* one of three foundational

scriptures] must not bring his 'Light of Asia' with him. The Sir Edwin Arnold of the forth or fifth century BCE had far slighter materials at his command: he was nearer the facts"; see Müller, "Buddhism," 330.

10. Nineteenth-century scholars were able to determine with relative accuracy the dates of the Buddha's birth and death using references in Buddhist scripture to non-Buddhist historical events with known dates. Most modern scholars fix the dates as either 566–486 or 563–483 BCE, as summarized in Ling, 45.

11. Perhaps the earliest printed life of Buddha was recorded by Ashvaghosa between the first and second centuries; see Ashvaghosa. My sources include many of those available to Arnold, mainly Alabaster and T. W. Rhys Davids, *Buddhism*. In addition, I have consulted twentieth-century retellings, for example, Snelling, and the exhaustive scholarly biography by Nakamura. I am aware that any short summary of this sort opens itself to criticism both for inaccuracy and for the particular interpretive slant of the author; this is unavoidable.

12. Along these lines, McKerlie wrote in 1890: "To consider the individual [Buddha] one must look on, not the miraculous conditions and fables related concerning him, but the historical facts of his existence" (McKerlie 303). See Caracciolo on the reception of the *Jatakas*. On the preference for the Pali canon, see Brear, 149.

13. For a summary of the "Eight Great Events" illustrated with ancient art, see Menzies, 33–51.

14. See, for example, Arnold, 4:85, and Phillips, 2.40 and 3.41. Graham provides a counter-point to my claim here, arguing that "part of Arnold's attraction to the East is in the eroticism he 'discovers' there" (Graham 128).

15. This is not the place to attempt a fuller treatment of the varieties of Lamarckism, Darwinism, Social Darwinism, and Spencerism that were part of the massive complex of discourses to which Phillips and Arnold, like many other Victorians, responded by confusing the distinctions between them. Though I hope not to perpetuate those confusions, I use the terms "Darwinism" and "evolution debate" to signify this complex of discourses at a general level. My primary sources, other than Darwin, are Beer and Crook. My discussion also is both indebted to and at variance with the treatment of Arnold's "spiritualized, creative evolution" in Clausen, "Sir Edwin Arnold," 179. For a somewhat more thorough consideration of these issues, see Franklin, "Memory."

16. It should be noted that Arnold too describes Buddhism in his "Author's Preface" as a "magnificent Empire of Belief," a "stupendous conquest of humanity" (Arnold, "Preface" 1, 3). The difference from Phillips is that Arnold does not carry the imperial conceit throughout the poem, nor does the poem portray East and West in a conflict for supremacy. Many readers, including Indians and Buddhists, have felt that the poem lives up to the author's claim that it "is inspired by an abiding desire to aid in the better mutual knowledge of East and West" (Arnold, "Preface" 6). For support of this claim, see Naravane.

17. The caveat to this claim concerning Buddhist non-violence is the history of Buddhism in Japan and the marshalling of it to serve Japanese imperial ambitions leading up to and during World War II. See Victoria, *Zen at War.*

18. On the Buddhist conception of the interconnectedness of all living beings and all actions, see Jean Smith 43, 100, 204, and 260. Especially illustrative is Thich Nhat Hanh's *Interbeing*, which places that doctrine at the center of Buddhist teaching. A not dissimilar concept can be found in the post-Darwinian theory of an organic

interdependence between all life forms within an ecosystem, as discussed in Crook (269). This, too, is why Buddhism and modern Western environmentalism have found much in common in the centuries following Darwin.

19. C. A. F. Rhys Davids, *Buddhism,* 99–100, comparatively analyzes the historical roots of these two alternative worldviews and ties them to a divergence between ancient Greek philosophy and ancient Indian philosophy.

20. Monier-Williams, an eminent scholar and critic of Buddhism, made this representative statement about Buddhist passivity in 1889: "According to Christianity:— Fight and overcome the world. According to Buddhism:—Shun the world, and withdraw from it" (Monier-Williams 559). One defender of Catholicism wrote in the *Dublin Review* in 1875: "The Eastern withdraws himself into contemplation, subdues every movement of passion, and longs vehemently for one only consummation, that the semblance of life, which he has, may be taken from him, and pain may cease with annihilation. The Western cannot learn this hopeless asceticism; he believes that the cycle of things is an evolution from mere potentiality to some large perfection; he worships progress, and looks out for the means of advancing society and mankind in its onward path" (*Dublin Review* 18). Note Eitel, 83–84, on Buddhism as fatalism.

21. See, for example, Phillips, 5.89. Phillips was not alone in viewing the Buddha as a great intellect, since, according to Brear, one appeal of Buddhism to some Victorian thinkers was "the sheer intellectual power of the system" (Brear 144).

22. On this understanding of karma and individual responsibility, see Fox, 116.

23. The traditional concept of *Bhavana,* mental or spiritual development, "presumes that the latent capacity we have needs to be cultivated," and "in Theravada Buddhism the way of escape from ignorance and craving is emphatically one of self-help" (Erricker 10; Fox 145). Some Victorians found this aspect of Buddhism compatible with their own ethic.

24. This did not stop some pro-Buddhist Victorians from trying to deny Buddhist atheism. See, for example, McKerlie and C. A. F. Rhys Davids, *Buddhism.*

25. See, for example, Arnold, 4:97. In addition, *The Light of Asia* often puts phrases into the mouth of the Buddha that are Biblical allusions. Clausen identifies many of these in his annotated critical edition of Arnold's text.

26. As Hauser, in annotating an 1890 edition of *The Light of Asia,* wrote in relation to Arnold 8:301: "If anyone hopes to arrive at a full understanding of this subject [nirvana], let them be well forewarned of its impossibility" (301). Others who joined the debate over the meaning of "nirvana" included Armstrong 187; Hardy 390, 395; Müller, *Chips* 227–28; Müller, *Lectures* 143; Rattigan 309; and, T. W. Rhys Davids, *Buddhism* 94).

27. The early French Buddhologists Burnouf and Bathélemy Saint-Hilaire strongly adhered to the interpretation of nirvana as annihilation, and it was their heavy influence on Müller (see *Chips,* 227–28, for instance), and his heavy influence on all subsequent scholars of comparative religion, that set the tone until the 1880s and1890s, at which point other theories of nirvana began to gain prominence, especially in the writing of the Rhys Davidses.

28. For one clear summary of *anatman,* see Rahula, 51–66. For a characteristically Victorian argument that Buddhist selflessness is nothing more than selfishness, see Eitel, 79, 83–84. For a discussion of Victorian distaste for this concept, see Almond, 88.

29. This parable was recounted in multiple sources available to Victorians, including T. W. Rhys Davids's widely read *Buddhism,* 133–34.

30. Clausen, "The Light of Asia", 251–52, outlines the ways in which Arnold's telling of Sujata's tale varies in significant ways from his primary sources.

2. Buddhism and the Emergence of Late-Victorian Hybrid Religions

1. Without delving into the history of the term "religion," I note that "the central explanatory category of religious studies, namely the notion of 'religion' itself, is a Christian theological category...forged in the crucible of inter-religious conflict and interaction" (King 40). As a result, one of the most common assumptions in the Victorian period and perhaps today is that a genuine religion must be based on creation and revelation by a monotheistic deity. In contrast, I use "religion" to mean any spiritual or ceremonial practice that is observed by an identifiable community over time and organized around agreed upon doctrines or rituals. The generality of this definition is unavoidable if one is to include the tribal religions of the upper Amazon as well as ancient Greek pantheism, not to mention Buddhism. Thus reference sources on religion tend to demur from offering any single definition. While, Émile Durkheim says religion is "'a unified system of beliefs and practices relative to sacred things,'" R. N. Bellah says it is "'a set of symbolic forms and acts which relate man to the ultimate conditions of his existence'" (qtd. in Bowker, *Oxford Dictionary of World Religions* xv). Such definitions exclude none of the religions discussed here, and I would challenge any definition that does.

2. Various scholars concur with the statement that all religions are syncretic; see Byrne, 99; Kraft, 143–44; and Shaw and Stewart, 7).

3. All references to Theosophy are to The Theosophical Society International, which should not be confused with the Theosophical Society Pasadena. Like all religions, Theosophy has experienced schisms. The most significant occurred in 1895 when William Q. Judge, one of the founders of the society in 1875, along with Helena Petrovna Blavatsky and Henry S. Olcott, chose to separate the American branch from Blavatsky's Eastern influence. Blavatsky and Olcott had moved their headquarters in 1879 to India where they built a center at Adyar in 1882. In 1929 the North American branch moved to Point Loma in California and later relocated to Pasadena. To confuse matters, there also is a major lodge belonging to the Blavatsky side in Wheaton, Illinois. I have chosen to focus on the international branch and not to include direct consideration of the California branch, even if there are significant similarities between the two.

4. Jean-Baptiste de Lamarck's *Zoological Philosophy* (1809) and Charles Lyell's *Principles of Geology* (1830–33) prepared the ground for the evolutionary theories of Charles Darwin and Alfred Russel Wallace after midcentury. My primary sources on the history of materialism are Frank Miller Turner, *Contesting Cultural Authority*, 262, and Richard C. Vitsthum, *Materialism: An Affirmative History and Definition*. Victorians were exposed to the pre-Socratic materialist philosophy and atomic theory of Democritus (c. 460—c. 370 BCE) and Epicurus (c. 340–c. 270 BCE) largely through contemporary translations of *De Rerum Natura* by the Roman poet Lucretius (98?–55 BCE). One well-know translation was made by H. A. J. Munro, in response to which Alfred Tennyson penned his less than flattering poem, "Lucretius."

5. These distinctions are evident throughout F. Max Müller's widely influential work *Natural Religion* (1889), which argues that it always had been his "endeavour to show that religion did not begin with abstract concepts and a belief in purely extramundane beings, but that its deepest roots can be traced back to the universal stratum of sensuous perception" (Müller, *Natural* 141). In other words, religious sentiment originated from the experience of the numinous in nature, awe and wonder at natural phenomena such as mountains, storms, the ocean, fierce animals, etc.

6. A version of this claim was made by Hudson Tuttle, *Arcana of Spiritualism: A Manual of Spiritual Science and Philosophy*: "A list of the names of those who have embraced Spiritualism would include the leading men of the nations—statesmen who wield the most power, scientists, and almost all the advanced and radical thinkers" (Tuttle 48). However, Tuttle does not note the largest category of eminent Victorians to dabble in Spiritualism: literary authors. That list includes but is not limited to Elizabeth Barrett Browning, Mary Elizabeth Braddon, Wilkie Collins, Edward Bulwer-Lytton, Charles Dickens, George Eliot, Alfred Tennyson, Elizabeth Gaskell, Margaret Oliphant, Marie Corelli, Thomas Hardy, Bram Stoker, Robert Louis Stevenson, and Arthur Conan Doyle. On the "new occultism" that followed the Spiritualism movement, see Alex Owen, *The Place of Enchantment*.

7. For more on spiritualist societies, see Oppenheim, *The Other World*, 49–57. On spiritualist publications, see Alex Owen, *The Darkened Room*, 22–24.

8. As evidence for Spiritualism as an organized religion, the United States saw the formation of the National Spiritualist Association of Churches in 1893, and Gordon J. Melton, *Encyclopedic Handbook of Cults in America*, defines "Spiritualism" as a religion, "a religion based upon the belief that mediumship, the ability demonstrated by a few selected persons to contact the world of spirits, proves that the individual survives bodily death" (Melton 118).

9. Mesmerism and hypnotism appear throughout subsequent literature, for example, in Edward Bulwer-Lytton's *A Strange Story* (1866) and as Marie Corelli's "Electric Principle of Christianity" in *A Romance of Two Worlds* (1886) (Corelli 211).

10. Frank Podmore, *Modern Spiritualism: A History and Criticism* (1902), makes this claim unequivocally: "Historically, moreover, Spiritualism is the direct outgrowth of Animal Magnetism" (Podmore xiv). Also see Oppenheim, 218–22.

11. As Maria M. Tatar, *Spellbound: Studies on Mesmerism and Literature*, puts this point, mesmerists "repeatedly stressed the empirical basis of animal magnetism in much the same way that Christian Science and spiritualism, lineal descendants of mesmerism, persistently underscore[d] the scientific foundations of their persuasions" (Tatar 6). Spiritualists claimed to practice a "scientific religion," as in Epes Sargent's *The Scientific Basis of Spiritualism* (1881).

12. Oppenheim organizes her invaluable study around the categories of Christian and anti-Christian Spiritualism. See Oppenheim, 63–110.

13. On the relationship between Spiritualism and Victorian progressivism, see Cottom, 130–31; Oppenheim, 94–96; and Turner, *Between Science and Religion*, 192–93. Turner also provides substantial consideration of the life and work of Frederic Myers.

14. Current scholarship speculates that between 40,000 and 110,000 witches were burned in Europe between 1450 and 1750; see Gibbons. According to the web source, "Major Events in the Burning Times" (which may have limited reliability), the last witch was burned in Europe in 1782.

15. It also is telling that, as Owen notes, "cross-cultural studies have indicated that major factors in determining the recipients of spirit possession are low status accompanying powerlessness, combined with a sense of personal deprivation"; in other words, poor women subjected to repressive men saw the séance as a ticket out of that condition (Owen, *Darkened* 49).

16. The use of "law" to designate the Dharma can be seen, for instance, in the title of Alabaster's influential 1871 work, *The Wheel of the Law,* and throughout Arnold's 1879 best-selling verse narrative of the life of the Buddha, *The Light of Asia,* which uses terms like "the great Law" (Arnold 8:212). For Victorian works that equate the Law of the Dharma to the law of evolution, either criticizing or celebrating the "scientific" qualities of Buddhism, see Eitel, 62 and 66; Lilly, 209, or *Literary Digest,* 162. For an analysis of the Victorian conflation of Buddhism and Darwinism, especially within Theosophy, see Clausen, "Victorian Buddhism," 7, and Bevir, "The West," 764.

17. My source here is Droogers, 9.

18. Shaw and Stewart further note that "many in religious studies now feel that the term is so tarnished that it is no longer usable" (Shaw and Stewart 5). The mid-twentieth-century trend in the study of religion was to dismiss "syncretism" as "a term of dubious heritage and limited usefulness, often employed to ascribe insincerity, confusion, or other negative qualities to a nascent religious group" (J. Smith 1042). Related observations can be found in Droogers, 9; Kraft, 142; and van der Veer, "Syncretism, Multiculturalism and the Discourse of Tolerance," 197.

19. I take this point from van der Veer, ibid.

20. Alex Owen, *The Place of Enchantment,* argues in this regard that "In certain respects the 'new' occultism," which encompasses what I analyze as late-Victorian hybrid religions, "represented a somewhat elitist counterpoint to the hugely successful Victorian spiritualist movement that had preceded it" (Owen, *Place* 5).

21. One exception to this claim may be Christian Science, which, like all late-Victorian hybrid religions, claimed a scientific basis but which did not to my knowledge derive this claim with any reference to Buddhism. The only treatment of Christian Science that I have read is Braud.

22. My primary sources on the early history of the Theosophical Society are Mead, Washington, and especially Gomes, *The Dawning of the Theosophical Movement.*

23. The term "Aryan," which since its adoption by the Nazis has been unavoidably considered racist and genocidal, referred in the nineteenth century to the ancient people and area of what is now Northern India or Pakistan, from which Siddhartha Gautama (c. 563–c. 483 BCE), and therefore Buddhism, issued. The "Aryan question" that interested Victorians, which was stimulated by the earlier discovery of the membership of English in the Indo-European language group, concerned the extent to which Northern European peoples were genetically or racially related to the people of Northern India, a question with implications for British occupation of India See Bachelor, 266, and van der Veer, *Imperial Encounters,* 134.

24. These statistics come from the website of the Theosophical Society International Headquarters in Adyar, India: http://ts-adyar.org/history.html. According to data provided via personal correspondence by Mr. Conrad Jameson, the Public Relations Officer in Adyar, in 2001 there were 1,081 Lodges across 51 different nations with a total of 31,996 memberships.

25. On the Mahatma letters and the related scandal, see Gomes, *Theosophy in the Nineteenth Century,* chap. 6. The letters themselves are preserved in The British

Library. The most vocal of Blavatsky's critics was William Emmette Coleman, who viewed Theosophy as an interloper on the territory of Spiritualism and who attacked Blavatsky in a series of articles with titles such as "A Splendid Fraud. Sources of Theosophical Literature—Where Blavatsky Got her Book." Blavatsky undeniably borrowed freely from a dizzying array of sources, and it is true that she did not quote or footnote according to Modern Language Association standards. On the other hand, *Isis Unveiled* contains between three and four thousand quotations and over 2,400 substantially accurate footnotes (Gomes, *The Dawning of the Theosophical Movement* 153). I would argue that regardless of Blavatsky's sloppy citation practices the end product is an original synthesis and a unique cultural artifact of the late nineteenth century. For a direct rebuttal of the plagiarism charge, see Hastings.

26. I am far from the first to describe Theosophy as a synthetic, if not hybrid, religion. An 1895 essay in comparative religion notes that Theosophy "professes to explain the doctrines and myths of all religions, and is in fact the boldest attempt ever made to achieve the colossal task of reconciling all the religions and philosophies of the world" (Snell 205). *Isis Unveiled* is nothing less than "The Key to all Mythologies," and while George Eliot's Mr. Casaubon was not up to the task Madame Blavatsky was.

27. As Blavatsky notes in this regard, "Plato never claimed to be the inventor of all that he wrote, but gave credit for it to Pythagoras, who, in his turn, pointed to the remote East as the source whence he derived in information and his philosophy" (*Isis* 2:39). These claims are supported by Clarke: "Pythagoras, who had a profound influence on Plato, is believed to have spent some time in Egypt where he learned about Indian philosophy; the synosophists were objects of considerable curiosity to thinkers in the ancient Greek and Roman worlds; and Buddhist monks were known in the Hellenic world" (Clarke 37).

28. The Essenes were an esoteric sect of Judaism that formed beginning in c. 150 BCE. Blavatsky argues that "the Essenes...were the converts of Buddhist missionaries who had overrun Egypt, Greece, and even Judea at one time, since the reign of Asoka the zealous propagandist" (Blavatsky, Isis 2:132). This theory was not uncommon in Victorian discourse; see Bunsen's *The Angel-Messiah of Buddhists, Essenes, and Christians* (1880). More recent scholars have argued that "there are clear indications that the Gnostic ideas, which played an important part in the early development of Christian doctrine, were influenced by Buddhist and Hindu thought" (Clarke 39).

29. Citing arguably mystical phrases that the New Testament attributes to Jesus, Blavatsky argues, "And, if we understand it rightly, we cannot avoid thinking that this 'secret' doctrine of Jesus, even the technical expressions of which are but so many duplications of the Gnostics and Neo-platonic mystic phraseology—that this doctrine, we say, was based on the same transcendental philosophy of Oriental *Gnosis* as the rest of the religions of those and earliest days" (Blavatsky, *Isis* 2:192).

30. Blavatsky had signaled early in volume one what sort of natural law she has in mind: "Is it too much to believe that man should be developing new sensibilities and a closer relation with nature? The logic of evolution must teach as much, if carried to its legitimate conclusions" (Blavatsky, *Isis* 1:v).

31. Sinnett develops his appeal to science throughout *Esoteric Buddhism*, as here: "In esoteric science, as in microscopy, the application of higher and higher powers will always continue to reveal a growing wealth of detail; and the sketch of an organism that appeared satisfactory enough when its general proportions were first discerned,

228 - Notes to Pages 71-79

is betrayed to be almost worse than insufficient when a number of previously unsuspected minutiae are brought to notice" (Sinnett, *Esoteric* 21). The microscope metaphor was common in Victorian discourse, as for example in George Eliot's Lydgate in *Middlemarch*.

32. Jean-Baptiste de Lamarck's *Zoological Philosophy* (translated in 1814) argued that acquired characteristics could be inherited, which was more palatable in general to progressive-minded Victorians than was Darwin's theory of evolution in *Origin of Species*, which argued for random selection and adaptation by mutation.

33. Concerning Annie Besant's role in British politics, feminist politics, and her combination of the two in activism in India see Beckerlegge, 235; Bevir, "A Theosophist in India"; Burfield; Dixon, 206; Ellwood and Wessinger; van der Veer, *Imperial Encounters*, 77; and Viswanathan, 177–207.

34. On Olcott's participation in the Singhalese Buddhist revival, see Godwin, 321–22, and, as the best general source, Prothero, *The White Buddhist*. Olcott penned *A Buddhist Catechism*, which still is used by Buddhists in Sri Lanka today, thereby creating his own hybrid of Buddhism mixed with a Protestant orientation and a Catholic genre.

35. For evidence for and against Blavatsky's purported sojourn in Tibet, see Blavatsky, *Isis Unveiled*, 2:598; "Mr. Lillie's Delusions"; Gomes, *The Dawning of the Theosophical Movement*, 9ff; Gomes, *Theosophy in the Nineteenth Century*, 215–223; Sinnett, *The Early Days of Theosophy in Europe*, 24; and Washington, 29. The question of whether Blavatsky had indeed spent time in Tibet was and still is debated because it is crucial support for her claim to have received the transmission of the "esoteric science" of Theosophy from the "Tashi Lama" over the course of years of residency, a claim that underpins the authority of her teachings (Blavatsky, Letter to Hartman 324).

36. This point comes from Dixon, 43.

37. On the association between the International Theosophical Society and the Hindu Arya Samaj in India, see Gomes, *Dawning*, 13, and the section "Pilgrimage to India," as well as Godwin, 320.

38. The Hinduization of Theosophy is blatant in Sinnett's *Esoteric Buddhism*. It adopts the story of "a Brahmin pundit" to the effect that Gautama Buddha, though a great teacher, had erred in democratizing the esoteric practices guarded by Brahmin adepts and thus "opened the doors of the occult sanctuary too widely" (218, 227). Sinnett then argues that the Buddha had to "re-incarnated himself, next after his existence as Gautama" as Sankaracharya (c. 788–820 CE), a Hindu reformer and proponent of Vedanta philosophy, in order to "repair certain errors in his own previous teaching" (219, 220).

39. One of many teachings ascribed to the Buddha on the Four Noble Truths can be found in the *Saccavibhanga Sutta*, *The Middle-Length Discourses of the Buddha*, 1097–1101. For an introduction to the Four Noble Truths, see Erricker, 35–59; Nhat Hanh, *Heart*, 3–46; Rahula, *What*, 15–50; Smith, 65–102; and Snelling, 43–46.

40. Turner, *Between Religion and Science*, 24, identifies these three scientific theories as definitive of Victorian scientific naturalism. As I. Salzer wrote in 1890 in reference to the Dharma, "Gautama Buddha's doctrine of continuous Change, or tendency towards Change within the Universe, is the only doctrine as yet known that includes all the elementary processes of this world, both physical and mental; it is the highest generalisation yet proclaimed by man" (Salzer 8).

41. If Theosophies cosmology is antithetic to Buddhism, it may have precedence in Hindu and Egyptian models. T. W. Rhys Davids notes that in the *Upanishads* "The belief in transmigration is here united with notion that soul go first to the moon, a theory...curiously common" (T. W. Rhys Davids, *Lectures* 82).

42. I will note only in passing that the model of spiritual progress within Theosophy is tied to a racial hierarchy. Blavatsky writes, for instance, that "Races of men differ in spiritual gifts," and Sinnett argues that each individual "has to live through a series of races on that planet" before progressing to the next (Blavatsky, *Isis* 2:588; Sinnett, *Esoteric* 95). Both state that the "Aryan race" of northern India and not the "white race" is the most evolved in the nineteenth century. One of Theosophy's founding principles concerns racial equality, yet its privileging of the Aryan race is far from disinterested. Is Theosophy racist, anti-racist, or, as I would argue, both? For the two sides of this argument, see van der Veer, *Imperial Encounters,* 77, and, on the other hand, Viswanathan, 177–207.

43. See Sinnett, *Esoteric Buddhism,* 65, and Besant (1895).

44. Blavatsky cites the skandhas many times; see, for example, *Isis Unveiled* 2:286–87, and *Key to Theosophy* 141.

45. Useful recent treatments of the Five Aggregates or the skandhas can be found in Erricker, 39; Nhat Hanh, *Heart,* 176–83; and Snell, 56–57.

46. On Freud and psychical research, see Oppenheim, 245–66, and Turner, *Between Science and Religion,* 109.

47. As a counterpoint, Sinnett does theorize a hell-like possibility for those who truly are not ready for spiritual progression, but this is the rare exception, a punishment place call "Avitchi" that is reserved for the few genuinely evil "aristocrat[s] of sin" (Sinnett, *Esoteric* 142). The very large majority of average sinners need not worry.

48. See Bevir, "A Theosophist in India." Van der Veer argues that "spiritualism and Theosophy have played a crucial role in the development of radical antiestablishment and anticolonial politics, both in Britain and India" (van der Veer, *Imperial* 77). In contrast, Viswanathan concludes that Annie Besant "attempted to forge through the theosophical movement a culture of universal brotherhood that was, at the same time, heavily marked by theories of racial fissures and regeneration" (Viswanathan 191). Both claims are supportable.

3. Romances of Reincarnation, Karma, and Desire

1. On the hypothesized link between Pythagoras and Buddhist reincarnation, see Arundale, 120; Buchner, 7; Bunsen, xii; Cook, 35–36; Cust, 42; and Wier, 56. Yang provides relevant analysis of eighteenth-century British conceptions about reincarnation.

2. My primary source on the debate over reincarnation in eighteenth-century Britain is Yang.

3. My source for this evidence of Corelli's popularity and sales is Federico.

4. Lewis Carroll alludes to this same metaphor for nirvana in *Alice's Adventures in Wonderland* when Alice pauses to contemplate the potential result of unchecked shrinking: "And she tried to fancy what the flame of a candle looks like after the candle is blown out, for she could not remember ever having seen such a thing" (56). This

metaphor became pervasive in late-Victorian discourse. See, for example, T. W. Rhys Davids, *Lectures on the Origin,* 101, which cites "Alice in Wonderland."

5. On the Victorian construction of Tibet and Tibetan Buddhism, see the works by Bishop, Flemming, McMillin, Venturino, and most especially Lopez.

6. We know that Haggard and Rudyard Kipling, who were close friends, supported one another's belief in reincarnation. For example, in his diary entry of 23 May 1918, Haggard wrote: "Also we [Kipling and himself] discussed the possibility (and probability) of reincarnation and agree that every year which passes draws back a curtain as it were, and shows us to ourselves in yet completer nakedness" (*Private* 138). We also know that Kipling had read comparative religious studies on Buddhism and might reasonably assume that Haggard had as well and that, in some of their many conversations and correspondences about Kipling's *Kim,* they discussed Kipling's Buddhist "Teshoo Lama."

7. For representatively unscholarly biographies of Corelli, see the works by Bagland, Carr, and Huff. Carr's 1901 biography makes this fabulous claim on Corelli's behalf: "Since St. John the Divine no one [before Corelli] had undertaken by a 'plain history of strange occurrences happening to oneself' to prove the actual existence of God and His Heaven" (Carr 41).

8. Corelli frequently distanced her own Spirit-based belief from Spiritualism, but we know that she had a connection to W. T. Stead, which "created a link with the contemporary spiritualist scene," and she finally confessed in her preface to *Life Everlasting* that her inspiration for *A Romance* had come from "a strange psychical experience which chanced to myself" (Kuehn 184; Corelli, *Life* 17). Similarly, Haggard in his twenties "discovered the new fad of Spiritualism" and, according to his autobiography, became a "frequent visitor" at the house of Lady Paulet, "a great spiritualist" whose séances he "used to attend" (Manthorpe 65; Haggard, *Days* 1:37). Something happened at one of those séances that disturbed him greatly, I suspect in part because he credited it as authentic paranormal phenomena. Though later he would attend several lectures by Arthur Conan Doyle on Spiritualism, he remained very critical of it.

9. Henkel argued along similar lines: "What Herodotus communicates on the religion of Egypt has to be taken with the greatest precaution. Egyptology has nothing to produce to sanction his statements on metempsychosis" (Henkel 106).

10. Note Victorian approaches to the "Aryan question": Hauser, 19; T. H. Huxley; Max Müller, *Lectures,* 31; Oldenberg, 5; T. W. Rhys Davids, *Buddhism,* 22, and *Lectures,* 23. Twentieth-century sources include Bishop, 120; Davies; and van der Veer, *Imperial,* 50and 134). Some Victorian versions of the life of the Buddha pointed out that Siddhartha was "an Aryan....a descendant of the Sâkas, or Sythians, who invaded India from the north about 600 B.C." and that he was "tall, handsome, with large blue eyes" (Hauser 19; Neale 441). Beyond simply refabricating a historical figure in one's own image, as is done in paintings of an Anglo-Saxon Jesus, this was a reclaiming of a racial origin and identity. As a result, "this Buddhism could...serve as a substitute self for Victorian Britain, a self present long ago in the very heart of the Orient" (Lopez 6).

11. On Haggard and Egyptology, see Pearson. Much has been written about race and racism in Haggard; see for example Malley, who notes that in creating Ayesha "Haggard uses the myth of the white queen (Sheba must also be a model) as a survival of an ancient white imperial presence in Africa" (Malley 286). On the similarities between Haggard's Kôr and Egypt, see Gilbert (126). It is not irrelevant to note that

Haggard, according to his nephew, " 'believed that he had lived before: as an ancient Egyptian, as a Zulu, as a Norseman' " (qtd. in Manthorpe 21).

12. For fuller development of reincarnation as a progressive evolutionary system, see Besant, *Reincarnation,* 11; Sinnett (any of his works); and Tuthill, 258.

13. On reincarnation compared and contrasted to genetic inheritance, see Arundale, 33; Besant, *Reincarnation,* 72; Henkel, 130; and Slater, 10.

14. Even so, one American author, Leo Michael, wrote a polemic entitled *She: An Allegory of the Church* (1889) in which he argues that Haggard's novel is an allegory in which Ayesha stands for the corrupted institutions of Christianity while the Theosophical spiritualism in the novel represents the true path for Christianity.

15. On the phallic nature of Ayesha's "fire of life" and Haggard's phallocentrism in general, see Gubar's "She and Herland," 144.

16. On Ayesha as a figure for the "New Woman" and as a perceived threat to Victorian masculinity, see the works by Gilbert, Gubar, Murphy, or T. Rogers.

17. Haggard echoed his character's sentiment in his autobiographical writing: "That all Love is immortal. It is God's light permeating the universe, and therefore incapable of diminution or decay" (Haggard, *Days* 2:259).

18. This contradiction between spirituality and sensuality has produced contradictory critical claims about Corelli's writing. While Kershner notes that "Corelli's religious vision—if we can call it that—was, like that of the Romantic poets or the Decadents, inherently sensual rather than ascetic," Siebers argues that "Corelli's brand of mesmerism is based on a kind of asceticism that rejects the body" (Kershner 75; Siebers 187). Both claims are supportable.

19. Corelli's protagonist in *Life Everlasting* repeatedly wonders about what has prevented her union with Santoris, as here: "Something opposing,—something inimical to my peace and happiness held me back" (*Life* 248). The texts hints that one partial explanation has to do with gender equality, though Corelli never would have expressed it that way: the protagonist demands her own spiritual power equal to that of the male counterpart. I believe that the author's sexual orientation also may have been a factor here.

20. Concerning desire, Haggard famously wrote in his 1887 essay "About Fiction" that "Sexual passion is the most powerful lever with which to stir the mind of man, for it lies at the root of all things human; and it is impossible to overestimate the damage that could be worked by a single English or American writer of genius, if he grasped it with a will" (Haggard, "About" 176–77). D. H. Lawrence would attempt just that: to grasp desire with will (or will with desire).

21. A similar argument was made by Howard, as in this statement: "According to them [fundamentalists], man is by nature sinful, and it is utterly futile to look to works for salvation: they therefore imagine that, if a man believes in their religious teachers—Christ of the Christians, and Mohamet of the Moslems—he will be saved, despite his whole life of sin" (Howard 144).

22. Corelli goes so far in her non-fiction work, *Free Opinions Freely Expressed on Certain Phases of Modern Social Life and Conduct* (1905), as to write: "IF YOU BELIEVE IN CHRISTIANITY, YOU MUST ALSO BELIEVE IN THESE THREE THINGS:—1. The virtue of poverty. 2. The dignity of labour. 3. The excellence of simplicity. Rank, wealth, and all kinds of ostentation should be to you pitiable—not enviable" (Corelli, *Free* 45).

23. For other Victorian scholarly commentaries on the Middle Way, see F. Max Müller, "Buddhism," 324, and T. W. Rhys Davids, *History,* 93.

24. T. W. Rhys Davids supports my claim here, for example, in the following: "I would just notice ... that it is craving thirst, and not desire, which in the Arahat is said to be extinct. The second division of the Noble Eightfold Path is the cultivation of right desires. It is only evil desires, the grasping, selfish aims, which the Arahat has to overcome; and those, unfortunately too numerous, writers who place nirvana in the absence of desire, are only showing thereby how exaggerated is the importance which they attach to isolated passages and to careless translations" (Rhys Davids, *Lectures* 203–4).

25. The level of threat that Buddhism posed to what I have generalized here as the Western "economic powerbase" is indicated especially by the fifth tenet of the Noble Eightfold Path, Right Livelihood, which proscribes against profiting from products that increase human suffering, including weapons, addictive substances, carcinogenic chemicals and foods, financial instruments that exploit the disadvantaged, and all products derived from exploitation. How many major industries would be entirely exempt?

4. Buddhism and the Empire of the Self in Kipling's Kim

1. Lycett can be taken as representative of the first position: "More than in any of his works, *Kim* demonstrates [Kipling's] love and understanding of India. He makes no attempt to portray the colonialist's existence as superior to the native's. Indeed his manuscript shows that they took special care to tone down any possible racialist traits in his European characters and to build his Asians—in particular, the lama, who had earlier been rather too ingratiating and childlike" (Lycett 331). Representative of the second position are Eung, Parry, and Suleri. Parry argues, for instance, "From the outset the two narratives [of the Great Game of British espionage and of the Buddhist pilgrimage] run together, but the demands of the Great Game are always more urgent and are from early on prioritized" (Parry 315).

2. Baucom further complicates any simply dichotomy as follows: "We might suggest that through the construction and collapsing of these dichotomies [English/Indian], Kipling erases any limit on the colonial state's boundaries, renders discipline everywhere, insinuates the police into every act of waywardness. We might also suggest the exact opposite: in the unmapped spaces written over the imperial map of India, and the de-Anglicization of the sahibized Kim, we could equally discover the subversion of all the works of imperial discipline" (Baucom 99).

3. See Said, *Culture and Imperialism*, 146.

4. One exception would be the very recent work, published and unpublished, by Venturino.

5. Some scholars have argued that Kipling chose Buddhism rather than Hinduism or Islam in part as a result of personal prejudice or out of a desire to create a non-aligned religious position that could therefore be more easily enlisted by the Empire. In this regard, see Islam, 37; Kaul, 435; and Reid and Washbrook. A contrasting position is offered by Rao, 132, and by McCutchan, who writes: "Kipling sets the lama's politically neutral religion against India's long history of religious, racial, and political strife.... The lama's foreignness exempts him from the century-old rivalries and hatreds that exist between the religions of India and between conqueror and conquered" (McCutchan 136). Both positions may be valid.

6. As Islam summarizes the first of these two points, though Kipling was "responsive to Christian ethical ideals" and "uses Christian symbols seriously," "there is in fact very little evidence anywhere in Kipling's writings of an adherence to articles of Christian faith" (Islam 32).

7. The Stupa at Amaravati was in use from the third century BCE until perhaps as late as the fourteenth century, by which time Buddhism had died out in the country of its birth. According to Knox, Colonel Colin Mackenzie visited the site in 1797. In 1821 he sent eleven stones to the Indian Museum in Calcutta, from which nine were sent on to the East India Company collection in Leadenhall Street. To that collection were added 121 more, and in 1874 some of them were erected in the Sculpture Court at the Southern Entrance of the new India Museum in South Kensington. In 1879–80 the collection was divided between the new Victorian & Albert Museum and the British Museum, where for sixty years they were on display in the main stairwell (Knox 18, 22). Kipling, like millions of other Britons, repeatedly saw these and other Buddhist artifacts in each of these locations.

8. As Hopkirk reports, in a letter from Lockwood Kipling to Sir Aurel Stein of 16 May 1902, "He enquired: 'I wonder whether you have seen my son's "Kim," and recognized an old Lama whom you saw at the old Museum and at the School'" (Hopkirk 42). In addition, Rudyard Kipling was influenced in his shaping of the character of the Lama by his reading of Tibetan travel literature, as discussed later in this chapter.

9. Here is how Kipling recalled his first exposure to Blavatsky's ideas: "At one time our little world was full of the aftermaths of Theosophy as taught by Madame Blavatsky to her devotees. My Father knew the lady and, with her, would discuss wholly secular subjects; she being, he told me, one of the most interesting and unscrupulous impostors he had ever met" (Kipling, *Something* 395).

10. In contrast to claims that Kipling was less sympathetic to Hinduism as a religion than to other religions, McCutchan develops the argument that Kipling in fact drew directly upon the Hindu tradition of *Varnashrama Dharma* in creating Kim and the Lama as representative, respectively, of the first and the fourth of four stages in the spiritual trajectory of a person's life prescribed within that Hindu doctrine.

11. Patrick Brantlinger makes this very argument: "Imperialism itself, as an ideology or political faith, functioned as a partial substitute for declining or fallen Christianity" (Brantlinger, "Imperial Gothic" 186). Critics of course have suggested as much in the case of Kipling's own beliefs.

12. On this British construction of "Mother India," see Roy, 90, or Reid and Washbrook, whose historical study concludes: "Conventionally, the ideal district Collector should be 'ma-bap' (mother-father) to his people" (Reid and Washbrook 18).

13. Concerning "interfering politicians in England," Kipling acidly commented: "They derided my poor little Gods of the East, and asserted that the British in India spent violent lives 'oppressing' the Native," when, he argued, England was a country in which sixteen-year-old girls were expected to work fourteen-hour days "hauling water up stairs" (Kipling, *Something* 419).

14. Especially relevant here is Richards's *The Imperial Archive*. My primary source on the Orientalist/Anglicist debate is van der Veer. For a differing but equally informed perspective to van der Veer's, see Suleri.

15. I make this claim without at the same time rejecting the argument that "What is totally elided in Kipling's narrative is the other story, that of native nationalism and

its own fantasies of religiously inflected masculinity" (van der Veer 94). My focus is rather on Kipling's contribution to discourses that raised India's unique cultural heritage into the consciousness of British readers, thereby laying the foundation for acceptance of Indian nationalism even while working against it.

16. The seminal texts on hybridity are those by Bhabha and Young, though I would return to Bakhtin's concepts of "hybrid constructions," or "hybridization," "organic hybridity," and "novelistic hybrid" (*Dialogic* 304–6, 320, 358, 361). Also relevant here are Lahiri and Pieterse.

17. The character of Hurree Chunder Moorkerjee has elicited strong stances on both sides of the critical polarization; see Rao, 149; and Roy, 78–79.

18. I draw here on Baucom, as when he writes: "Creighton's decision to re-Orientalize Kim reflects his decision to guarantee English rule in India through the pursuit of knowledge rather than the cultivation of Englishness" (Baucom 99). He also argues that "in contributing to the Anglicization of India, Colonel Creighton finds himself in the odd position of Orientalizing England" (Baucom 95).

19. Note further references to the love between the Lama and Kim, and Kim's devotion to the Lama, see *Kim*, 70, 90–91, 103–4, 121, 123, 165, 189, 213, 270, 274, and 288. Annan's treatment of the relationship between Kim and the Lama concludes, "Both find enlightenment and freedom—the comprehension of the order of things—through love" (Annan 327). Other considerations of the function of their love in the novel can be found in Fraser, 62; Howe, 337; Kindead-Weekes, 439; and Sullivan, 150, 166, and 173.

20. In contrast to my argument here, Thrall argues: "Kim's true allegiance to the lama is filial rather than spiritual: love, not a search for ultimate truth, keeps him at the lama's side" (Thrall 53). While his is one of the most thorough readings of religion in *Kim*, he too neglects the Buddhist content of the novel and therefore sees the relationship between the two characters largely in terms of fellowship and loyalty.

21. For a counter-example to this claim of mine, see Victorian, *Zen at War*.

22. Most modern scholars fix the dates of the life of the Buddha as either 566–486 or 563–483 BCE, as summarized in Ling, 45.

23. Examples of the "Greco-Buddhist sculptures" in the Wonder House—perhaps the very one's that Kipling had seen there—are held by the British Museum, photographs of which can be viewed on the British Museum website (*K* 6).

24. The details in this paragraph about the pilgrimages of Fa Hian and Huan Tsang are from Allen, 205, which provides a detailed account of how Cunningham and subsequent archaeologists in India reconstructed the pilgrimages in order to locate the ancient holy sites.

25. Other widely read works by Samuel Beal that Kipling also may have read include *The Romantic Legend of Śākya Buddha, A Translation of the Chinese Version of the Abhinis.kraman.asūtra* (1875) and *Si-Yu-Ki: Buddhist Records of the Western World, Translated from the Chinese of Hiuen Tsiang (A.D. 629)* (1884).

26. I thank my mother, Margaret Trotter Lane, for her personal assistance in locating these Biblical passages.

27. Along these lines, Roy, whose thesis concerns the construction of national identity, notes that the "trope of pilgrimage in Kim, pilgrimage without a specific local object—the River of the Arrow is, like the idea of the nation, mythical and internal and therefore necessitates travel to all places—serves to concretize and make visible the form of the nation" (Roy 85). In this case, however, it would not matter

what the object of the search is as long as it is as yet unfound, which still leaves open the question of why the River of the Arrow.

28. See Allen, 256. For a sample of the Waddell-Führer public debate, see Führer's letter and Waddell's response in "Note to Above Letter."

29. In addition to Waddell, Das's *Indian Pandits in the Land of Snow* (1893) recounted the life of "The Great Tashi Lama," who was born in 1737 in Tashi-lhunpo, or "Teshoo Lomboo," and was synonymous with "Teshoo Lama" (Das, appendix 16, 27). Hopkirk writes that he consulted "a Tibetan-speaking scholar, formerly with the Victoria and Albert Museum," who told him that "Teshoo Lama" simply means "Learned One" (Hopkirk 40). Lopez notes that Madame Blavatsky praised Tibetan "Teshu Lamas," by which he claims "the British referred to the Panchan Lama" (Lopez, *Prisoners* 36). Finally, according to McMillin, we know that Kipling had read the travelogues of George Bogle, who in 1774 had visited the Tashilhunpo monastery of the Pachen Lama and whose descriptions of Teshoo Lamas influenced Kipling (McMillin 80).

30. Kipling revered Edwin Arnold. He reports in an 1888 letter that he was very pleased to hear of Arnold's praise for *Departmental Ditties* (1886) and *Plain Tales from the Hills* (1888) (Kipling, *Writings* 136). Lycett suggests that "Arnold probably encouraged the Kiplings to visit Kamakura, twenty miles outside Yokohama, the site of a great bronze and gilt statue of Buddha," which inspired the 1892 poem "Buddha at Kamakura" (Lycett 250). One of the most direct allusions in *Kim* to Arnold's *Light of Asia* occurs when the Lama states, "As a drop draws to water, so my Soul drew near to the Great Soul which is beyond all things" (288). Arnold's famous line, which may itself come from a Buddhist source, is, "the Dewdrop slips / Into the shining sea!" (Arnold 8:216).

31. To take a few examples from the end of Edwin Arnold's *The Light of Asia*, where the Buddha says, "If ye lay bound upon the wheel of change / and no way were of breaking from the chain, / The heart of boundless Being is a curse, / The Soul of Things fell Pain," "the wheel" is synonymous with Kipling's Lama's Wheel, the "chain" refers to the chain of rebirths, and the last two lines allude to the First Noble Truth, which states that suffering is an intrinsic aspect of lived existence (Arnold 8.210). This stanza—"Before beginning, and without an end, / As space eternal and as surety sure, / Is fixed a Power divine which moves to good, / Only its laws endure"—begins a long discourse on the Dharma in which "law" is roughly synonymous with Kipling's Lama's Law (Arnold 8.211). Phrases like "Power divine" represent a quasi-Christian deification. Arnold's Buddha then spends a dozen stanzas romanticizing the Dharma, showing it to have a hand in all things great and small. The poem gives an accurate sense that within the Dharma all natural and human systems are interconnected in an ethically ordered universe, but then attributes to it anthropomorphic features and a creating force that are largely antithetical to Buddhism. The treatment of the Dharma ends with this famous stanza, which, like much of the poem, simultaneously captures a not unreasonable interpretation of Buddhist doctrine while thoroughly Westernizing it: "Such is the Law which moves to righteousness, / Which none at least can turn aside or stay: / The heart of it is Love, the end of it / Is Peace and Consummation sweet. Obey!" (Arnold 8.214).

32. For examples of Victorians who perceived a compatibility between Buddhism and Darwinian theory see *Dublin Review* 19; Eitel 63–66; Lilly 213; *Literary Digest* 162; and T. W. Rhys Davids, *Lectures* 94. This Victorian understanding laid the

groundwork for "new age" and postmodern ecological conceptions of the interconnectedness of systems from spheres as seemingly diverse as quantum mechanics, microbiology, and ethics, a trend perhaps initiated by Huxley's *Evolution and Ethics* (1893). For more in this regard, see Jacobson, 19–35.

33. For some introductions to the Three Marks of Existence, see Erricker, 38; Nhat Hanh, *Heart,* 131; and Snelling, 53–54.

34. This is confirmed in Kipling, *Writings,* 169.

35. In *The Imperial Archive,* Richards develops a more specific argument about Tibet as the imagined repository of knowledge within an Empire that increasingly conceived itself as founded not on military force but on domination through "intelligence," a message that Kipling built into *Kim* and that the novel helped to perpetuate. Richards writes, "In the late nineteenth and early twentieth centuries, the prevalent model for the archival confinement of total knowledge under the purview of the state was Tibet, an imagined community that united archival institutions and persons in one hieratic archive-state" (Richards 11).

36. Along these same lines, Guy Boothby's novel *Dr. Nikola* (1896) recounts the penetration by Westerners of a secret Lamasery in "Thibet" that harbors occult knowledge—dating "from before the apotheosis of the ever-blessed Buddha"—for extending human life indefinitely, in which the monks are described thusly: "A more disreputable-looking crew I can unhesitatingly assert I had never seen before...[;] hardly a face among them that did not suggest the fact that its owner was steeped to the eyebrows in sensuality and crime" (Boothby 44, 159, 245).

37. On perceived similarities (and, it was thought by some, causal links) between Catholicism and Lamaism, see Lopez, *Prisoners,* 15–45.

38. The ox is a familiar symbol in Buddhist allegory for the uncontrolled will, the head-strong mind, the ego. See, for example, Rahula's *Zen and the Taming of the Bull.*

39. Though L. Austine Waddell wrote in places scathingly about the indigenous practices of Tibetan Buddhists, he also summarized some Buddhist doctrines with great respect, as he does here in introducing his interpretation of The Wheel: "Indeed, it would scarcely be going to far to say that at the period before the epoch of Alexander the Great, in the valley of the Ganges, and at a time when writing was still unknown in India, an Indian anchorite evolved in the main by private study and mediation an ontological system which, while having much in common with the philosophy of Plato and of Kant, and the most profound and celebrated speculations of modern times (such as those of Bishop Berkeley, and Schopenhauer, and Hartmann), yet far surpassed these in elaborateness. And as this bold system formed the basis of Buddhist ethics, its formulas came to be represented for teaching purposes in concrete pictorial form in the vestibules of the Indian monasteries and temples, as they still are in Tibet and China" (Waddell, *Tibetan* 107).

40. The six realms of existence depicted between the spokes of the Wheel are, very briefly: the realm of devas or gods, the realm of the jealous titans or demi-gods, the realm of the "hungry ghosts," the realm of tormented beings (partial corollary to the Christian hell, though not eternal), the realm of the animals, and the realm of the human beings.

41. If the "logic was unanswerable," the reader is not given that logic, other than the Lama's conclusion that he had been "tempted" and was misguided in returning to the hills to search for the River of the Arrow. There is no precedent of which I am

aware for interpreting a connection between those two particular "houses" in the chain of dependent origination, though all of the links in the chain are interpreted as both causes and effects of all the others. The image of the woman giving birth indicates rebirth into a new life of suffering, which is what the Lama would avoid by finding the River. "The Child" may point figuratively to the Lama's childhood in the mountains, to which he was "tempted" by nostalgia to return, or to Kim, a child by whom he unknowingly was "tempted" to return there. The "House of the Senses" may point to the fact that the Lama was misled by Kim's sensual engagement with "the world" to pursue the pleasures of his own senses. I also do not know if "houses" is a term used by Tibetan Buddhists or if Kipling might be mixing the Wheel with the astrological zodiac.

42. Victorian sources that discuss the doctrine of dependent origination and its portrayal in the Wheel include Monier-Williams, *Buddhism*, 102–4, and T. W. Rhys Davids, *History*, 101–8. More recent sources include Erricker, 45–49; Nhat Hanh, *Heart*, 221–49; Rahula, *What*, 53–54; and Snelling 62–65.

43. An even stronger response can be seen in D. H. Lawrence a generation later. He traveled to Ceylon in 1922 to visit Earl and Achsah Brewster, who were exploring Buddhism, and exchanged a series of letters with them mentioning Buddhism, as here in a letter from 30 August 1926: "What irritated me in you in the past was a sort of way you had of looking on Buddhism as some sort of easy ether into which you could float away unresisted and resisting. Believe me, no truth is like that. All truth—and real living is the only truth—has in it the elements of battle and repudiation.... You've got to get out of the vast lotus-pool of Buddhism on to the little firm island of your own single destiny. Your island can have its own little lotus pool, its own pink lotus. But *you yourself* must never try again to lose yourself in the universal lotus pool: the mud is too awful" (Lawrence, in Brewster 104–5). Also see Doherty.

44. An example here is Parry's assertion that the "essential 'artifice' of the novel is the pretence throughout that Kim can serve the Lama's quest and the needs of the Great Game," which, I am arguing, is to reproduce the pretense of Western discourse that no other way of knowing is possible (Parry 315).

45. It should be acknowledged that Kipling capitalizes on Kim's rough adherence to the precepts of a *chela* in order to generate sexual tension, especially in the series of exchanges with the Woman of Shamlegh, and to perpetuate the novel's misogynistic portrayal of women primarily as prostitutes. Perhaps the sympathetic portrayal of Gobind Sahai, the Sahiba, counterbalances this. However, perhaps Virginia Woolf is correct in her assessment of the limitations of the masculine point-of-view of novelists like Kipling: "It is not only that they celebrate male virtues, enforce male values and describe the world of men; it is that the emotion with which these books are permeated is to a woman incomprehensible" (Woolf 2514). Suffice it to note here that Buddhist ethics contains explicit instructions concerning "sexual misconduct," and Kim appears to reference these in his exchange with the Woman of Shamlegh.

46. See, for example, Eitel, 80, and Monier-Williams, 559.

47. Sullivan, one of the most astute readers of Kipling, argues that "The powers of contemplation, meditation, vision, repose and nonaction—are subverted at the end of the novel by the plot, by the ideology, and by the lama's final act. By choosing freely to return from nirvana for the sake of Kim, the lama commits an action that is at once human, loving, sacrificial and also supportive of official ideology" (Sullivan 176–77). The first part of this statement represents a misreading based on a lack of

understanding of Buddhism and an attachment to the active/passive dualism; the second sentence even so remains accurate. The Mahayana and Vajrayana *bodhisattva* ideal is precisely to gain enlightenment but then to choose to remain in this world in order to compassionately guide other beings toward nirvana. For a summary introduction to this concept, see Erricker, 66–68, or Snelling, 68 and 82–83. For a reading of the ending of the novel more attuned to this understanding while not entirely incompatible with Sullivan, see Kinkead-Weekes, 439. Also relevant is this statement from Irigaray: "Love takes place in the opening of self that is the place of welcoming the transcendence of the other" (Irigaray 115).

48. It could only have been disturbing to Victorian sensibility that Buddhism is in this sense more individualistic than Protestant individualism. This suggests an inverse logic behind Victorian attacks on the concepts of karma and *anatman* (the "no self" doctrine), namely that Buddhist individual moral responsibility is threatening not for its divergence from but rather for its very similarity to Protestant individualism, which it therefore threatens to displace with a form of individuality that at the same time does not "free" the individual from the necessity of social responsibility. As Max Weber, Raymond Williams, and many other critics have argued, Protestant individualism effectively serves capitalism. I would argue that, in contrast, Buddhist individualism threatens the lasses-faire worldview.

49. For a useful analysis of the Cartesian *cogito*, see Strozier's chapter "Descartes, Interiority, and Identity." I also would agree with Strozier's argument that the "autonomous subject was never relinquished, not even during the era of the greatest poststructural influence," which is to say, that even postmodern theory has not been able to escape entirely from the dominant Western paradigm of the individual self, which, I would add, has never entirely shaken off the Christian body/soul dichotomy (Strozier 54).

50. T. W. Rhys Davids made this same point in 1896: "Secondly, it is the belief common to all schools of the Buddhists that the origin of sorrow is precisely identical with the origin of individuality. Sorrow is in fact the result of the effort which an individual has to make to keep separate from the rest of existence" (T. Rhys Davids, *History* 81).

51. In this same vein, Caroline Rhys Davids was even less polite than her husband in describing how Buddhism obviates the "inner mannikin [sic]" of the "animistic soul" as well as the myth of the "absolutistic self" (C. Rhys Davids, *Buddhism* 55, 56).

52. One primary source on eternalism and annihilationism is *The Connected Discourses of the Buddha*, 2:1393–94. Recent commentaries include Gowans, 67–68, and Rahula, *What*, 66.

53. Giles refers here to David Hume's argument in *A Treatise on Human Understanding* (1748), one of the few Western philosophers until the twentieth century whose understanding of identity approached the Buddhist theory of selfhood as consisting of Five Aggregates that do not compose an integrated, essential self. On Hume in relation to Buddhism, see Giles, "No-Self"; Gowans, 80; and Jacobson, 62, 158, and 160.

54. Considerations on karma as "character" are widespread; see, for example, Bettany, 155; Burnouf, 12; Eitel, 73; Lilly, 204; and, more recently, Fox, 115 and 131.

55. For another example of a Theosophical interpretation of the multi-layered self, see Sinnett, *Early Days*, 103. The Theosophical conception of the "higher self" likely owes a debt to Matthew Arnold's *Culture and Anarchy*, as discussed in Whitlark, "Matthew Arnold and Buddhism," 26.

56. For a fuller response to Caroline Rhys Davids and to all who attempt to find in Buddhist scripture a basis for belief in an eternal soul, see Rahula, *What* 55–66.

57. The sutras attribute this point to the Buddha many times, as here he is quoted in the *Cūlasaccaka Sutta:* " 'Bhikkhus, material form is impermanent, feeling is impermanent, perception is impermanent, formations are impermanent, consciousness is impermanent. Bhikkhus, material form is not self, feeling is not self, perception is not self, formations are not self, consciousness is not self. All formations are impermanent; all things are not self' " (*Middle* 322).

58. The original source of the story of Nagasena and King Milinda is the *Milindapahna,* or *The Questions of King Menander,* of which there are many versions, including Mendis. Discussions of this story are numerous; see Oldenberg, 254–58; T. Rhys Davids, *Buddhism,* 95; and, more recently, Giles, *No Self,* 130; and Gowans, 82.

59. This argument of Nagasena's to King Milinda was effectively reproduced in the eighteenth century by David Hume in *A Treatise of Human Understanding* (1748), which uses the example of a ship, the parts of which are gradually replaced over the years until not a single part belonging to the original ship remains. Is this the same ship or a different ship; where is the essence of ship? Approaching the Buddhist theory of the Five Aggregates, Hume wrote: "When I enter most intimately into what I call *myself,* I always stumble on some particular perception or other, of heat or cold, light or shade, love or hatred, pain or pleasure. I never can catch *myself* at any time without a perception, and never can observe any thing but the perception" (Hume 252).

60. I borrow the concept of "monological," as opposed to "dialogical," from Bakhtin.

61. I use the term "hail" in the sense developed by Althusser in his definition of "interpellation" (Althusser 174–75).

62. By "soft imperialism" I mean to acknowledge that Kipling favored the hegemony of cultural incorporation over military domination of India and that in places *Kim* reproduces this view. Kipling's view was representative of an attitude prevalent among the Indian Civil Service, as Reid and Washbrook argue. Richards argues in this regard that "what *Kim* figures more clearly than any other Victorian text is a world in which colonization through ethnocide, deportation, and slavery...has begun to give way to colonization through the mediated instrumentality of information" (Richards 23). A related claim appears in Eung (727). Suleri goes a step further in claiming that "if one of the manifestations of the anxiety of empire is a repression of the conflictual model even where economic and political conflict is at its most keenly operative, then Kipling's transcriptions of such evasion point to his acute understanding of the ambivalence with which empire declares its unitary powers" (Suleri 115). Though this charge is largely accurate, the reading of which it is a part fails to perceive other potential readings available in the text in the process of projecting onto the novel the very imperial condescension that it claims to find there.

63. A twenty-first-century example of this aspect of Buddhism is provided by the teachings of Thich Nhat Hanh, the first of whose "Fourteen Mindfulness Trainings" reads as follows: "*Aware of the suffering created by fanaticism and intolerance,* we are determined not to be idolatrous about or bound to any doctrine, theory, or ideology, even Buddhist ones. Buddhist teachings are guiding means to help us learn to look deeply and to develop our understanding and compassion. They are not doctrines to fight, kill, or die for" (Nhat Hanh, *Interbeing* 17).

64. Discussions of the Buddha's dialogue with Vacchagotta and then Ananda may be found in Gowans, 67; Rahula, *What,* 66; Santina, 153; and, in a widely read nineteenth century source, Oldenberg, 272.

65. According to canonical scripture, the Buddha saw nihilism as another form of attachment to self, and one of the sources of human suffering as described in the second of the Four Noble Truths, as here: "And what, friends, is the noble truth of the origin of suffering? It is craving, which brings renewal of being, is accompanied by delight and lust, and delights in this and that; that is, craving for sensual pleasure, craving for being,...and craving for non-being" (*Middle* 1099).

66. For a formal analysis of tetralemma logic in relation to artificial intelligence systems, see Sawamura and Mares.

67. Though I would not agree with every criticism leveled at postcolonial theory by Erin O'Connor, I think he has it right when he says that "the scholarship aimed at demystifying Victorian literature's ideological complicity with empire is itself an integral part of the narrative tradition it seeks to expose" (O'Connor 240).

68. While Kim is figured as a disciple to the Buddha as Ananda was the Buddha's discipline, in the Jataka tale that the Lama twice tells of the older elephant liberated from the leg iron by the younger elephant, Kim is figured rather as himself the Buddha who frees Ananda. See *Kim*, 165–66and 192. As Sandra Kemp notes, the Jatakas, the folkloric collection of stories about the Buddha's birth and former lives, which was translated by T. W. Rhys Davids in 1880, were a primary influence on Kipling's writing: "Kipling's father shows his acquaintance with them in *Beast and Man in India* (1891), and they were among the source material for Kipling's *Jungle Books, Just So Stories* and *Kim*" (Kemp 32). As Kipling wrote in a letter to Edward Everett Hale, 16 January 1895: "The idea of beast-tales seems to me new in that it is a most ancient and long forgotten idea. The really fascinating tales are those that the Bodhisat tells of his previous incarnations ending always with the beautiful moral" (Kipling, *Writings* 46). Having consulted several sources that would have been available to Kipling—including Jacobs (who used Rhys Davids's translation), Speyer, and *Tibetan Tales*—I have been unable to locate the particular tale recounted by Kipling's Lama, which inclines me to think that Kipling invented it, drawing on the Jatakas as a pattern. On the influence of the Jataka tales on Kipling, see Caracciolo.

69. At the peripheries of Western discourse, from perspectives as disparate as New Age Wicca and twenty-first-century quantum physics, Kim's dissolution of the separating slash in "physical/mental" or "material/spiritual" is entirely natural. As Richard King notes, "Today, comparisons are made between quantum mechanics and the 'new physics' on the one hand with the non-substantialism and non-dualism of Mahāyāna Buddhist thought" (King 152). I leave the question of the supportability of those comparisons to others. One recent example from popular culture is the film *What the #$*! Do We (K)now!??*

Conclusion: The Afterlife of Nirvana

1. Recent scholarship confirms Everett's observation. Clausen notes that "perhaps the most significant controversy, however, was over the nature of Nirvana" (Clausen 9). Whitlark observes that in the 1880s–1890s "the nature of nirvana was relatively common topic of conversations among people more interested than knowledgeable" (Whitlark, "Nirvana Talk" 17). Almond concurs: "Of all the aspects of Buddhist doctrine with which the Victorians dealt, the question of the nature of Nirvana aroused the most interest and the most controversy" (Almond 102).

2. One frequently cited example of the Buddha's discussion of annihilationism and eternalism is in his dialogue with Vacchagotta and then Anatta found in *The Connected Discourses of the Buddha*, 2:1393–94. For analysis of this dialogue, see Gowans, 67; Rahula, *What*, 62–66; Santina, 153; and, in a widely read nineteenth-century source, Oldenberg, 272.

3. As Everett summarized this well-known point in 1882: "The question [what is nirvana?] was forced upon him by his disciples. They begged him to give an answer. He simply refused to have anything to do with it. He told them that it was of no practical concerns, and pointed them back to the path which they were to tread" (Everett 432–33). Also in this regard see Huxley, *Evolution*, 102, 160, and Oldenberg, 263.

4. For other, representative statements about Nirvana attributed to the Buddha, see, for example, the *Middle Length Discourses*, 536, 540, and 613. Statements in the sutras about Nirvana are quoted and analyzed in Oldenberg, 263–85, and T. W. Rhys Davids, *Buddhism*, 110–11.

5. Colebrooke's monograph, which was delivered to the Royal Asiatic Society, was published in 1837 as part of *Essays on the Religion and Philosophy of the Hindus*. On Colebrooke, also see Droit, 50 and 175.

6. One version of the anti-indigenous argument ran as follows: "The only ground, therefore, on which we may stand, if we wish to defend the founder of Buddhism against the charges of Nihilism and Atheism, is this, that, as some of the Buddhists admit, the 'Basket of Metaphysics' was rather the work of his pupils, not of Buddha himself" (Müller, *Chips* 281). Other examples of the anti-indigenous argument can be found in Ambereley, 313; Gordon, 527; and Müller, *Lectures*, 144.

7. Here is a fuller statement of Rhys Davids's position: "What then is Nirvāna, which means simply going out, extinction; it being quite clear, from what has gone before, that this cannot be the extinction of the soul? *It is the extinction of that sinful, grasping condition of mind and heart, which would otherwise, according to the great mystery of Karma, be the cause of renewed individual existence....* Nirvāna is therefore the same thing as a *sinless, calm state of mind;* and if translated at all, may best, perhaps, be rendered 'holiness'—holiness, that is, in the Buddhist sense, *perfect peace, goodness, and wisdom*" (Rhys Davids, *Buddhism* 111–12).

8. For other examples of Victorians who understood Nirvana neither as annihilation nor as "absorption" but rather as achievable in this life, see Huxley, *Evolution*, 126, and Oldenberg, 283–84. One thoughtful philosophical analysis of this understanding of Nirvana can be found in Gowans, 135–47.

9. On the linkage between Schopenhauer and Buddhism, I am indebted to various sources, including, Droit, 45, 76, and 91–103; Welbon, 154–93; and Dumoulin. Also relevant are Batchelor, 250–71; Clarke, 76–79; and Schwab, 427–34. Taylor concludes that Schopenhauer's pessimistic assessment of the human condition "appears to have been lifted directly from Buddhism," and that his philosophy recommends "a kind of existence divested of will, evidently coinciding exactly with the *nirvana* sought by the Buddhist" (Taylor 176).

10. "Cult of nothingness" was coined as a descriptor of Nirvana by Victor Cousin in 1829, as discussed in Droit, 84. Droit also more fully articulates the point: "The last half of the nineteenth century believed, with increasing firmness, that Schopenhauer and the Buddha were saying the same thing. Pessimism and nihilism were lastingly associated with Buddhism in the European imagination, beginning with the decade of the 1850s" (Droit 93).

11. Another example of this argument is Ambereley, writing in 1872: "Nirvâna, in short, is the abstraction of theologians; the bliss of heaven is the hope of the masses" (Amberley 313).

12. An introduction to the influence of exposure to Eastern religions and philosophies on the American Transcendentalists can be found in various sources, including Clarke, 84–92; Dejong; Fields, 60; Godwin, 309; and Schwab, 200. The best sourcebook I have found on the impact of Eastern thought on the United States is Tweed and Prothero.

13. This claim stands despite the existence within Buddhist mythology of the realm of *devas* or gods, as pictured in one segment of the Wheel of Becoming. This "heaven," as it sometimes is translated, is not eternal: gods too are subject to karma and may be reborn in lower realms. Also, I am aware that my claim may fail to account for the modern Japanese Pure Land sect, about which I am largely uninformed but which I understand posits a heaven-like afterlife.

14. My use of male pronouns throughout does not represent a lack of awareness but rather reflects the highly gendered nature both of Nietzsche's philosophy and of the Western ideology of the self-made man.

15. Fox writes in a similar vein: "They [early Buddhists] had known the moment of awakening to Something that transcended the world: their logic had taught them this Something was, in fact *no* thing, since it could not be categorized or expressed, but that it was not *nothing*, since nihilism was not a tenable position. There was, then, a Real and it was not simply the world *as one usually understood it;* it could be known only when one had abandoned all the logical presuppositions with which one became burdened from infancy" (Fox 93).

16. Turner goes so far as to argue that the Christian afterlife serves a critical social function in preserving an order that protects the power of the wealthiest because it provides the promise of a "Heavenly reward" that will make up for the inequality of temporal life. Thus anything that undermines belief in the eternal soul threatens to undermine the dominant social order. See Turner, *Contesting Cultural Authority,* 110.

17. Neither Nietzsche's theory of the will to power nor his theory of nihilism are limited to the work titled *Will to Power;* both are rooted in his writings as a whole. Because *Will to Power* is one primary work from which I have drawn, the reader should be informed that it consists of a series of aphoristic fragments written by Nietzsche but compiled and edited after his death by his sister, Elisabeth Förster Nietzsche, and others. Thus philosophers consider it less authoritative than Nietzsche's fully finished works. On this point, see Kaufman, 15–20. The sources that I have consulted suggest that Nietzsche's conception of nihilism in *Will to Power* is consistent with that found in his finished works; I leave the details of that debate to professional philosophers.

18. On Nietzsche's nihilism and his distinction between active and passive nihilism, I have consulted, in addition to Nietzsche himself, works by Barnes, Beardsworth, Caygill, Clemens and Feik, Conway, Bret W. Davis, Glicksberg, Kaufmann, Ratschow, and Solomon.

19. Brobjer provides analysis and a timeline of Nietzsche's reading in Oriental philosophies, in particular the early German scholarship on Buddhism. On Nietzsche's debt to Schopenhauer, see Solomon, 105–9, as well as sources that treat Schopenhauer's and Nietzsche's contact with Buddhism: Batchelor, 250–71; Clarke, 76–84; Droit, 143–48; Schwab, 426–38; Welbon, 154–93.

20. In contrast to the summary treatment here, Conway offers a sophisticated analysis of Nietzsche's "will to power" as less a quality of individual volition or "metaphysical will" than a "trans-human cosmological hypothesis," which strikes me as akin to D. H. Lawrence's vitalism and not necessarily opposed to Buddhist dependent origination (Conway 128).

21. I draw in this paragraph upon Kaufmann, who, among other Nietzsche scholars, traces the parallels between central Nietzschean concepts across his writings.

22. Kaufmann observes in this regard that "negatively, the doctrine of eternal recurrence is the most extreme repudiation of any deprecation of the moment, the finite, and the individual—the antithesis of any faith which pins its hopes on infinite progress, whether it be [biological] evolution...or the endless improvement of the human soul" (Kaufmann 277).

23. For a limited perspective on nihilism in these and other modernist authors, see Glicksberg. Also relevant is Kevin Bell.

24. General sources on Conrad and Buddhism include Brashers, Julkarni, Lombard, Saravan, Stein, and, especially, the works by Caracciolo. On Eliot and Buddhism, see Caracciolo, Gillis, and McConnell.

25. On Nietzsche's early study of Buddhism see Bell, 7 and 105; Bret W. Davis; Doherty; and Widmer, 115.

26. As Michael Bell observes in this regard, "To some extent, Lawrence's understanding of Nietzsche was through the popular conception by which the 'will to power' was effectively identified with the assertive will Birkin sees in Gerald Crich" (Bell 7).

27. A small sample of the criticism on Lawrence's individualism is represented by Brown, Langbaum, Rooks, and Zytaruk.

28. For this same reason, Bell argues that in *Women in Love* while Gerald represents Nietzschean active nihilism, "Birkin's concern for psychic wholeness and renewal makes him the more truly Nietzschean figure," the Dionysian Nietzsche (Bell 105).

29. As Doherty puts this point in relationship to *Aaron's Rod:* "Thus 'nirvana' is a type of solipsistic idealism, the attempt to 'lose yourself' in a woman or in humanity or in God....At the same time, however, as the text is actively subverting the nirvana 'ideal,' it suppresses a more crucial indebtedness to Buddhism" (Doherty, "Nirvana" 57).

30. What I am calling Lawrence's "red Nirvana" points to the privileging of the figure of the phallus within his vitalism. I avoid this point because it opens into complex critical debates concerning the degree of Lawrence's gender bias and sexism that are at once too significant and too peripheral to the present purposes to be addressed in this context. Another point that requires mention, if only in a footnote, is that Lawrence attempted to translate Buddhism into his phallic vitalism, as in this excerpt from a letter of 8 November 1927 to the Brewsters: "Did you know that in ancient Buddhism, the 'stupa' occupied the holy central position in the cave, or the temple: and when the Buddha figure was invented, the standing Buddha took the place of this stupa. Now it looks to me as if this stupa was just the monumental phallic symbol....And the standing Buddha has still a phallic quality" (Lawrence in Brewster 153).

31. On Sartre's concept of nihilation, see, for example, 104 and 775–76, as well as analysis in Barnes and Solomon.

32. The concept of freedom is integral to Sartre's philosophy, as analyzed in Solomon, 248, 271, 285, and 314.

33. Note the Russian contribution to modern nihilism and its subsequent association with revolutionary politics (as in Joseph Conrad's *The Secret Agent* [1907]) in Clemens and Feik, 22–32; Goudsblom, 8; and Olson, 515.

34. Indeed, I suggest that the "postmodern condition" in part describes the outcome of the historical fact that the "democratization of the humanist tradition has place[d] the 'nothing is true' theory within everyone's reach" (Goudsblom 179). Nihilism, now ubiquitous, is the source of postmodern irony. I further agree with Clemens and Feik that the era in which we live "is nihilistic not only because it is witness to the ungroundedness of all values, but also because it cannot recognise this becoming-nothing of its ground" (Clemens and Feik 20–21). I believe this is the hypocrisy of those who live in denial that nihilism underlies the corporate-capitalist state, or, worse, who, like some politicians, cynically claim values that their actions belie.

35. This describes Buddhism as a "meta-ethics," which as it happens is one way that defenders of existentialism describe its ethical orientation, as for example in Solomon, 316.

36. See for example Jones, *The New Social Face of Buddhism.*

37. On the current state of Buddhism in the West, see Coleman.

Bibliography

Alabaster, Henry. *The Wheel of the Law: Buddhism Illustrated from Siamese Sources.* London: Trübner & Co., 1871.

Albert, Eliot. "The Shattering of the Crystal Spheres: 'rolling from the centre toward X.'" In *Nihilism Now! Monsters of Energy,* edited by Keith Ansell Pearson and Diane Morgan, 1–17. New York: St. Martin's, 2000.

Alexander, Sidney Arthur. *Sakya-Muni: The Story of Buddha.* Oxford: A. Thomas Shrimpton & Son, 1887.

Allen, Charles. *The Search for the Buddha: The Men who Discovered India's Lost Religion.* New York: Carroll & Graf, 2002.

Almond, Philip C. *The British Discovery of Buddhism.* Cambridge: Cambridge University Press, 1988.

Althusser, Louis. *Lenin and Philosophy.* Translated by Ben Brewster. New York: Pantheon, 1969.

Ambereley, John R. "Recent Publications on Buddhism." *The Theological Review* 9 (1872): 293–317.

Anderson, Jerome A. *Reincarnation, A Study of the Human Soul In its Relation to Re-Birth, Evolution, Post-Mortem States, the Compound Nature of Man, Hypnotism, etc.* 4th ed. San Francisco: Lotus Publishing, 1896.

Annan, Noel. "Kipling's Place in the History of Ideas." In *Kim,* edited by Zohreh T. Sullivan, 323–28. Norton Critical Edition. New York: W. W. Norton, 2002.

Archer, Mildred, and Ronald Lightbown. *India Observed: India as Viewed by British Artists, 1760–1860.* London: Victoria and Albert Museum, 1982.

Armstrong, Richard A. "Buddhism and Christianity." *The Theological Review* 7 (1870): 176–200.

Arnold, Edwin. *The Light of Asia: Being The Life and Teaching of Gôtama, Prince of India and Founder of Búddhism.* 1879. Edited by I. L. Hauser. Chicago: Rand, McNally, 1890.

Arnold, Edwin. *The Light of Asia, or The Great Renunciation (Mahābhinishkramana), Being the Life and Teaching of Gautama, Prince of India and Founder of Buddhism (As told in verse by an Indian Buddhist)*. 1879. Adyar, India: The Theosophical Press, 1997.

Arnold, Matthew. *Culture and Anarchy*. 1869. Edited by Samuel Lipman. New Haven: Yale University Press, 1994.

Arundale, Francesca. *The Idea of Re-birth: Including a Translation of an Essay on Reincarnation by Karl Heckel*. London: Kegan Paul, Trench, Trubner, & Co., 1890.

Ashvaghosa. *The Buddhacarita; or, Acts of the Buddha. Complete Sanskrit text with English translation*. Edited by E. H. Johnston. Delhi: Motilal Banarsidass, 1972.

BBC News. "Buddhism Becomes Second Religion." 4 March 2003. http://news.bbc.co.uk/2/hi/uk_news/england/2820377.stm.

Bagland, Eileen. *Marie Corelli, The Woman and the Legend, A Biography*. London: Jarrolds Publishers, 1953.

Bakhtin, Mikhail. *The Dialogic Imagination: Four Essays*. Edited by Michael Holquist. Translated by Caryl Emerson and Michael Holquist. Austin: University of Texas Press, 1981.

Ballard, Frank. *Why Not Buddhism?* No. 10. The Christian "Why Not?" Series. London: Charles H. Kelly, 1915.

Barnes, Hazel E. Introduction to Jean-Paul Sartre, *Being and Nothingness: An Essay on Phenomenological Ontology*. Translated by Hazel E. Barnes. New York: Philosophical Library, 1956.

Batchelor, Stephen. *The Awakening of the West: The Encounter of Buddhism and Western Culture*. Berkeley: Parallax Press, 1994.

Bathélemy Saint-Hilaire, J. *The Buddha and His Religion*. 1860. London: Bracken, 1996.

Baucom, Ian. *Out of Place: Englishness, Empire, and the Locations of Identity*. Princeton: Princeton University Press, 1999.

——. "[The Survey of India]." In *Kim, by Rudyard Kipling*, edited by Zohreh T. Sullivan, 351–58. Norton Critical Edition. New York: W. W. Norton, 2002.

Baudrillard, Jean. *Simulacra and Sumulacrum*. Translated by Sheila Faria Glaswer. Ann Arbor: University of Michigan Press, 1994.

Beal, Samuel. *The Romantic Legend of Śākya Buddha, A Translation of the Chinese Version of the Abhiniṣkramaṇasūtra*. 1875. Delhi, India: Motilal Banarsidass, 1985.

——. *Si-Yu-Ki: Buddhist Records of the Western World, Translated from the Chinese of Hiuen Tsiang (A.D. 629)*. 1884. New York: Paragon Book Reprint Corp., 1968.

——. *Travels of Fah-Hian and Sung-Yun, Buddhist pilgrims, from China to India (400 A.D. and 518 A.D.)*. London: Trübner, 1869.

Beardsworth, Richard. "Nietzsche, Nihilism and Spirit." In *Nihilism Now! Monsters of Energy*, edited by Keith Ansell Pearson and Diane Morgan, 37–69. New York: St. Martin's Press, 2000.

Beckerlegge, G. "Professor Friedrich Max Müller and the Missionary Cause." In *Religion in Victorian Britain. Volume V: Culture and Empire*, edited by John Wolfe, 177–220. Manchester: Manchester University Press, 1997.

Beer, Gillian. *Darwin's Plots: Evolutionary Narrative in Darwin, George Eliot and Nineteenth-Century Fiction*. London: Routledge and Kegan Paul, 1983.

Bell, Kevin. *Ashes Taken for Fire: Aesthetic Modernism and the Critique of Identity*. Minneapolis: University of Minnesota Press, 2007.

Bell, Michael. *D. H. Lawrence: Language and Being.* Cambridge: Cambridge University Press, 1991.

Bellah, Robert. *Beyond Belief: Essays on Religion in a Post-Traditional World.* New York: Harper and Row, 1970.

Besant, Annie. *The Self and Its Sheaths: Four Lectures.* Benares: Theosophical Publishing Society, 1895.

Bevir, Mark. "A Theosophist in India." In *Imperial Objects: Essays on Victorian Women's Emigration and the Unauthorized Imperial Experience,* edited by Rita S. Kranidis, 211–27. New York: Twayne, 1998.

———. "The West Turns Eastward: Madame Blavatsky and the Transformation of the Occult Tradition." *Journal of the American Academy of Religion* 63.3 (Fall 1994): 747–67.

Bhabha, Homi K. *The Location of Culture.* London: Routledge, 1994.

Bigandet, The Right Rev. P. [Paul Ambrose]. *The Life or Legend of Gaudama, The Budha of the Burmese, with annotations. Notice on the Phongies, or Budhist Religious, and The Ways to Niban.* Rangoon: Pegu Press, 1858.

Bishop, Isabella Bird. *Among the Tibetans.* New York: Fleming H. Revell, 1894.

Bishop, Peter. *The Myth of Shangri-La: Tibet, Travel Writing and the Western Creation of Scared Landscape.* Berkeley: University of California Press, 1989.

Blavatsky, H. P. *Isis Unveiled: A Master-Key to the Mysteries of Ancient and Modern Science and Theology. Vol. 1: Science.* 1877. Pasadena, CA: Theosophical University Press, 1972.

———. *Isis Unveiled: A Master-Key to the Mysteries of Ancient and Modern Science and Theology. Vol. 2: Theology.* 1877. Pasadena, CA: Theosophical University Press, 1972.

———. *The Key to Theosophy: Being a Clear Exposition, in the form of Question and Answer, of the Ethics, Science, and Philosophy for the study of which the Theosophical Society has been founded.* New York: Theosophical Publishing Company, 1889.

———. Letter of 19 November 1877. *The Canadian Theosophist* (September–October 1990; January–February 1991).

———. Letter to Hiram Corson. 16 February 1875. In *Some Unpublished Letters of H.P. Blavatsky,* edited by Eugene Corson, 127–29. London: Rider & Co., 1929.

———. Letter to F. Hartmann. 3 April 1886. *The Theosophical Quarterly* (April 1926): 324.

———. "Mr. Lillie's Delusions." Letter to the Editor. *Light* (9 August 1884): 323–24.

———. *The Secret Doctrine: The Synthesis of Science, Religion, and Philosophy.* London: Theosophical Publishing Company, 1888.

Bloomfield, Maurice. "Essentials of Buddhist Doctrine and Ethics." *International Journal of Ethics Devoted to the Advancement of Ethical Knowledge and Practice* 2, no. 3 (April 1892): 313–26.

Bode, Mabel. "Women Leaders of the Buddhist Reformation." *Journal of the Royal Asiatic Society of Great Britain and Ireland* 25 (1893): 517–66, 763–98.

Brandon, Ruth. *The Spiritualists: The Passion for the Occult in the Nineteenth and Twentieth Centuries.* New York: Alfred A. Knopf, 1983.

Brantlinger, Patrick. "Imperial Gothic: Atavism and the Occult in the British Adventure Novel, 1880–1914." In *Reading Fin de Siècle Fictions,* edited by Lyn Pykett, 184–209. London: Longman, 1996.

———. *Rule of Darkness: British Literature and Imperialism, 1830–1914.* Ithaca: Cornell University Press, 1988.

Brashers, H. C. "Conrad, Marlow, and Gautama Buddha." *Conradiana* 1 (1969): 63–71.

Braud, Ann. "The Perils of Passivity: Women's Leadership in Spiritualism and Christian Science." In *Women's Leadership in Marginal Religions: Explorations Outside the Mainstream,* edited by Catherine Wessinger, 55–67. Urbana: University of Illinois Press, 1993.

Brear, Douglas. "Early Assumptions in Western Buddhist Studies." *Religion: Journal of Religion and Religions* 5 (Autumn 1975): 136–59.

Breckenridge, Carol A., and Peter van der Veer, eds. *Orientalism and the Postcolonial Predicament: Perspectives on South Asia.* Philadelphia: University of Pennsylvania Press, 1993.

Brewster, Earl, and Achsah Brewster. *D. H. Lawrence: Reminiscences and Correspondence.* London: Martin Secker, 1934.

Brobjer, Thomas H. "Nietzsche's Reading about Eastern Philosophy." *Journal of Nietzsche Studies* 28 (2004): 3–35.

Brown, Dennis. *The Modernist Self in Twentieth-Century English Literature.* New York: St. Martin's Press, 1989.

Buckley, Jerome Hamilton. *The Triumph of Time: A Study of the Victorian Concepts of Time, History, Progress, and Decadence.* Cambridge, MA: Harvard Belknap, 1966.

Buddhaghosa, *Visuddhimagga.* 5th century CE.

Budge, Wallis. *Egyptian Ideas of the Future Life.* 1899. New York: University Books, 1959.

Bulwer-Lytton, Edward. *A Strange Story.* 1866. In vol. 10 of *The Worlds of Edward Bulwer Lytton.* New York: P. F. Collier and Son, 1901.

Bunsen, Ernest de. *The Angel-Messiah of Buddhists, Essenes, and Christians.* London: Longmans, Green, 1880.

Burdett, Carolyn. "Romance, Reincarnation, and Rider Haggard." In *The Victorian Supernatural,* edited by Nicola Brown, Carolyn Burdett, and Pamela Thurschwell, 217–38. Cambridge: Cambridge University Press, 2004.

Burfield, Diana. "Theosophy and Feminism: Some Explorations in Nineteenth-Century Biography." In *Women's Religious Experience,* edited by Pat Holden, 27–56. Totowa, NJ: Barnes & Noble Books, 1983.

Burnouf, Eugène. *L'introduction à L'historie du Buddhisme Indien.* 1844. Edited and translated as *Legends of Indian Buddhism* by L. Canmer-Byng and S. A. Kapadia. New Dehli: Ess Ess Publications, 1976.

Burton, Antoinette. *At the Heart of Empire: Indians and the Colonial Encounter in Late-Victorian Britain.* Berkeley: University of California Press, 1998.

Byrne, Peter. *Natural Religion and the Nature of Religion.* London: Routledge, 1989.

Caracciolo, Peter. "Buddhist Teaching Stories and Their Influence on Conrad, Wells, and Kipling: The Reception of the Jataka and Allied Genres in Victorian Culture." *Conradian* 11.1 (1986): 24–34.

——. "Buddhist Typologies in *Heart of Darkness* and *Victory* and Their Contribution to the Modernism of Jacob Epstein, Wyndham Lewis, and T. S. Eliot." *The Conradian* 14.1–2 (1989): 67–91.

Carpenter, J. Estlin. "The Obligations of the New Testament to Buddhism." *Nineteenth Century, a Monthly Review* 8 (1880): 971–94.

Carr, Kent. *Miss Marie Corelli.* London: Henry J. Drane, 1901.

Carrington, Charles. The Origins of *Kim.*" In Rudyard Kipling. *Kim,* edited by Zohreh T. Sullivan, 278–82. A Norton Critical Edition. New York: W. W. Norton, 2002

Carroll, Lewis. *The Adventures of Alice in Wonderland.* 1865. Peterborough, ONT: Broadview Press, 2000.

Caygill, Howard. "The Survival of Nihilism." In *Nihilism Now! Monsters of Energy,* edited by Keith Ansell Pearson and Diane Morgan, 189–97. New York: St. Martin's, 2000.

Cerullo, John J. *The Secularization of the Soul: Psychical Research in Modern Britain.* Philadelphia: Institute for the Study of Human Issues, 1982.

Clarke, J. J. *Oriental Enlightenment: The Encounter between Asian and Western Thought.* London: Routledge, 1997.

Clarke, James Freeman. "Buddhism; or, the Protestantism of the East." *Atlantic Monthly* 23 (1869): 713–28.

Clausen, Christopher. "'The Light of Asia': An Annotated Critical Edition." Ph.D. diss., Queen's University, 1972.

——. "Sir Edwin Arnold's *The Light of Asia* and Its Reception." *Literature East & West* 17 (1973): 174–91.

——. "Victorian Buddhism and the Origins of Comparative Religion." *Religion: A Journal of Religion & Religions* 5 (1975): 1–15.

Clemens, Justin, and Chris Feik. "Nihilism, Tonight...." In *Nihilism Now! Monsters of Energy,* edited by Keith Ansell Pearson and Diane Morgan, 18–36. New York: St. Martin's Press, 2000.

Coates, John D. "The 'Spiritual Quest' in Rider Haggard's *She* and *Ayesha.*" *Cahiers victoriens & edouardiens* 57 (2003): 33–45.

Colebrooke, Henry Thomas. *Essays on the Religion and Philosophy of the Hindus.* London: Trübner, 1837.

Coleman, William Emmette. "The Sources of Madame Blavatsky's Writings." In *A Modern Priestess of Isis.* Translated by Walter Leaf, 353–66. London: Longmans, Green, 1895.

——. "A Splendid Fraud: Sources of Theosophical Literature—Where Blavatsky Got Her Book." *The Daily Examiner* (San Francisco), July 8 1888: 12.

Collins, Mortimer. *Transmigration.* London: Chatto & Windus, 1883.

Collins, Richard. *Buddhism and 'The Light of Asia.'* Victoria Institute: London, 1893.

Collins, Steven. *Selfless Persons: Imagery and Thought in Theravāda Buddhism.* Cambridge: Cambridge University Press, 1982.

Collins, Wilkie. *The Moonstone.* 1868. 2nd ed. Oxford: Oxford University Press, 2000.

——. *The Woman in White.* 1860. Oxford World Classics. Oxford: Oxford University Press, 1999.

Colombo, Reginald Stephen. "Buddhism." *The Nineteenth Century* (July 1888): 119–35.

The Connected Discourses of the Buddha. 2 Vols. Translated by Bhikku Bodhi. Boston: Wisdom Publications, 2000.

Conrad, Joseph. *Heart of Darkness.* 1901. Boston: Bedford/St. Martin's, 1996.

——. *The Secret Agent: A Simple Tale.* 1907. Oxford: Oxford University Press, 1998.

Conway, Daniel. "Revisiting the Will to Power: Active Nihilism and the Project of Trans-human Philosophy." In *Nihilism Now! Monsters of Energy,* edited by Keith Ansell Pearson and Diane Morgan, 117–41. New York: St. Martin's Press, 2000.

Cook, Keningale. "The Ancient Faith of Egypt." *Dublin University Magazine* 90 (1877): 27–51.

Corelli, Marie. *Free Opinions Freely Expressed on Certain Phases of Modern Social Life and Conduct.* London: Archibald Constable, 1905.

——. *The Life Everlasting, A Romance of Reality.* 1911. Los Angeles: Borden, 1966.

——. *A Romance of Two Worlds.* 1886. Los Angeles: Borden, 1947.

Cowell, E. B. "Jataka; or, Stories of the Buddha's Former Births." *Westminster Review* 145 (June, 1896): 622–34.

Crook, Paul. "Social Darwinism: The Concept." *History of European Ideas* 22.4 (1996): 261–74.

Countess of Jersey. "Buddhism, and Christianity." *National Review* 4 (1884–85): 577.

Cust, Robert Needham. "The Philosophical Aspect of the Idea of Metempsychosis." *Calcutta Review* 107 (July 1898): 42–78.

Dall, C. H. A. "Legend of Buddha and Life of Christ." *Unitarian Review* (Boston) 18 (September 1882): 230–41.

Darwin, Charles. *The Descent of Man and Selection in Relation to Sex.* 1871. 2nd ed. New York: Appleton, 1874.

——. *On the Origin of Species by Means of Natural Selection, or the Preservation of Favoured Races in the Struggle for Life.* 1859. 2 vols. New York: Appleton, 1897.

Das, Sarat Chandra. *Indian Pandits in the Land of Snow.* Calcutta: Baptist Mission Press, 1893. Repr. Calcutta: Firma K. L. Mukhopadhyay, 1965.

——. *Journey to Lhasa and Central Tibet.* 2nd ed. London: John Murray, 1902.

Davies, A. "The Aryan Myth: Its Religious Significance," *Studies in Religion* 10.3 (1981): 290–95.

Davis, Bret W. "Zen after Zarathustra: The Problem of the Will in the Confrontation between Nietzsche and Buddhism." *Journal of Nietzsche Studies* 28 (2004): 89–138.

Davis, Charles Maurice. *Mystic London.* New York: John W. Lovell, 1890.

Davis, Mary F. *Danger Signals: An Address of the Uses and Abuses of Modern Spiritualism.* New York: A. J. Davis, 1875.

Dean, Susan Thach. "Decadence, Evolution, and Will: Caroline Rhys Davids' 'Original' Buddhism." In *Women's Theology in Nineteenth-Century Britain: Transfiguring the Faith of Their Fathers,* edited by Julie Melnyk, 209–31. London: Garland, 1998.

de Harlez, C. "Buddhist Propaganda in Christian Countries." *Dublin Review* 107, 3S24 (1890): 54–73.

De Jong, J. W. "A Brief History of Buddhist Studies in Europe and America." *The Eastern Buddhist* 7.1 (1974): 55–106.

de Purucker, G. *Occult Glossary: A Compendium of Oriental and Theosophical Terms.* 1933. Pasadena, CA: Theosophical University Press, 1953.

Dillon, E. J. "Ecclesiastes and Buddhism." *Contemporary Review* 65 (1894): 153–76.

Dixon, Joy. *Divine Feminine: Theosophy and Feminism in England.* Baltimore: Johns Hopkins University Press, 2001.

Doherty, Gerald. "The Nirvana Dimension: D. H. Lawrence's Quarrel with Buddhism." *D. H. Lawrence Review* 15 (1962): 51–67.

——. *Oriental Lawrence: The Quest for the Secrets of Sex.* New York: Peter Lang, 2001.

Doyle, Arthur Conan. *The History of Spiritualism.* 1926. Vols. 1 and 2. New York: Arno Press, 1975.

Droit, Roger-Pol. *The Cult of Nothingness: The Philosophers and the Buddha.* Translated by David Streight and Pamela Vohnson. Chapel Hill: University of North Carolina Press, 2003.

Droogers, André. "Syncretism: The Problem of Definition, the Definition of the Problem." In *Dialogue and Syncretism: An Interdisciplinary Approach,* edited by

Jerald Gort, Hendrik Vroom, Rein Fernhout, and Anton Wessels, 7–25. Grand Rapids, MI: William B. Eerdmans, 1989.

Dublin Review. "Modern Society and the Sacred Heart." 25.49 (July 1875): 1–21.

Dumoulin, Heinrich. "Buddhism and Nineteenth-Century German Philosophy." *Journal of the History of Ideas* 42.3 (July–September 1981): 457–70.

Eitel, Ernest J. *Buddhism: Its Historical, Theoretical, and Popular Aspects.* 3rd ed. Hong Kong: Land, Crawford, 1884.

Eliot, T. S. *On Poetry and Poets.* London: Faber, 1957.

Ellinwood, F. F. "Buddhism and Christianity—A Crusade Which Must Be Met." *The Missionary Review of the World* 4 (1891): 108–17.

Ellis, Peter Berresford. *H. Rider Haggard: A Voice from the Infinite.* London: Routledge & Kegan Paul, 1978.

Ellwood, Robert, and Catherine Wessinger. "The Feminism of 'Universal Brotherhood': Women in the Theosophical Movement." In *Women's Leadership in Marginal Religions: Explorations Outside the Mainstream,* edited by Catherine Wessinger, 68–870. Urbana: University of Illinois Press, 1993.

Erricker, Clive. *Buddhism.* Lincolnwood, IL: NTC/Contemporary, 1975.

Everett, Charles C. "Recent Studies in Buddhism." *The Unitarian Review and Religious Magazine* (Boston) 18 (1882): 421–36.

Federico, Annette R. *Idol of Suburbia: Marie Corelli and Late-Victorian Literary Culture.* Charlottesville: University of Virginia Press, 2000.

Fields, Rick. *How the Swans Came to the Lake: A Narrative History of Buddhism in America.* 3rd ed. Boston: Shambhala, 1992.

Flanders, G. T. *Christ or Buddha?* Salem, MA: Bates, 1881.

Fleming, Peter. *Bayonets to Lhasa: The First Full Account of the British Invasion of Tibet in 1904.* New York: Harper, 1961.

Foley, C. A. "The Psychological Basis of Buddhist Ethics." *Journal of the Royal Asiatic Society of Great Britain and Ireland* 26 (1894): 321–33.

Ford, James L. "Buddhism, Mythology, and *The Matrix.*" In *Taking the Red Pill: Science, Philosophy, and Religion in The Matrix,* edited by Glenn Yeffeth. Dallas: Benbella Books, 2003.

Forlong, J. G. R. "Buddhism: Through What Historical Channels Did It Influence Early Christianity?" *Open Court. A Fortnightly Journal, Devoted to the Work of Establishing Religion and Ethics upon a Scientific Basis* 1 (1887–88): 382, 416, 439.

Forster, E. M. *A Passage to India.* 1924. New York: Harcourt, 1984.

Fox, Douglas A. *The Vagrant Lotus: An Introduction to Buddhist Philosophy.* Philadelphia: Westminster Press, 1973.

Fox, St. George Lane. "The Neo-Buddhist Movement." *Time, a Monthly Miscellany* 22, NS1 (1890): 597–602.

Franklin, J. Jeffrey. "The Counter-Invasion of Britain by Buddhism in Marie Corelli's *A Romance of Two Worlds* and H. Rider Haggard's *Ayesha: The Return of She.*" *Victorian Literature and Culture* 31.1 (spring 2003): 19–42.

——. "Memory as the Nexus of Identity, Empire, and Evolution in George Eliot's *Middlemarch* and H. Rider Haggard's *She.*" *Cahiers victoriens & édouardiens* 53 (2001): 141–70.

Fraser, Hilary, Stephanie Green, and Judith Johnston. *Gender and the Victorian Periodical.* Cambridge: Cambridge University Press, 2003.

Fraser, Robert. *Victorian Quest Romance: Stevenson, Haggard, Kipling, and Conan Doyle*. Plymouth, UK: Northcote House, 1998.

Gagnier, Regina. "The Law of Progress and the Ironies of Individualism in the Nineteenth Century." *New Literary History* 31 (2000): 315–36.

Gaskell, Elizabeth. *Cranford*. 1851. Oxford: Oxford University Press, 1998.

Gates, William. *Letter to Katherine Tingley*. May 8, 1912. Pasadena, CA: Theosophical Society Archive, 1919.

Giddens, Anthony. *The Consequences of Modernity*. Stanford: Stanford University Press, 1990.

Gilbert, Sandra M. "Rider Haggard's Heart of Darkness." In *Coordinates: Placing Science Fiction and Fantasy*, edited by George E. Slusser, Eric S. Rabkin, and Roberts Scholes, 124–38. Carbondale: Southern Illinois University, 1983.

Giles, James. "The No-Self Theory: Hume, Buddhism, and Personal Identity." *Philosophy East & West* 43, no. 2 (April 1993): 175–200.

——. *No Self to be Found: The Search for Personal Identity*. Lanham, MD: University Press of America, 1997.

Gillis, Everett A. "The Spiritual Status of T. S. Eliot's Hollow Men." *Texas Studies in Literature and Language* 2 (1961): 464–75.

Gilmour, David. *The Long Recessional: The Imperial Life of Rudyard Kipling*. New York: Farrar, Straus and Giroux, 2002.

Glicksberg, Charles I. *The Literature of Nihilism*. Lewisburg, PA: Bucknell University Press, 1975.

Goldfarb, Russell M., and Clare R. Goldfarb. *Spiritualism and Nineteenth-Century Letters*. Cranbury, NJ: Associated University Presses, 1978.

Godwin, Joscelyn. *The Theosophical Enlightenment*. Albany: State University of New York Press, 1994.

Gordon, Rev. M. L. "Mill's Use of Buddhism." *Bibliotheca Sacra: A Theological Quarterly* (London) 42 (July 1885): 527–35.

Goudsblom, Johan. *Nihilism and Culture*. Totowa, NJ: Rowman and Littlefield, 1960.

Gowans, Christopher W. *Philosophy of the Buddha*. London: Routledge, 2003.

Graham, Colin. *Ideologies of Epic: Nation, Empire, and Victorian Epic Poetry*. Manchester, Eng.: Manchester University Press, 1998.

Green, Robert Frederick. "Christianity and Buddhism." *Proceedings of the Literary and Philosophical Society of Liverpool* 44 (1890): 299–322.

Gubar, Susan. "She and Herland: Feminism as Fantasy." In *Coordinates: Placing Science Fiction and Fantasy*, edited by George E. Slusser, Eric S. Rabkin, and Robert Scholes, 139–49. Carbondale: Southern Illinois University Press, 1983.

Haggard, H. Rider. "About Fiction." *Contemporary Review* 51 (February 1887): 172–80.

——. *Ayesha: The Return of "She."* 1905. In *The Classic Adventures: Ayesha: The Return of She, Benita: An African Romance*. Poole, Eng.: New Orchard Editions, 1986.

——. *The Days of My Life, An Autobiography*. 2 Vols. Edited by C. J. Longman. London: Longmans, Green and Co., 1926.

——. *The Private Diaries of Sir H. Rider Haggard 1914–1925*. Edited by D. S. Higgins. New York: Stein and Day, 1980.

——. *She*. 1887. Oxford World's Classics. Oxford: Oxford University Press, 1998.

——. *She and Allan*. 1920. New York: Ballantine Books, 1978.

Haggard, Lilias Rider. *The Cloak That I Left: A Biography of the Author Henry Rider Haggard K. B. E.* London: Hodder and Stoughton, 1951.

Hardy, R. Spence. *A Manual of Buddhism, in Its Modern Development.* Translated from Singhalese Mss. 1853. London: Williams and Norgate, 1860.

Hartnell, Elaine M. "Morals and Metaphysics: Marie Corelli, Religion, and the Gothic." *Women's Writing* 13.2 (June 2006): 284–303.

Harvey, Peter. *An Introduction to Buddhism: Teachings, History, and Practices.* Cambridge: Cambridge University Press, 1990.

Hastings, Beatrice Hastings. *Defence of Madame Blavatsky.* Worthing, Eng.: Hastings Press, 1937.

Hauser, Mrs. I. L. "Preface to Notes." *The Light of Asia. Being The Life and Teaching of Gautama, Prince of India and Founder of Büddhism.* 1879. Chicago: Rand, McNally & Company, 1890.

Heckel, Karl. "The Idea of Re-Birth." Translated by Francesca Arundale. In *The Idea of Re-Birth, Including a Translation of an Essay on Re-Incarnation by Karl Heckel.* London: Kegan Paul, Trench, Trübner, & Co., 1890. Hesse, Herman. *Siddhartha.* 1922. Translated by Sherab Chödzin Kohn. Boston: Shambhala, 2000.

——. *Siddhartha.* 1922. Translated by Joachim Neugroschel. New York: Penguin 1999.

Hoare, John Newenham. "The Religion of the Ancient Egyptians." *Littell's Living Age* 140, 5S25 (4 January 1879): 33–41.

Hodgson, Richard. "Account of Personal Investigations in India, and Discussion of the Authorship of the 'Koot Hoomi' Letters." *Proceedings of the Society for Psychical Research* 3 (1886): 207–380.

Holmes, Oliver Wendell. Review of *The Light of Asia. International Review* 7 (1879): 345–49.

Hopkins, R. Thurston. *Rudyard Kipling: A Literary Appreciation.* London: Simpkin, Marshall, Hamilton, Kent, 1978.

Hopkirk, Peter. *Quest for Kim: In Search of Kipling's Great Game.* Ann Arbor: University of Michigan Press, 1996.

Howard, Mrs. Charles L. "The Doctrine of Reincarnation." *The Metaphysical Magazine* 8 (May and June 1898): 141–48.

Howe, Irving. "The Pleasures of *Kim.*" In *Kim,* edited by Zohreh T. Sullivan, 328–37. A Norton Critical Edition. New York: W. W. Norton, 2002.

Huff, Chester Clarence. "The Novels of Marie Corelli: Their Themes and Their Popularity as an Index to Popular Taste." Ph.D. diss. Boulder: University of Colorado, 1970.

Hume, David. *A Treatise of Human Understanding.* 1748. Edited by L. A. Selby-Bigge. Oxford: Oxford University Press, 1965.

Humphreys, Christmas. *The Development of Buddhism in England, Being a History of the Buddhist Movement in London and the Provinces.* London: Buddhist Lodge, 1937.

——. *Studies in the Middle Way: Being Thoughts on Buddhism Applied.* 1940. 3rd ed. London: George Allen and Unwin, 1959.

Huxley, Aldous. *The Doors of Perception.* New York: Harper, 1954.

Huxley, T. H. *Evolution and Ethics.* 1893. Edited by James Paradis and George C. Williams. Princeton, NJ: Princeton University Press, 1989.

Irigaray, Luce. *Between East and West: From Singularity to Community*. Trans. Stephan Pluháček. New York: Columbia University Press, 2002.

Islam, Shamsul. *Kipling's Law: A Study of His Philosophy of Life*. New York: St. Martin's, 1975.

J. M. M. "Buddhism." *Journal of Sacred Literature and Biblical Record* 35 (1865): 281–300.

Jacobs, Joseph, ed. *Indian Fairy Tales*. New York: Putnam's Sons, 1903.

Jacobson, Nolan Pliny. *Understanding Buddhism*. Carbondale: Southern Illinois University Press, 1986.

Jacolliot, Louis. *The Bible in India: Hindoo Origins of Hebrew and Christian Revelation*. 1870. New York: Carleton, 1877.

Jay, Elisabeth. *Faith and Doubt in Victorian Britain*. Houndmills, Eng.: Macmillan, 1986.

Jensen, Lionel M. *Manufacturing Confucianism: Chinese Traditions and Universal Civilization*. Durham: Duke University Press, 1977.

Johnson, Samuel. *A Dictionary of the English Language*. London: W. Strahan, 1755.

Johnston, J. Wesley. "Christ and Buddha: Resemblances and Contrasts." *Methodist Review* 80 (1898): 32–40.

Jones, Ken. *The New Social Face of Buddhism: A Call to Action*. Boston: Wisdom Publications, 2003.

Julkarni, H. B. "The Buddhist Structure and Significance in Joseph Conrad's 'Heart of Darkness.'" *South Asian Review* 3 (1979): 67–75.

Kerouac, Jack. *The Dharma Bums*. 1958. New York: Penguin, 1986.

Kaufmann, Walter. *Nietzsche: Philosopher, Psychologist, Antichrist*. Cleveland, OH: Meridian Books, 1956.

Kaul, Suvir. "*Kim*, or How to Be Young, Male, and British in Kipling's India." In *Kim*, edited by Zohreh T. Sullivan, 426–36. A Norton Critical Edition. New York: W. W. Norton, 2002.

Keely, E. W. "Christianity and Reincarnation." *The Metaphysical Magazine* 8 (August 1898): 235–37.

Kellogg, S. H. "Kingdom of, Life of, and Legend of Buddha." *Bibliotheca Sacra* 39 (1882): 458.

——. *The Light of Asia and the Light of the World*. London: Macmillan, 1885.

Kemp, Sandra. *Kipling's Hidden Narratives*. Oxford: Basil Blackwell, 1988.

Kemp, Sandra, and Lisa Lewis, eds. *Writings on Writing by Rudyard Kipling*. Cambridge: Cambridge University Press, 1996.

Kershner, R. B. "Modernism's Mirror: The Sorrows of Marie Corelli." In *Transforming Genres: New Approaches to British Fiction of the 1890s*, edited by Nikki Lee Manos and Mer-Jane Rochelson, 67–86. New York: St. Martin's, 1994.

King, Richard. *Orientalism and Religion: Postcolonial Theory, India, and "The Mystical East."* London: Routledge, 1999.

Kingsford, Anna, and Edward Maitland. *The Virgin of the World of Hermes Mercurius Trismegistus*. London: George Redway, 1885.

Kinkead-Weekes, Mark. "The Ending of *Kim*." In *Kim*, edited by Zohreh T. Sullivan, 436–41. A Norton Critical Edition. New York: W. W. Norton, 2002.

Kipling, Rudyard. *Kim*. 1901. Edited by Alan Sandison. Oxford World's Classics. Oxford: Oxford University Press, 1998.

———. *Something of Myself* (1937). Vol. 24 of *The Collected Works of Rudyard Kipling.* New York: AMS Press, 1970.

———. *Writings on Writing by Rudyard Kipling.* Edited by Sandra Kemp and Lisa Lewis. Cambridge: Cambridge University Press, 1996.

Kling, Blair B. "*Kim* in Historical Context." In *Kim,* edited by Zohreh T. Sullivan, 297–309. A Norton Critical Edition. New York: W. W. Norton, 2002.

Knight, William. "The Doctrine of Metempsychosis." *The Fortnightly Review* 30, NS24 (1878): 422–42.

Knox, Robert. *Amaravati: Buddhist Sculpture from the Great Stupa.* London: British Museum Press, 1992.

Kraft, Siv Ellen. "'To Mix or Not to Mix': Syncretism/Anti-Syncretism in the History of Theosophy." *Numen: International Review for the History of Religions* 49.2 (2002): 142–77.

Kuehn, Julia. *Glorious Vulgarity: Marie Corelli's Feminine Sublime in a Popular Context.* Berlin: Logos, 2004.

Lahiri, Shompa. *Indians in Britain: Anglo-Indian Encounters, Race and Identity, 1880–1930.* London: Frank Cass, 2000.

The Lalita-Vistara: Memoirs of the Early Life of Sakya Sinha. Chps. 1–15. Translated by R. L. Mitra. Delhi, India: Sri Satguru Publications, 1998.

Lamarck, Jean-Baptiste de. *Zoological Philosophy.* 1809. Translated by H. Elliott. London, 1914.

Langbaum, Robert. *Mysteries of Identity: A Theme in Modern Literature.* New York: Oxford University Press, 1977.

Langdon, Samuel. *Punchi Nona: A Story of Female Education and Village Life in Ceylon.* London: T. Woolmer, 1884.

Lawrence, D. H. *Aaron's Rod.* 1922. London: Penguin, 1995.

———. *Lady Chatterley's Lover.* 1928. London: Penguin, 1994.

———. *Phoenix: The Posthumous Papers of D. H. Lawrence.* Edited by Edward D. McDonald. New York: Viking, 1936.

———. *Reflections on the Death of a Porcupine and Other Essays.* 1925. Bloomington: Indiana University Press, 1963.

———. *Sons and Lovers.* 1913. London: Penguin, 2006.

———. *Women in Love.* 1920. Oxford: Oxford University Press, 1998.

Legge, F. "The Origin of Modern Occultism." *The National Review* (London) 14 September 1889: 10–22.

Lillie, Arthur. *Buddhism in Christendom; or, Jesus the Essene.* London: Kegan Paul, Trench, & Co., 1887.

Lilly, W. S. "The Message of Buddhism to the Western World." *The Fortnightly Review* 78 (July/December 1905): 197–214.

Ling, T. O. *A Dictionary of Buddhism.* New York: Charles Scribner's Sons, 1972.

Literary Digest. 1:6 (31 May 1890): 162.

Littell's Living Age. "A Buddhist 'Matthew Arnold.'" No. 1351 (April 23, 1870): 235–38.

———. "The Contrast between Buddhist and Christian Teaching." No. 2198 (7 August 1886): 381.

Lombard, François. "Conrad and Buddhism." *Cahiers d'études et de recherches victoriennes et édouardiennes* 2 (1975): 103–12.

Long, J. Bruce. "Reincarnation." In *Encyclopedia of Religion,* edited by Lindsay Jones, 7676–7681. 2nd ed. Farmington Hills, MI: Thompson Gale, 2005.

Lopez, Donald S., Jr. *Curators of the Buddha: The Study of Buddhism Under Colonialism.* Chicago: University of Chicago Press, 1995.

——. *Prisoners of Shangri-La: Tibetan Buddhism and the West.* Chicago: University of Chicago Press, 1998.

Low, Gail Ching-Liang. *White Skins / Black Masks: Representation and Colonialism.* London: Routledge, 1996.

Loy, David. *Nonduality: A Study in Comparative Philosophy.* New Haven: Yale University Press, 1988.

Lucretius Carus, Titus. *De rerum natura: libri sex.* Translated by H. A. J. Munro. Cambridge: Deighton, Bell, 1886.

Lycett, Andrew. *Rudyard Kipling.* London: Weidenfeld & Nicolson, 1999.

Lyell, Charles. *Principles of Geology.* 1830–1833. Lehre: Verlag von J. Cramer, 1970.

MacDonald, Frederika. "Buddhism and Mock Buddhism." *The Fortnightly Review* 37, no. 221 (May 1885): 703–13.

Malley, John. " 'Time Hath No Power against Identity': Historical Continuity and Archaeological Adventure in H. Rider Haggard's *She.*" *English Literature in Transition, 1880–1920* 40, no. 3 (1997): 275–97.

Manthorpe, Victoria. *Children of the Empire: The Victorian Haggards.* London: Victor Gollancz, 1996.

Marshall, P. J. *The British Discovery of Hinduism in the Eighteenth Century.* Cambridge: Cambridge University Press, 1970.

Mason, Philip. *Kipling: The Glass, The Shadow, and the Fire.* New York: Harper & Row, 1975.

Maugham, W. Somerset. *The Narrow Corner.* 1932. New York: Penguin, 1993.

McConnell, Daniel J. " 'Heart of Darkness' in T. S. Eliot's *The Hollow Men.*" *Texas Studies in Literature and Language* 4 (1962): 141–52.

McCutchan, Corinne. "Who Iås Kim?" In *Transforming Genres: New Approaches to British Fiction of the 1890s,* edited by Nikki Lee Manos and Meri-Jane Rochelson, 131–51. New York: St. Martin's, 1994.

McDonough, Sheila. "Sense and Sensibility: A Survey of Western Attitudes to Hinduism, Buddhism, and Islam as Expressed in Various Editions of the Encyclopaedia Britannica." *Cahiers d'histoire mondiale: Journal of World History* 9, no. 3 (1966): 771–84.

McKerlie, Helen Graham. "Western Buddhism." *Asiatic Quarterly Review* (London) 9, no. 17 (January 1890): 192–227.

McLeod, Hugh. *Religion and Society in England, 1850–1914.* New York: St. Martin's, 1996.

M'Clintock, John, and James Strong. "Transmigration." In *Cyclopaedia of Biblical, Theological, and Ecclesiastical Literature,* vol. 10, 524–25. New York: Harper & Brothers, 1886.

McMillin, Laurie Hovell. *English in Tibet, Tibet in English: Self-Presentation in Tibet and the Diaspora.* New York: Palgrave, 2001.

Mead, Marion. *Madame Blavatsky: The Woman behind the Myth.* New York: G. P. Putnam's Sons, 1980.

Melton, J. Gordon. *Encyclopedic Handbook of Cults in America.* New York: Garland Press, 1992.

Menzies, Jackie. *Buddha: Radiant Awakening.* Sydney: Art Gallery of New South Wales, 2001.

Michael, Leo. *She: An Allegory of the Church*. New York: Frank F. Lovell, 1889.

The Middle Length Discourses of the Buddha: A New Translation of the Majjhima Nikāya Translated from the Pali. Translated by Bhikkhu Ñāṇamoli, edited and revised by Bhikkhu Bodhi. Boston: Wisdom Publications, 1995.

Mill, John Stuart. *The Collected Works of John Stuart Mill*, edited by J. M. Robson. Toronto: University of Toronto, 1963–1985.

Monier-Williams, Monier. *Buddhism, in Its Connexion with Brāhmanism and Hindūism, and in Its Contrast with Christianity*. London: John Murray, 1889.

——. "Buddhism and Christianity." *Evangelistic Repository* 68 (1891): 478–84.

Morgan, Sue. *Women, Religion, and Feminism in Britain, 1750–1900*. New York: Palgrave Macmillan, 2002.Müller, Friedrich Max. "Buddhism." *The Quarterly Review* 170 (April 1890): 318–46.

——. *Chips from a German Workshop. 1. Essays on the Science of Religion*. 1867. Chico, CA: Scholars Press, 1985.

——. "Christianity and Buddhism." *The New Review* 4 (1891): 67–74.

——. "Esoteric Buddhism." *Nineteenth Century* 33 (May 1893): 767–88.

——. *Lectures on the Science of Religion; with a Paper on Buddhist Nihilism, and a Translation of the Dhammapada or "Path of Virtue."* New York: Charles Scribner, 1872.

——. *Natural Religion*. The Gifford Lectures. London: Longmans, Green, and Co., 1889.

Murphy, Patricia. "The Gendering of History in 'She.'" *Studies in English Literature, 1500–1900* 39, no. 4 (Autumn 1999): 747–72.

Nakamura, Hajime. *Gotama Buddha: A Biography Based on the Most Reliable Texts*. Vol. 1. Translated by Gaynor Sekimori. Tokyo: Kosei, 2000.

Naravane, V. S. "Edwin Arnold and The Light of Asia." *Indian Horizons* 29, no. 1 (1980): 17–33.

Neale, E. Vansittart. "Buddha and Buddhism." *Macmillan's Magazine* 1 (1860): 439–48.

Neff, Mary K. "How Many Objects Has the Theosophical Society?" *The Theosophist* (May 1935): 118.

Neufeldt, Ronald. "In Search of Utopia: Karma and Rebirth in the Theosophical Movement." In *Karma and Rebirth: Post Classical Developments*, edited by Ronald W. Neufeldt, 233–55. Albany: State University of New York Press, 1986.

Nhat Hahn, Thich. *The Heart of the Buddha's Teaching: Transforming Suffering into Peace, Joy, and Liberation*. New York: Broadway Books, 1999.

——. *Interbeing: Fourteen Guidelines for Engaged Buddhism*. Edited by Fred Eppsteiner. 3rd ed. Berkeley: Parallax, 1998.

Nietzsche, Friedrich. *The Anti-Christ*. 1895. Translated by H. L. Mencken. New York: Alfred A. Knopf, 1923.

——. *The Will to Power*. 1883–1888. Edited by Walter Kaufmann. Translated by Walter Kaufmann and R. J. Hollingdale. New York: Random House, 1968.

Niles, Henry Thayer. *The Dawn and the Day; or, The Buddha and the Christ*. Toledo, OH: The Blade Printing & Paper Company, 1894.

Nixon, Judith V. *Victorian Religious Discourse: New Directions in Criticism*. New York: Palgrave, 2004. Noakes, Richard. "Spiritualism, Science, and the Supernatural in Mid-Victorian Britain." In *The Victorian Supernatural*, edited by Nicola Bown, Carolyn Burdett, and Pamela Thurschwell, 23–43. Cambridge: Cambridge University Press, 2004.

Nobel Prize Committee. "The Nobel Prize for Literature, 1907." In *Kim,* edited by Zohreh T. Sullivan, 290–96. A Norton Critical Edition. New York: W. W. Norton, 2002.

O'Connor, Erin. "Preface for a Post-Postcolonial Criticism." *Victorian Studies* 45.2 (January 2003): 217–46.

Olcott, Henry Steel. *A Buddhist Catechism: According to the Canon of the Southern Church.* Colombo, Ceylon: Theosophical Society, 1881.

——. "The Genesis of Theosophy." *The National Review* (London) 14 (October 1889): 208–17.

Oldenberg, Hermann. *Buddha: His Life, His Doctrine, His Order.* 1881. Translated by William Hoey. London: Williams and Norgate, 1882.

Oppenheim, Janet. *The Other World: Spiritualism and Psychical Research in England, 1850–1914.* Cambridge: Cambridge University Press, 1985.

Oswald, Feliz L. "Was Christ a Buddhist?" *The Arena* 3 (1890–91): 193–201. Oulton, Carolyn W. de la L. *Literature and Religion in Mid-Victorian England: From Dickens to Eliot.* Houndmills, Eng.: Palgrave, 2003.

Owen, Alex. *The Darkened Room: Women, Power, and Spiritualism in Late Victorian England.* Philadelphia: University of Pennsylvania Press, 1990.

——. *The Place of Enchantment: British Occultism and the Culture of the Modern.* Chicago: University of Chicago Press, 2004.

Paley, William. *Natural Theology: Selections.* 1802. Edited by Frederick Ferré. Indianapolis: Bobbs-Merrill, 1963.

Parker, W. B. "The Religion of Mr. Kipling." *The New World* 7(1898): 662–70.

Parry, Ann. "Recovering the Connection between *Kim* and Contemporary History." In *Kim.* Edited by Zohreh T. Sullivan, 309–20. A Norton Critical Edition. New York: W. W. Norton, 2002.

Parsons, Gerald. "Introduction: Victorian Religion, Paradox and Variety." In *Religion in Victorian Britain.* Vol. 1. Edited by Gerald Parsons, 1–13. Manchester: Manchester University Press, 1988.

——. "From Dissenters to Free Churchman: The Transitions of Victorian Nonconformity." *Religion in Victorian Britain.* Vol. 1. Edited by Gerald Parsons, 67–116. Manchester, Eng.: Manchester University Press, 1988.

——. "Reform, Revival, and Realignment: The Experience of Victorian Anglicanism." In *Religion in Victorian Britain.* Vol. 1. Edited by Gerald Parsons, 14–66. Manchester, Eng.: Manchester University Press, 1988.

Pater, Walter. *The Renaissance: Studies in Art and Poetry.* 1873. Oxford: Oxford University Press, 1998.

Pearson, Keith Ansell, and Diane Morgan. "Introduction: the Return of Monstrous Nihilism." In *Nihilism Now! Monsters of Energy,* edited by Keith Ansell Pearson and Diane Morgan, 1–17. New York: St. Martin's Press, 2000.

Pearson, Richard. "Archaeology and Gothic Desire: Vitality beyond the Grave in H. Rider Haggard's Ancient Egypt." In *Victorian Gothic,* edited by Ruth Tobbins and Julian Wolfreys, 218–44. New York: Palgrave, 2000.

Peiris, William. *The Western Contribution to Buddhism.* Delhi: Motilal Banarisidass, 1973.

Pels, Peter. "Occult Truths: Race, Conjecture, and Theosophy in Victorian Anthropology." In *Excluded Ancestors, Inventible Traditions,* edited by Richard Handler, 11–41. Madison: University of Wisconsin Press, 2000.

Pember, G. H. *Theosophy, Buddhism, and the Signs of the End.* London: Hodder and Stoughton, 1891.

Phillips, Richard. *The Story of Gautama Buddha and His Creed: An Epic.* London: Longmans, Green, 1871.

Pieterse, Jan Nederveen. "Hybridity, So What? The Anti-hybridity Backlash and the Riddles of Recognition." *Theory, Culture & Society* 18, nos. 2–3 (April–June 2001): 219–45.

Pirsig, Robert M. *Zen and the Art of Motorcycle Maintenance: An Inquiry into Values.* New York: William Morrow, 1974.

Podmore, Frank. *Modern Spiritualism: A History and Criticism.* 2 vols. London: Methuen, 1902.

Prothero, Stephen. "From Spiritualism to Theosophy: 'Uplifting' a Democratic Tradition." *Religions and American Culture* 3, no. 2 (Summer 1993): 197–216.

———. *The White Buddhist: The Asian Odyssey of Henry Steel Olcott.* Bloomington: Indiana University Press, 1996.

The Quarterly Review. "Buddhism." 170 (1890): 318–46.

Rahula, Walpola. *What the Buddha Taught.* New York: Grove Press, 1974.

———. *Zen and the Taming of the Bull: Toward the Definition of Buddhist Thought.* London: Gordon Fraser, 1978.

Rajapakse, Vijitha. "Early Buddhism and John Stuart Mill's Thinking in the Fields of Philosophy and Religion: Some Notes toward a Comparative Study." *Philosophy East and West* 37, no. 3 (July 1987): 260–85.

Rao, K. Bhaskara. *Rudyard Kipling's India.* Norman: University of Oklahoma Press, 1967.

Rattigan, William H. "Three Great Asiatic Reformers: A Study and a Contrast." *London Quarterly Review* 92 (1899): 291–312.

Rawlinson, H. G. *Intercourse between India and The Western World: From the Earliest Times to the Fall of Rome.* 2nd ed. Cambridge: Cambridge University Press, 1926.

Reed, Edward S. *From Soul to Mind: The Emergence of Psychology from Erasmus Darwin to William James.* New Haven: Yale University Press, 1997.

Reid, Fred, and David Washbrook. "Kipling, *Kim,* and Imperialism." *History Today* 32 (August 1982): 14–20.

Rhys Davids, C. A. F. *Buddhism: A Study of the Buddhist Norm.* New York: Henry Holt, 1912.

———. *Buddhist Psychology: An Inquiry into the Analysis and Theory of Mind in Pali Literature.* London: G. Bell and Sons, 1914.

Rhys Davids, T. W. *Buddhism: Being a Sketch of the Life and Teachings of Gautama, the Buddha.* 1877. 21st ed. London: Society for Promoting Christian Knowledge, 1907.

———. *Buddhist Birth Stories; or, Jātaka Tales. The Oldest Collection of Folk-Lore Extant: Being the Jātakatthavaṇṇanā, for the first time Edite in the Original Pāli.* Vol. 1. Edited by V. Fausböll. Boston: Houghton, Mifflin, 1880.

———. *Buddhist India.* 1903. Delhi: Indological Book House, 1970.

———. *The History and Literature of Buddhism.* 1896. Calcutta: Susil Gupta, 1962.

———. *Lectures on the Origin and Growth of Buddhism.* 1881. Hibbert Lectures. Allahabad, India: Rachna Prakashan, 1972.

Richards, Thomas. *The Imperial Archive: Knowledge and the Fantasy of Empire.* London: Verso, 1993.

Robertson, James. *The Rise and Progress of Modern Spiritualism in England*. Manchester: "The Two Worlds" Publishing Company, 1893.

Rogers, H. T. *Buddhaghosha's Parables*. Translated by F. Max Müller. London: Trübner, 1870.

Rogers, Terence. "Restless Desire: Rider Haggard, Orientalism and the New Woman." *Women: A Cultural Review* 10.1 (1999): 35–46.

Rooks, Pamela. "D. H. Lawrence's 'Individual'...." *DHL Review* 23 (1991): 21–29.

Root, E. D. *Sakya Buddha: A Versified, Annotated Narrative of His Life and Teachings; with an Excursus, Containing Citations from the Dhammapada, or Buddhist Canon*. New York: Charles P. Somerby, 1880.

Roy, Parama. *Indian Traffic: Identities in Question in colonial and Postcolonial India*. Berkeley: University of California Press, 1998.

Said, Edward W. *Culture and Imperialism*. New York: Alfred A. Knopf, 1993.

——. *Orientalism*. New York: Pantheon, 1978.

Saint-Hilaire, J. Barthélémy. *La Bouddha et Sa Religion*. Paris: Librairie Académique, 1860.

Salzer, I. *Buddhism, Positivism, and Modern Philosophy*. Calcutta: J. Larkins, 1890.

Sandison, Alan. Introduction to *Kim*. Oxford World's Classics. Oxford: Oxford University Press, 1998.

Sarvan, Charles Ponnuthurai, and Paul Balles. "Buddhism, Hinduism, and the Conradian Darkness." *The Conradian* 26, no. 1 (1994): 70–75.

Sargent, Epes. *The Scientific Basis of Spiritualism*. Boston: Colby and Rich, 1881.

Sartre, Jean-Paul. *Being and Nothingness: An Essay on Phenomenological Ontology*. 1943.Translated by Hazel E. Barnes. New York: Philosophical Library, 1956.

Sawamura, Hajime, and Edwin D. Mares. "How Agents Should Exploit Tetralemma with an Eastern Mind in Argumentation." *Lecture Notes in Artificial Intelligence* 3371 (Spring 2004): 259–78.

Schopenhauer, Arthur. *The World as Will and Representation*. 1818 and 1844. 2 vols. Translated by E. F. J. Payne. New York: Dover, 1966.

Schwab, Raymond. *The Oriental Renaissance: Europe's Rediscovery of India and the East, 1680–1880*. Translated by Gene Patterson-Black and Victor Reinking. New York: Columbia University Press, 1984.

Scott, William Stuart. *Marie Corelli: The Story of a Friendship*. London: Hutchinson, 1955.

Shanks, Andrew. *Civil Society, Civil Religion*. Oxford: Blackwell, 1995.

Shaw, Rosalind, and Charles Stewart. "Introduction: Problematizing Syncretism." In *Syncretism/Anti-syncretism: The Politics of Religious Synthesis*, edited by Charles Stewart and Rosalind Shaw, 1–26. London: Routledge, 1994.

Shelley, Percy Bysshe. *A Defense of Poetry*. 1821. Boston: Ginn, 1903.

Siebers, Alisha. "Marie Corelli's Magnetic Revitalizing Power." In *Victorian Literary Mesmerism*, edited by Martin Willis and Catherine Wynne, 182–202. Amsterdam: Rodopi, 2006.

Silk, Jonathan A. "The Victorian Creation of Buddhism." *Journal of Indian Philosophy* 22 (1994): 171–96.

Sinnett, A. P. *The Early Days of Theosophy in Europe*. London: Theosophical Publishing House, 1922.

——. *Esoteric Buddhism*. 1883. 7th ed. Boston: Houghton, Mifflin, 1887.

Slater, T. E. *Transmigration and Karma*. London: Christian Literature Society for India, 1898.

Smiles, Samuel. *Self Help*. 1859. Project Guttenberg Ebook. http://manybooks.net/titles/smilesaetext97selfh10.html. 29 November 2007.

Smith, Jean, ed. *Radiant Mind: Essential Buddhist Teachings and Texts*. New York: Riverhead Books, 1999.

Smith, Jonathan Z. *The HarperCollins Dictionary of Religion*. New York: Harper-Collins, 1995.

Smith, Warren Sylvester. *The London Heretics, 1870–1914*. New York: Dodd, Mead, 1968.

Snell, Merwin-Marie. "Modern Theosophy in Its Relation to Hinduism and Buddhism." *The Biblical World* (March–April 1895): 200–205, 259–65. Snelling, John. *The Buddhist Handbook: A Complete Guide to Buddhist Schools, Teachings, Practice, and History*. Rochester, VT: Inner Traditions: 1991.

Solomon, Robert C. *From Rationalism to Existentialism: The Existentialists and Their Nineteenth-Century Backgrounds*. Lanham, MD: Rowman & Littlefield, 2001.

Speyer, J. S. *The Jātakamālā, Garland of Birth-Stories of Āryaśūra*. 1895. Delhi: Motilal Banarsidass, 1971.

Stein, W. B. "Buddhism and *Heart of Darkness*." *Western Humanities Review* 11 (1957): 281–85.

Steiner, Rudolph. *Theosophy: An Introduction to the Supersensible Knowledge of the World and the Destination of Man*. 1924. New York: Anthroposophic Press, 1971.

——. *Theosophy of the Rosicrucian*. 1907. London: Rudolph Steiner Press, 1954.

Stephens, Winifred. Introduction to. *L'introduction à L'historie du Buddhisme Indien* (1844), *by* Eugène Burnouf. Edited and translated by L. Canmer-Byng and S. A. Kapadia as *Legends of Indian Buddhism*. New Dehli: Ess Ess Publications, 1976.

Stevens, Wallace. *The Collected Poems of Wallace Stevens*. New York: Alfred A. Knopf, 1977.

Stewart, Susan. *Nonsense: Aspects of Intertextuality in Folklore and Literature*. Baltimore: Johns Hopkins University Press, 1979.

Strozier, Robert M. *Foucault, Subjectivity, and Identity: Historical Consciousness of Subject and Self*. Detroit: Wayne State University Press, 2002.

Suleri, Sara. *The Rhetoric of English India*. Chicago: University of Chicago Press, 1992.

Sullivan, Zohreh T. *Narratives of Empire: The Fiction of Rudyard Kipling*. Cambridge: Cambridge University Press, 1993.

Swenson, Don. *Society, Spirituality, and the Sacred: A Social Scientific Introduction*. Toronto: Broadview, 1999.

Tatar, Maria M. *Spellbound: Studies on Mesmerism and Literature*. Princeton: Princeton University Press, 1978.

Taylor, Richard. "Arthur Schopenhauer." In *Nineteenth-Century Religious Thought in the West*. Vol. 2. Edited by Ninian Smart, John Clayton, Steven Katz, and Patrick Sherry, 157–80. Cambridge: Cambridge University Press, 1985. Telang, Kashinath Timbak. *The Bhagavadgita with the Sanatsugatiya and the Anugita*. Oxford: Clarendon, 1882.

The Theosophical Society International Headquarters. "Early History." Adyar, India: 2002. http://ts-adyar.org/history.html.

Thrall, James H. "Immersing the *Chela*: Religion and Empire in Rudyard Kipling's *Kim*." *Religion & Literature* 36, no. 3 (Autumn 2004): 45–67.

Tibetan Tales, Derived from Indian Sources. Translated by F. Anton von Schiefner and W. R. S. Ralston. London: Trübner & Co, 1882.

Tromp, Marlene. "Spirited Sexuality: Sex, Marriage, and Victorian Spiritualism." *Victorian Literature and Culture* 31, no. 1 (2003): 67–81.

Turner, Frank Miller. *Between Science and Religion: The Reaction to Scientific Naturalism in Late Victorian England.* New Haven: Yale University Press, 1974.

——. *Contesting Cultural Authority: Essays in Victorian Intellectual Life.* Cambridge: Cambridge University Press, 1993.

Tuthill, William Burnet. "Development through Reincarnation." *Metaphysical Magazine* 4 (October 1896): 250–61.

Tuttle, Hudson. *Arcana of Spiritualism: A Manual of Spiritual Science and Philosophy.* London: James Burns, 1876.

Tweed, Thomas W., and Stephen Prothero. *Asian Religions in America: A Documentary History.* Oxford: Oxford University Press, 1999.

Upham, Edward. *The History and Doctrine of Buddhism.* London: R. Ackerman, 1829.

van der Veer, Peter. *Imperial Encounters: Religion and Modernity in India and Britain.* Princeton: Princeton University Press, 2001.

van der Veer, Peter. "Syncretism, Multiculturalism and the Discourse of Tolerance." In *Syncretism/Anti-syncretism: The Politics of Religious Synthesis,* edited by Charles Stewart and Rosalind Shaw, 196–211. London: Routledge, 1994.

Venturino, Steven J. "Where Is Tibet in World Literature?" *World Literature Today: A Literary Quarterly of the University of Oklahoma* 78, no. 1 (Winter 2004): 51–56.

Victoria, Brian Daizen. *Zen at War.* 2nd ed. Lanham, MD: Rowman & Littlefield, 2006.

Viswanathan, Gauri. *Outside the Fold: Conversion, Modernity, and Belief.* Princeton: Princeton University Press, 1998.

Vitsthum, Richard C. *Materialism: An Affirmative History and Definition.* Amherst, NY: Prometheus Books, 1995.

Waddell, L. Austine. "The Buddhist Pictorial Wheel of Life." *Journal of the Asiatic Society of Bengal* 61 (1892): 133–55.

——. *Tibetan Buddhism.* 1894. New York: Dover Publications, 1972.

Walker, E. D. *Reincarnation: A Study of Forgotten Truth.* 1888. New York: University Books, 1965.

Wallace, Alfred Russel. Letter to H. P. Blavatsky. 11 January 1878. Published in *Theosophist* (April 1906): 559.

Washington, Peter. *Madame Blavatsky's Baboon: A History of the Mystics, Mediums, and Misfits Who Brought Spiritualism to America.* New York: Schocken Books, 1993.

Weber, Max. *The Protestant Ethic and the Spirit of Capitalism.* Translated by Talcott Parsons. New York: Scribner, 1958.

Welbon, Guy Richard. *The Buddhist Nirvāna and Its Western Interpreters.* Chicago: University of Chicago Press, 1968.

Westminster Review. "Buddhism: Mythical and Historical." *Westminster Review* 66 (1856): 162–81.

Whitlark, James. "Matthew Arnold and Buddhism." *The Arnoldian: A Review of Mid-Victorian Culture* 9, no. 1 (Winter 1981): 5–16.

——. "Nineteenth-Century 'Nirvana Talk.'" *South Asian Review* 5, no. 2 (July 1981): 17–33.

Widmer, Kingsley. "Lawrence and the Nietzschean Matrix." In *D. H. Lawrence and Tradition,* edited by Jeffrey Meyers. Amherst: University of Massachusetts, 1985.

Wier, John. "Forms of Belief in Transmigration." *Methodist Review* 76 (1894): 565–73.

Wilkinson, C. W. *Edwin Arnold as Poetizer and as Paganizer.* London: Funk and Wagnalls, 1884.

Wilkinson, John Gardner. *The Manners and Customs of the Ancient Egyptians, including Their Private Life, Government, Laws, Arts, Manufacture, Religion, and Early History.* London: John Murray, 1837.

Williams, Patrick. "*Kim* and Orientalism." In *Kim,* edited by Zohreh T. Sullivan, 410–25. A Norton Critical Edition. New York: W. W. Norton, 2002.

Winter, Alison. *Mesmerized: Powers of Mind in Victorian Britain.* Chicago: University of Chicago Press, 1998.

Woolf, Virginia. "From *A Room of One's Own.*" In *The Longman Anthology of British Literature.* Vol. 2C. Edited by David Damrosch, Kevin Dettmar, and Jennifer Wicke. New York: Longman/Addison-Wesley, 2003.

Wright, B. *Interpreter of Buddhism to the West: Sir Edwin Arnold.* New York: Bookman, 1957.

Wurgaft, Lewis D. *The Imperial Imagination: Magic and Myth in Kipling's India.* Middletown, CT: Wesleyan University Press, 1983.

Yang, Chi-ming. "Gross Metempsychosis and Eastern Soul." In *Humans and Other Animals in Eighteenth-Century British Culture: Representation, Hybridity, Ethics,* edited by Frank Palmeri, 13–30. Hampshire, Eng.: Ashgate, 2006.

Young, Robert J. C. *Colonial Desire: Hybridity in Theory, Culture and Race.* London: Routledge, 1995.

——. *White Mythologies: Writing History and the West.* London: Routledge, 1990.

Zirkoff, Boris De. Preface to *H. P. Blavatsky: Collected Writings 1874–1878.* Vol. 1. Adyar, India: The Theosophical Publishing House, 1966.

Zytaruk, George J. "The Doctrine of Individuality: D. H. Lawrence's 'Metaphysic.'" In *D. H. Lawrence, A Centenary Consideration,* edited by Peter Balbert and Phillip L. Marcus, 237–253. Ithaca: Cornell University Press, 1985.

Index